THE ONE YOU WANT
TO MARRY

(And Other Identities I've Had)

THE ONE YOU WANT
TO MARRY

(And Other Identities I've Had)

A Memoir

SOPHIE SANTOS

TOPPLE
BOOKS

Little
a

Published by TOPPLE Books & Little A, New York

www.apub.com

Amazon, the Amazon logo, TOPPLE Books, and Little A are trademarks of Amazon.com, Inc., or its affiliates.

ISBN-13: 9781542020404 (hardcover)
ISBN-10: 1542020409 (hardcover)
ISBN-13: 9781542020411 (paperback)
ISBN-10: 1542020417 (paperback)

Cover design by Zoe Norvell
Cover photography by Mindy Tucker
Interior photo credits: Unless otherwise noted, all photos are courtesy of the author. *Titanic* still: © 20th Century Fox/Paramount/Kobal/Shutterstock; Nick Nolte mugshot: Kypros/Shutterstock.

Printed in the United States of America

First edition

To my parents, who will now know how insane

their daughter truly is

CONTENTS

A Note from TOPPLE Books

How do you find your true voice when you've spent most of your life just trying to fit in?

In Sophie Santos's hilarious, cringeworthy memoir, she recounts her early life as an army brat, when her sharpest survival skill was thriving in any environment—every new school, dance class, football practice, her father's Filipino-Spanish family, and eventually the Alabama home where she and her southern belle mother settled down. Sophie had an ability to succeed in any social situation. But with mounting anxieties in college, as a sorority sister caught up in the pursuit of an engagement before graduation, Sophie finally had a dramatic realization that the life she'd spent so long cultivating was not the one she wanted. After so many years of playing a role, who was she? In *The One You Want to Marry (And Other Identities I've Had)*, Sophie opens up about important issues of race, sexuality, and mental health, all with her signature wit.

Far more than a coming-out story, Sophie's brilliantly funny memoir shows the long journey beyond realizing your path—those years and moments where you stumble along, until you finally find your footing. Any person who has ever wanted to fit in and struggled will relate deeply, laugh loudly, and root for Sophie throughout this remarkable memoir.

—**Joey Soloway,** TOPPLE Books editor-at-large

Author's Note

Some names and details have been changed, but the story itself is true, cross my heart and hope to die, stick a needle in my eye.

Preface

I was a late bloomer. Not physically. Those awkward melons came in too early for my liking. In fact, I had hoped they'd never make an appearance. But emotionally, I was a step behind. On second thought, two steps behind. Let's kick it back to December 26, 2004. I had just crashed my new moped while going full *Motocross Madness* down our gravel driveway. I had begged my mom and stepdad for a 250cc dirt bike, but instead Santa delivered a dinky bright-red Scoot-N-Go. It was a present I did not deserve, and yet it did not live up to what I wanted. I still rode that electric scooter like the dirt bike I'd longed for, and I took off like a bat out of hell.

Which is not something I recommend.

On my first ride down the driveway, I went full throttle, lost control, crashed into our neighbor's pristine fence, and shattered the scooter's headlight. Only ~~fifteen~~ five minutes in, and I had ruined my Christmas present.

I hobbled into the garage, where my stepdad, Buck, was puffing on a Swisher Sweet.

"Ya did some damage, kid," he drawled with a shrug. "Don't worry. Go talk to your mom. I have no idear where she got that thing."

That didn't make sense. It didn't make sense because my *mom* hadn't gotten me the scooter.

Santa had.

I was thirteen years old.

Buck's words stunned me more than the initial crash. I let out a guttural "MOM!" and raced inside the house.

"What is it, sweet thang?" she asked. She was lounging on the living room couch in the perfect reading position, at an angle of repose that meant, *I'm relaxin', honey.*

"*Buck,*" I said with a hard *K*, "told me to ask you where you got my moped, but Santa got it for me. Why would he say such blasphemous words?"

Mom put down *The Four Agreements*, a book that was on her coffee table for more than 50 percent of my childhood. She folded her reading glasses and took in the skin dangling from my chin.

"Also, I might have wrecked the moped."

"I thank we need to talk," she sweetly drawled. My mom's voice sounds like what I imagine the liqueur Southern Comfort sounds like. It's comforting, sweet, but right when you get too comfortable, it'll bite you in the ass to remind you it's in charge. That day was a taste of the comfort. I thought she might be about to break it to me that Santa had cancer.

"I mean, Santa's real," I scoffed.

Her hazel eyes looked me squarely in my big brown eyes.

"I'm sorry, honey. He's *naaaaaht.*"

My mouth opened, and I froze. I would have preferred him to have cancer. Every memory I had of Santa Claus flooded to the front of my brain, like a bad trip through Willy Wonka's Tunnel of Terror, floating down the colorful river on the never-ending haunted gondola ride, seeing flashes of the presents my parents had given me. The carrots half eaten by the reindeer. The oddly cropped selfies of his white-as-snow beard he'd left behind. Was I supposed to believe the reindeer hoofprints on the steps were fake too?!

I stood there with my well-developed rack, eyes welling up with tears, spinning out faster than my scooter. I tried to give my best Detective Olivia Benson, swiping away the tears as they fell.

"And the Easter Bunny?" I croaked.

"Just me," she said with a half smile.

"I'm only going to ask you this once. What about the tooth fairy?"

She confessed. "I have all your teeth hidden around the house."

No further questions.

I'm not, well, the most observant person—even to this day. My girlfriend hides my Christmas presents in plain sight, confident that I won't notice them. There is, likely, a present from her sitting on my desk right now. With my name plastered on it, accompanied by a large, blinking neon sign that reads, THE PRESENT WRAPPED IN BRIGHT ORANGE IS FOR SOPHIE. And yet, nothing. Truly amazing.

But a house full of children's teeth seemed a damning secret to keep.

I was gutted. *I should have you arrested.* I thought of all those times I'd gone back to class after the holiday break, confidently standing up for Mr. Claus's existence. I'd take my seat at a desk in the front row and whip my head around to face the other children.

"Of course Santa is real. How else do you explain *this?*"

I'd pull out a photograph from my JanSport backpack to reveal a close-up (yet out of focus) shot of Santa's eyes and beard with a tiny crumb tucked into the hair. The other children sat in what I'd assumed was stunned silence. I turned back in my seat toward the board, smiling like I'd won.

Back with my mom, I took a strangled breath. My parents had led me right out in front of a firing squad, believing I was invincible.

My mom's words echoed in my head. "We took a picture of one of the Santa figurines, honey." Mom collected Santas of the world from Hallmark and Cracker Barrel—a new one every year. I had the privilege of helping her place them all around the house each Christmas. There was a Brazilian Santa and an Irish Santa. I had a feeling that this particular photo was from Cracker Barrel's Caribbean Santa.

"Why would you lie to me?" I hissed, silently drumming up the worst word I could call my backstabbing mother: *turd.*

"Your dad and I wanted to give you the best Christmas possible. It was a fun game for us. We really enjoyed playin' Santa."

A game. Interesting. I hadn't realized my dignity was something to play with—but there we had it. It was a game—and the game was now officially over. I lunged into her arms, curled up on the couch, and wept, tears sliding down into my cleavage. Christmas would be changed forever.

That was the first time I realized I was a late bloomer—but it wouldn't be the last.

Years later, I was sitting across from my retired lieutenant colonel dad at a strip-mall Mexican restaurant. He had taken me to lunch on my break from rehearsing for one of the spring college plays, *The Government Inspector*. I was in the stupid *The Government Inspector* because I was robbed and didn't get cast as Maureen in *Rent*. I was still very much working through it.

I had ordered a chimichanga, the perfect entrée for stuffing face to avoid parental questions. Our conversation started with the usual college catch-up: "How's class?" "How's your house?" "How's that friend who you haven't mentioned in years, but I'm gonna bring her up because that's all I really know about your social life?" Then:

"So, kiddo—you got a boyfriend?"

"No," I said with a huge wad of chimichanga tucked into my cheek. My dad cut a piece of his own chimichanga and placed it sharply into his mouth. *Please don't ask me if I have a girlfriend. Please don't ask me if I have a girlfriend. Please don't ask me if I have a girlfriend,* I chanted in my mind, hoping he would hear my plea. It's not that he had asked me the question in the past—but at that moment, I *did* have a girlfriend, and I knew I wouldn't be able to lie.

Without missing a beat, he said, "You got a girlfriend?"

BOOM. Just like that, my casual, avoid-everything lunch had turned into a high-stakes interrogation. Okay, sir! You can put away the warfare tactic. I worried my dad was about to start waterboarding me about these women I was *allegedly* dating.

"No," I said, taking another whopping bite of chimichanga, trying not to choke.

"All right." He sat there as I avoided eye contact with him.

Mind-numbing silence.

I chewed for what felt like two hours. *Is this really how long it takes to break down a flour tortilla?* Tossed back some ice-cold water and looked up. I somehow squeaked out, "Actually, yeah. I have a girlfriend."

"Well, what's her name?"

What's her name . . . ? Nice try, Colonel! You're just using the pride-and-ego-up approach to get her information.

"Rylee. Her name is Rylee."

"How long have you been dating?"

"Six months."

"Six months!" He sounded a little shocked. Not because it was a woman, apparently, but because I had been dating someone for six months and had yet to even hint at it.

"Mm-hmm," I said, trying to stuff the rest of the chimichanga, the beans, and the entire platter of chips and guac into my mouth.

"Well, kiddo—you always had good female relationships."

He said it nonchalantly. Like we were talking about my favorite color. Within two seconds, I was transported back to the Willy Wonka Tunnel of Terror. My dad's voice echoed in my head, *"You always had good female relationships,"* as I glided further and further into my past. I saw the faces of all my friendships throughout the years. All the burned mixtapes accompanied by handwritten letters about why "Fall for You" by Secondhand Serenade was our "friendship" song, all the times there was that one girl in school whom I'd spend every waking moment with. "Good morning! It's me again! I know we don't have plans, but I brought you breakfast!" The (. . . many) times I had kissed my best friend in high school because it was a dare but then couldn't stop thinking about it as I watched the rain fall so gracefully against the windowpane.

I came to, drenched in sweat, as my dad was asking for the check.

"Female friendships." It was the final nail in the coffin of gaydom. I was in a trance as we walked out of the restaurant, got into his car, and drove back to campus. I have no memory of getting out of the car and walking into the building for rehearsal, but suddenly I was sitting in the lobby of the theater building.

Alone. No one had returned from break yet, and it was just me, myself, and the faint sound of "Take Me or Leave Me."

Oh, and you're sharp, Maureen.

All of a sudden, I let out a huge laugh.

I had accepted that I was gay. I mean, I was in a relationship, HELLO! But this was different. My dad had called out something that appeared to have been there all along. The thing was—he was right about my relationships. My bonds with "females" have been as strong as Rosie the Riveter's upraised fist throughout the years. These friendships were nuclear, man. Like superhuman. Like my superpower. It was like I was Luke Skywalker and had just realized that the Force had been inside me all along.

What I wanted to know was, how the *fuck* did I not see the signs?

PHASE ONE

→

"Rocket Power Realness"

You're made from good loins.

—My grandfather Bobby Rouse, 1991

Chapter One

GRAND ENTRANCE

I agreed to be born. To an unborn child, the transformation into a literal baby is a heavy task, and not just because I was a heavy child at eight pounds and eleven ounces. I'd like to consider myself a reasonable person, but I needed to know, if I were to leave my little chamber, that I'd have a say in how things went: a full head of hair, a sunny disposition, good lungs for screaming, etc. Listen, I liked to be prepared, sue me. Alas, I was an unborn child, and I didn't quite know how to tell my mom my terms of departure.

So there I was, floating in the amniotic fluid, content with that being my home, but Mom had other plans. A week after missing her due date (I was still waiting for my demands to be accepted), my very preggers mom was in sheer agony and doing whatever she could to get me out of her. Despite her best efforts, all the spicy food in the world, raspberry (sweet) tea, squat jumping, and witchcraft chanting wouldn't work. Little did she know, I was in there sucking down all that jambalaya, the rhythmic chanting lulling me to sleep as I waited for our negotiation to be completed.

My dad was stationed overseas in Germany and had sent my mom back to the States—to Biloxi, Mississippi, to be exact—so she could be with her parents, Bobby and Sally. Dad wanted to make sure I was born on American soil so that I could have the chance to become president. Very high expectations from the start. I'd like to officially state that, Dad, sorry to disappoint, I do not want to be president . . . yet. However, Obama, if *you're* reading this, DM me.

My mom was at her wits' end. She called my dad and told him that if I didn't arrive soon, and if *he* didn't arrive soon, she'd take it upon herself to figure out other ways to hurry me up. A few options being: castor oil, a bumpy car ride, or hiring tiny men to jump up and down on her stomach like a trampoline.

It was a standoff.

As she was about to call in the tiny-men brigade, Dad managed to squeak into town, fresh flattop and all. His military airlift command flight landed, and Mom insisted they race to the hospital—only to discover I was still not ready. Her gynecologist told her that I was so far up, I was *"stuffed inside her esophagus,"* and that she and my dad should try having sex. That night, my mom—who was "uncomfortably" pregnant—stripped off all her clothes, stared at my dad, and asked, "You ready?"

He responded, "Let's just get this over with."

And what do ya know? It worked—two days later.

On the morning of May 18, right before she was about to dig into Grandpa Bobby's famous biscuits and gravy, Mom yelled, "My wahter broke!"

Dad jumped to his feet and said, "Attention!"

Grandpa Bobby, a.k.a. Papa, drawled from the living room, "THE PIPE'S BROKE?"

"WAH-TER. My wah-ter broke!"

"Susan! We don't have time for this," Dad said. But he was no match for the southern exchange. Mom entered the living room, holding her stomach. "Daaad, my wahter broke."

"Oh! Good lord, shit. SALLY! We gotta go to the hospital! Susan's wahter broke!"

Grandma Sally, who was in the process of curling her hair, shot back from the bathroom coolly, "You're outta your damn mind if you think I'm goin' to the hospital lookin' like this," and continued to methodically take out her hair rollers. Mom made herself a plate and sat down at the kitchen table with a bath towel in between her legs.

"I'm gonna have my biscuits first, so y'all can meet me in the car in five."

The four of them loaded into the Buick and finally rushed her to the hospital, bath towel and all, on the nearest military base, with the nurses saluting my dad as he wheeled my mom into her room. Still, I made everyone wait even longer. There was no way in hell, no matter how long my mother labored (more than twenty-four hours), that I was ready to make an appearance.

Thus, I was born via emergency cesarean, brought about by my parents' sad sex. In my humble *opinión*, the term *C-section* doesn't do it justice. *Cesarean* sounds so elegant—regal even—and that is how I entered the world, theatrics and all. My full head of hair was very King Arthur suave (thanks, Mom and Dad), so I just needed a tiny flower crown and sword, and I was ready to make my mark as Sophie Elizabeth Santos!

Mom and Dad had planned to name me Ben-Bob, after Dad and Grandpa Bobby, but they got a girl. Thank God. If I'd been gifted a name like Ben-Bob, I would have wanted to open a gator-wrestling school. They also tossed around naming me Vanessa, because I'd been conceived in a van on the beach. Ultimately, they settled on Sophie Elizabeth and called me by my middle name, with me not deciding which one I'd like to be called for years to come.

I wish I could say it was all smooth sailing once I had raised my tiny fists into the air for the first time, but I was rushed to the baby ICU—with an IV stuck in my head that created a bald spot I have to this very day—and my mom fell ill, so the delivery room conversation turned quickly to "Is Susan gonna die?" which was "just lovely," as she has since said. Being an overachieving nurse herself, Mom eventually noticed that something was wrong with her chart. Every time they gave her medication for the presumed infection, her fever spiked.

"It's called drug fever," she told the nurse taking care of her.

"I don't understa—"

She grabbed the nurse by the neck and said they needed to get her off the meds stat.

"Ma'am . . . well . . . if we do that, you might die . . ."

"I guess we'll find out," she said with total confidence.

That night, she was released and ate at the officers' club on base, and I was bundled up and smiling at Mom, who had nursed herself back to health.

The better-late-than-never child. Not to mention, my parents had me in their midthirties, which was not only late for their generation but was somehow rude.

My dad's parents arrived the next day and greeted me. While my Spanish grandma, Carmen, said, "Oh my God . . . how beautiful," on repeat, my Filipino grandpa, Pee-Paw, kept pulling his son to the side to insist that I be raised Catholic. Grandpa Bobby nudged my mom and whispered, "You're made from good loins. She is too." Grandma Sally, overhearing, snapped and said, "Enough of that, Bobby!"

I was the product of a southern-immigrant military family, destined to be Sophie Santos (ish), of the House of the Hard Head, One of a Kind, Queen of the Stunted Late Bloomers, and Certifiable Smart-Ass. Two weeks later, we flew to Germany, and I became a European baby, baby, but only for a year.

If I had had any say about it, I would have kept us in Europe, baby. I loved being a European baby. I'd don my baby berets and eat my tiny schnitzels. Alas, I still couldn't communicate, so I didn't have a say in the family plans. I guess we were destined for Kansas, home of the wheat fields, one of the many stops on our upcoming US World Tour. Unfortunately, as much as I wanted to keep calling the shots, I was no longer in charge—and my life was about to become a circus.

DAY CARE
Location: Fort Riley, KS
"Female Friendship": Kira
Favorite Time to Hang: Nap time

Kira was the first of many "female friendships" I had growing up. I threw myself into at least one friendship like this every time my family moved. Most were fleeting, but each—at the time—was my very *best* friend.

Kira and I were attached at the hip. I have often found myself attracted to shiny, pretty things—and Kira was the shiniest *and* prettiest thing at my day care. She had the best OshKosh B'gosh overalls, and her pink sparkle shoes were top-notch. We spent lunchtime, story time, and nap time practically on top of each other. My day-care teacher Audrey warned us several times to stop the nap-time chitchat. We'd close our eyes, pretend we were asleep, and then—moments later—pick up where we'd left off: an inane, unending discussion about Andrew, who we both agreed looked like a ginger-haired Cabbage Patch Kid and was possibly an actual doll. Eventually, Audrey got fed up with our antics and separated our cots.

"You!" she said, pointing at me. It felt like a gunshot to my heart. "Over there." She pointed to the opposite side of the classroom.

"You!" she said, pointing at Kira. Another gunshot. "Don't move."

I looked across the room, which had instantly transformed into a desert wasteland, too far and too treacherous to traverse. I dragged my cot and furiously set it up on the other side of the room. And then I did the only thing I could think of: I threw a hissy fit.

I wailed and wailed, pining over my lost love. Audrey must have been made of steel, because she didn't move a muscle. I waited for her to be distracted by another classmate who had just learned to climb and was apparently training for Everest. I dragged my cot back over to Kira's.

"What are you doing? You're going to get us both killed," she whispered.

"I don't care. I missed you too much."

The noise from our muffled conversation must have gotten Audrey's attention, because I felt my sorry five-year-old ass moving inches away from Kira. I looked up to see Audrey staring over my cot, dragging it—with my body splayed across it—even farther away. She stuck me by the trash can.

I kicked the trash over in protest.

When Audrey extended our punishment to a full week of separation, I cried more than I did when my mom dropped me off every morning—which is to say, a lot.

Chapter Two

THE ~~NANNY~~ BABYSITTER DIARIES

My first memory is of being absolutely gobsmacked by *The Wizard of Oz*. Actually, for honesty purposes, my *very* first memory happened when I was three: I was getting out of Grandpa Bobby and Grandma Sally's car, when their friend slammed the heavy Buick door on my tiny index and middle fingers, causing me to yelp for the heavens. Despite my throbbing fingers, we made our way to Catholic Mass (Grandma Sally was Baptist and lost the annual coin toss). I guess Jesus's birthday was more important than my would-be potential as a featured pianist at the New York Philharmonic. I sat in the front pew, holding ice on my fingers (which still have indents to this day). If I had known the impact of a middle finger, I would have used mine—ice pack and all—to show my disdain for their friend (and God). Instead, I cradled it through the hour-long ceremony as it withered away before my eyes. Grandma Sally whispered to me, "We'll only be goin' to the Baptist church from now on."

Therefore, my infatuation with *The Wizard of Oz* was actually my second memory. I was obsessed with Dorothy, a girl from humble beginnings who found herself in a world of infinite possibilities. From an early age, I was certain I was also destined for more (cue the opening number).

That infatuation, a product of my bad habit of die-hard obsessing, was something my parents weren't prepared to manage. I wore out the VHS tape of *The Wizard of Oz* within two weeks. Grandma Sally sewed me my very own Dorothy blue-and-white gingham dress to wear to day care and bought the much-needed accessories: the wicker basket for Toto, a stuffed Toto (who was a nondescript white dog, an oversight that I noticed, but moving on . . .)—and, of course, the ruby-red slippers. The costume's debut was a hit.

My classmate Andrew said, "Bluuuuue."

I nodded in agreement.

Naturally, I wore it the next day, and then the next. And then the next.

Mom would strip me down after class, throw my dress in the wash, and lay it out on my chair each morning for my triumphant return. After two months, Dad was genuinely concerned. He pulled my mom aside one night and said, "Maybe something is wrong with her."

My mother responded, "If she decides to wear it down the aisle, then her husband can deal with it."

For the record, we also used an Easter basket instead of a picnic basket, and the last time I checked, Dorothy didn't wear purple socks.

Unfortunately, I have to report that my *wife* will have to deal with the dress.

I don't know what it was about the yellow brick road that had me gassed up. Maybe it was just because I was five and loved the Lollipop Guild? Or maybe it was the idea that, if I clicked my heels three times, anything was possible. That attitude was something my parents instilled in me. Either way, I've been a head-in-the-clouds type of gal ever since. Which was also my downfall. I was naive to a fucking fault.

I was also living in Kansas at the time, so there's that.

After Germany, even though my family's zip code changed a thousand times, we never went far. We just jumped from cornfield to cornfield in Kansas and Missouri. Mom was stuck working long nursing shifts at the hospital, and Dad was off on whatever base we were currently stationed at, playing "military games." Which—what even are those?

Mom was getting her PhD and had rented a thimble of an apartment on campus for the two of us to live in during the week while she went to school. The apartment had two rooms, and the bedroom was basically in the kitchen, and the kitchen was in the toilet. Still, even a small second apartment maxed out our budget, so we embraced the ever-popular midwestern hobby: couponing. I loved coupons. I'd open the newspaper, and, before checking out the latest *Calvin and Hobbes*, I'd gather the coupons like they were gold and rub them on my face. So colorful and so mysterious!

On the weekends, we'd go back home to my dad and our dogs Sam (half Lab / half Great Dane / whole Lotta Ass) and Ginger (our Miss Priss mutt). Sometimes Dad would visit the tiny apartment during the week. When he was there, I was banished to the couch every night, but I would walk in unannounced and tuck myself under the covers to take back my domain. We'd play Pretty Pretty Princess and watch *The Wizard of Oz*, and I'd fall asleep, splayed octopus-style, between them.

Then it happened. As the mystique of Dorothy wore off, the Spice Girls invaded the US and my household, otherwise known as the second British invasion, blah blah girl power—ya know what I mean?

I had the CDs. I had the movie, *Spice World*. And of course, I had all five "Girl Power" Galoob dolls. If I could have turned myself into one with a tiny headset, looking through the clear plastic of the box, and shelved on aisle four of Toys "R" Us, I would have. My mom fed the obsession so I could have five best friends. I practiced their moves to every music video so that if they ever needed a replacement, I'd be the first they'd call. I imagined their agent calling our home number.

Alas, the call never came, and due to their demanding work schedules, Scary, Sporty, Baby, Ginger, and Posh couldn't make time for me. I was instead left with a cast of not-so-famous babysitters.

That's when Audrey entered our lives long term and became my favorite person in the world. Audrey was the cold-blooded preschool teacher who'd thrown a wrench into my romance with Kira, but Audrey and I were destined for better things. Mom was working full-time AND studying AND trying to stop me from packing up my things and becoming a Spice Girls roadie. It had become a lot. Dad, ever the career military man, was off driving doughnuts in tanks (or whatever tankers not at combat do, although he'd say we're always at combat). So Mom shamelessly asked my twenty-one-year-old teacher to be my live-in babysitter[1] for an indefinite amount of time. Shockingly, Audrey said yes, despite having a stable job with health benefits. We'll never know why.

She moved into the bedroom next to mine with two massive suitcases and a bunch of loose clothes in hampers. I was slightly on guard re: cot incident. Audrey's approach to the nannying profession was unconventional, in that she recognized that I was a tiny person who had wants and needs. Sleeping in? No problem. Eating sweets? Sure! Waiting until the last moment to make me do homework? You bet your bottom dollar. She let me be a kid, which was a refreshing change from the regimented military lifestyle my dad had been trying to create, sir, yes sir! Turned out, Audrey was a supercool lady and the exact opposite off school premises. *Well, my, my, my. Nice to finally meet you.* Audrey and I would cut up all the time. We'd drive down the highway in her beat-up Toyota Corolla (Kelley Blue Book not approved), the passenger's seat floorboard taped with cardboard to cover the gaping hole, belting out Carly Simon's "You're So Vain," screaming the lyrics. Carly seemed to really resonate with Audrey. *Are they friends?* I felt a tingling sensation when singing the songs. Unsure what that feeling was. Rage? I kept shouting because Audrey shouted, and that seemed like what we were supposed to do.

"Again! Again!" I'd yell. We'd play it until our ears bled.

Before she moved in, I was a shy child who hid behind my mom's legs any time there was a chance of social interaction. I walked everywhere in tandem with Mom, like I was a third limb. Once Audrey became my nanny, things changed. I walked in tandem with *her* instead. Crop-top attitude and all.

One afternoon, Audrey and I were hanging out on the living room couch, chatting about her problems—a favorite pastime of ours. Audrey said that her friend Theresa was dating a real piece of work, and I pretended to know what that meant. Suddenly, Audrey jumped to her feet.

"Let's go for a walk," she said.

"Why?"

"Because we're gonna get you some friends."

"I don't want new friends," I protested, looking at my Spice Girls dolls. That didn't matter—we were already out the door, on a mission. We walked up and

---

[1] Okay, nanny. But don't let the word *nanny* make you think we lived in the Pembrooke and ate shallots. We had free housing from the government and lived off canned goods.

down the street until we spotted a group of girls, and Audrey gave the order: "Let's start with them."

"Ughhhh, no—I'm okay," I said, trying to take up my usual position behind her legs.

"Heyyy, girls," Audrey said. She smiled from ear to ear. Her "Rachel" hair shimmered in the light. *Do my eyes deceive me? Is Audrey shiny and pretty?* "This is Elizabeth. I'm Audrey. We live down the block."

"Hiiii," they all said back, totally lacking enthusiasm.

"Go for it," Audrey whispered in my ear. And I did what I had to do; I walked up to them. My heart was in my throat.

"I'm Elizabeth. Can I play?" I said, looking at the hopscotch pattern they'd drawn on the ground.

"Sure . . . ," one girl answered. I attempted to hopscotch awkwardly a few times.

"Is your mom inside?" Audrey asked the girl.

"Yeah."

"Audrey, what are you doing?" I asked, rushing to catch up as she walked toward the house.

Audrey waved me off. She knocked at the front door, and it was opened by a certified WASP wearing a Talbots cardigan nearly buttoned up over a shirt with a Peter Pan collar. (Yes, I knew all those references then.)

"Hey there! I'm Audrey, and this is Elizabeth. We're new to the neighborhood. The girls were hitting it off, and we were wondering if they could have a playdate."

"I suppose," the woman replied, looking us over. "But only after my girls finish their reading."

I looked up at the frail woman and quickly ducked behind Audrey.

"Girls, come inside!" the woman called like she was Kitty Montgomery from *Dharma and Greg*. Her diamond tennis bracelet glinted in the sunlight as she beckoned them in.

Audrey faked a smile. "Got it. Okay, we'll come back then."

The girls ran past us as the woman gave us one look up and down, then disappeared behind the large, intimidating door. I watched through the sliver in the curtain she had also drawn in the front window as they all sat down on the couch and opened their chapter books.

"Why'd you make me do that?" I asked once we'd left, my head hung low.

"Because you need friends, Elizabeth. You can't hang out all day with only grown-ups."

Wait, why? And whatever, can't a kid prefer adult company? And I had Audrey. And kindergarteners scared the hell out of me. Small children know things, and they aren't exactly tight-lipped—a dangerous combination.

Despite our initial effort and Audrey's concern for my social skills, we never went back to that house, but the interaction had a lasting effect. For the next few months, Audrey was determined to make me smarter than those snooty girls.

"Please don't make me read another book!" I'd whine over the top of *The Odyssey*. *Damn*, just like that, cold-blooded Audrey could reemerge.

Audrey taught me good things, like how to spell M-I-SS-I-SS-I-PP-I and not to shout, "I love brown people!" whenever I saw brown people in a mall. And—unbeknownst to her—she expanded my knowledge of what underwear could look like. I walked into her room one day when her back was to the door. I had a bad habit of not knocking and also of not respecting "boundaries." Clothes were strewn all around. And there it was, something I'd never seen before. A tiny, lacy red string balled up on the ground. It was lifeless and sad, yet thrilling. *That's not what* my *underwear looks like.* Hanes Her Way didn't make anything even close to that. I wanted to steal it so I could investigate. Sadly, I didn't have the courage, but I asked my mom about it later, who introduced the word *thong* into my vocabulary.

After Audrey'd drop me off at school, I'd spend all day at my desk thinking about her. What she was doing, what she might be wearing, and if she had other thongs in different colors. As soon as the bell rang, I'd rush out of the building and see her waiting for me. She'd smile and open the door, and I'd plop onto the front seat.

"My teacher says I'm not supposed to say 'thong' in class anymore."

"Ugh, it's probably because she doesn't know what thongs are," she'd say with an eye roll.

Audrey was a free spirit, like my mom, and as much as he thought of Audrey as part of the family, it drove my dad nuts. In some ways, I can't blame him for being uptight. He was trying to lead the troops at home, and Audrey, my mom, and I all had pots and pans on our heads. That, and Audrey was routinely trying to sneak me out of school. Despite being completely charmed by her, I always wanted to ask my mom's permission. I was a strict rule follower. The thought of being sneaky was terrifying.

"Wait, what? You wanna call the school and tell them she's sick?" my mom asked Audrey.

"Yes! It'll be so fun! I used to skip school when I was younger."

"I guess that's fine. Just don't tell her father because he'll . . . ," my mom said, then mimed strangling herself. Mom would routinely poke fun at Dad for being uptight, and when he would tell us to behave, she'd normally respond with "Aye, aye, Hitler," or "Where's the mud, Mr. Stick?"

On that particular occasion, Audrey had used the Saint Patrick's Day parade as the reason for my truancy. Because she deemed viewing the floats from the ground insufficient, although it seemed fine to me, I followed her lead, and we sneaked into the 30 Rock of Kansas City.

"Act like you belong here," she whispered.

It was hard to blend in because everyone inside was wearing some version of a fancy suit with big briefcases and stilts for shoes. Audrey was wearing a white tee with trendy mom jeans, and I was in a purple windbreaker. We clearly did not belong there.

We made our way into the elevator and took it to the highest floor. The doors pinged open onto a boring-ass office filled with cubicles and conference rooms. Audrey and I walked briskly to the nearest window, looked out at the floats, and then got the hell out of there before anyone could call security.

My little five-year-old self felt a major rush from being *bad*. Audrey was like an intense girlfriend—exciting but dangerous. I would have followed her to the dark side of the moon.

Perhaps I lied to the school about being sick one too many times that year, because karma is a bitch, and she doesn't take days off. One night, Audrey tried to tuck me into bed as I wiggled out of the sheets.

"Stay tucked in, Miss Priss! I don't want you catching pneumonia!"

"Pneumonia?"

"Yeah—it's like the flu but WAY WORSE," she said and laughed.

I stared back at her, my eyes the size of Magic 8-Balls.

"It's just a saying," she told me, trying to brush it off. "'Don't catch pneumonia.'"

Had she not realized I was one obsessive little kid? I started drilling her relentlessly.

"You're not gonna catch pneumonia. It will never happen, home skillet. You gotta stop being such a worrywart." She kissed my forehead and left.

I pulled the covers up to my head as she flicked off the light and my glow-in-the-dark stars glowed overhead.

"It's just a saying," I told myself.

Two months later, I was hospitalized. With pneumonia. For eight days. I still don't really know how I caught it, but I'd be lying if I told you it wasn't that bad. I got deathly ill. It started with a cold, which turned into the flu, which turned into hospital-ridden, IV-stickin', almost-gettin'-held-back-in-school pneumonia. This worrywart (who believed she caught the infection because her babysitter had jinxed her) was totally buggin'. After I spiked a fever of 105 degrees, my parents rushed me to Children's Mercy Hospital. Shout-out to Dr. Baulk (and my mom) for saving my life.

I had been lying in bed for hours, and the nurse had stuck me at least ten times without finding a vein, when someone knocked on the door. *This better be the head of the hospital telling me he's firing that poop.*

"Come in," Mom said as I turned my face to the side, pretending to be asleep.

"Hi, Elizabeth." I recognized Audrey's voice but kept my face turned. "Is she sleeping?"

"I think so," Mom whispered back.

"I can come back. I'll let her sleep."

They whispered back and forth for a while, and I kept up my charade. Giving the silent treatment to someone who came to visit you in a hospital wasn't the nicest thing to do, but it was her fault. I had PNEUMONIA.

Finally, I whipped my head back and hit her with, "You said I wouldn't get pneumonia!"

Audrey just stood there, stricken. "I know," she said. "I didn't think you would. I'm really sorry, Elizabeth."

"I have PNEUMONIA. *Talk* to the hand."

"I know you do. I'm sorry. It was a joke."

I kept my cold stare leveled right at her lying face.

"And it wasn't a funny joke at all," she continued. "Can you forgive me?"

I turned my head away and stared at the bars of the hospital bed. I tried to let it drag out—but eventually I couldn't take it anymore. My heart belonged to Audrey. She was my favorite person in the world besides my mom—and sometimes over my mom! I didn't want her to think I was holding a grudge. *People die from thinking that.* I turned back to her.

"I guess I forgive you," I said with a pout. It was our first real fight.

She smiled.

That fight was the only rough patch we endured. In fact, we had two blissful years together, until she met Bob. Bob was a midwestern engineer who was from Minnesoooootahh. He was totally unworthy. I just knew I was going to lose her forever.

"Don't marry him," I begged her.

"This won't change anything between us—I promise." She gave me the tightest hug, but I knew, deep down, that everything *would* change.

Mom held her face and gave her a kiss on the cheek. Dad gave her a big hug and then patted me on the back. I noticed he was sad, too, and we all watched her drive away that evening into the sunset. Not really, because it was in the dead of winter, and I think her car got stuck, but you get the idea.

I lost my first love the day Bob proposed, but I'd always known it wouldn't work between Audrey and me. The age difference was too big. At the very least, she had helped me beat the "hiding behind women's legs" phase, and I was ready to be out in the world on my own. Her work was done.

KINDERGARTEN
Location: North Kansas City, MO
"Female Friendship": Patricia
Favorite Phrase: "I want you to draw me like one of your French girls."

My best friend in kindergarten, Patricia, was a rug rat. She had bright-orange hair and freckles on her face and arms. We liked to play outside in the dirt. With Mom's permission (and since it was the nineties and boundaries weren't a thing), her mom would throw me in the shower with Patricia, because it was much easier to get it done all at once. I couldn't help but peek at Patricia's body. She had freckles everywhere! But also, mainly because her belly button was weird as hell. It stuck out and looked like a prune.

"It's an outie belly button," my mom explained.

I loved Patricia's outie.

At that moment in time, I shifted my obsession from *Spice World* to *Titanic* and watched it on repeat. After Audrey, I'd become a bit of a romantic. I was enamored with Jack drawing Rose and wanted to re-create it. One night, I asked Patricia to pose while I drew her naked body with some markers and white computer paper. I paid very close attention to her figure (especially the outie belly button). I thought I was drawing this:

It looked more like this:

The next morning, I tattled on myself. My mom told me that drawing your friend naked was inappropriate for my age. Probably for most ages.

Chapter Three

UNIFORM LIFE

Without any brothers or sisters, my closest fashion influencers were my parents. It seemed to me that Dad wore his BDUs, a.k.a. battle dress uniform, twenty-four seven, despite not being at war, but that was above my pay grade. His hairstyle was a flattop for the twenty-two years he was in the military, and I never saw him with stubble until he was sixty.[2] Mom was a typical nineties mom—midlength hair that she'd blow out every morning; high-cut, camel-toe Levi's mom jeans; and Chico's for a night on the town. A real Geena Davis vibe. She'd always wear a full face of makeup, and she dyed her hair light auburn from a L'Oréal box every six weeks (except when she had the red skunk look in '03, which we do not mention) like clockwork.

I thought her hair was light auburn naturally until I walked in while she was buck-ass naked, painting dye on her white hair. *Who is this person?* Whoever that was, that look wasn't going to work for me.

Deeming the style my parents were serving insufficient, I took my cues from television. I *strictly* identified with the threads of the teen boys on the Disney Channel. The layered tees of Max Keeble (the more layers, the better) and

---

[2] Dad has since felt like he had a lot of catching up to do and has rocked in no particular order: the goatee, the Jack Dorsey, and the Lorax.

the Hawaiian shirts of Louis Stevens gave me some inspo—Disney Channel boys were the shiznit.

I talked constantly—to anyone who would listen—about how much I admired the Disney Channel boys.

"Real talk! Max Keeble is my favorite because he has confidence! And nerdy swag. And has a dry and witty personality. Which I, too, have!" (I've called my elementary school teachers to verify this.)

My parents must have thought I was head over heels, but I didn't want to date those boys. I wanted to *be* them.

I couldn't put my finger on it at the time, but I could feel it in my growing bones. They all dressed in baggy clothes. I dressed in baggy clothes. I didn't have facial hair and neither did they. Our voices essentially sounded the same—so obviously we were, in fact, the same. Looking back, I now know I'm describing a lesbian of the time.

I wanted to be Aaron Carter—a lesbian—and it was there in the blue-print. I didn't have the language for that, so I wished I was a boy. Some nights, I fell asleep hoping it'd happen overnight—that I'd wake up under my bright-blue baseball-and-football sheets and be transformed into a skinny preteen boy. I'd knock over all my sports trophies because of my clumsy boy legs. I'd hit my head on my bedpost because I was so tall. It'd solve all my problems. This is also slightly the inverted plot of *The Luck of the Irish*, another Disney Channel movie.

I hated everything girlie. I joined Girl Scouts because I wanted, badly, to be a Boy Scout—camping, building fires, howling in the woods like a hyena—and then I immediately quit when the Girl Scout troop leaders began trying to teach us sewing. Unless I was going to stitch my own wound from falling out of a tree, it wouldn't help me.

Therefore, it was settled. From the ages of seven to about twelve, I chose a daily uniform that consisted of cargo shorts, closed-toed suede Birkenstocks, and Hawaiian buttoned-up shirts. This was a major contrast from the slap bracelets, Claire's platform flip-flops, and Xtina patchwork jeans that the other girls were wearing. I was beginning to learn how to express myself through my clothing, but the resulting look was less *Magnum, P.I.* hottie and more Nick Nolte's mug shot from his 2002 DUI arrest.

From time to time, I'd swap in a Harley-Davidson tee or my best dress shirt—a mint-condition, silk Spider-Man button-down that was only to be worn on special occasions such as class photo day or saluting my father as he arrived home from work.

Walmart crew socks were 100 percent always worn until the heels were threadbare, and the only accessories were a scrunchie that took up permanent residence on my wrist and the occasional puka-shell necklace from a Beta Club convention to Gulf Shores. Each component was assembled in that specific order. I wore it *avec confiance.*

I rounded out the look by parting my hair carefully down the middle like a butt crack and brushing the sides back until there were no flyaways, however long it took. When I was satisfied, I secured my ponytail in a death grip. Not even a Category 5 hurricane could get this baby to come loose. I'd wet the whole masterpiece down to give it that classic "I know what hair product is" look.

There were very few girls whose style I wanted to emulate or whom I identified with—and one of them was a cartoon character: Reggie from *Rocket Power.* The other, of course, was my soul sister—none other than Andy from *Motocrossed.*[3]

For the woefully unfamiliar, *Motocrossed* is a made-for-TV movie about motocross-racing fraternal twins. It should be in the canon. The hotshot, Andrew, breaks his leg, and then his sister—Andrea a.k.a. "Andy"—impersonates him in the life-changing race he had just qualified for. When I first saw

---

[3] Motorcycle screeches across the page.

Andy chop off her hair, I lost my shit. I begged my mom for weeks, "Pleeeasse let me cut my hair short." A request she met consistently with a hard, multiple-syllable "nooo."

I was a pretty typical nineties kid. I spent a lot of time stuffing my face with cardboard pizza—Lunchables Edition—and smashing Capri Suns like a frat boy with Bud Light on spring break. I've actually had Capri Sun cocktails in the years since, and I must say—it ain't bad. Nostalgia in a pouch, baby.

Nineties food was the shiz. Packed with sugar, loaded with plastic, and so colorful it made your eyeballs bleed funky purple like the Heinz EZ Squirt ketchup. Mom liked to call us a Stouffer's family because we lived off Stouffer's family-size boxed dinners. Except on special occasions, like my parents' anniversary, when we'd all dine at the Peppercorn Duck Club at the Hyatt. I would watch the roasting ducks behind the glass, thinking, *Ahhh! What a romantic night for the three of us.*

Mom wore the Stouffer's badge with honor because we were not able to have traditional home-cooked dinners because I had TWO working parents. She made sure to remind me that they BOTH had ambition. Most moms I knew were stay-at-home moms. Whenever I'd visit a friend's house, I'd see their fridge loaded with snacks that their mom had made from scratch. I'd ask her why she didn't cook me three-course meals like Patricia's mom.

"Why don't you ask those moms if they know how to write a research proposal and if they could win a grant?" she'd say without skipping a beat. She'd toss me a Dunkaroos to shut me up.

We were never in one place long enough for me to make a lot of friends or settle into a neighborhood. We were always at the ready. Just when I'd picked out a color swatch for my room, my mom and dad would walk in and break the news about a new duty station. We flipped more houses than the Property Brothers. The ringmaster was Uncle Sam, and when he said, "You're moving," we moved, clown car and all. In fact, military life had all the circus trappings—lots of bright distractions, avant-garde costumes, and it's never quite clear what the point of it all was. I had just settled into my first grade classroom when my parents sat me down on the couch and told me we were moving . . . again.

It sucked hard. I was really breaking the ice with this one American Girl Samantha look-alike named June. *I think she might even call me her friend by the end of the week,* I'd thought.

Too bad.

We packed up and were gone.

I learned how to be a shape-shifter. I could like whatever the cool kids were into to get them to like me. You into Hot Wheels? Great—me too. How about lava lamps? I know I don't own a tunic, but I swear I'm a hippie. Often the boys would raise an eyebrow when I showed up resembling them ("You wear boys' clothes?" "Yup!"). But the awkwardness was always short-lived. I'd win over any class—and thank God because that uniform was the only piece of armor I had.

I learned to take control and keep it by any means necessary. By age six, I knew how to network like a profesh, and by age seven, I could travel anywhere solo. I knew how to grab my baggage from baggage claim by myself. *For the love of Southwest, do not buy a black suitcase. Or at least tie some colorful ribbons on it so that yours stands out.* Moving made me a master of first impressions. Every school was a new audition, and I had my headshot at the ready. Moving also meant I had to be a master at cutting bullshit and getting to the good stuff. I knew I had only half a year tops, so I wasn't interested in small talk. I needed to know Ashley's deepest, darkest secrets stat.

That's not to say there weren't metaphorical dodgeballs to avoid. Especially when my family interjected themselves. I was sitting in a new class minding my own business when all of a sudden the lights turned off and a full, illuminated sheet cake was presented in my honor. *Stop, please! No one knows me! I've only been here for two weeks.* But over time, I got really good at rolling with whatever came my way. *Yeah, this is the limited-edition Hot Wheels cake, no biggie. I'm humble.* On the outside, I was charming left and right, nothing short of tap dancing, but on the inside, I was hyperventilating. It got hard to keep a grasp on reality and who I was.

A Seven-Year-Old's Guide to Moving A Lot

1. If flying Southwest, be nice to the stewardess so she'll give you a wing pendant to wear during the flight. She might even bring you into the cockpit to meet the pilots.[4] Again, assuming you're flying Southwest.

2. If you're the new kid at school, be quiet at first. You don't want to seem too eager. This is your opportunity to suss out who's who.

3. Don't make friends with the first person you meet. I don't know why, but it will never work out, and it will be awkward.

4. Find out what activities the kids in your class do and then ask your parents to sign you up. (I became a big fan of jump roping and cartooning.) Be a yes-man!

5. Don't fight your parents on moving. It won't work. You can, instead, make them feel really guilty, and so they will buy you stuff. They might even gift you a Game Boy Pocket.

6. Be friends with the teacher, but do it discreetly. You want to keep both the teachers and the students on your side.

7. If you're riding in an RV with your grandparents who have kindly taken you on a trip to see the Four Corners, don't make your seventy-one-year-old grandpa sleep on the floor—unless he grabs your knee and jokes, "This is how a horse bites an apple." Then it's fair game. I understand this has nothing to do with moving, but it's important nonetheless.

The pro was that the military lifestyle afforded me the luxury of starting over, which most kids don't get. If I wasn't jiving with a particular class, I knew the clock was ticking before I'd get a permanent hall pass.

Plus, I always had my mom—my best friend and confidante. She'd do anything (except let me cut my hair) to keep me safe and happy. She gladly mined the boys' racks at Sears to suit my tastes. My dad seemed to love that his daughter was a tomboy. When he was going through a motorcycle phase, he decided he'd buy me a biker jacket and chaps because my mom wouldn't let me ride on the

---

[4] I can't say for certain this will hold up by the time you read this book.

back of his bike unless I was clad entirely in leather. I was thrilled. And when the seventy-year-old Harley-Davidson owners mistook me for my dad's son, I thought I had died and gone to heaven.

"These look good on him! Nice look, son," he said.

"*Her,*" Dad corrected the man at the Harley store. I looked up. "My *daughter,*" he said.

Dammit. The jig was up. So what if he had mistaken me for a boy? I felt like a boy. Dressed like a boy. And the more I thought about it, the more it seemed impossible that puberty would change me. There was certainly no way I was going to dress like the girls at school. I was going to stay the same forever. I mourned the idea of changing. It would mean losing myself. I was afraid I'd cross over during puberty, forgetting I was ever a boyish girl and losing the memory of all the adventures I used to go on.

Everyone was supportive of my self-expression, except for my grandmother.

Sally Rouse, RN, was a pistol, a pistol that fired without warning. She ruled over my mom's family with an iron fist. You couldn't disgrace Sally Rouse. Hell, you couldn't even disagree with her. She strong-armed my mom into beauty pageants, starting at ten years old. Mom told me that their relationship only got better once Grandma Sally was diagnosed with Alzheimer's. "She stopped being . . . well, a bitch," Mom lamented over a cigarette. Sally was tall, lanky, catlike, and—at less than 120 pounds—could somehow lift her entire kitchen table so she could clean underneath it thoroughly. A stubborn woman, rooted in her southern ways, Grandma Sally was equally loving and mean. In one conversation, she would go from complimenting a person to reading them for filth.

"That's a cute top."

"Thanks, Grandma."

"But if you want to wear it, you need to lose weight."

I had that exact conversation with my grandma Sally on more than one occasion. Most of the time, it was her way or the highway. Grandpa Bobby had a full ride to Mississippi State on a football scholarship. After his first semester, Grandma Sally told him to come home to Moss Point—or she was gonna leave him. He came home.

But Grandma Sally worked the late shift at the hospital for an entire decade to put her son and daughter through school—she liked to remind my mom of that as well. And also knit dresses for my stuffed lamb, Lammy (whom I

still have, thank you very much). Grandma Sally loved to go shopping. She was the first person in line at five a.m. on Black Friday, anxiously awaiting the doors of Belk (an off-brand JCPenney) to open. She locked herself in her room out of protest when Waldoff's (no, not Waldorf's) went out of business. I'd travel down to Mississippi for a week in the summer. Grandma Sally and I would hop in the big Buick, crank up Alison Krauss—"Did you know she has a flat nose?" my grandma would quip—and head to the big city of Hattiesburg. We'd walk into Sears, and she'd steer us directly to the girls' department.

"No. No. Um . . . no," I'd say as she sharply flourished each cami and denim skort in front of me. With one rack exhausted, she'd turn, undeterred,

to the next and start riffling through it. Grandma Sally rarely smiled, and her shoving clothes into my face with a judging expression was a slightly horrifying experience.

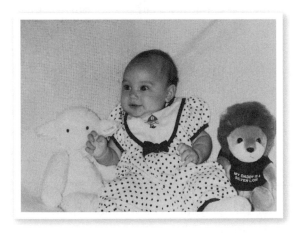

After about twenty minutes of her pulling out clothes, showing them to me, my avoiding eye contact, and then her—begrudgingly—putting them back, she'd purse her lips and, without speaking, we'd take the escalator up to the next floor: the boys' department.

I was home.

I'd run straight for the cargo shorts and the button-up shirts, pressing them to my face in delight, not unlike the coupons. She'd passive-aggressively hold the clothes away from her body as I gathered them, and then I'd ask a retail gal to let me try them on. My grandma would purse her lips again in a rare moment of near defeat and deliver a backhanded compliment to anyone within range.

"A very bright lip color you've chosen, my dear," she'd deadpan to the saleswoman, who'd put a hand to her mouth as if she'd been slapped.

Sally would sit in the dressing room with me as I, deeply embarrassed to undress in front of her, tried on the clothes. She'd look away until I said, "Ready," and then she'd look up, nod her reluctant acquiescence, and then look away again so I could move on to the next item. By the end of every shopping trip, her head would be in her hands. All that mattered was, she swiped the card and we'd be on our way. *Sorry, Grandma, you made me gay.*

She was likely hoping beyond hope that one day I'd change my mind and blossom into the southern belle she clearly wanted. As my childhood passed, it became evident this "boyish phase" of mine wasn't disappearing so easily.

Chapter Four

FIRST LESBIAN SIGHTING

I don't know why it started happening. I just remember walking down the stairs to say hey to my mom before I got lost in my head for the rest of the day. The least I could do was squeeze her into my busy first grade schedule! As my foot hit the bottom step, I heard something like a sudden gunshot, followed by a ringing in my ears. I felt disoriented and scared. I rounded the corner, wanting to run into my mom's arms, and saw her calmly fiddling with her Mr. Coffee. She turned around and smiled. I watched her mouth the words, *Hey, honey,* but I couldn't hear anything. Her voice sounded muffled, underwater. She walked over and gave me a big hug, like things were normal, as I stood silent, frozen, and terrified. I closed my eyes—and all of a sudden, the ringing stopped. I could hear everything clearly again.

I didn't know it at the time, but I'd just had my first panic attack. When the second followed weeks later, I told my mom I was hearing voices. I suggest you don't ever say that, unless you're literally hearing voices.

My mom, a very calm nurse, asked me kindly, "Are people talkin' to you?"

I thought about it for a moment. I knew the difference between *I see dead people* and *I talk to myself because I'm a bored and* perhaps *lonely only child.* This was not the time to bring up my imaginary friend, Lucy, but something was wrong. I didn't know how else to describe it. Mom arranged for me to see her therapist, Barbara.

I imagine there's a rule that all therapists must be named Barbara, Bec, or Carol. Their profession is locked once their birth certificates are signed.

I've had two of the three. And both happened to be lesbians. To round out the triumvirate, I watch the movie *Carol* monthly and consider it part of my therapy routine.

Barbara had a typical therapist's home office. Half-dead exotic plants, check. Beige furniture that every depressed person in a ten-mile radius has wept on, check. Closed blinds that let in the faintest sunlight, hitting her face in streaks, check.

"Describe the voices you're hearing," Barbara said to me in a low register that could be described as the audio version of Klonopin.

"I'm not hearing voices. I hear . . . I hear . . . ," I mumbled. I felt badly about not being able to articulate what was happening, and I just wanted to get out of her office, so I backtracked.

"I don't know what I hear, but it's not voices!" I laughed hysterically. I didn't want Barbara to think I was crazy. Hysterically laughing didn't help my case.

She didn't laugh along with me. Looking back, I realize that I didn't have the wherewithal to say, *It's like a gunshot! I'm underwater! ALSO, MY DAD KEEPS CHOOSING THE MILITARY OVER ME, AND IT'S GIVING ME ABANDONMENT ISSUES! AND YOU KNOW WHAT? IT'S NOT COOL FOR YOUR BEST FRIENDS TO BE YOUR TEACHER, BABYSITTER, AND MOM. AND WHILE WE'RE AT IT, I AM TIRED OF LIVING OUT OF BOXES, BARBARA!*

Barbara was stumped (some therapist), so she told my mom to watch and see if it happened again.

Those moments were often triggered by three things: my dad being stationed far away from us, being alone, and watching Harry Potter. Seriously. I had undiagnosed OCD and anxiety that started appearing during childhood. Sure, I'd shut doors multiple times and tap on my desk. I'd check the stove repeatedly when my mom wasn't looking (she was always looking). Those were small potatoes compared to what would develop.

As the first few notes of the John Williams orchestration would play, I'd think, *Okay, don't ruin* Harry Potter *with your anxiety.* But, seeing as I had OCD, I had to say it two more times. Everything needed to be in sets of three. Per the rule of comedy? No idea. Regardless, I'd repeat the phrase, *Don't ruin* Harry Potter *with your anxiety. Don't ruin* Harry Potter *with your anxiety.* If something scary or sad flashed across my brain while I recited those thoughts—like Large

Marge's popping eyes from *Pee-wee's Big Adventure*—I needed to start over. I was afraid that a negative thought would ruin my protection from the anxiety. I had no choice but to begin the repetition again once I thought of a positive image and fixed it in my mind. "Don't ruin *Harry Potter* with your anxiety," I'd chant while trying to think of Audrey picking me up from school.[5] Then I'd feel bad because I'd missed the opening scene while I'd been talking in my head. So I'd say to myself, "Ugh, I ruined the movie." To which I'd reply, "You didn't ruin the movie. But if you stop talking, you'll be able to enjoy yourself . . . stupid." And thus, I now had to repeat that phrase. Two hours and thirty-nine minutes would go by, and as the ending credits scrolled, I had repeated that loop in my mind for a grand total of 3,333 times.

Why would I put myself through this wonderful time? Because I was scared that something would happen to my mom. That was my number one fear, closely followed by getting pregnant by hugging. If I didn't do things in sets of threes, I believed my mom would get hit by a car, die in an airplane crash, have an aneurysm—the list goes on—and it'd all be because of me. I almost deleted this section because, as I typed it, Word shut down and crashed my computer. *I take that as a sign! I take that as a sign! I take that as a sign!*

Of course her horrible demise would be brought on because I didn't ENJOY A HARRY POTTER MOVIE. You couldn't convince me otherwise. And sometimes, when I was really on an OCD high, I'd hold my breath as I said the sentences three times. Future free diver alert!

For a while, Dad was stationed in Fort Hood, and because Mom wasn't always able to take off work, I had to fly alone to see him. The flight wasn't scary, but being separated from my mom was.

When I got to Texas, he expected me to act like an adult. As a seven-year-old, I loved being an adult at some moments, but not all the time. I sought constant care and affection. Often at night, when Dad went to bed, and I'd lie awake tucked in on the couch, listening to the clock on the wall, the gunshot feeling would reemerge with a vengeance. The ticking of the clock grew louder in my head until I ran into my dad's room, convinced the clock would grow hairy arms and eat me for a late-night snack, hoping he would be my protector. Instead, he told me sternly, "Go back to bed, Elizabeth."

---

[5] Nicole Kidman is my current positive image.

Maybe it's all in my head, I thought.
It certainly was.

After the love of my life, Audrey, married someone else, I figured I'd be Home Alone from then on. I mean, Kevin McCallister did it. In my *opinión*, I didn't need looking after anymore. My mom, on the other hand, thought differently.

Mom had finished her PhD by then (werk) and become a professor of nursing. She regularly dropped hints to her students that she was in need of babysitters.

"If any one of y'all want a side job, I need a babysitter. I'll give ya extra credit."

No shame.

At this point, Mom started trying to put her foot down and keep us in one town, for fear I'd start Bubble Wrapping myself if we had to move again.

Afternoons were mostly spent hanging out by myself, with my head in the clouds. I had to find things to do to keep myself occupied. Like throwing a baseball across the yard and going to the other side to pick it back up and throw it again. Or hopping on the trampoline, bouncing high so I could see the neighbor kids on the other side of the fence. I even tried hide-and-go-seek, but that got really dark. It was what it was. To be honest, being alone is something I still have a hard time dealing with. *What if I choke on a piece of General Tso's chicken in my New York apartment? Who will perform the Heimlich? Will I be able to run to my downstairs neighbors in time?* I've since googled how to perform the Heimlich maneuver on yourself and still have no idea how to do it.

I yearned for a connection. One student who answered the babysitting call to duty was Cheryl. She had sandy-blonde hair that hit right below the ears and wore shiny Doc Martens. To my eyes, she was a very tall version of Aaron Carter. She always wore a wallet chain on her belt loop that had a shiny carabiner with her keys attached. Ah yes, my very own "ring of keys" moment. It's defined as the moment when "a young girl feels something when a soft butch walks through the door." Thank you, Alison Bechdel.

Unlike Alison, I was completely and utterly clueless.

I liked Cheryl. She didn't exactly rise to my Audrey level of "shrine made out of chewed gum" worship, but it was close. She'd take me outside to play, and she'd let me talk to her about all the stress in my young life.

"I have to eat vegetables," I'd say with a sigh.

"Vegetables are good for you," she would say. "*I* eat them."

Well, if Cheryl eats vegetables, then I should eat vegetables too!

"Does Cheryl have a boyfriend?" I asked my mom one afternoon. I had a habit of not keeping my nose out of other people's bizness.

"No, but I think she has a girlfriend," Mom replied.

"Girls can have girlfriends?" I spurted out, nearly squishing my Kool-Aid Bursts Tropical Punch.

"They can, honey. Some girls like boys, but some girls like girls." My mom could have stopped there—she'd already just expanded my understanding of the world exponentially—but Mom loved using technical terms. I knew to use *vagina* by age four and understood what *conjugal visits* were by age six. Can't remember why she'd brought up conjugal visits. I'd rather leave that stone unturned.

"She's a lesbian," Mom continued.

"A lezbiahn?" It sounded funny and didn't quite come out of my mouth right. "Lesss-bia? Lesbon?"

"Lezzzbeeeinnn," my mom corrected. *Ahhhh.* It sounded like a Japanese car.

By age seven, I knew what a lezzzbeeeinnn was. Sort of.

I didn't quite understand, but all I needed to know was that Cheryl was cool and I liked having her around. One day, Cheryl and I were at her apartment on campus because my mom needed me to be watched for the afternoon. (I promise I'm fine solo! *Has panic attack in closet.*) I loved going to Cheryl's apartment. It had a mattress on the floor and a lava lamp in the corner. Very bohemian. We were midway through *Titanic* when I looked over and saw that she had fallen asleep. Cheryl was a hardworking student nurse who took the graveyard shift and also sometimes looked after a precocious child.

I loved naps—so if she wanted to take one, that was okey dokey with me. I took the opportunity to inspect her.

The "lesbian."

I counted two eyes. Two ears. Ten fingers. The "lesbian" seemed normal. She had a pretty, feminine face, but her clothes reminded me more of a boy's.

Like mine, I thought. *Maybe I'll look like a lesbian when I grow up.* Her pants sagged, again like Aaron Carter's—but even then, this was different. I continued to examine the short hair framing the very soft face. I wanted to get closer. I sneaked around the back of the couch, and that's when I saw it. A *marking* on the back of her neck. I almost fell over. *Should I lift up her hair?* The only time I had seen a neck mark like this, it was the plug on Neo in *The Matrix.* The ceiling fan blew aside a little hair right on cue, and I saw that it was in the shape of a sun. What could this mean? Maybe she wasn't normal after all. I still couldn't help but be drawn to the "lesbian." Regardless of whether she'd taken the red pill or not, she at least resembled a girl, and I now knew that alien-lesbian girls could cut their hair short. I was excited about the possibility of using this as ammunition in convincing my mom to let me cut mine.

I was not successful.

Not only did Cheryl have a girlfriend, but Cheryl and Bonnie got engaged within a few months[6] and threw a party to "celebrate their commitment." And luckily for me, my mom and I were invited!

"Are they getting married?" I asked when I saw the save-the-date magnet made out of tree bark, with a photo of Cheryl and her girlfriend holding their beautiful white dog.

"Yes, they are, sweetie."

I lit up. "Lesbians can get married?"

"Well," she said, "no. *Technically,* they can't. It's not legal. But they love each other very much and wanna celebrate that."

"Why isn't it legal?" I pressed.

"Because the government is full of rats and shit people,"[7] she said. My mom kept it real.

The reception after the lesbian commitment ceremony, or LCC, was extraordinary. They'd rented out the second floor of a bar and set up a trifold poster board—just like I had in science fair!—with pictures of Cheryl and Bonnie tightly holding one another, both "out-butching" each other. I saw a banner

---

[6] Lesbians move in fast, or as we like to call it, "U-hauling," because we are obsessed with unboxing videos.

[7] Up until 2015, when gay people wanted to marry, they had commitment ceremonies. Certain states allowed legal marriage for same-sex couples in 2004. And one or two states even let us tip our hats and walk through silently.

in the background that read LILITH FAIR. *Must be some type of flower festival,* I thought. And what do ya know—there were other lesbians at the reception.

There's more than two?

It was amazing. I got to work examining all the lesbians with their leather vests and three-piece suits. I'd sneak up behind them to get a better look and then run away.

They all had that tough look. Like the saloon barfly guys I'd seen in the John Wayne movies my grandpa watched. There were a lot of odd birds there, and I was totally digging it.

We danced all night at the LCC reception. Me in my Birkenstocks and Cheryl in her Doc Martens.

Back at school the next week, I told my classmates all about going to my first LCC and shared my new understanding of "lesbians." *What do you know, girls can like girls!*

Shockingly to me, not everyone shared the same affection for the term *lesbian*. Later that day, my classmate Samantha walked past me on her way to the carpool lane, unable to let it go.

"My daddy says that boys can only like girls. And girls can only like boys. *You* have to like boys."

"As if! That's not true!" I yelled back, but she was already in the car before I could make my case. I ran home from school to clear this up.

"Dad! Someone told me that I have to like boys. What if I don't want to like boys, and I want to like girls?"

"That's okay. You love who you wanna love," he said, giving me a pat on the head.

Victory was mine.

Dating was not anywhere in my immediate plans—but I did, desperately, want to prove my classmates wrong. Specifically, that sourpuss Samantha.

I went back to school the next day and proudly told her that my dad had confirmed it.

"People can love whoever they want, and you're just jealous that you didn't get to dance at the LCC." I stuck out my tongue.

I was vindicated, but not for long. Just a few years later, I'd find out about Santa Claus, and my sense of superiority would be shaken.

I obsessively asked my mom if her friends had boyfriends.

"No, Cynthia's a lesbian," Mom said.

"What about Candice?" I asked.

"Candice's also a lesbian."

"Are Cynthia and Candice dating?" I asked.

"No, honey. Not all lesbians date each other."

I beg to differ.

I started to think that my mom might be part of some secret society, one with special handshakes and grand plans to take over the world hidden under the floorboards of their sensible homes. It seemed to me that most of her friends—with the exception of Clementine, a white woman who converted to Buddhism because she wanted to make her life more interesting—were lesbians. I was starting to wonder if everyone was gay!

Mom had a time-share in Key West and would fly out every spring and fall to hang out with them.

The Key West Lesbians.

I'd imagine them all just hanging out with their big, fancy Russian borzoi dogs (Mom confirmed) and wearing big Coke-bottle glasses, puffing on pipes, reading Roald Dahl to one another. In my mind, they never caused too much of a ruckus because nobody wanted to risk getting too close to the $4,000 dogs for fear they'd shatter into a million pieces. They weren't the type of dogs you'd play with. These were dogs that looked like Italian fine-porcelain sculptures—and every once in a while reminded you they were alive when their tongues ventured out of their frozen bodies.

Over time, I became pretty sure that my mom, although married to my dad, was also a lesbian. So sure, in fact, that I finally asked her.

"Are *you* a lesbian?"

"No, I'm a *heeeteroosexxxual.*" My mom was really committed to correct vocabulary.

"So why do you hang out with so many lesbians?"

"Because they make better friends.[8] My straight friends are so caught up with their kids and husbands. And they're just *fun,* ya know?"[9]

---

[8] Yes, we do.
[9] Yes, we are.

SECOND GRADE
Location: North Kansas City, MO
''Female Friendship'': Miss Narum
Favorite Gossip: ''Mia said the C-word''

I spent my time in second grade with my teacher, Miss Narum. She was beautiful, my very own Miss Honey from *Matilda* who radiated warmth like the scent of fresh-baked cookies. I'd hang out by her desk and ask her the difference between a pentagon and a hexagon even though I already knew the answer. When another kid would come up, asking for help, I'd give Miss Narum a nod, like, *Handle the children, I'll be back later.*

It wasn't always peaches and cream, as Grandpa Bobby would say. I got caught up that year in a tangled, lying mess when I spread a rumor that Mia (the popular girl) was calling everyone the C-word. I don't know how it started, but one day, one kid said it, and the next, it was on everyone's lips. The principal had forbidden us to curse or it would be straight to suspension. I appointed myself the C-word police because I wanted to be a hero in Miss Narum's eyes.

I dare you to say, "See you next Tuesday," I thought. Mia was laughing with another girl when I heard what I swore was the *C* sound. I ran to Miss Narum. The jury is still out about whether she actually said the rest of the word.

She didn't.

I told Miss Narum the truth after Mia had been sent home. It was the only time I had purposely lied, and after I fessed up, Miss Narum punished me by making me stand against the wall during recess. I felt betrayed. Everyone else knew I was a liar, liar, pants on fire. The other kids shook their heads as they walked past me to play four square. I couldn't do anything except suffer the humiliation. After twenty minutes, Miss Narum called my name, and I followed her inside.

"I like you, Elizabeth. But what you did was not nice."

I guess it worked. She likes me.

"I know. I'm sorry."

I dedicated a section of my notebook to her. I drew her along with peace signs and that weird pointy *S* we all loved so much. Miss Narum and I developed a bond so tight that—with my parents' permission—she once picked me up after school and took me on a date to Chuck E. Cheese. I set out with my lady, dressed in the mint-condition Spider-Man shirt. We ate pizza, and she watched, waiting for me at the bottom, as I successfully went down the slide. She dropped me off back at my parents' house, and I ran up to my room, drunk on the thrill of having had a date with the teacher. The next day, I had a little extra swagger as I walked into class.

My attitude for the rest of the year was, *Ha-ha, suckers! I got to hang out with Miss Narum after hours.*

But I kept the date our little secret. That one was for me.

Chapter Five

LOOK 'EM STRAIGHT IN THE EYE

If you remember anything from reading this book, let it be these three tenets I learned to live by:

Rule Number One: Always keep an industrial-strength fireproof safe packed with your passport, a gallon of bottled water, and flashlights (don't forget the batteries). You never know when there will be a fire, a giant mudslide, or an invasion of chemical, biological, radiological, or nuclear warfare a.k.a. CBRN.

Rule Number Two: The enemy is everywhere, at all times. We are targets of outside forces with ulterior motives. Be aware of your surroundings, respond and report, and don't make yourself a target. If a friendly British couple at dinner on vacation is speaking to you, and their questions get too specific, change the subject. Better yet, punch them. They are most likely terrorists.

Rule Number Three: There is only one way to put a toilet paper roll onto a dispenser. The roll must be facing toward you like a little waterfall—which makes it easier to pull the roll—with no more than two squares hanging down. I'm sure you've seen the memes. Why is it easier this way? Have you ever tried grabbing the paper when it's draped down the other side? It'll be too far out of reach, and you'll face-plant from missing the paper, break your back, and find yourself lying on the floor for hours until someone (hopefully) finds you, by which time you might be dead. It's true. We must not have that.

As much as I'd love to make this chapter all about toilet paper (or acid shit, or punching friendly terrorist-tourists), it's not. These are just a few of the many ~~disciplinary teachings~~ neuroses that my dad instilled in me from an early age.

My dad, who operated sixty-eight tons of weapon machinery, also happened to be very concerned with toilet paper position, getting a real shine on the bathtub, and every door being shut when you are not in the room. I can't imagine how his child could have OCD. I held up my grandfather's funeral to fix every toilet paper roll in the funeral home. I've been late for professional meetings because I was busy fixing the stalls in the office bathroom. Don't get me started on what I'm like at an airport.

Right before Christmas 2000, my family was packed and ready to set out on our annual trip to Jacksonville to visit my dad's side of the family. We were about to pull out of the driveway when my dad presented my mom and me with an itinerary.

"Okey dokey! The Santos family is off. This is for you . . . Mother," he said in an exaggerated accent that somewhat resembled Sean Connery's as he handed her a Xeroxed copy of a legal pad page. "This is for you . . . Daughter," he said, again with what I thought was a British accent?

"Are we ready?"

Mom and I exchanged glances. Our dogs, Sam, Ginger, and now Shadow, a schnauzer my mom had forced on my dad, all side-eyed me. Then Mom smiled back at him, her eyes narrowing, like, *Get on with it.* I looked down at my copy.

"0800–1100, drive through Missouri," he read.

"Why can't you just use normal time?" I asked him.

"*Civilian* time," he corrected me, "is way more confusing. You never know if it's a.m. or p.m."

"Just say a.m., Dad."

"No, no, no. Too many words. Add the time you want to twelve, subtract the previous number, multiply the circumference of the earth, apply Archimedes' principle—and voilà! You've got military time. Easy as pie."

Sure, Dad.

"1100, we'll swing by a drive-through, slowing down just fast enough to grab the food, 'if you don't grab it, we won't have it,' then hop back on the road," he continued. "1400–1405, gas up the tank. And 1405–1800, drive the rest of the way until we touch down in Atlanta at the Best Western. All of this is assuming no extra stops for gas, but I know this car burns twenty-five miles to the gallon."

I held the extra-crisp sheet of paper in my hand and frowned. "What about bathroom breaks?"

He squinted at the itinerary.

"I mean—if that's necessary, but the schedule's pretty tight," he said. "Might be best to do it after 1200 because of traffic."

Noon, Dad.

I squirmed in my seat, feeling the urge to pee at the mere thought of no bathroom breaks for the next four hours, if I was lucky. Mom sighed and stretched her arm to the back seat to give me a pat on the leg as my dad turned the key in the ignition. Her manicured red fingernails glimmered in the sunlight. The car was awkwardly silent. Dad laughed.

"What? Ha-ha. Oh, come on, kiddo—of course you can go to the bathroom. There's a bottle in the back."

More silence.

"Nutter Butter?" he asked, offering me a cookie from a package he'd stashed in the cup holder.

I stared at the cookie over the shoulder of the seat and declined. He gave a "suit yourself" shrug as I pressed my forehead against the cold window, and Sam tried to lick my hand.

That was my dad. Road trips consisted of fixed itineraries, work parties required extensive coaching the night before, and family cruises meant 136-page Anti-Terrorism PowerPoint training manuals with quizzes (something my dad has said I should keep on hand and refer to in the present day).

Yes, I know, I know—you're also probably speculating about what the hell was in the Anti-Terrorism PowerPoint training manual with quizzes. I'll spill. Let's see. Pictures of burning cars, blurred figures staring into peepholes, and security-camera footage of students in trench coats with AK-47s. You know—imagery you want to see right before you go on a vacation. My dad literally said, "I know there are a lot of slides, but PLEASE review it at least once (the answers to the quizzes are in the notes)."

Because of my dad's training as a high-ranking Tanker, US Army Ranger, and hard-ass, his thinking always stemmed from the military. A cultural invasion was always imminent. We can't be so sure the Spice Girls aren't Russian operatives. I was equipped to go to war, if need be. Except against the Spice Girls. I would betray America in a heartbeat for them.

Dad didn't use Venmo until two years ago, and when I left my college USB drive in his desktop computer, he went apoplectic about his security clearance. 'Cause I bet the terrorists are thinking, *You know how I'll take down America? SOPHIE SANTOS'S THUMB DRIVE.*

Despite it all, I thought my dad was a brown Captain America. As a kid, I loved that he was a high-ranking military officer. Most people would nod and say "Ahh!" when they heard. The occasional bro-ey guy still salivates when I say that Dad was a Tanker in the military and later in his career used to write speeches for the general.

"Whaaa? Who?"

"I don't know . . . *the* general?" I'd say.

"Coooool, bro. *The* general."

In addition to preparing me for any possible natural or man-made disaster or impending terrorist attack (grenade shrapnel rises from the detonation, lying on the floor reduces exposure), my dad also trained me since infancy to talk to adults like a fellow adult.

"Okay, kiddo," he'd say. "Next week, we're going to *the* general's house for the New Year's afternoon reception. There are going to be a lot of important people there, and we need to make a good impression."

We? Of course—we.

"You're a big girl now," he told me (I was eight), "and you need to conduct yourself in an adultlike manner." (Still eight.) "Let's talk about a proper hand-shake. When people come up to you, you're going to square up, extend your hand, look 'em straight in the eye, and give them a firm handshake. No dead fish."

He flopped his hand in a relaxed fashion, pointed to it, and mouthed, *Bad.*

"You're a strong woman," he said (I was very much a child), "and you are not weak. You're a Santos."

We practiced the handshake a few times, trying to out-firm each other. I wanted him to know that my eight-year-old hand was no wimp! I let go of his hand and then headbutted him. He headbutted me back. We then pressed our foreheads together, growling and wrestling, until the weaker one (my dad) caved.

I walked around the house with a little red spot on my forehead from our match, grinning from ear to ear.

We had a foot in two worlds: military and civilian, and I loved getting to go to the base with him, even though the mandatory car search at the entrance always made me think that I'd somehow brought an IED—a device I'd never seen in real life. Once we were cleared, I'd flash my military ID to the MPs like I was in the Secret Service, and we'd go on in. It was a rush and a relief to realize I hadn't brought an IED after all.

Notice the fingertips touching.

On our way to the general's house (or anytime), we'd sing one of the army's "jodies": "R is for Ranger! A is for airborne! N is for never stop! G is for going strong! E is for every day! R is for Ranger!" I guess they couldn't come up with something else for *R*.

At the reception, all the men were clean-shaven, just like my dad, in their "blues," and seemed very tall. Their hair looked like perfectly mowed lawns on top of their heads. Military parties were cocktail affairs, except that everyone was wearing the same costume. And then I saw women in uniform, with their tight doughnut buns, sharp bone structure, and their doofy husbands in civilian wear. *And did I see she parted her hair down the middle like a butt crack?* I couldn't believe it.

"Just like G.I. Jane," my dad said, nudging me. My dad loved Demi Moore and let me watch the 1997 flick because, according to him, it presented a strong woman in the military. That strong woman also happened to be naked a lot. Leave it to my dad to ignore the uncomfortable parts.

I was procuring a piece of cheese on a stick when the first couple approached Dad and me. The anticipation built. I'd been training for a week with my dad, and this was my moment. I felt like I was about to attempt to shoot the winning goal for the World Cup. I tucked the cheese into my pants pocket to free up my hands.

"Elizabeth, this is Colonel Redacted and his wife, Mrs. Censored."

"Nice to meet you, Elizabeth," said the colonel. I grabbed his outstretched hand, looked him straight in the eye, and tightened my grip.

"Whoaaaa! You've got a firm handshake!" he said.

"No dead fish," I said, giving him a toothy grin and a wink.

He let out a breathy chortle, as if to say, *Mm, yes—I hate dead fish.*

"My wife throws out dead fish like she's a sailor, and we HATE the navy," the colonel said. His wife didn't seem to think this was funny—but whatever, all eyes were on me.

"Hooah!" I said back. The chant of army officers surely had to be an ace in the hole. I smiled at my dad. I was killing it.

"Hooah! What a nice daughter you have, Major." He saluted my dad and was off. I wanted to take a bow, but why lose the crowd once you've already won 'em? I gathered by the twinkle in the colonel's eye that my dad had risen to the occasion.

Success.

And that wasn't my only brilliant-daughter moment that night. I gave out several top-notch handshakes, including to the surprisingly short general, who—due to the strength of my grip—wanted to recruit me on the spot. My firm, bony handshake seemed to make me the prince of the party. I was Ben Santos's daughter, and I was there to make him proud.

When we got home that night, my right hand was sore. We both knew it was celebration time. Dad loosened his "straight tie" and marched upstairs to change into his civilian attire—which normally meant a vacation T-shirt, cargo shorts (perhaps I did take some clothing cues from him), and slaps. (Slaps are flip-flops—and, as far as I know, my dad is the only one who calls them this.) I changed into my pajamas and tossed my pants on the ground, and then I saw the melted cheese in the pocket. Whoops. A small bump in a more or less perfect night.

I waited for him to come down to enjoy the evening's dessert; he was a dessert fiend. His favorites were, in no particular order, Long John doughnuts with icing, Ritter Sport chocolate, chocolate malts, ice cream, and cake. When we went out to eat, as soon as the server would come over, he'd say, "Can I see your dessert menu?"

"Dad! We can't have dessert before dinner."

"Says who?"

This night, he served us bowls of Blue Bell ice cream, and we sat on the couch watching Allison Janney decide which turkey to pardon on *West Wing* until he fell asleep. He always fell asleep in front of the TV—even though when I'd poke him, he'd say, "I was just resting my eyes."

⟆⟆↗

I always wanted to make my dad proud, even though I didn't really understand him or what it was like for him to be a first-generation American. Back in the forties, Filipinos could enlist in the military in order to become US citizens. Pee-Paw, wanting a better life, sailed the world with the US Navy—first as a steward's mate and then as a yeoman. While docked in Spain, he walked into the restaurant my grandma Carmen was working at, took one look at her, and told her, "You're the most beautiful woman I've ever seen. I have to marry you."

Pause. I'm happy it worked out, but what the hell was that? Pee-Paw, you didn't even know her! What if she was crazy? And, Grandma, what if HE was crazy? Men kill women all the time!

Turns out the only kind of crazy they were was for each other. They wrote letters back and forth until his grand return. However, because he was enlisted, he had to ask his ranking officer if he could marry her. The officer tried to make him reconsider.

"You know Spaniards. She's just trying to get citizenship."

The joke was on them, because she wasn't. In fact, she was offended. When it came to applying for citizenship, the judge overseeing their case didn't mince words. "Señorita Beltran, it seems to me you're trying to use Mr. Santos to become a citizen!"

"I don't need to be an American, Your Honor. I'm Spanish."

The judge was shocked, and they signed the citizenship papers right then and there. Never fuck with a hardheaded Spanish woman.

My grandpa sailed back to Spain, and they got married in her little historic town of Lucena del Cid. The entire town showed up. A true old-timey love story.

My grandparents loved America and—like all immigrant families—had to learn how to assimilate into American culture. My dad was in first grade when they moved from Morocco and back to the States, and he spoke only Spanish. Upon entering school on the base, they spoke only English, and it was time to sink or swim. Nevertheless, the Santoses loved being American. My grandfather was a proud member of the US Navy, and his son, my dad, inherited that love—for America, not the navy.

Dad's love manifested into his adoration for the military. The (many) homes we lived in over the years were filled with replicas of memorials, soldiers standing together, Tankers, Stivers prints, and Dad's framed unit guidons and unit flags. That was punctuated by family portraits of the three of us, with my mom's jovial smile and my dad's serious expression. A mirror image of Pee-Paw and Grandma Carmen's in their Florida home.

There were glimpses of our heritage, but it was a crowded field because of "Army Strong." Luckily, I got a full immersion into our heritage when I visited Grandma Carmen and Pee-Paw in the land of swamps and gators.

Walking in, you were hit with the aroma of Filipino adobo and a fresh batch of *lumpia*. *Lumpia* was for special occasions—and the arrival of the firstborn and his family was the epitome of a special occasion. Grandma Carmen, in a polka-dot, short-sleeve navy blouse with navy slacks; gold medals of patron saints hanging from her neck; and clutching her rosary, would come and kiss my face. She was eye level until I hit my growth spurt—after which she could fit right under my chin. She'd greet me holding a bowl of fruit and cheese and gift me with rosary beads before I even had the chance to sit down. She'd stare at me through her big-rimmed, tinted glasses, just saying, "Oh my God." Pause. "Oh my God, you're so beautiful," in an accent that made it sound like she had gotten off the boat the day before. Only to put me in full flamenco dress moments later, begging me to learn Spanish. At ninety years young, she hasn't changed a bit.

Pee-Paw, on the other hand, was a man of few words. I could never tell if this was because English was his second language or because he simply chose not to speak. My grandma, in all her glory, was high on Spanish culture. We always talked about Spain, we traveled to Spain, her (may I say stunning) relatives visited from Spain. Most days, Pee-Paw would sit in his recliner in his blue slippers, watching TV, dressed in a button-down with a crucifix hanging from his neck like he was ready for the usual day at the office, even though he was twenty years into retirement.

A typical convo between us at the end of a visit went like this:

"Hey, Pee-Paw."

"Hi, Elizabeth."

"I'm gonna go. We're leaving."

"Okay. Okay. I love you," he'd say, smiling, and I'd pat his soft hand. I mean, really freaking soft.

"Love you too, Pee-Paw." I'd go in to kiss his cheek, and he'd wince a little bit. He didn't appreciate physical affection. Can you blame him? He was just trying to watch *Jerry Springer*. He'd reach into his pocket and slip me a crisp $100 bill.

And that was it. It wasn't always hundreds—but as a pesky kid, I knew that saying those three little words could help me get rich quick. Just twenty dollars goes a long way when you're eight. Heck, it goes a long way even now. My parents didn't like him throwing his money at me, but even when I refused (and I did, at first—I swear), he wouldn't take no for an answer. After all, he showered my two cousins with hundos all the time because they lived near him. It was my turn, *Dad!* Money fills a void, *Dad!* You're always gone, *Dad!* I started to make my goodbyes while my parents were still in the kitchen, saying goodbye to Grandma Carmen. I had to be quick. Pee-Paw and I needed to exchange words faster than a drug dealer with a DEA agent in the next room.

In the car, my dad would ask through the rearview mirror, "Did Pee-Paw give you money, Elizabeth?"

"No . . . he . . . gave me a big hug."

Pushes cash deeper into pocket.

When we visited, I'd sleep the first night in the tiny spare bedroom, which was decked in crosses, shrines of Jesus, and ornate photos of my pee-paw and Grandma Carmen looking very serious. And like clockwork, the following morning, I'd pack my bags and stay at my cousins' instead. Grandma would show up every morning with another rosary, reminding me that I'd left mine behind.

In third grade, I enrolled in a private religious school, the one and only private religious school I ever attended. I was very disappointed when I learned we didn't get to wear uniforms, which my cousins did at their private schools. What a letdown! However, the private religious school had an art program—one so prestigious that any parent would trade their lesser-talented child to get in. We learned methods like acrylic painting and encaustics. Every grade had a huge art project they'd create together to display in the school. Our class project was to turn our floor into a papier-mâché rain-forest extravaganza!

Once we had learned about our new assignment, the other students' families took them on trips to the Amazon—the actual, literal rain forest—for inspiration. I begged my mom to take me to Brazil too.

She took me to the Rainforest Cafe at the mall.

Let's pause for a moment. The Rainforest Cafe was not Brazil—it was even better. You were taken on your safari to chow down on dishes such as Anaconda Pasta and the Sparkling Volcano. Then, midway through devouring your dino nuggets, there was a huge rainstorm, and it sounded like panthers were going to pounce down from the trees and eat you and your nuggets. The birds fluttered overhead. And there was a massive elephant in the corner of the restaurant that trumpeted loudly. Wussy kids cried around you. It was epic. We survived. The storm lifted, and my nuggets were intact. On top of that, the servers' uniform would have fit nicely in my closet. I wanted to work at the Rainforest Cafe.

Brimming with mist-machine inspiration, I chose to make the prehensile-tailed tree porcupine (not to be confused with the Malayan porcupine or god forbid a hedgehog). I *chose* the prehensile-tailed tree porcupine because I felt a connection with it. I knew that if I pulled off an outstanding porcupine, I'd win big at animal making. Actually, there is no award for this—but in my mind, I would win.

And as I was a budding perfectionist, my animal needed to look supreme.

The centuries-old phenomenon that is papier-mâché (since 200 BC, to be exact) was the best art project to give us pesky third graders. It felt like slime, and nineties kids (and, interestingly enough, kids today—and also maybe all kids ever) were obsessed with slime and dough and putting their tiny fingers into gross things that felt like boogers.

My dad was totally committed to helping me achieve the best and most lifelike prehensile-tailed tree porcupine that had ever been crafted. Projects were our thing. Dad and I didn't talk about our feelings, so we spent our time doing things, while Mom filled the role of full-time therapist and sounding board on life ("Are you sure that if I accidentally swallow soap, I won't die?").

Dad and I started plotting the project right away at the dining room table.

"We'll get pipe cleaners for the barbs, and we need to get papier-mâché for the body," I said. "And a balloon! Can't forget the balloon. But the feet will be difficult."

"I think we can get a baby doll to use for the feet," Dad said.

This stumped me. "What would we use it for?"

"We'll just chop off the hands and feet."

"Really, Ben?" Mom called from the living room over her copy of *Alone Is Where the Heart Is!* "You're gonna destroy a doll?"

"Why not?" he asked, smiling. He turned to me. "What do you think, kiddo?"

I closed my eyes to picture the hands and feet of a baby doll and then opened them and looked at the photo we had printed out of the animal.

"The feet look pretty identical," I agreed. *Hooah.*

We didn't waste any time getting our hands on a baby doll at Hobby Lobby. Despite not knowing their very public position on gay rights—or my position, seeing as I was a tiny human—I'd like to think it was a big eff-you to them because I was about to destroy the product I was buying from their store. I was not a sweet little innocent straight kid coming to paint a ceramic whale—I was, unbeknownst to us all, an ambiguously queer, androgynous nightmare child. Rawr.

I looked at our victim with pity in the shopping cart, but Dad and I were two people gunning for an A, and nothing could stop us.

When we got home, Operation Mad Scientist began. We used brute force and scissors to rip off the doll's hands and feet. Mom came down to the basement and nearly fainted at the sight of the massacre. Baby-doll appendages were strewn all over. The body had been thrown into the corner and was lying on its stomach. Papier-mâché was dripping everywhere. It was a true crime scene. Robert Stack even appeared in a trench coat and intoned, "True story, of extraordinary people and extraordinary circumstances."

I understand now that our zeal over the mutilation could have been foreshadowing a larger issue down the road—and contrary to what I thought, the issue wasn't *how are we ever going to pay for art school?*

We chiseled the Styrofoam to make the head and blew up the balloon to set the body overnight. After the papier-mâché did its thing, we attached the doll extremities to the prototype. Once the body was constructed, it was time to get down to bizness. Every bit of felt fur needed to be smooth. I groomed him meticulously before attaching the long pipe-cleaner quills. And finally, I carefully painted the dark-brown feet like a Mark Rothko prodigy. Mom pitched in by helping me with the accompanying report, spending hours researching via the hefty Encyclopedia Britannica, the animal's eating habits—because, of course, I was actually supposed to be learning something. Who knew? After 336 hours working on the model, lightning flashed, and Perry the Porcupine was ... ALIVE!!!

The day I presented the prehensile-tailed tree porcupine, I'm pretty sure my teacher lost her goddamn mind. It was perfect. It looked lifelike! Dad had procured color-coded ties to affix Perry to his tree branch. Dad and I stood there, smiling from ear to ear. Another girl, Shelby, handed her "clearly made in a rush at three a.m." toucan up the ladder to her overworked father, who hung his head in defeat. It was our proudest moment as a father-daughter team.

That was my dad and me at our best, with some massive project that required critical-problem-solving skills and gave me the opportunity to best a whole lot of other third graders. It was the last project I did at that school—because, while the teachers were training artistic savants, it turned out that we (their students) could only do math at a first-grade level. Once that became apparent, my parents pulled me out so fast, I barely had time to scream, "But what about my mosaaaaiiiic?!"

Perry lived with us until he passed away in 2010.
He received a proper burial.

Right before I started fourth grade, we moved back to Fort Leavenworth. There was a bakery outside the base called Annie's Cakes, and my dad and I would often drop in there on the way home from school. Annie's was a small, locally owned shop with handcrafted cakes.

Annie had her own style. The design of her cakes was impeccable and quirky. Her clown cake was my favorite—little men hugged the cake, as if holding on for dear life. These clowns weren't made out of inedible fondant—they were artful, three-dimensional icing masterpieces.

One afternoon, my dad and I popped our heads into the bake shop. I often got giddy wondering if I would ever meet the real Annie. There were a few women who worked there, but no one ever introduced themselves. A portly woman came out of the back. She was the same height as Dad. Covered in flour. An image out of a storybook.

"What can I help you with?" the woman asked.

Am I finally meeting the real Annie? I wondered.

"I'd like to sign up for classes!" Dad announced.

I smacked my forehead out of embarrassment. He always had such confidence.

"What?" he asked, looking at me.

The woman sized him up and gave him a tired smile.

"Sure. One sec."

She wiped her hands on her apron and left the room.

"Come on, *Dad*," I said. "You're not really gonna sign up for classes, are you?"

"'Course I am! Why wouldn't I?" He had a glint in his eye I hadn't seen before. I should have known something was up because of his excited waddle as he'd walked into the store—a waddle I inherited, by the way.

I looked up, and the woman was back, standing in front of us. She laid out a few forms, and I tried to make eye contact with her so we could shit on him together—but we were not in cahoots. He was right, I guess. He wanted to do it, so he should be able to do it.

Dad was by the book, but he did love an occasional unconventional moment, like signing up to make cakes or getting monthly pedicures because "they make my toes look real good."

Dad filled out a form that I could barely see from my height. He gave her his credit card, and we were off. I wanted to ask him questions about this new hobby, but before I could open my mouth, he cranked up the car radio, and AC/DC's "Thunderstruck" drowned out any chance of conversation. I air-guitar soloed all the way home, and he jumped in at the red lights.

Besides, my dad was not one for small talk. If I'd asked, *Why are you baking?* he'd have hit me back with, *Why not?* And if I were to ask, *What inspired you to learn the art of cake making?* he'd respond, *I wouldn't say inspired. I just like cake.* And that would be that. On the flip side, if *I* suddenly wanted to bake, then I would definitely have given anyone who'd listen a long-winded monologue about my recent obsession with my Easy-Bake Oven and how I'd always wanted to "challenge" myself.

I ran into the house, my arms numb from playing pretend guitar for the four-minute-and-fifty-two-second song.

"Dad's gonna be a baker," I told Mom, spilling the beans before he could get in the door.

"A baker? Your dad doesn't know how to bake," she said.

"Sure I do!" Dad said. So confidently. Too confidently.

"Honey, you can do anything you put your mind to," she said, kissing him on the forehead. Which in Southern Speak means, *Fat chance—I'll watch while you fall on your ass.*

"Hey! I'm serious," he said.

I exchanged a look with my mom.

"He's taking classes at *Annieee's.*"

I smirked and shook my hand to the side of my body, like I had seen in Eddie Izzard's *Dress to Kill* with both my parents. A constant joke that ran through the house if one secretly thought opposite of what they had just publicly stated. Normally he'd join me. This time, he did not.

"They have classes? When do you start?" she asked him.

"Monday."

"Do you need to buy anything for the class?"

He pulled out the piece of paper that Annie[10] had given him. I sat next to my parents at the kitchen table as we discussed what he needed to prep for his class. Whatever my dad was fixated on, whatever his new passion was—that's what we talked about as a family. Like the one time he wanted to run a naked 5K and asked us to come cheer him on.

Over the next few days, I got to help him put his baking kit together: a rolling pin, a whisk, a fine-mesh sieve, a pastry brush, a tiny blowtorch, a fluted pastry wheel, a cake pan, a round cake pan, a rectangular cake pan, and a piping bag for colored frosting. Who knew you needed so many pans! All in the name of avoiding a soggy bottom—right, Mary Berry? And while he was making the cakes for class, I'd sit on the counter and watch him. It was kind of nice. Or I'd often spy on him from afar, watching him struggle to get the layers of the cake to sit neatly on top of each other. Laughing to myself before he turned around and noticed me—at which point I'd duck into the hall closet.

After weeks of practice, he started to get really good. And I got to reap the benefits.

For my birthday, he spent hours making me the clown cake that I'd admired at Annie's Cakes. And it was just like the cake in the shop. Actually, it was even better. The clowns were hanging on for dear life.

---

[10] Jury's still out on if the woman was Annie or just a woman named Diane.

Chapter Six

FINDING GOD

"Mom? I don't know how to tell you this, but I found God," I whispered into the phone.

"WHAT?" Smoke started coming out of the phone.

"I found God," I repeated, trying to feign a confidence that I didn't actually feel. "The worship leader was gonna call you, but I told her not to. I wanted to tell you myself."

"I'm callin' your father!" Mom said and hung up the phone.

I stood in the middle of the empty mess hall with a nauseated feeling in my stomach. I had messed up big-time.

I had found God earlier that day in the middle of the woods of Missouri, at the Grand Oaks Baptist Assembly summer camp. I didn't expect to find God, nor did I initially think that was even a possibility, but that day, I had accepted the Lord and Savior Jesus Christ into my nine-year-old heart—purely out of jealousy of my fellow campers.

To say that I was jealous is an understatement. I'd moved far past my early years of hiding behind women's legs and fully into a phase where I wanted to stand in front of them. I was the kid who'd stop what everyone else was doing so I could stand on the sofa and start singing Alison Krauss's "When You Say Nothing at All" for no reason, at All.

To say that the camp was in the woods is an overstatement. In my memory, we were deep in a thick forest, but recently I researched the camp and—turns out—it's in a suburban area that happens to have trees. Three trees in total. It was next to a highway, with a strip mall a few yards away that had a flickering neon sign reading GOGO GIRLS. Grand Oaks Baptist Assembly summer camp was made up of makeshift cabins from the early forties that resembled army barracks or public restrooms, and they were only held up by the strength of prayer to the Good Lord.

If you look past the homophobia, bigotry, snakes, pushy moms, and Joel Osteen–style, veneer-capped smiles, Baptist churches are the best. Those queens are theatrical AF, and that was very on brand for me. When I was growing up, my family attended services for Episcopalians, a.k.a. "diet Catholics," where—if you look past their tolerance, inclusivity, ordination of women, and official affirmation of LGBTQ+ people—it was a snooze fest. Mass was somber, and the reverends spent a lot of time swinging scented, smoky balls. I needed more drama in my life.

Anyone with a left tit could see they were the hip denomination. Baptist services were full-on spectacle soft-rock concerts that would make Matchbox Twenty seem amateur. They'd have a Trans-Siberian Orchestra light show with confetti cannons blasting and extremely good-looking people strumming blinged-out guitars in leather jackets. I'd sing, "God is SOOOO good! He died, he died, he died on wooooood!" while playing my air guitar. My dad and AC/DC had prepped me for this.

The Baptist camps were no different. Each session had some sort of theme (such as "unhinged") that the camp would revolve around. We'd have mini stages where we would put on plays and our own soft-rock concerts (dedicated to God, of course), with ~~kids~~ me vying to lead the band.

I ended up at camp mostly because I was now attached at the hip to a kid named Bette. Bette's real name was Elizabeth, but our teacher, Miss Smith, didn't want to have two Elizabeths in class, so she gave her a nickname, which Bette despised. I didn't care because I got to keep Elizabeth.

At the time, I had no idea what Baptists believed in, but I knew they were more fun than spending the summer with the sleepy Episcopalians or in the house staring at my parents. Bette's social world revolved around church—and so now, mine did as well. I also think my mom thought she'd raised a strong daughter with a mind of her own who would not get sucked in by the Baptists.

My mom knew plenty about the Baptist Church. She had lived it. My grandma, the almighty Sally Rouse, forced my mom to go to church with her every Sunday until she got Alzheimer's and forgot she was Baptist. Unlike me,

Mom would not categorize a Baptist congregation as *fun*. I begged her to let me go to the camp.

"Elizabeth, don't be fooled by the damn smoke screen. They are cultish, mean-spirited, and have a weird obsession with water."

"I don't know . . . one singer at Bette's church had hair like Jesse McCartney. Jesse McCartney is a teen heartthrob." Gotta hand it to the Baptists—they really package it up and sell it to you.

Mom looked to the side, contemplating. I could tell she was still mad at Bette's mom for taking me to church without telling her. *And* for putting on scary movies during our sleepovers, knowing full well that any slightly scary thing would create an issue she had to deal with, i.e., me sleeping in her bed for two weeks. We'd watched *Children of the Corn*, *Pet Sematary*, and *Old Yeller*—all to the same effect. To this day, I'm so petrified of scary movies that I insist, for my mother's sake, we move on.

"I've never been camping! I wanna go camping! I wanna be one with the woods!"

In the end, Bette's mom convinced my mom it would be "good for the girls to get out of the house." Bette's mom was a typical Bible-thumping, backwoodsy, gun-toting, Greta-Van-Susteren-loving woman. I used to stay up late at Bette's house, watching Greta with her mom until I fell asleep. We'd recline in the rocking chairs, and in my best announcer voice, I'd say, "GRETA VANNNN SUSTERENNNN" while she laughed at me.

Bette's mom signed us up and off Bette and I went. Sitting in Bette's mom's van as she smoked a cigarette, I was sent off into a fever dream by the puff of smoke. I imagined us singing by the fire, playing outside games, and getting that fresh, woodsy air.

I was wrong.

It was a weeklong sleepaway camp in the middle of the woods (or three trees). Far from the parents and close to God. God is certainly closer in the woods—but so is poison-ivy rash, mosquito bites, and beaver fever, a really fun way to say the horrible sensation of giardia.

If Elizabeth is in the middle of the woods and a tick sucks her life away, can God hear her?

The camp was coed. *Whoa.* It turned out the real reason that Bette wanted to go was because there was a cute boy she was crushing on who'd be there.

Camp was crawling with prepubescent horndogs. It was a place to sneak away to the empty chapel to hold sweaty hands and look off into the distance, unsure about the strange feeling in your guts. The lucky among us would even get to suck face like two codfish, scaly lips and all.

I spent most days running around with Bette and two randos who turned out to be boy crazy too. I certainly was not. I thought Bette had invited me so that we could spend the week together (four days, to be exact). But I was cast aside for swoopy-haired Blake.

Camp started off pretty chill *(see? Told you, Mom)* with tug-of-war, paddle-boating around the lake, and Manhunt. But oh, what a fool I was. Missouri might not be the Bible Belt, but it's the buckle. It gets frequent visits from the Westboro Baptist Church and is home to the belief that there's a war on Christmas. God came down and made Missouri His thirteenth disciple.

After I had just put up my paddleboat, then came the Bible study . . . Bible songs around the campfire . . . even Bible-themed talent shows, as I would come to learn.

"Here's where you will get to put on a play, if that's your thing!" one of the camp counselors—who was a closeted Phish head, judging by the amount of tie-dye he wore—told us, gesturing toward a tiny stage.

"This will be perfect for our Spice Girls tribute, Bette," I whispered, giving her a nudge.

"We're thinking more John 3:16, ladies," he said, clearly overhearing my very private convo.

And then full-on church . . . I guess I had forgotten that church would be a major part of a church camp. And the church "lifestyle" infiltrated the rest of the camp. For example, we had to swim in the pool with our shirts on. Yes, even the boys. But if you had good eyesight, you could look through a boy's plastered wet tee (past the "God Is Dope" logo) and make out the tiny outline of a nipple. (Cue "Temptation" by Destiny's Child.)

We thought we were so cool and promiscuous.

At one of the first evening services, we had just finished singing an original a cappella arrangement of "This Little Light of Mine" (while I slammed a bongo). The young pastor—who, with his boy-band blond hair and Life Is Good attire, was a certified hottie—asked the band to play an inspirational song. The *Tiger Beat* cover model vibe was just a front. Only later did I realize he would have condemned me to the eternal fire, prepared for the devil and his angels, if he'd gotten one whiff of the gay.

As the song began, he told us that there was a reason we were all there together. And that reason was God. Which, I felt, could have gone without saying. But then he started to go on about how not everyone had accepted God. And for those people, it was time to come home.

I looked straight ahead in horror. *WTF?* I didn't want the other kids to know my dark secret—I hadn't accepted God. *Or have I?* I was christened, but I'd only been a baby, and it was only a few droplets of water. It wasn't really my choice. I had never come *home*.

"Do you accept the Lord Jesus Christ?" he asked us. "If you're ready for the next step, come forward." I watched as a few kids quietly walked down the aisle. Kids in the pews cheered them on in a low-key but supportive way.

I clapped along with the other kids. My first reaction was *look at these suckers*, but I quickly looked around and noticed that, apparently, I was the only one who felt that sentiment. This sort of thing was normal. *Da fuck?* I mean, *Da what?*

I wasn't able to sleep that night. I tossed and turned on the hard piece of plastic that was serving as my mattress. I was sweating through my clothes, in part due to the ninety-degree, midwestern, capital *H* for *Humidity* heat, and also due to a fear that I might fall off the top bunk. (Thinking it would be "fun" to be on the top bunk was now coming back to haunt me.) But more than that, I felt guilty—like I was supposed to be one of those kids headed down the aisle. I began to rethink my reason for being there. Bette spent a lot of time going on about the cute basketball boy, but I thought her crush was stupid. I had to find God—we needed to talk. *He* was the only guy I was interested in.

Every day after that, at the end of worship service, the pastor would say, "If you're ready to accept the Lord and Savior into your heart, then please come forward." Each day, more kids cheerfully walked down the aisle toward a new life. The low-key cheering had gotten rowdy.

"You go, Stephen!" echoed throughout the room. Kids slapped the pews in a fever. They were high off God. If God were a drug, they'd done a whole bag of Him. I felt envious of the Lord-acceptors stepping forward.

At night, around the campfire, the "chosen" kids would sit next to the pastor as if they were special. I'd watch them from a separate log, alone, as they talked about the man upstairs. The hurt of not being a part of the club brewed inside me. I wanted in—stat.

It was my fourth day of camp when the pastor addressed the crowd of overheated, sweaty kids again. "Now's the time I'd like to welcome anyone who'd like to come forward and acknowledge they accept the Lord and Savior Jesus Christ into their hearts."

I had had enough. It was time to get saved.

The young pastor had a charming way of speaking, and the urgency in his tone had grown steadily over the past few days. Today was the last day of camp—it was now or never. I wouldn't get a chance to be saved again if I didn't do it right then. I felt myself being pulled forward as if God were saying, *Left foot, right foot, left foot.* I pushed past Bette, who gave me a "what the hell are you doing?" look, and I embraced the pastor. I wanted to turn around and tell Bette, *I was you only a few short days ago. Come get saved with me*, but I assumed she'd learn in her own time. I felt the cheers behind me. I felt the hoots and hollers. I put the residue of God on my gums like a drug-starved addict.

The pastor gave me a tight squeeze and, as a tear fell onto his cheek, said, "God bless you."

"God bless you too," I said, welling up with emotion.

I hadn't actually found God—I wasn't even sure what that meant—but I tried to make myself believe that I had found God. It felt weird to lie to a pastor, but I couldn't turn back now.

A woman from the church who hadn't cut her hair since birth took me into a room with the other "found God" youths. Each of us had our own nice lady.

"I'm so happy to hear you've accepted the Lord and Savior into your heart," she said.

"Me too," I responded.

She stared at me. Clearly I was supposed to say more.

"But how do I actually *know* that I've found Him?" I added.

The woman looked confused.

Uh-oh, the jig is up.

"He's always there. He's all around us."

"Right . . . I guess I'm confused because I feel like I definitely found Him—but I also am not sure?"

The woman told me to close my eyes and to see if He came to me. I squeezed them tight.

God? Are you there?

Nothing.

"Your relationship with God is personal. I'll leave you be," she said. "We have all the time in the world," she added.

Oh, really? Then why am I in a tiny room separated from Bette?

She left me alone while I tried to find Him, and I closed my eyes tightly once more.

Can You please show Yourself so I can leave this room? I'm tired and scared and am pretty sure the lady will take away my "found God" card if You don't wave Your staff and cape around in my brain. Thanks. I looked to see if anyone had heard my thought. No one seemed to have noticed.

Then I saw why. All the kids had the same expression on their faces—like they were in a trance. I spotted Bette's boy toy, Blake, who looked somber and perplexed. Some of the other ladies had placed their hands on top of their kid's head, and those kids were doing some weird chanting.

One by one, the kids left the room. Blake walked past me, and I whispered, "Hey, what's the deal with the chanting?"

"What chanting?" he asked. Then he hugged a few of the counselors and left.

What chanting?! Are you kidding? Oh, no, no, no. Get me out of here!

I felt my lie being exposed.

Plus, the heat in that room was too much for my body to handle. I knew God had died for my sins, but I wasn't prepared to die of heatstroke for Him. *I ain't ready—no thank you.* The walls were closing in. I had no other choice. The only way I knew to get out of this one was to tell the long-haired woman that I had found Him. I waved her over.

"I found God!" I whisper-yelled.

"Thank heavens, you did?! I'm so glad to hear that!" She gave me a big hug.

As she hugged me, I felt more guilt—but like she said, my relationship to God was personal, which to me meant that even if it was made up, it still wasn't her bizness.

"Yes—me too," I told her. "Imagine if I hadn't!"

She asked if I wanted her to tell my parents about my new salvation, and I quickly told her no—I wanted to do it because my mom would be so proud of me and would want to hear it directly from me!

"While we prefer to tell your parents, we respect your choice," she said.

Yeah, you're not gonna spoil this for me. And don't you think you're gonna try to brainwash my mom either. I saw what you did to Blake!

Then she gave me a little pamphlet about God and "The Word." I went back to my bunk and felt weird. Shame. I didn't like that this God guy had gotten into my head. He was all around me—even though I didn't want Him to be there. All the kids were hanging out, shooting the shit. They didn't seem to be aware of what had happened.

Bette asked, "How'd it go?"

"Fine. I found Him."

"Good." She turned to one of the other girls in our room. "So do you think Blake will meet me near the docks to codfish me?" *No—he's one of them now. Also, he ain't all that and a bag of potato chips, Bette.*

I walked to the communal phone in the mess hall, tail between my legs, and dialed my home number. But of course, not until I waited for another camper to finish crying to their mom . . . *Jesus, Danielle.*

I confessed I'd found God—Mom only said, "What!" and then, "I'm calling your father."

After she'd hung up on me, I dialed again. And again. Until she answered the third time. Pure silence. She liked to do this when I was really in trouble—make me speak because she was too exhausted to get into it.

"Mom . . . I'm sorry. I messed up," I said quietly so the other kids wouldn't hear. I had messed up because I had let the Baptists take me, after my mom had warned me not to.

She was silent for another half hour, so I continued the verbal diarrhea.

"It's not like they're gonna call you! I told them not to."

"Wouldn't pick up even if they tried!" she said. "You and I are gonna talk when you come home. And I'm gonna have a word with Bette's mom."

"Please don't be mad at me," I said, lowering my voice even more. At this point, it was almost inaudible. "I didn't actually find Him. I only *told* them I found Him. But, Mom, I'm not saved, and shouldn't I be saved?" I also wanted that ceremony where I'd be dunked in the water at Bette's church to seal the deal, because it seemed like a very regal thing to do, but I decided that now was not the time to admit my secret.

"You're already saved! You were christened when you were *bornnn*." It still amazes me how many syllables Mom can use to make a word.

"Does that count?" I asked, immediately feeling better.

"We're not Baptists, Elizabeth. I'll see you when you get home." It was a relief to know that I already had Him. I felt better about my immortal soul but immediately started to dread seeing my mom the next day.

In my bunk, I wrote down a few questions to God with permanent marker on notepad paper I'd found crumpled up on the floor that had John 3:16 printed at the top.

"Hey, God. Why are You being such a poop? Like, come on, man, it's not that hard to say hello for ten seconds. You really left me hung out to dry back there. You seem to talk the talk, but You can't really walk the walk, ya know? Anyway, can You please tell me why I'm supposed to believe in You so much? And will You tell me why Bette cares more about Blake than about me? I dropped everything in my life to come to this stupid camp, and she left me in the dust. Will I ever like boys like Bette does? 'Cause right now, I only like Bette, and that's fine with me. When I wake up, You better have written me back or else. Bye. Elizabeth."

I woke up the next morning and found my piece of paper right under my face where I'd left it, unchanged except for a couple of drool droplets. He was officially the first man who I didn't find as attractive as everyone else did, and He wouldn't be the last.

Chapter Seven

STRIP LIMBO

In my opinion, our society gives young boys too much credit for being the horniest. We know when boys are up to something because there's visible proof: crusty socks and hardened boxers stuffed into the bottom of hampers. I'd wager that a lot of girls are just as horny. We just have the gift of being able to hide it better. Sorry, boys. While you may not see evidence, just know the couch armrest is our best friend.

I remember the first time I got horny. Full-body, shakingly, never-going-to-be-the-same horny. It came out of nowhere and hit me in the face like the blast of air that strikes you in the eyeball at the eye doctor. It all started at the apex of horniness: an all-girls sleepover. My first *group* sleepover.

Yes, I had spent the night at a friend's house before (come on, I wasn't a loser), but most of the time, it was three people max. And there was always the one girl who got homesick, would call her mom by ~~9:00 p.m.~~ 2100 to be picked up, and then it was back to me and just one other friend. I never did well in trios, so I'd politely tell the deserter, "We'll miss you!" as the car door slammed, only to breathe a sigh of relief and head back inside to do what I really wanted to do with my *one* friend: learn Destiny's Child's choreo.[11] Overnights weren't sleepovers—those were a way of life. They were what you did when the sun went down, and your parents didn't want to come get your ass because they were too tired and had already cooked supper.

---

[11] Yes, I realize they were a trio, but let's be honest: Michelle was always deadweight.

Real, multi-person sleepovers, I'd come to learn, were totally different. There was nothing—I repeat, *nothing*—that could beat a sleepover. It was a who-let-the-dogs-out party. It was a chance for networking. A chance to hang out with kids who normally wouldn't give me one-on-one time.

And, as I'd later find out, a sleepover was a chance for me to strip down to my XL training bra and let my freak flag fly.

This first, lady-boner-inducing sleepover happened one night when I was in fourth grade, when my basketball team, the Gruesome Hoopsters, got together at Michelle's house. Michelle was the coach's daughter, and this Michelle was no deadweight.

After going undefeated for the third week in a row, the team was on a high. Nothing could stop us. We all hugged and high-fived and were ready to let off some steam at the much-anticipated weekend hang. We were more amped than Sum 41's "In Too Deep" music video by the time Michelle's sleepover came around.

The night before, my parents had helped me pack my bag. Last-minute packing was not an option with my dad. "You need your ready bag at the ready. The platoon will leave you and you will die!" Mom sat on the floor, carefully folding and then putting my clothes into my bag, as I hugged her neck and told her how much I'd miss her. I was already having separation anxiety. She grabbed my toothbrush and wrote our landline number (even though I could recite it by heart) on a slip of paper with a huge, swirly *LOVE, MOM*. Dad gave me a flashlight (in case of a power outage, duh), his camouflage sleeping bag he used in the army, and slipped me a ~~box cutter for escaping~~ Ritter Sport chocolate. The next afternoon, my mom and I drove over to Michelle's house.

When we arrived, any anxiety I'd felt had vanished, and all the parents were laughing and beaming at the prospect of the night ahead for them: a night alone—one night and one night only. I was surprised they were so excited to get the hell out of there.

"She's your problem now," I heard one of the dads say with a chuckle to the hosts as he escorted his daughter in, gave her a fist bump, and bolted before she could change her mind. No tearful goodbyes?

A few of the moms had also packed bags: wine, jumbo acrylic wine tumblers with straws, youth sports uniform catalogs, and a little Percocet. They were clearly staying too.

My mom never tried to join that clique. I asked her why she didn't want to stay.

"What am I supposed to talk to them about? I don't have shit in common with those women," she responded.

Mom didn't have time for fake friendships. She taught me the most valuable lesson of all: "Don't hang with nobody who sucks your energy. It ain't worth it. Life's too short." She gave me a tight squeeze, looked me in the eye, and said, "You're gonna be fine. It's one night!" and headed back to her child-free home.

She had decided early on that I was a child who didn't need a lot of supervision and told me, when I would spiral, to "trust myself." But that didn't mean shit when the anxiety set in. *She* wasn't worried; *I* was worried about the sleepover. *What if I pee in my sleep? What if I sleepwalk? What if I have a seizure? I'll embarrass myself and will never be able to look my teammates in the eye again.* I'd have to hang up my Adidas high-tops—and that would be that.

I am relieved to say I didn't do any of those things.

But what I *did* do, I never saw coming.

At the start of the sleepover, we all shuffled downstairs and marked our territory by tactically throwing our sleeping bags over the perfect spot on the floor. I chose right in front of the TV. I had to be a front-row bitch. And it was—oh, what do ya know?—conveniently located next to Michelle, who I was trying to cozy up to. Being friends with her equaled more playing time. Remember, coach's daughter. Social hierarchy starts being established at vernix caseosa[12], I'm pretty sure. Then we all immediately attacked each other. With my extensive Disney Channel research, I'd thought that an all-girls sleepover meant we'd lightly hit each other with pillows and french braid each other's hair. Once the Mountain Dew adrenaline kicked in, it was quite the opposite. We started whacking each other with pillows. Hard. Terrorizing each other just like I imagined the boys did. Worse, actually. We had some shit to work out.

Sleepovers are not a time for kids to huddle in twos in the corner, quietly sharing secrets. Sleepovers are full-on group affairs, deciding who's going to be who in the Spice Girls so we could perform the choreo to "Spice Up Your Life" for the drunk parents. After we'd wrapped up our performance, the parents would make us all leave the house to do some activity that was too structured

---

[12] I learned vernix caseosa from my mom by age ten.

for drunk adults—like a neighborhood scavenger hunt. The moms held their big wine acrylic tumblers that said "Sip Happens" as we ran around looking for clues that were never found, neither by us nor the parents.

"Really, Greg, you drove to Topeka to plant the last clue?" one mom said.

"You told me to go big, Sharon."

Once we'd exhausted ourselves looking in trees and inside random old people's mailboxes, Papa John's pizzas were waiting back at the house to go IN on.

What goes up must come down, and after two or three cans of Mountain Dew and orange soda, we all crashed harder than Katherine Heigl's career. To relax, we decided to watch a movie. I don't know who signed off on it or if the parents were just too drunk to notice, but Michelle picked the romantic sports drama *Love & Basketball*. So far, this was the *best* sleepover I'd ever been on. No seizures yet.

Love & Basketball is, hands down, one of the best films ever made. A Gina Prince-Bythewood film for the girls—as well as a true depiction of what love can be like. Not to mention, we were a basketball team! The film even had "basketball" in its title!

Love & Basketball is not an appropriate film for ten-year-olds.

Which meant it was the *perfect* film for the sleepover.

Michelle popped in the DVD, and we all slinked into our sleeping bags.

The movie started off as a pretty tame story about a boy and a girl who lived next door to one another and who both loved basketball. Honestly, it was a story about *a girl* who loved basketball. And she was good at it. One night after the high school dance, the boy and girl were just messing around in a bro way when she planted one on him and they fell into the bushes outside her house.

My stomach did a soft flip-flop.

Why would she kiss her friend? More importantly, why did my stomach do that flip-flop?

They kept kissing and then climbed through the window into the bedroom. The boy reached over the bed and somehow pulled out a package that looked a lot like a WARHEAD candy—small, blue, and wrapped in cellophane. But inside was a white . . . balloon?

Instead of blowing that balloon up, it looked like he put it in his pocket. Then the girl's eyes got really wide. Like he had said something alarming, although he wasn't speaking. *Hmm. That's weird. Why would she be so alarmed?*

Did he hit her funny bone? Why would he take out a balloon and not blow it up . . . that's stupid. Oh, wait . . . I think they're . . . No. Are they? They ARE! SEX?! ARE THEY HAVING SEX?! Or . . . at least what I think is SEX?!?! Calm down, Santos—you don't want everyone to know you just mind-shouted sex. I stifled my screaming in my brain. A couple of "ooooooo"s murmured through the room. I wished everyone would shush so I could keep trying to figure out if this was actually the legend called *sex.* My mom had said the penis entered the vagina, but I did not see either happen here.

Something was brewing inside me, and I pulled my sleeping bag up to my chin. They stared into each other's eyes as he did a few push-ups on top of her. Then out of nowhere, down below near my butthole started to thump along to the music. As he pushed up, the area near my butthole . . . pushed up. Thump. Thump. Thump. Then the scene faded out. I was paralyzed.

I thought that would be the end of the naughty stuff, until a few scenes later, when they were in a college dorm. He pointed to his mini basketball hoop and suggested they play a game: strip basketball.

My stomach did another flip-flop.

I had obviously heard of basketball before. *Duh, I'm in a basement with all my teammates at this very moment.* But not *strip* basketball.

As the one on one game started, it was clear that Monica wasn't playing well. *Get your head together, girl! Or you're gonna start losing your clothes!*

I was very concerned about her performance. When she took off her shirt, I started to sweat.

They kept taking off more clothes. And more clothes. I felt like my stomach was on a roller coaster.

Then I saw myself in the movie. Taking off my clothes. Wanting to lose, which was the first time I had ever had that feeling. *What's happening to me . . .*

I sank deeper into my sleeping bag. My lower region was throbbing. It was warm. Aching. Like I had to pee but different. Like I might poop but out of a completely different region. Could I poop out of my . . . I was writhing as I crisscross-apple-sauced my legs. I had to hold my legs down with my mind because I was sure people would start to notice. *I can't be the only one about to hit the ceiling.* I didn't want to look around the room.

It. Was. Dead. Silent.

If someone laughs right now, I'm gonna lose it. Don't ruin this for me!

I sank even deeper into my sleeping bag. At this point, the only thing I could hear was the thing near my butthole, who was clearly trying to talk to me. I had never heard it speak, and I wasn't ready to hear what it had to say. I pressed my butt down firmly to quiet it and squished the area like a bug. To make matters worse, I was sweating down near my butt, like I had just played a big game. The pool of sweat was only amplifying my discomfort.

Monica lost, by the way. Unlike last time, however, I didn't get to see them go all the way.

I discovered the rest of the movie was a letdown.

No more sex? Come on! Even *Life-Size's* Tyra Banks's cameo couldn't capture my interest.

I would've given up Lammy to rewind the movie. The DVD player was within reach. *Everyone wants to see it again, right? Come on, Santos, think. What if I excuse myself to use the bathroom and then accidentally trip? I'll face-plant into the "rewind" button. . . . No. That won't work.* I tried scheming up other ways including downright asking if we could watch all the basketball scenes over again, which just so happened to include the one in the bedroom. I never got the shot. By the time the credits were playing, I was pretty sure I had actually sweated through my sleeping bag.

Is it me, or is it hot in here?

Game over.

Except, it wasn't game over. *Something* was still happening downstairs. The pulsing had only amplified. My ~~vagina~~ tootie was talking to me. (You see, despite my mom's best efforts to raise a linguistically precise daughter, I thought of all boys' and girls' parts as *tooties*. And the name stuck.)

Now that I'd been introduced to strip basketball, Tootie was urging me to play. I felt her hiss, "Get a game together!" But I had the wherewithal to see if anyone else would bring it up first.

The lights flipped on, and I saw a million stars.

No one else needs to take a breather? We're gonna turn off the moment that fast? Cool, cool, cool.

I quickly checked to see if I was sitting in a puddle. Visibly, I was clean.

"Let's play a game," one of the girls said.

It's happening.

"Want to play limbo?"

UGH. LIMBO?

"Yeah!" the other girls screamed. Apparently, their tooties were *not* talking to them.

Someone grabbed a broom from the closet, and I had to cross my legs, because I was sure that everyone could see Tootie trying to claw her way out of my pants. "HIIIII, GIRLS! WANNA PLAY? THE PLEASURE IS ALL MINE . . ."

SHUT UP! I told her.

My teammates giggled and ducked under the broom (some incorrectly, I might add). I shimmied underneath, wishing someone would pipe up about the risqué game we had all watched moments prior.

Limbo was G-rated. I almost couldn't take it anymore. I wanted to blurt out, *WE'RE ALL THINKING IT, RIGHT? IT'S MOIST IN OUR PANTIES.* But I was fully aware that if I asked everyone to strip, I'd be seen as the freak.

I was the one who asked everyone to strip.

"Maybe we should do what they did in the movie," I suggested lightly.

Luckily, some other girl backed me up.

"What she said."

She and I gave each other a knowing nod. If our tooties could have high-fived, they would have.

"Okay. Hmm. Are we allowed?" Michelle asked.

IDK. It's your house, bitch. (I didn't say that—Tootie said that.)

The voices of assent started as a murmur but quickly turned into shouts. "Yes! OMG, YES!"

We took turns holding on to the broom and limboed under it. If you fell, you took off a piece of clothing. That was the rule.

Kelsey was the first to fall. She took off her shirt. Unlike me, she appeared not to have developed, and I envied her tiny beestings. I was worried that my miniature beanbags would be too intimidating for this crowd. But Kelsey wasn't the only one shirtless for long. One by one, the girls started to fall. And soon, most of the party was shirtless. And we were all into it! Except for Meagan, who sulked in the corner. She frowned and told us, "I will not be participating."

The rambunctious energy grew like it did when the kids were walking down the aisle to be saved. Except that God was nowhere in sight, and I liked it that way. He was a gross boy, and I didn't want Him near me. Being sinful was way more fun. After several rounds, I realized I was just too damn good at this limbo shit. Finally, I fell (on purpose).

FREEDOM!

There we were, all running around. I grabbed the broom and hoisted it over my head like the tribe leader I was. I could finally see everyone's bodies. Their circles around their daggers looked different from mine. Pink. Some girls didn't even have daggers. I didn't realize we could look different.

Michelle gave me a smile like, *this is the best day ever.* I went up to go and hug her but was sidetracked by someone nudging me, thanking me for starting the most brilliant game ever.

"Don't thank me, thank Toot—" I started to announce.

At this point, we were laughing and talking so loudly that Michelle's parents came downstairs to check on us, and then the situation turned into total chaos.

"What are you doing?" they yelled, and everyone grabbed their shirts. The scramble was overlaid with cries of, "Who started this?"

Damn. Our wild strip-limbo party was over. The parents squinted at each of us, but we all avoided eye contact.

I knew we had done something wrong.

I don't know who told. Probably Meagan, who thought it was "gross." We all went to our designated sleeping spots, deflated. So much for picking a spot next to Michelle—she had fled the scene and was sleeping in her room. *Ugh! It never works out, even when I preplan.*

I'm sure the parents wanted to send us all home, but at this point, they were in the bag and it would have caused more of a frenzy than necessary. The wash of shame was creeping up my extremities and overtaking my entire body, but Tootie was pulsing more than ever. The harder she pulsed, the more shame overtook me.

"Come on . . . let me come out. I thought we were friends!" Tootie said.

"You ruined everything!" I screamed back at her.

Would I be kicked off the team? *For once, I wish Dad had a transfer at the ready so we could get. The. Fuck. Out. Of. Dodge!*

I went upstairs to ~~grab some water~~ assess the situation, and Sharon was cleaning up in the kitchen.

"Thanks for letting me stay over, Miss Sharon."

A sigh. "You're welcome, Elizabeth."

"Sorry about before. Let me know if you need any help cleaning up." I had to cover my tracks.

She politely told me that she was practically done, and I walked back downstairs.

Ughhhh. Does she think I started it? No way! I offered to help her! My record is clean!

I played the scenario over and over and over in my head for the next eight hours. The magic of the sleepover was broken, and my OCD had returned.

In the morning, my mom picked me up—and before my butt had hit the seat, I told on myself. I always told on myself.

"I don't know if Miss Sharon told you or not, but . . . there might have been a game of strip limbo . . . and I might have started it?"

Beat.

"Are you mad at me?"

She looked forward, and her eyes narrowed. Darting to the left and right. *What is she thinking? Am I grounded for life?*

"You need to be careful, Elizabeth, because I don't want you to cross a line," she finally said. "I don't want you to get kicked off the team."

She said those words: *kicked off the team.* The exact thought that had been running on a loop through my brain.

Mom always had a way of saying exactly what I was thinking. The good and the bad. She was a soothsayer. A sounding board that kept me on the straight and narrow. She was my gut check. I loved it when she was honest about the good stuff. Or sometimes, if she didn't think something was that bad, then I knew I had only made up the worst-case scenario in my head. I hated it when she was honest about the bad stuff. And today was a case of the bad stuff. My stomach dropped—but not in a good way like it had before.

I knew that I had fucked up.

"It won't happen again," I said.

"Good. I just don't want the other girls' parents to not let you hang out with them," she cautioned me.

I didn't want that either. But I wanted to feel that rush again. I thought about the night before, mixed with shame and full-on excitement. My tootie had calmed down, but I knew she had awoken.

FIFTH GRADE
Location: Roeland Park, KS
''Female Friendship'': Olivia
Favorite Pop Star: Selena

Olivia was one of my mom's students (shocker), and she babysat me from time to time. She was my first brown babysitter, and I felt a kinship that I hadn't felt before.

"YOU DON'T KNOW WHO SELENA IS?" she shouted when I asked her about a curious DVD on her coffee table.

"SIT DOWN RIGHT NOW! I'M TELLING YOUR MOM THAT YOU WILL BE HOME LATE TONIGHT!"

"Is J.Lo 'Selena'?"

Wrong thing to say. I thought Olivia was gonna put me out onto the street. After cursing my mom for never showing me the iconic 1997 film, she sat me down and held my head so I couldn't look away as I watched *Selena*.

My life changed in a flash. The journey.

"She was murdered?" I screamed. "Why would you show me that?"

"BECAUSE SHE IS YOUR SISTER. YOU NEED TO KNOW YOUR ANCESTORS."

I DON'T KNOW WHAT IT MEANS, BUT IT SEEMS IMPORTANT.

We discussed Olivia's thoughts about Yolanda—"never trust a fan club"—for the rest of the car ride home. I was officially in mourning.

"Mom, I'm wearing all black for the next week," I said as I entered the house.

"Honey?"

"We failed her. We failed Selena."

Chapter Eight

MOM, DAD, I WANNA PLAY FOOTBALL

At this point in my life, I had been to seven schools and lived in eight cities, and I was pretty sure I was about to turn into a Birkenstock. For your sanity, stop trying to keep track of schools and years. There are times when I have no flippin' clue where we were. If I could say I grew up in one town for my entire childhood, I would, but honestly, I find that type of stability horrifying.

Clear your head. Go grab some water. And have a quick pee (in my case, three times). 'Cause things are about to get more complicated.

My dad had decided to take a new-duty station in South Korea, and I was thrilled—until I learned I wasn't going with him. I had practically packed my bags and learned all the current K-pop moves when my mom told me we would be staying in Kansas. Cue the record scratch. He was going to be stationed in South Korea for two years, and I couldn't process it. I took every opportunity to tell Mom that I wanted to live overseas, not to mention, I needed to get out of town after the strip-limbo incident.

"Elizabeth, I'm doing the best I can—please don't fuck with me."

That stopped my campaign. I zipped my lips but was aggravated that we were still landlocked while Dad got to go overseas. Dad had an opportunity with the military, but Mom believed that a move like that might tear apart their relationship. Dad thought our family could get through anything. We'd lived apart so many times before. He made the difficult decision to take the post.

I was heartbroken that he'd be so far. I begged him to leave the military after the two years in South Korea were over. "Can this be the last time? Please? Please, I want you to stay. I want you to be at home."

I saw the weight of that request—one that I thought was simple—on his face, but he looked me in the eye and said, "When I come home from South Korea, I'll get out of the military."

His mood shifted to lighten things up. "Come on, kiddo, time's gonna fly! I'll be back before you know it."

"But who's gonna read Harry Potter with me?" I asked him.

"We'll read it over the webcam, kiddo! It'll be like I'm right there."

A webcam, I'll have you know, is an inanimate object that fools you into thinking someone is "right there." The house felt empty without my dad. Because he was stationed in Asia, when I was waking up, he was going to bed. Still, I thought it was cool having a dad overseas. He'd send me K-pop, rice-ball snacks, and FILA kicks, and I felt like a jet-setter.

I missed my dad, but I was happy to be with my best friend: my mom. Unlike my dad, she didn't treat me like I was a private in the army—in fact, she had only one unbreakable rule: don't be a little shit. Dad would travel back and forth between the United States and Asia, and they'd find ways to coparent me while he was abroad.

In the meantime, I was now in sixth grade and very rooted in my tomboy, baby-dyke ways. I was coming into myself and loving who I'd become. I had also become utterly obsessed with the desire to play football—and I would not let it go. I grew up watching the Chiefs (yes, before they were good, shout-out to Mahomes). I asked my parents the same question a million times.

"Mom, Dad, can I play tackle football?"

Dad was apprehensive because he didn't want me to get hurt, and Mom would say things like, "Honey, I don't know," or, "We'll talk about it." It was never talked about unless I brought it up, and the conversation never got far. It always ended with, "No—you're already too busy," or, "How about we sign you up for flag football?" Flag football—I kept having to remind them—was not *real* football. *Besides, I'm tackling people during recess flag football anyway.*

I fantasized about wearing the oversize pads and a mesh jersey with "Santos" slapped on the back. Boys would give me nice-play! pats on the butt. I wanted to be Keanu Reeves in *The Replacements* or Sunshine in *Remember the Titans*—heck, I'd even settle for being Rudy in *Rudy*.

I'd imagine John Madden and Pat Summerall on CBS announcing the new star player (me) in a misty dream sequence:

Pat Summerall: Annnd herrrrre comes Santos! Boy, I gotta say—I've never seen a player more dynamic and agile than number one. Where did she come from?

John Madden: I don't know, Pat, but the Kansas City Under-150-Pound League better be thanking their lucky stars. I see a bright future for this young player. She might be small, but she sure knows how to play the game.

I'd imagine throwing the pigskin down the field, a Hail Mary pass, and it sailing straight into my teammate's hand.

Pat Summerall: Holy mackerel! Did you see that?

John Madden: Of course I saw that! Are you kidding me? She's got an arm like Joe Namath!

I'd jump up and down, and my teammates would hoist me onto their shoulders. Our breaths would be visible in the ice-cold air, and I'd rip off my helmet, ceremoniously letting my hair down.

My parents would smile, wave, and call out, "That's our kid!"

IRL, that wasn't happenin', and I was starting to get discouraged. *Why can't I play football? Everyone else plays football!* It was a thing that kids did when they were eleven. One day, when my dad was in town, I was jumping on the trampoline, trying to see into the neighbors' house, when my parents, together, told me they wanted to talk to me. They brought me into their room. Whenever we had family conversations, we'd always cozy up on their bed together.

"Your mom and I talked," Dad said. "We've agreed to let you play football."

"ARE YOU KIDDING ME?" I punched the air in excitement. "Thank you! Thank you! Thank you!"

"But we want to talk to you about what you're getting yourself into," Mom said, getting straight to business.

Rats. There was always a *but*.

"You know, *some* people might not be okay with this," Dad continued.

"What do you mean?" I asked.

"*Some* people might not like a girl playing football," Mom stated. She had a way of saying "*some* people" like they were troublemakers.

I shrugged. "No biggie."

"We just want you to be aware that *some* people might be weird about it. We need you to be brave, Elizabeth. You *are* brave. We're proud of you, kiddo," Dad said.

"Okay, Mom. Okay, Dad. You're embarrassing me."

They each kissed my forehead, got up, and went back to whatever the hell it was that adults did. Spreadsheets? I still don't know. I sat there for a moment in my glory, but somewhere around the edges, an icky, tingly, scared feeling started creeping in. I had spent so much time obsessing over getting to play that I had forgotten (or hadn't thought about) what it might be like to actually be the only girl on the team.

I soon found out I wasn't just the only girl on the team—I was the only girl in the league.

The next week, my dad and I drove to the tackle football sign-ups. The walk into the football facility, with the gravel crunching beneath our feet, was the longest walk of my entire life.

A woman greeted us inside the weight room.

"Here for cheerleading?"

What a stupid question, I thought. For years, my teachers had been saying, "There are no stupid questions, only stupid answers," but this was, irrefutably, a stupid question. A cheerleader can look like anything, and stereotypes are bullshit. But I did not—I repeat, I did NOT—look like a cheerleader. I waddled when I walked. A waddling cheerleader? Please—spare me.

Oh. Maybe these are the "some" people.

"Nope. She's here for football," said my dad.

"Oh. It's . . . uh . . . over there," she said, pointing a lax finger to the next table. What a sight that table was! Happy little boys were with their dads. Norman Rockwell–esque. The boys were all talking to each other. Tackling one another. Way better than the girls, who were taking mimed "photographs" of each other with their fingers.

Dad and I made a beeline for the football table. I'm sure I got a few stares from other people in the facility, but I kept my eyes on the table and didn't look anywhere else.

"My *daughter*," my dad proudly said to the sign-up volunteer as he placed a hand on my shoulder, "is here to sign up for football."

It'd be juicier to tell you that we got pushback. That those *some* people called us troublemakers. That they had public demonstrations outside the football complex, holding signs that said, DOWN WITH THE FOOTBALL GIRL! That my dad called the president (because top security clearance meant he knew the prez). That the president declared, "I'll be there first thing." That he flew in, and we marched back to the football fields with the Secret Service following us—but not before my dad and I got a tour of Air Force One and a photo op. That I signed my name, and that those *some* people finally told me I could play for as long as my heart desired.

The sign-up volunteer simply handed me a form and told me to fill out my weight and age. After all, it was club football. Virtually anyone who met the age and weight requirements was accepted.

Luckily for me, there were no tryouts. Very lucky indeed, because, despite my love for the game, I'd never actually played *real* football.

They put me in shoulder pads and forced a helmet onto my head, which was the size of a small boulder. The helmet was snug and a tad claustrophobic. Dad peered in through the grid of the face mask and tapped the top of the helmet, signaling me to take it off. Practice started in a week.

My first practice was hell. They made us do "Six Inches," an agonizing death workout where participants raised their legs off the ground six inches and then held them there for an eternity. We ran drills by running fast through tires (video

games at Adventure Landing with the cousins hadn't prepared me for this one bit) and jogged laps around the football field with pads on. *I thought we were gonna play football—what the heck is this?* I might have been husky for a girl, but now I needed to learn how to hit, tackle, block, and run while wearing twenty pounds of equipment.

I was sore for a week.

"Why does my stomach hurt?" I asked my dad the next morning. I lay on the floor, unable to move.

"Because you did ab exercises, kiddo! They're good for you!"

"Hellllp. Make it stop," I begged like I was crawling across the desert, searching for water.

Back at practice, I wanted them to put me at quarterback, but they decided to make me a defensive end. My job was to tackle. A skill, I'd realized, that satisfied my bloodlust.

I was simultaneously taking dance lessons (Mom, a former dancing star, encouraged me). I danced for ten years and, no matter the effort, I was never able to do the splits. Once football started, I'd show up to dance class looking freshly battered. I bruise easily, so I had about ten bruises on a rotating basis on my arms and legs. My dad would drive me there and then wait with me until class started. The instructor would come out, horrified at the sight of my new bruises, and glare at my father.

"No . . . no . . . no . . . Miss Ibsen, my daughter plays football!" Dad proudly told her, smiling.

Slam.

When my grandparents found out that I was playing football, Grandma Sally scolded my mom.

"You always do this, Susan. She's gonna get killed! Is this payback for all those pageants I put you through?" she asked, clutching her tissue. She always had a tissue.

"Calm down, Sally. Elizabeth's fine." Papa tucked a pinch of dip behind his lip and looked around for his spit cup.

"Bobby, that's disgusting. Put this in your mouth after." She handed him a Werther's Original.

Of course, the decision to let me play football had nothing to do with revenge against Grandma Sally, but you'd think it did by the way she carried on about it. Even though she thought I might break my face and ruin my pageant "potential," both she and Papa would come to my games and cheer me on. Papa proud on the sidelines and Grandma sitting in a lawn chair with her head in her hands. Grandpa Bobby, a former football player himself, was about six three and strong as an ox. He looked like Elvis, but he had the build of Dick Butkus. He'd give me tips and practice with me in the living room, laughing as my arms flailed while he held me away at arm's length, one finger against my forehead.

"You little devil," Papa would say.

I finished the season second-string, but I was the first girl the town had heard of who played tackle football.

Okay! It's true. I'll say it: I was a trailblazer. Stop flattering me!

SIXTH GRADE
Location: Roeland Park, KS
''Female Friendship'': Miss Rast
Favorite Pickup Line:
''May I go to the restroom?''

Miss Rast was kind of a babe and tough as nails, and it was hard for me to even breathe around her. I immediately saw that she was playing hard to get, but I would take many opportunities to prop myself against her teacher's desk and (cough) charm her.

"Miss Rast," I'd croon.

I'd look at my nails and then to the side like I was Two-Bit from *The Outsiders*, a character I'd just discovered from the Scholastic Book Fair. Without her glancing up, her blonde ponytail talked for her.

"Yes?"

"Can I go to the restroom?"

"I don't know, Miss Santos, *can* you?"

Cold. Real fucking cold. I shrank in my clothes and pretended to kick rocks.

"*May* I go to the restroom?"

I was fine with the chase. She taught me how to speak good and to care about maths.

My infatuation with Miss Rast was very real to me. Was I latching on to her because she was the only stable thing in my life? Maybe. After I finished sixth grade, every few years, we used to talk on the phone, and she'd update me on her life. I'd called the elementary school, and they gave me her number. I've since lost that number and don't know her married name. I've long searched to find her current whereabouts. If you're out there, Miss Rast, I love you.

Chapter Nine

WHERE TO SIT IN A PRISON YARD

I often think of where I'd sit in prison. If I were to ever go to prison. Like, if I ever accidentally brought an IED onto a military base. (I still haven't ever seen one. Please don't put me on a national-security-threat list.) I have a fear of going to prison, and there's no mystery about why. Military kids are given a military ID at age ten, and I lost mine because . . . hello, I was ten. When I told my dad, he scolded me for an hour about how someone had probably stolen my identity and was now using it in Indiana. Then he made a call, put me into the car, and we drove to the military base and pulled into the United States Penitentiary.

The notorious United States Penitentiary, known as the Harvard of prisons. Ya know, formerly home to the Birdman of Alcatraz, Michael Vick, and even George "Machine Gun" Kelly—not to be confused with Machine Gun Kelly. We parked. I gawked at him and then scanned the tall, ominous tan building with barbed wire all around it. It was the exact place that my parents told me I wasn't allowed to go near, so why were we here now?

We walked into the building and waited in a small room with fluorescent lights, with a tired security guard behind a glass window. *I guess this isn't so bad.* Then an MP came out through a buzzed door with an extra gate attached and escorted me into a menacing, desolate cement-block room. I noticed a table in the center with handcuffs attached. All the room needed was torches on the wall, and I'd have been sure they were about to flay me right then and there. The table seemed to telescope away from me as I gaped at it. I looked back at my stoic dad as the gate slammed and locked behind me with a huge KA-CHUNK. The MP motioned for me to sit, and then he silently filled out a huge stack of paperwork.

The scratching of pen against paper was somehow my worst nightmare.

More silence and scratching.

Without a word, he got up and disappeared into the darkness. I could make out a figure opening another door at the far side of the room, and then he was gone.

The MP left me alone in that room for twenty minutes, wringing my hands. *Welp, might as well say goodbye to my clothes.* I patted my cargo shorts like a sad puppy—hoping to god I hadn't brought the pocketknife that I didn't own. Right as I was about to give myself a full cavity search, the MP returned, and instead of bringing me a bright-orange prison uniform, he brought a newly printed ID.

"You know your way back out?" he asked as he sat down again and continued to do paperwork. *Chyeah . . .* I wobbly stood up and walked toward the locked door. I stood there, and before I could knock, another KA-CHUNK and SQUEEEK, and I was let back into the real world. The sun on my face never felt so good.

For the next ten years, I thought that's what happened when you lost your military ID: you were taken to prison. But when I lost my ID again in college (not due to drinking or anything), my dad admitted that I could just go to the commissary, and they'd print me out a new one in fifteen minutes.

"WHAT? I THOUGHT YOU HAD TO GO TO PRISON!"

"I wanted to teach you a lesson," he said with a shrug.

I've been scared of prison ever since. And I often wonder, if I had to go for real, where I'd sit in the prison yard. I'm white, but not white enough to sit with the Aryan Brotherhood. I'm Spanish, but not Latino—and seeing as I don't speak Spanish, I would be booted before I could mumble, *"Lo siento."* And I wouldn't be able to sit with the Asians, because no one knows I'm Asian. (I know you picked this up because you assumed I was Puerto Rican.) Plus, Filipinos are often told that we're not Asian *enough*. That's the thing. I'm not enough of one thing, which is kind of the biggest head trip there is when it comes to being multiracial. That and *is this Goya product we're using tonight for Pee-Paw, Grandma Carmen, or Grandma Sally's black-eyed peas . . . ?*

It's a hard world. Let's hope I never have to go to prison.

All this is to say: I'm an "Other."

Other **definition:** being the one or ones distinct from that or those first mentioned or implied.

This was *Merriam-Webster's* definition. I have not a flippin' clue what the census thinks it means.

I'm an Other because of my parents, naturally. Today, interracial marriages are not uncommon. At the time that my parents—a southern white woman and a Filipino/Spanish man—hooked up, they were a sight to be seen walking together down the street.

I'd like to think that, instead of the race issue, it was really because he was a foot shorter than she was.

There is clear evidence to the contrary.

Mom once dropped my baby butt off at a walk-in day care on the base. When she returned, they wouldn't give me back.

The woman looked at me, "Santos" name tag on my shirt; looked back at my mom; then looked at me. Then she said, "That's not your daughter. I can't let you take her."

My mom can quickly go from zero to one hundred. I can't remember what happened that day—because, once again, I was a baby—but I'd like to think she stopped nothing short of becoming the Hulk . . . that she grew ten times her size to hover over the woman and demanded, "GIVE ME MY DAUGHTER, GODDAMMIT, or I'll tear this place to smithereens!"

This was the first of many cases of false assumption that have plagued us.

For at least the first decade of my life, I didn't notice. The first time I became aware that I was an Other was in sixth grade, in Miss Rast's class. And no—it wasn't because of how I was dressed. That's a whole different kind of Other.

It was in Miss Rast's class that I first took a standardized test, otherwise known as the stupidest test known to humankind! I hated standardized testing so much that I took a cue from my Baptist days. I prayed. I prayed long and hard that my teacher would forget to hand out the tests.

She didn't forget.

Miss Rast passed out the packets, and we sat quietly awaiting instructions. Miss Rast, the love of my life, suddenly became a robot.

"We're now going to begin our state-mandated test. Please do not pick up your pencils until you have been asked to do so. If at any time you have a question, wait until we get through a section, and *then* you may raise your hand. Please remain quiet."

In my head, I heard the deranged clowns say, *Please keep all hands and feet inside the car. You are strapped in! This roller-coaster ride to hell is happening whether you like it or not—ha-ha-ha!*

Miss Rast continued. "We're going to start by filling in a few demographics. Please fill in your name."

Should I put in my actual first name or the name I preferred? Already, I felt like a failure. I decided to choose my battles wisely and begrudgingly bubbled in "Sophie."

We then had to fill in the little bubbles of our date of birth, birthplace, and gender. This I could do, and I sat up straighter in my chair. Then, finally, we were onto the last part of the data collecting: our ethnicity. The choices swirled in front of my eyes, each contradicting the one that came before it. "White, not Hispanic," "Hispanic, not white," etc. The bubbles taunted me like my very existence was a sick joke.

"We will now begin the math portion," Miss Rast announced. "You have sixty minutes. Your time starts now."

I still hadn't picked which bubble to fill in for my ethnicity. I started to debate why one choice was better than the others. The voices arguing for each bubble fought like a jury inside my brain.

The minutes were ticking by. I was still hung up on the census survey while everyone else was now on the math portion. "If Isabella has four white friends, and I have one brown friend, how many snooty test makers does it take to make one kid feel excluded from a goddamn census survey?" I glanced around the room, then guiltily turned my attention back to my paper. I wasn't allowed to move a muscle—this was a totalitarian regime, and The Man would think I was cheating.

I raised my hand. Miss Rast walked over to me.

"I don't know what to put."

"What do you mean?"

"I don't know what ethnicity I am. It says 'Hispanic, not white.' I'm both."

"Pick what you feel is best. You're not going to be graded on this portion."

In other words, she abandoned me—no child left behind, my ass. I now had to, as a confused sixth grader, decide who I was.

I filled in the "white, not Hispanic" bubble and felt a swell of guilt. Like I had forsaken my Jacksonville family and all our ancestors. Though I had made a choice, and that part felt good! I had answered the question. I'd chosen my bubble. I felt a sense of warmth wash over me. I looked up at the clock, and twenty minutes had already passed. That meant I only had forty minutes left to do the math section, and—despite being able to calculate that amount of time pretty quickly—I sucked at maths. I sank back in my chair.

Just as I went to turn the page, my eye caught on another bubble: Asian / Pacific Islander.

I forgot about Pee-Paw!

That evening, I went home, slumped onto the couch, and tossed my dirty backpack onto the opposite couch (a disgusting habit that I still have). Sam curled up next to me and nudged me with his wet nose. My mom walked in.

"How'd the test go, honey?"

"Fine. I killed the essay. But, *Mom!* They asked us all these questions that we didn't cover in Miss Rast's class. It's not fair!"

Mom kissed my head and said, "I'm sure you did fine, honey. I can get you a tutor."

"Ew, no. Also. They made us fill out questions about our race." I told her about the contradictory bubbles.

"Just put white, honey," Mom said. She opened her new book, *Sanity: Is It Really All That?*

"I'm not *just* white."

"It doesn't matter." Her drawl sounded even more intense than usual. "It's all a crock of horseshit, anyway."

I went into my room, opened the door, and almost got hit by a baseball. My room was still decorated floor to ceiling in SPORTS! I sat on my twin bed and looked at a photo of my parents and me. It *was* a crock of horseshit, but I still felt lost. I felt white around my mom, but something was off. Sam peeked his head into my room, and I gave him a nod. He understood. *A dog always understands.* He hopped onto the bed and tried to put his entire human-size body into my lap.

The next day, I called my dad via webcam. Over the video call, I brought up my conversation with Mom, and he almost jumped through the computer screen.

"You're BROWN! Elizabeth! Look at me. You're brown!"

"I know, but Mom thinks I'm white. I *am* white."

"Yes. You are—partly. But not completely. Pee-Paw is Filipino. Look at your skin." He held up his arm to the webcam. It was certainly brown. It was also hard to really tell . . . we're talking about a 2001 webcam.

"What about the Spanish side? It said, 'white NOT Hispanic.'"

My dad just said, "Naaah—you're brown. You're brown."

"Thanks, Dad."

So that clears things up. Mom thought I was white. Dad thought I was brown. And I still had no idea what was going on or when my dad was coming back.

"Good news, though," Dad continued. "You'll get to meet the rest of our family when we go to *Spain* this summer."

"Yeah! You're right." I felt better once he reminded me.

"Love you bigger than a dinosaur."

"Love you bigger than *ten* dinosaurs."

His screen went black. I wanted to be both, equally, but I felt like it would be easier to just say I was white and leave the rest alone. I didn't have time to juggle my identity while also juggling how to deal with Dad living across the world. All the K-pop in the world, all the frozen MREs he'd send me so I could eat lunch like a soldier, all the times I stood up at Career Day and said, "My dad's not here because he's in Korea fighting the enemy. Which is way cooler than your dads who work in HR," didn't really cut it. I wanted him home. I thought about what we'd do if he could squeeze through the webcam and appear in person—even for an hour.

"Hey der', kiddo. I only have an hour, but I wanted to come and see you."

"You're back?"

"I am. Let's go do brown things!"

"YES!" I'd jump on his back, with my arms around his neck, and we'd fly up in the sky (because if he can jump through a webcam, he can fly, duh) to travel to Saint Augustine and go have flan at our favorite Spanish restaurant. I know Spaniards are white, but flan rocks, and that's what we liked to do.

He didn't come through the camera. I pushed it off the top of the computer because I didn't want to stare at it anymore.

I still didn't have total clarity about my ethnicity, but I would be getting more clarity about our family dynamic.

Before long, we were off to Spain. Unbeknownst to me, it'd be our last hurrah.

Chapter Ten

¡VIVA ESPAÑA!

Every year in July, thousands of people flock to Pamplona, Spain, for the Fiesta de San Fermín, where they sprint down a very narrow cobbled street as bulls are unleashed behind them. The winners get—I guess—spared? And the losers get a trip to the morgue. It's a tradition about machismo, and it's for people with egos big enough to think they can outrun an angry, thousand-pound, horned beast. Naturally, my dad wanted to do it.

And, judging by the book my mom had recently purchased, *Ten Vacations That Will Solve Your Problems!* she wouldn't mind too much if a bull potentially ran over him. It was a win-win, so we were off to Spain. The land of paella and siestas.

The trip to Spain was a family affair. Attendees were Mom, Dad, Grandma Carmen, Pee-Paw, and my mom's best friend, Libby. Libby, a.k.a. Aunt Libby, a.k.a. my fairy godmother, was a southern tugboat captain and queen of the ocean. I was named after her. She had to be a descendant of Rosie the Riveter, and underneath the waders, she wore jeans, a tucked-in blouse, and pearl earrings as she sailed the open seas. Libby and my mom had been best friends since high school. Libby joined so she could also run with the bulls.

Dad had made us get to the airport four hours early. There was no rushing through Kansas City International à la the McCallister family. In fact, we had time to get to the airport, back home for Dunkaroos, and back again. Instead, we stood in line together at the gate, arms linked, so we'd be first on the plane, even though we had assigned seat numbers.

My Spanish ancestors were welcoming me to Spain—and my Filipino ancestors were begging me to leave as the plane landed. For those who aren't history savvy, Spain conquered the Philippines in 1521—so the fact that my Filipino grandfather was so enamored with the enemy (my Spanish grandmother) was perplexing. *You don't fall in love with the enemy!* That was rule number one—I didn't need my dad's handbook to tell me that. That's like dating a Jet when you're a Shark and the Jets stole land from you five hundred years ago. Well, it happened, and that's how my dad was made—and thus, me.

People usually think "Santos" is Spanish, but it's actually from my Filipino side—which, again, is also part Spanish . . . because of the conquering. If I say that "Santos" is actually Filipino, history-savvy people often say, "So . . . you're Spanish!" And I reply, "Ah, yes, thank you. No one has ever made that point to me." Actually, I usually respond with, "I'm Spanish *and* Filipino, so I like to conquer myself," which puts an end to the conversation.

At the time, I was still figuring all this out, and my only example of what it was like to travel overseas was *Passport to Paris*. I had watched enough Mary-Kate and Ashley films to know that this trip to Spain would be a "passport to fun." The twins had found their crushes, so maybe I'd secretly find my own Euro boy hanging in front of a café, smoking a cigarette. He'd be 'laxing on a Vespa and wearing a half helmet. We wouldn't be able to understand each other, but we'd just stare into each other's eyes for hours, which would be satisfying enough.

I walked out of the airport and expected to see my European crush loitering right there. Sadly, there was only a snot-nosed kid pushing his sister.

As this was a Santos trip, I learned more rules from the Santos handbook. Rule Number Four: always know three phrases in the destination country's language: "Where's the ice cream?" "Where's the bathroom?" and "What hotel did you say you were staying at because you're asking too many questions and it sounds like you might be a terrorist?" Luckily for my dad (who only spoke Spanish *un poquito*), we had my grandmother with us—the only translator we needed. Sort of. Grandma Carmen speaks a blend of Catalan and Spanish, so depending on the region we were in, we could be SOL. We could have the UN called on us when asking for ice cream.

We spent the first days in Bar-they-lona at our cousins' beautiful villa. Aunt Libby and I stayed in a washroom that had been converted to sleeping quarters.

I slept on a cot, and she slept on the floor. Perhaps this was because I'm the precious only child. Fans blasted my face in the humid room.

During the day, we'd hang out at my cousins' pool, which was made of *cuerda seca* glazed tile. Judging by the decor, I thought they must be royalty. They ate like royalty too. Each meal would be seven courses, to the point that I'd be begging to tap out right before midnight. But, like, if they had gorgeous tile and enough food to feed the masses, why the hell didn't they have AC?

The next destination was Lucena del Cid, the small town where Grandma Carmen was born and raised. It was an old-world setting, with cobblestone streets and tiny shops. I spent the majority of my time hanging with my great-uncle Fernando, who was a Spanish Don Rickles. We were able to communicate despite the language barrier by playing with our food at dinner. I'd scare my mom with the shrimp heads from the paella. "Ahhh, it's attack of the shrimp! *Booga booga!*"

"Be careful around Uncle Fernando. He used to get me into trouble when I was five years old and he would pretend to give me alcohol," my dad warned. *HOW OLD IS THIS GUY?*

We were fed by Raquel, my grandmother's sister-in-law. She was even shorter than my grandmother—which I didn't think was possible.

Maybe it was the excitement in the air and the sight of the art-house-style posters in storefront windows, but I quickly went from wanting to meet other prepubescent nonconformists to wanting to see a bullfight.

That's right. A real, live bullfight. I already had a few matador figurines my grandma had gifted me, but I wanted to see one in the flesh.

"I wanna see a bullfight!" I told my family.

"Mom . . . what did you do?" my dad asked Grandma Carmen suspiciously.

"What do you mean, me? I'm an angel," Carmen said, smiling back at him.

"You're gonna see me run with the bulls, kiddo," my dad said. "You can see a bull then. Do you wanna run with me?"

"Ben! She's eleven. She's *not* running with the BULLS!"

"Come onnnn. She's fast!"

"Oh my God . . . ," my grandma said, clutching her cross.

Aunt Libby piped up. "I'll throw her on my back. It'll be fine!"

"How 'bout I buy all of you your own bulls, if y'all let it go?" Mom asked us.

"Yeah, yeah, sure, sure," Grandma Carmen said.

Grandma Carmen had three go-to English phrases: "Oh my God, you're so beautiful." "I love you, sweetheart" (when she used the word *sweetheart*, it probably meant she had forgotten your name). And "Yeah, yeah, sure, sure" which meant "shut up." Most often, "Yeah, yeah, sure, sure" was reserved for my dad, who had a habit of trying to tell our matriarch what to do.

That was that. No bullfight. No red cape. That didn't mean Spain didn't have other things to offer.

That night, Dad asked me if I wanted to walk up a small cliff the next morning to watch the sunrise.

"She's not gonna get up, Ben," Mom said before I could respond.

"'Course she will . . . ," Dad said doubtfully.

"'Course I will!" I declared.

"You're gonna get up? At six a.m.? Without kickin' and screamin'?"

"Well . . ." I shuffled my feet. "Six in the morning?"

"Sunrise is actually at 0430," Dad said.

Mom smiled at me like she had won.

When I say that I had never been more tired in my life than that morning, I had never been more tired in my life, and that's including the time I pulled an all-nighter on Adderall, almost passing out in the shower, before my Spanish final, oddly enough. I regretted promising my dad as soon as he came into my room.

"Wakey wakey!" He had a tank top with "Branson, MO" shellacked (as he'd put it) on the front and had clearly already had his Wheaties, a.k.a. The Breakfast of Champions, by the spring in his step.

Wanting to prove my mom wrong, I bounded out of bed with my own "Branson, MO" tank top, Nike shorts, fanny pack, and Doc Martens fisherman sandals already on. Damn right, I'd slept in them.

Mom was in the kitchen, pouring herself a cup of coffee. I thought she was gonna keel over when she saw me.

"Well, if my eyes do deceive me!" she said with some sass before her face turned to disappointment. "Now, why do you get up for him and not for me?"

"It's not every day we're in Spain, Mom."

"Aren't you tired?" she prodded, stirring her coffee.

"NO!" I said and followed my dad. I turned back and mouthed, *Yes!* I had to give her a win too.

Dad and I climbed the cliff together. The cliff was more or less a tiny mountain, and it zigzagged. I panted as we kept climbing upward. Dad stopped to breathe in the fresh air.

"You okay, kiddo?"

"Mm-hmm." I slipped but caught myself, hoping he hadn't seen it.

I looked down at the houses below. They were old, all different heights, with chipping paint. They had clothes drying on lines. The houses had history and were much more appealing than the little boxes I was used to seeing in suburbia. Once we got to the top, there was an open-air hut that I poked my head into, imagining that whoever lived here probably wouldn't have ever had the luxury of sleeping in. The town had been around since the age of Thor—and the hut smelled like it too. My dad beckoned me to come over to him, and we sat down on the ledge together outside.

"I used to do this with my dad," he said as we looked out over the buildings and the sun rose. "And now you and I are doing it together." He gave me a little nudge. And I nudged him back, harder.

It was nice. We hadn't spent much time together lately, and the hiking trip (which it certainly was) almost made up for the fact that he'd been away for practically a whole year.

We made our descent. I walked into the house, immediately went into my room, and got back into bed.

"That's the Elizabeth I know," Mom said and joined me for a nap that turned into a siesta.

The final leg of the trip was to Pamplona. Dad and Libby donned the white-on-white outfits, with the red scarf and waist sash (which apparently isn't actually to attract the bulls, because they are color-blind, but to honor San Fermín). I also got my own makeshift outfit. I hadn't found a hunky guy with a beret, so I became that guy with a beret. Mom, Dad, and I had stopped by a farmers market, and I'd spotted it hanging there—an upgrade from my German baby beret. From a satellite, I looked like a large boob.

The people were packed like sardines in the narrow cobblestone streets of Pamplona. And since some Spaniards like to be natural, it smelled like sardines too. People were hanging out of windows to get a look at the main event. If anything were to go awry, the bulls weren't the only thing that would stampede. I couldn't see anything from where I stood a ways back in the rambunctious crowd, but suddenly I noticed that something was happening above my head. A man was trying to steal my beret, but my mom smacked his hand away in two seconds.

Don't fuck with me, I saw her eye-say to the man. *She means bizness.*

All of a sudden, a rocket was fired, and the crowd cheered. The *mozos*, as they called the participants, were running down one of these narrow roads to get away from the bulls. Apparently.

"The *mozos* are running down a narrow road!" a man cried.

Then another rocket, and the bulls were released. I tried to squeeze through the crowd but couldn't get past anyone. *Oh no! Is my dad okay?* There was the thundering of the hooves. The crowd was cheering even louder. *This sucks! I wanna see!*

About two minutes went by, and my mom said, "Let's get out of here! It's over!"

"It's already over? Is Dad okay?"

"He'll either meet us at the beer hall, or he'll call us from the hospital."

Dad was more than fine and was drinking water with Aunt Libby when we met up with them. They were laughing!

"I touched one!" he told us.

"And I pushed a guy in front of one," said Aunt Libby.

In fact, a bull had a late start (something I totally understand), so Dad and Aunt Libby ran back up the path, to run alongside the last bull. What rebels!

Nothing could top that day, and our trip was coming to an end. I was sad to leave Spain. I felt like I had just gotten into the Spanish way of life.

"Please let us live here!" I begged.

"No can do, kiddo. But we can always visit."

Normally, when you return home, the vacation fades away, and you're forced back to reality. Except the reality I returned to wasn't the new school year or jet lag.

One afternoon a week after our return, my parents said that we needed to talk and brought me into the living room. This was in direct contrast to how we all usually sat on their bed. Mom sat on the love seat, and Dad sat on the couch. I don't remember a lot of what was said, but it all led up to this:

"Your mom and I have decided to not be married anymore." Dad tried to look stoic.

I looked between both of them, trying to understand. But we had just gone to Spain! We had all been laughing together. What do you mean—*not married?* I begged them to reconsider.

"You love each other, though!"

"We do, and we love you."

Dad's eyes filled with tears. I had never seen my dad cry before. It was over. I started to cry too.

"If we're all sad, then why are we doing this?" I continued.

I looked at Mom. She looked like a dam that was about to burst. Her face was sunken, and her red hair was going in every direction from the sweat.

Dad just shook his head. "I think I'm going to go now, but I'll see you tomorrow, kiddo."

"Can't we have just one more night? All of us together?"

"I'm sorry, but . . ."

Dad got up, kissed my forehead, and walked out the door. I didn't know where he was going. I heard him mumble something to Mom about an apartment and "yeah, I have some stuff—thanks."

I curled up into Mom's arms and wept. I had never felt so much pain in my life.

"Me too, honey," she said. "Me too."

My dad got an apartment in a complex about ten minutes away from our house that should have been called "Sad. Single. Dads." The complex was a step down from what I was used to. Guys in white tank tops with their feral kids running around. Older men smoking on cement porches. Had all these people pissed off their wives? Dad's apartment was barren, with only a few paintings that hadn't been hung yet and a dining room with a small table and two chairs. He didn't have a couch. The TV was on the floor, with some of his favorite Star Wars movies stacked next to it. I went to my room and noticed I had a small twin bed with brand-new sheets.

"What do ya say, kiddo? Want to go out and grab some stuff for your room?"

We went to Target, and I picked out a few items. *I guess having brand-new stuff isn't so bad.* But the rush from our shopping spree was fleeting. I felt my anxiety starting to come back. The first night I had to sleep at his place, I suffered separation anxiety from my mom. This unfamiliar apartment wasn't home. Our home was on W. 54th Terrace. I wanted to scream at him, *JUST COME*

BACK. I'LL CONVINCE MOM TO RECONSIDER. But it didn't matter. My parents' marriage was over—and my wounds were only beginning to cause me pain.

The day the divorce was final, I came home and saw that all the carpet had been ripped up around the house. I saw my mom standing there, drenched in sweat, exhausted, and I ran to her and held her because I knew, then and there, that our lives would be different.

To make matters worse, with two homes to shuttle between, I had to learn how to be more responsible with my stuff.

I played the violin in elementary school. And a violin is not a hard thing to keep track of. Except when your parents live in separate houses.

I'd be having dinner with my dad when I'd get that gut feeling of terror. *H-E-Double-Hockey-Sticks. My violin.*

"Dad . . . ?"

"What, Elizabeth?"

"I left my violin at Mom's."

His face showed complete disapproval and disappointment.

"You have to be more responsible! Think, Elizabeth. Think." That was his go-to line when I messed up. *Think.* As he shook his head and his nostrils flared, I'd get up, walk over to his beige slimline phone, and call Mom. Her sweet southern voice was exactly what I needed to hear.

"What is it, honey?"

"I left my violin at your house!" I said and started trembling. I couldn't take the wrath of another parent.

"It's okay, honey! Can you put your dad on the phone?"

I overheard him saying a few *yeps* and *uh-huhs* and, "She needs to be more responsible." Within a few minutes, we were in his Chevy Malibu, off to Mom's.

This happened a few more times.

Once he was no longer living at home, I wanted him to make good on his promise to leave the military. And he did. He kept his promise. My mom attended his retirement ceremony. She had been there through it all and still offered her support. I stood by his side, dressed in khakis and a green polo (for the army), as my dad was awarded for his twenty-two years of service. It felt like the end of an era. I had gotten what I wanted: my dad back. Only this time, even more was about to change.

Chapter Eleven

ARAB, AL, POPULATION 8,320

My mom moved on from my dad quicker than you can say *yeehaw!* I had just mastered keeping track of my violin when Mom started sneaking around the house, whispering on the phone with an unknown subject. I say sneaking, but she didn't do a good job because she had to drag the landline into her room, and it stuck out from underneath the door.

"Who . . . are you talking to?"

"A friend, honey. I'll just be a minute."

Three hours later, Mom would appear in her pajamas, by which I mean an oversize painter's shirt, basketball shorts, and her omega gold necklace. She'd be flushed and smiling.

The ~~friend's~~ culprit's name was Buck, and he lived in Bermuda.

"Bermuda? What's Bermuda?" I asked.

"It's a little island. A British territory. I think I'm gonna go."

"TO BERMUDA?"

My mom was officially dating again.

Buck happened to be the first man who gave Mom attention after the divorce. She was like a baby owl and imprinted on him through the landline. I could tell because Mom reverted to a full-blown teenager. Here are the fabulous ways he won my mom over:

1.   He listened.
2.   He sent her a carton of (duty-free) extra-long Marlboro Lights.
3.   He helped pick out the ticket she bought to Bermuda.

She came back with a new tan line, a new Myspace-official status, and had big news for me.

"YOU'RE GETTING MARRIED?" I yelled over a drive-through burger she'd bought to bribe me.

"I love him. He's my dream man."

"YOU JUST MET HIM!" *There's no way you can fall in love with someone and want to uproot your whole life in two months!*[13]

"He treats me the way I should be treated, Elizabeth. I really love him. I *need* this."

"Will he be okay that I play football?"

"Oh yes, honey. He's extremely supportive."

She then blasted Keith Urban's "Somebody Like You" on the car stereo and sang it at the top of her lungs. *I bet you put that on your Myspace profile too.* It was like her inner southerner had cranked the dial way up and it'd gotten stuck on max.

I was silent. I wasn't ready for her to move on from our old life. Not yet. Correction. *I* wasn't ready to move on. Again, I had just figured out how to keep track of my things. (Make sure you duct-tape the violin to your body, so there's absolutely no chance it will be forgotten.) I didn't need another curveball. I liked living by ourselves. We had a good thing going. I was comfortable.

Still, she decided it was time for us to meet. The car pulled up from the airport and, I kid you not, Buck opened the car door, put one snakeskin cowboy boot down and then another. He stood up. I stared at the Wrangler jeans and the tucked-in, cream-colored, brushed-alpine flannel shirt. On his face was a thick gray Tom Selleck mustache that clearly took a lot of testosterone to grow. His coiffed gray hairdo was a foot tall.

This was not my dad.

This was not a midwesterner. People were rubbernecking as they drove past our house. *What in the tarnation?*

---

[13] Listen, I wasn't a lesbian yet.

Although they had both served in the military (Buck had been drafted to fight in 'Nam), he couldn't have been more opposite of my by-the-book—and yes, sometimes anal-retentive—military dad. Buck smoked Swisher Sweets and was 'Murican. He was as tall as a tree. Once again, the opposite of my dad, who was five eleven with good inserts. (Sorry, Dad.)

"Hi, partner," he said to me in a drawl similar to my mom's. He stood with his hands on his hips. His chewed nails gripped the sides of his washed jeans.

"Hi. Nice to meet you."

"Y'all talk!" said Mom. "I'm gonna bring your stuff inside. I'm so happy you're *heeuhr*! You're both *heeuhr*!"

Both? I live here, Mom.

"Thanks, babe," he said, winking at her.

Mom took his Carhartt tan coat and his one-piece tattered-horse-leather duffel bag inside.

"So . . . I play football. Are you cool with that?"

"Fine by me."

I figured he was okay.

He made himself comfortable, as my mom made him a ham sandwich and helped pick out the pieces from his mustache.

A few days later, Mom was in Alabama visiting Buck's parents, and I'd decided to spend the weekend at my friend Devon's because I didn't want to be left alone with the possessed Furby that lived in my basement, eager to suck my soul and eat my corpse for dinner. Mom called with more news.

"Now . . . I wanna talk to you about somethin'. We're thinkin' of moving to Alabama, honey."

"ALABAMA!" I reached out to grab my friend Devon's hand. *Please hold me.*

"It's so gorgeous down here, and I think you're really gonna love it. I loved living in the South. And I really wanna be close to Mother. I don't have that much time left with her." Grandma Sally had been diagnosed with Alzheimer's a year before.

"I want to talk about it when you get home," I said sternly.

I did think I had a say. I was an equal member of the household!

"Okay, honey. We can talk about it." She had a sincerity in her voice that meant two things: Yes, we would talk about it, and I'd get my say. But also—her mind was already made up, and the plan would be in place before I could bring out my PowerPoint presentation (thanks for the training, Dad).

Still, I wasn't going to Alabama without a fight. I didn't want to move. It was one thing to keep going from town to town because of my dad's job. But the idea of moving to an unfamiliar area for a guy who I was pretty sure she'd found on Craigslist seemed totally ridiculous. And for love? *Bye.* And to the South? And as much as I'd fantasized about living in California or Europe, I had never—not once—dreamed of putting down roots in the South.

In the words of Regina Spektor, *No, thank you, no thank you, no thank you!* I gave her my eleven-year-old blessing.

Buck and Mom got married three months[14] after the initial phone call on the day before my twelfth birthday.

"THE DAY BEFORE MY BIRTHDAY?"

"It's not *on* your birthday, sweetie."

Red flag, red flag, red flag.

It wasn't like I was some big birthday person. I didn't do "birthday months," because it was just such a Leo thing to do—and I was a Taurus. But Mom and Buck couldn't have waited until the next week? My gifts were still waiting to be wrapped! I was livid.

"Now, Elizabeth, please don't be selfish. We have planned a big birthday party in the park for you. *I* got all your relay activities[15]. *I* bought your cake. *I* helped you send out the invitations[16]. Please lay off."

My parents' wedding had been a lavish spectacle: the gowns, the military uniforms, the swords! Buck and Susan had a backyard barbecue. We all wore identical white button-downs and Wrangler jeans. The ceremony was held on the new deck (that Buck had built) at Buck's sister's house. One of the Key West Lesbians officiated.

Buck's parents lived in a small town called Boaz—and since he won rock, paper, scissors (which I'm pretty sure he managed to cheat at), we settled in a town only forty minutes from there and four and a half hours from Grandma Sally and Papa. This made no sense because she had said she wanted to live closer

---

[14] Again. This was a shock. I hadn't fulfilled my lesbian destiny.

[15] Burlap potato sack racing, piñata, "what we admire about each other" game.

[16] All from Target with special boxes that said, "Check yes if going" or, "Check no if you suck."

to *her* parents—but what Buck wanted, Buck got. We packed up our house in Kansas and loaded up the car.

Not only was I about to be shipped off against my will, it meant I was leaving Devon.

I wrote her a letter goodbye (a habit I have horribly kept), folded it like a little paper football, and gave it to her the last night I slept at her place.

On the day we left, she stood outside the car. I hugged her so tightly, I figured our bodies had melded together and she could come with me.

As I hopped into the car, I said, "Please tell Miss Rast I love her."

Devon sat on her bike and watched as we pulled out of the driveway.

The town Buck chose was called Arab, Alabama[17].

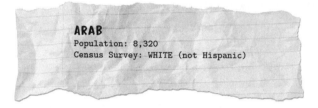

ARAB
Population: 8,320
Census Survey: WHITE (not Hispanic)

Yes, I lived in a town called, Arab, Alabama. Wikipedia makes itself very clear: "Not to be confused with Arabs."

Legend has it, Arab was originally meant to be named after a man called *Arad* Thompson. Back in the olden days, towns were named at post offices, and the weather forecasts were made based on a groundhog's shadow. The town clerk delivered the new name to the post office and only after he had left, the post office discovered the name had been misspelled. Despite realizing the mistake, they were too lazy to fix the one-letter error. Or they didn't care. Or maybe the clerk had to run an errand that he was late for and didn't have time to confirm with the post office if it was to be "Arad" or "Arab"—and his tardiness set in stone the worst name in history for a southern town.

Maybe, but we'll never know.

So I moved to an all-white town bearing the most racially inappropriate name imaginable. To make matters worse, our town's mascot was called the Arab

---

[17] Under no circumstances do you called it AH-RAB. Or AIR-AB. Or AIR-RAB. It's called AY-RAB. I'm the idiot here—people made fun of me because I *mispronounced* Arab for a solid three months. Kids would ask me, "Why're you calling it that? What's WRONG with you?"

Knight. 🌟 He was a knight in shining armor who happened to be Arabian—meaning from Arab, Alabama, not the Middle East.

According to the census survey then and now, the town was technically 99.6 percent white. (I was the 0.4 percent.) I was *the diversity hire* for the town. All you had to do was put my face on a brochure—which is sad for people of color, because on a scale of one to Selena, I'm a Britney . . . Bitch.

The house Buck chose looked like a shack to me. He called it a "fixer-upper." It was on Mockingbird Road, and if you drove past the run-down trailers and past the chicken farm—

"What is that smell?" I asked as I breathed through my mouth, hyperventilating.

"Chicken farms, girlie!"[18] Mom said, smiling.

Buck added, "That's their shit. Don't it smell good?"

"I love it," my mom said back as she took a deep inhale.

Stranger danger! This is not my mom!

If you went past the deathly smell, past the one Martha Stewart home that was halfway down the street, and then down a long gravel driveway, you'd find our house tucked away.

"Isn't this wonderful?" Mom asked. "You can't see our house from the road. It's a little hideaway!"

Why would you want to . . . ?

My mom gave me a tight squeeze. I took one look at the shingle-board house and thought, *If I huff and I puff, I can definitely blow this place down.*

"Don't worry," Buck said to me. "We got big plans for this house. Don't we, babe?" He was already moving some lumber.

I walked around to the back of the house. There was a towering American flag and about five acres of land. On the other side of our fence, I saw cows grazing. One cow looked at me and mooed. I mooed back.

"Well, if we're gonna make this work . . . I want a tree house and a pool," I said as they came around from the front.

"Done!" Buck said. He dusted off his hands.

---

[18] If you've never had the pleasure of smelling chicken shit, all you need to know is that it smells like if a dog managed to dig up a century-old corpse, eat it, then roll around in rotten salmon he found in a river of sewage, then fart on you, and even then . . . it was still a two on the scale of *bullshit smells I should never encounter.*

"Really?" I asked, confused and a little disappointed. Yes, I wanted a pool and tree house, but him denying me would have been cause for an annulment. The ink had barely dried!

"Oh yeah, honey," my mom said. "Buck's good with his hands. Aren't ya, babe?" They kissed in front of me, and I wondered if they could get started on the pool stat so I could go ahead and drown myself.

And good news! The chicken-shit smell immediately permeated my Spider-Man silk shirt.

Arab was the epitome of the South. Missouri seemed like a raindrop compared to the flood of Christianity Arab was drowning in. People went to church in the Midwest because it was practically a tax write-off. People *lived* at church in the South. There were Wednesday youth services, Friday evening services, Saturday, and the traditional Sunday service, so again, it's cheaper to claim a pew and sleep there.

Arab was a dry town because the church argued that alcohol poisoned "the children." They had pencils they handed out at stop signs, hoping to infiltrate the school. Did it make it harder to get a beer? Nope! In fact, it was easier.

You wanted to practice any religion besides Baptist or Methodist Christianity? You had to drive twenty minutes to the neighboring town. Mom and I went to the Episcopal church in Guntersville, and we didn't tell a soul. Buck thought it was in his best interest to stay home.

You were judged by your decision to say either "Roll Tide" or "War Eagle," the two big university battle cries—and trust me, you had to choose one or they'd slap your back for you to cough out an answer.

Sweet tea was shot up intravenously.

And people were painstakingly nice. Mom tried to enforce the southern "yes, sir" thing for two seconds until I looked at Buck gnawing on a corn on the cob and said, "No." I knew respect—I had learned it from Dad's military parties—but I wasn't about to incorporate that into my repertoire. N.O. (MA'AM.)

You were a person of color? You had to live in a town twenty minutes away called Guntersville. Luckily, it was near a beautiful man-made lake, with excellent hiking. The hippies and free thinkers who lived there were probably jarring their moonshine before they gave it to children.

Arab, by contrast, was a sundown town until 1990. I didn't even know such a thing existed until in high school, when my lifeguard coach said she wouldn't give me a ride home from Guntersville.

"Yeah, girl. I can't roll up with my boyfriend's rims blinged out. Sorry."

WHAT?

"Look around, Santos. You're one hoop earring away from deportation in that place."

You wanted to eat at a "nice" restaurant like Bob Evans, Red Robin, or the ~~Waffle~~ Huddle House? You had to drive a minimum of forty minutes. You wanna see a movie? Fifty minutes. The closest town where we could do anything besides doughnuts in a high school parking lot was Huntsville.

And the most important thing about Arab: no one ever leaves.

Living in Arab was a massive change from the relatively happening midwestern cities I'd grown up in. That and my cholesterol was in jeopardy because of the number of fried Oreos I ate.

The first night we were in Arab, I got bit in the ass by the South.

Mom and Stepdad were sitting in the living room of my step-grandfather's house, laughing and talking. Buck's father, Walter, was a hardcore-military World War II vet. I also decided pretty early on that he was a jerk (not because he was a vet but because of what happened next).

I was outside, throwing a ball for Walter's German shepherd, but I quickly grew bored. The dog did not. I left him there and ran back inside, and then I felt the sharpest pain in my leg.

I came into the kitchen with chunks of my leg in my hand. My mom and stepdad wrapped my leg, scooped me up, and drove me to the ER.

In the exam room, the doctor assessed me.

"Cain't do stitches for a dog bite," he said. "I can only do butterfly Band-Aids. If you put on some ointment, you can prevent it from scarrin'."

My mom was distraught—but that didn't stop her from ever-so-subtly demonstrating her nursing knowledge to the doctor.

"Because she could have a fulminating infection that could lead to necrotizing fasciitis and amputation?"

"Correct," the doctor said.

I didn't know what the rest meant, but *AMPUTATION?* Apparently, stitching a bite was unsafe. Animal bites carry a high risk of infection, and stitching a wound increases the likelihood of amputation. Look it up. The mouth is nasty, y'all.

The doctor bandaged me up, and we headed home with my leg in a plastic sack. As we drove, my mom and stepdad made jokes about how the scars they each had were badges of honor.

"Will they put the dog down?" I asked.

"We're gonna talk to Walter about it." Mom looked at Buck, concerned.

Let the record show that my step-grandpa did not put him down. In fact, he blamed *me* for the dog bite—in front of the dog.

We got back to the house, which didn't have any furniture yet. I spent my first night there lying on the floor, my leg in plastic wrap, in great pain. Should have known right away that the event put a curse on our time there.

The next day, I started my new school. Middle school.

I had to take the bus.

I had never taken a school bus before.

That first morning, I boarded and walked all the way to the back. At the next stop, an older degenerate—who was in eighth grade but looked like he was sixteen, because he was sixteen—sat directly behind me. He wore shit kickers and a T-shirt that said "TOOL." The degenerate said "hi" to me by placing a tiny speaker in the crevice between my seat and the window and then blaring "Colt 45" by Afroman.

"HEY! Shrimp Fried Rice!" he drawled. He shout-rapped along as the song played explicit lyrics that I knew weren't meant for my virginal ears.

I kept my eyes directly forward.

"I said, Shrimp Fried Rice!"

I clutched my backpack.

He shouted on top of the blaring music, "HEY, PONYTAIL! WHAT DO YOU THINK ABOUT MY SONG?"

"I . . . I . . . I don't really like it. Can you turn it off?"

"What'sa matter, Shrimp Fried Rice? You don't like it?"

That's what I said. I also now realized he was calling *me* "Shrimp Fried Rice," which was a line directly pulled from his song, which went, "I ate that p#$Sy like shrimp fried rice."

I was conflicted. On the one hand, he recognized my Asian-ness. On the other hand—

"Hey! Shove it, Jeb!" a gruff female voice piped in.

I looked up and noticed that a girl about the same age as me, in a T-shirt, long basketball shorts, and Jordans was in the seat in front of mine. She had blonde, shoulder-length hair, parted down the middle—just like a butt crack.

I could tell immediately that she was a part of my tribe.

"Whatever, Shayna! Tell Shrimp Fried Rice to perk up!"

"I'm Shayna," she told me. "Ignore Jeb."

"Thanks. I'm Elizabeth."

"You talk funny!" she said and laughed. "Where are you from?"

"Kansas. We just moved here."

"Y'all ever been to the South before?"

"Yeah." Beat. "You sound funny," I poked back. Then she strung a few sentences together that I took as a warm welcome to school, but I couldn't quite make them out.

She turned back around in her seat.

After the shrimp-fried-rice incident, I convinced my mom to drive me to school by insisting "they're gonna beat me up because I don't sound like them." It worked, but a new problem arose. I was late to school several times because we got stuck behind a tractor (cursing).

The promise of an impending pool and tree house faded once we settled into our new home. For one, Buck's previously coiffed gray hair was now always sweaty, and his clothes reeked of stale cigar smoke. He traded in that cream alpine flannel for darker colors that hid the dirt, and his Wrangler jeans had cigar burns on them.

Buck was a rugged, blue-collar Alabama boy who had been living in Bermuda because the cost of living was dirt cheap. (Later, I'd come to wonder if it was also because Bermuda was far away from his exes.) He was a contractor, a handyman, and a . . . I actually have no idea what he did. He had a plumbing license—that I do know—and was an electrician at one point. A self-made ex-pat whose assets were in all cash.

Honestly, Buck just bothered me. My mom waited on him hand and foot and paid for everything.

"Does Buck work?"

"He works on the house, honey!"

I'm all for the wife being the breadwinner. Mom was proud of it too. But Buck wasn't cooking or cleaning or being a productive member of the family. Once the construction on the house was done, I mostly saw him watching TV or hanging out in his toolshed, untwisting and retwisting a loose bolt.

There were times when he'd fly back to Bermuda, and I hoped he'd get lost in the Bermuda Triangle. *Ah—so tragic that we'll never know what happened to his plane.*

Sadly, he never did.

I hated spending time with him outside. He would just toss his Swisher Sweets, still fully lit, onto the lawn. I imagined the grass catching fire from the cigar and—within an instant—burning down our few acres of yard and then our house. Secretly hoping he'd go up in flames with it—but not my mom. She and I would drive away, never to return. By the time I looked back up from the smoldering butt, he'd have another Swisher Sweet in his mouth.

I thought Buck's whole "American by birth, southern by the grace of who cares" attitude was whack. He'd get mad about really inconsequential things, like me calling his brand-new, bright-red Hennessey VelociRaptor 6X6 pickup truck a "car"—as if me calling it a "car" would make it sprout fairy wings and fly him to dine with the Disney princesses. He loved dogs more than people, and I will never trust men who cry at the death of an animal but not of a person. He said "idear" instead of "idea."

And he wasn't my dad.

After Dad had adjusted to the shock waves that were sent through his body when his daughter was transplanted across many state lines, he went to Maryland to work for the government, now as a civilian. There weren't any jobs in Alabama; Maryland was no farther from Alabama than Kansas was. All of my childhood, I had felt it was my dad's choices keeping our family apart, but now it was my mom's.

Buck still had one important redeeming quality: he was supportive of me playing tackle football.

It turned out that football meant something very different in Alabama. Tossing the pigskin was just a thing people did in the Midwest, but football was a whole way of life in the South. Have you even heard of Bear Bryant? People there would name their firstborn after him in 'Bama. And SEC didn't stand for US Securities and Exchange Commission. It stood for NCAA Southeastern Conference Football[19].

I was not prepared.

My mom and I drove to the town's youth football practice field.

"Here for cheerleadin'?" asked a woman at the sign-up table. She had a platinum-blonde hairdo bigger than an Easter basket. Once again, I was not a cheerleader, and by Alabama standards, I was even less of a cheerleader.

"No. She's here for football," my mom said in a dismissive tone.

"I see. Well, then. It's . . . inside? The boys are inside, ma'am. Okay, next. Next, please." Then she whispered to the woman sitting next to her as a pudgy man with a toothpick in his mouth made direct eye contact with me.

The weight room was small, with tin walls, and it was occupied by burly southern men and boys who all looked like Ham Porter from *The Sandlot*. It was a different picture than the Norman Rockwell scene I had witnessed only a year before. The boys were bigger, and their bulging arms had farmer's tans. Some had clearly started to hit puberty. I saw a boy who could only be described as Mount Kilimanjaro. *Let's hope I don't have to come into contact with him, ever.* I stepped onto the scale, and a man scribbled my weight on a legal pad. I grabbed shoulder pads and gear to try on. I kept to myself because I didn't want another "shrimp fried rice" incident. I signed out the gear, and we stepped outside.

Then a bald man with no neck popped his head out.

"Santos?" he called.

"Yeah? I mean, yes, *sir*?" I had been practicing . . .

"Can you come with me for a moment?"

Ughhhhhhh. This is it. This is the "some" people. I'm done for, and they didn't even give me a chance.

He sat me down at a folding table with another man, and my mom quietly sat by my side.

---

[19] The greatest conference in college sports. I have since fully committed.

"Here's the thing. Hi. Didn't introduce myself. I'm Coach Randy—this is Coach Carlisle." He stuck out his hand.

"Nice handshake ya got there!"

I know . . .

"Anyhoo. Ya know, we looked at your chart, and you're just shy of being in the lower weight class by about ten pounds." When he said "ten," it sounded like "tin."

"We think you might do better in that class," he continued. "Mom?" He looked at her. "Do you think y'all can make the lower weight class?"

THIS IS ABOUT WEIGHT! I felt a huge rush of relief. But no, no—I didn't think we could do that, if that meant having to shed "tin" pounds off my husky body.

"I mean, we can try," my mom said doubtfully.

"Listen, no pressure. If it happens, great. If not, we'll put you on the heavy-weight team. But the boys are bigger, and it might be safer not to—okay, Mom?"

Mom and I discussed it in the car, and then Mom drove me straight to the Burger King drive-through, and we ordered the usual: double cheeseburger, large fries, and three packets of barbecue sauce. The next week, I was in the heavyweight class and was placed on the Broncos, led by Coach Randy himself.

He gave me a smile as I walked onto the field.

"Santos!"

I ran up to him.

"Guess the other weight class didn't work out, hun? Ah, shoot—least you're stuck with me." He smiled, and then the smile turned into a grimace.

GOD PLEASE DON'T MAKE ME DO SIX INCHES!

"Errrbody on the ground now! Gimme Six Inches!"

I was immediately thrown back into drills.

The coaches made me left tackle and defensive end—positions that, in the pros, were reserved for men who weighed about two hundred pounds, and that's the lower end. Peewee football was no different—it was just scaled down proportionally. So there I was, going up against boys built like shithouses.

I was put up against our record-setting linebacker, Rogers, in a one-on-one-tackle drill. Winner gets a tackle; loser gets the wind knocked out of them. I hit him as hard as I could. He didn't push back.

"Rogers! What the heck are you doin'? You're a disgrace!" Coach Randy yelled. He blew the whistle, and we went again. I hit Rogers. He stood there.

"Rogers! You gotta be kidding me. Stop foolin' around!" yelled the coach.

"I ain't gonna hit no girl."

Coach Randy grabbed his whistle again and blew on it.

"I need everybody to take a knee and listen up! I said, take a knee, dog-gonit!" We all dropped to the ground. "Santos is your teammate. She's not your sister. She's not your mom. She's not the cute girl in class you have a crush on."

Awww—thanks, Coach.

"She's your teammate. She's wearing the same jersey as you. So when you hit her, you hit her just as hard as you'd hit Jones or Martin. Got it?"

Muffled and inaudible yessirs were heard.

"What did you say?"

"YES, SIR!"

"Good! Now, Rogers! What do *you* gotta say to that?"

I put my finger down on the grass in the three-point stance. My heart was pounding. I looked into Rogers's eyes. He seemed scared and, frankly, confused. Everything he had been taught went out the window. It was something else I learned living in Arab. Gender roles were set in stone. You never hit a girl! Girls belong in the house. Boys belong in the yard. If you hit a girl, how's she gonna cook you dinner?

Then Rogers's expression changed, and he zeroed in on me like I was dead meat.

Wait, I thought. *Wait a minute. Wait, Coach . . . I think I'm good. Treat me like a girl. Treat me like a—*

Coach Randy blew his whistle. Before I knew it, my ass was on the ground, gasping for air.

"Atta boy!"

Rogers offered me his hand, and I took it and weakly got up. The blow had hurt like hell, but it also felt like an initiation. For the first time since starting the sport, I felt like an equal. With every hit, I became stronger, better, faster, and meaner. And before I knew it, I was a starter on both offense and defense.

Gaining acceptance from my teammates was just half the battle. Getting support from the rest of the league was different. There'd be groans from other players and coaches on competing teams about not wanting to play against me. But my team stuck up for me, and Coach Randy would say, "Yeah, I wouldn't want to go up against her either. She's gonna kill you."

Every time I'd hit the field, I'd beat their guys and sack their quarterback.

Meanwhile, I continued to take dance classes. Just like back in Kansas, my teacher in Alabama would shake her head as Buck dropped me off, covered in bruises. I didn't correct what they were thinking. In fact, I made sure to limp a little bit as I entered the room.

I finished the season with five quarterback sacks—including knocking Mount Kilimanjaro on his ass[20]—and with new friends from my team. I'd also gained a reputation in the town, and other girls started showing up on the sidelines to cheer me on. Dad was so proud that he even penned a sonnet, and I'd love to share it with you, but the permissions were too expensive.

With seventh grade ending, it was time to sign up for middle school ball. By the time tryouts rolled around, all the other players had definitely hit puberty, and everyone was much bigger than I was. The coaches decided to try me at quarterback. Turned out, I wasn't great at throwing the football. But I was too small to play defensive end or right tackle. Nevertheless, I showed up on time to the locker room with the rest of the team, changing behind a little folding screen they had set up, so I could hear the coach's inspirational chats.

Then something happened. In the middle of training that summer, *I* hit puberty.

---

[20] I don't know why I lied. I absolutely ran away from him. As soon as the ball was hiked, I ditched hitting him, and ran as far as I could in the opposite direction.

Just kidding. Here's Dad's poetry:

PIGSKINS AND PONYTAILS

Pigskins and ponytails
or so the story's told,
Ain't for the faint of heart
it's only for the bold.

Faces stare across the line
their bodies caked in mud,
Steam rises from their sweat
here and there, a drop of blood.

Defense in, cries the coach
quickly trot eleven,
Helmets held in their hands
looks like they're in heaven.

Fifty-two! yells the crowd
let her play for sure,
Our girls came to see her hit
they want to be like her.

Time again they crash the line
looking for a little width,
Quickly plugging all the gaps
is a lineman? called Elizabeth.

—*Ben Santos*

PHASE TWO

$\longrightarrow$

"The One(s) You Want to Marry"

It's painful to be beautiful.

—My mom's friend Dorinda, 1998

Chapter Twelve

PUBERTY, PART I

I was in the middle of seventh grade when it happened. I woke up one day, as per ushe, ten minutes before I needed to go to school. I always set three alarms. One was to wake me up. The second to make sure that, when I fell back asleep, I didn't fall into a deep REM cycle. The third meant I actually had to get up now because my mom was about to go apeshit.

That morning, my mom had already opened my door multiple times, as all three dog-barking alarms were now going off at full blast together because of my option to "snooze" each one.

"Elizabeth, I'm leavin'—and if you're not ready in five, then you're on your own," she said before slamming my door so hard, a baseball rolled off the shelf.

Getting left behind would be bad. I couldn't drive, and I wasn't friends with the neighbor kid who drove a tractor. I sleep-drunkenly grabbed an outfit from the floor (or maybe the hamper), dressed, and swished some water through my braces. With just enough time for a quick pee, I was about to pull up my pants when I saw it. The kiss of death. The thing I had sworn would never happen to me. My period.

No no no no no no no.

I guess I thought that if I dressed like a boy and acted like a boy, then my period would mistake me for a boy and pass me by.

It did not.

"ELIZABETH!" my mom yelled out with a hard pronunciation on the *Z*.

I put my face close to my Hanes Her Way to double-check and then quickly moved it away in half disgust, half discombobulation. It smelled like pennies had spilled into my underwear.

Is this what a period smells like?

"Elizabeth! You have five seconds to get your ass in the car!" She meant bizness.

I knew she was about to leave me behind, yet I didn't want to tell her. I was too embarrassed. Getting your period was the A-number-one girliest thing in the world. But if I didn't tell her, then I was about to be the girl who had bloody pants in class. I shuddered. It had become my number three fear at age twelve, behind my mom's demise and me getting pregnant from hugging. (Also, once pregnant, then having the baby in Walmart. I had watched *Where the Heart Is* too many times.) Despite my mom showing me countless birthing videos—which looked like the scene from *Men in Black* where the alien, covered in alien goo, breaks through the flesh of the farmer's body (I was fascinated and prepared!)—and her reassuring lectures in the car ("I've told you a thousand times. The penis has to enter the vagina. Did Ryan do that when he hugged you?"), my brain couldn't make sense of the miracle of life.

I pulled up my pants, walked down the hallway, and went into the kitchen, where my mom was lathering on lipstick one more time, as if to hold her tongue.

"Mom."

"What?" she asked sharply. I thought her head was gonna snap off.

"I think I—I mean, I don't know. I—"

She glared at me.

"Gay-et. Ian. The. Car," she told me through gritted, perfect white teeth.

"I think I started."

My mom's face switched from an episode of *Snapped* to sympathetic in two seconds.

"Oh, honey—it's okay. It's okay—I promise. Here. Let me see if I still have some pads lyin' around." My mom had undergone a hysterectomy a couple of years before, so there was only a fifty-fifty chance. And let me tell you—she *loved* to tell ya about that hysterectomy. No period! No problem!

She checked the cabinets in the middle bathroom. No one ever used that bathroom except for guests—of which we had none—but someone, somehow, had left a box of pads in there. A ghost? A young girl who died from getting her period and bled out on the floor?

"Wait, I think I also see a tampon—"

"NO!" I was horrified. Too girlie, and I was not ready for anything to be inside Tootie.

Mom grabbed a ghost pad and stayed in the bathroom with me.

"Want me to show you how to use it?"

"NO, MOM!" I said, mortified. I shut the door.

"I think I saw some instructions in the back of the cabinet," she said through the door.

I remained silent. Not that I usually had great boundaries about privacy. When I was five years old, any time I heard the shower crank on, I'd immediately hop off the couch and walk into my mom's bedroom—no knock, no kind of warning, just good ol'-fashioned intruding. She'd be standing there, naked, bunching her red hair up into an oversize shower cap.

I'd strip down, stretch out my arms, and scream "NAKED PEOPLE!" while running toward her to give her a bear hug. It was our thing. She'd let me shower with her, but not before throwing an oversize shower cap onto my head. That was my happy place. It was a perfect illustration of my relationship with my mom . . . close—way too close—and codependent as hell.

I felt a sense of comfort with my mom that not many kids did with theirs. My mom, PhD, RN, CNL, FAAN, didn't really have any boundaries with other people's bodies. Like that one time I was so constipated that my mom inserted a suppository for me. Or the other time we took mother-daughter glamour shots, nude, covered strategically with feather boas.

The real image is 36 x 24, with an oil-painting finish, and is currently hung over my mom's fireplace.

Nothing was off-limits. But as a twelve-year-old, humiliated and betrayed by my own biology, I decided to draw the line at her showing me how to use a pad. I was too proud to have my mom and her fingers that close to my free-flowing 'gina.

I rummaged through the cabinet and found the instructions stashed in the box. I took out the little piece of paper that was folded like an accordion, then took one glance at the wrinkled instructions and changed my mind. I hated reading instructions. I tossed them in the trash. Why did they have to over-complicate it? It wasn't that hard—there's really no need for detailed pictures of each step. *See . . . I'll spread out the wings like so . . . and with a quick flick of the wrist, they are now . . . stuck to each other.* I tried to unstick them, but the pad had balled up. Rummaging through the trash can, I saw where it was outlined how that could happen in the third image.

"How's it going in there?" my mom called through the door. Her tone had shifted entirely to caretaker, and I thought I might even get to skip school.

"FINE!"

It wasn't fine. I put whatever sticky part was left on my underwear, pulled up my pants, and exited the bathroom. *Ugh.* Immediately, my stepdad's dog ran up to me and tried to bury his nose in my crotch.

What had started off as a horrible day continued to be a horrible day. Mom did not let me stay home from school.

The moment I stepped into the building, I felt like everyone was looking at me. Like I had the plague—complete with boils the size of Idaho. *They know,* I thought. *They 1,000 percent know.*

They didn't know. Or shit, maybe they did!

Mom offered to buy me tampons, but I declined. For the next year, I pro-ceeded to waddle around one week a month. Complete with my pads stuffed into my cargo short pockets. If this was being a woman, then I wanted no part of it. However, that attitude was about to change.

In sixth grade, most boys are short, gangly, and awkward—and then one summer, they shoot up two feet, grow a peach-fuzz mustache, speak two octaves lower, outgrow their shoes, and are recruited by the NBA. My puberty was just as drastic, except the difference between them and me was they became more manly and I became a *wuhman.* The cargo shorts and butt-crack hairdo were so ten minutes ago, and suddenly I started my period, was speaking two octaves higher, my B-cup blossomed into a B-plus, and I was recruited by the DAR. Instead of my button-downs, I wanted shirts with the top buttons missing, the ones that blonde beach babes wore in the black-and-white murals at Abercrombie stores.

The moment I turned thirteen, a transformation began. During childhood, I had high hopes I would turn into a merman like Cody Griffin in *The Thirteenth Year*, but although I was sans fins, the results were just as alarming. That summer, I grew three inches and lost twenty pounds.

The onset of puberty left me like a newborn deer—weak, new to the world, and barely able to stand.

I was now a lady . . . ish.

I gave my Harley-Davidson T-shirts, my cargo shorts, *and my mint-condition Spider-Man button-down* one last hug and thanked them for their service before shoving them into the bottom of my ClosetMaid steel dresser. My enthusiasm for "girls' things" came upon me so suddenly that my mom thought someone had eaten her daughter. I asked her to take me clothes shopping because I was thirteen years behind schedule. My mom dutifully agreed and decided to bring me to the store she knew best: Chico's.

Mom was the epitome of a mama bear who would protect me at any cost. Years later, she kicked her friend to the curb who thought I was rude for not stopping a work call *for this book* to introduce myself . . . Betty. And I would have done the same for her. However, I couldn't support her cluelessness when it came to shopping for a teenage daughter. It was . . . tragic. It's not like she was friends with anyone who had kids. Remember—she hung out with the Key West Lesbians, who were far more concerned with keeping the carpets clean than having children. Even now, she'll send me links to jeans or boots she finds on the discount site Zulily and I have to kindly say, "I'll get back to you," hoping she'll forget.

Nevertheless, we Chicoed.

Chico's marketed themselves as a place for the bold and unconventional. In fact, it was very clear from the moment we walked through its doors that Chico's was a place for women who liked the color turquoise and who wanted to be Salma Hayek but worked in sales at an insurance company.

Mom and I went bold.

I skimmed through the "petites" section, which my mom assured me was the "juniors" section. I wasn't well versed in hot-girl attire, but I had a big feeling this wasn't it. The one sequin-embellished blouse I tried on came up to my navel, and it wasn't a belly shirt. At five six, I was definitely not petite. I asked my mom to take me to my OG happy place: Sears.

Even in Sears, the girls' department felt so foreign. Where was Grandma Sally when I finally needed her? In Mississippi, that's where. I didn't have a feminine style of my own (*Teen Vogue* wasn't knocking on my door to do a beauty profile), so I tried to copy the outfits the popular girls in class would wear: Red polyester scooped necks. Skinny faded jeans. Floral swing blouses. My mom offered up a plaid sleeveless shirt. A tank with rings sewn into the neckline. Mossimo. (Yes, Lori Loughlin's husband's brand.) We purchased a pile of clothes—a lot of denim and accessories to boot—and then Mom bought me a set of Bobbi Brown makeup at Belk for being a good sport.

My mom was a champ throughout the entire transformation. I overhead her on the phone telling Libby, "Guess she's doing the girlie thing now. My head spun a one-eighty, but la-dee-da!"

In other words, she didn't mind.

Now that I had the clothes (sort of) down, it was time for the hairdo. I thought if I just took my hair out of its ponytail, it'd look exactly like the other girls' hair at school. Never mind it'd been in a death grip for the past six years. If I had ever let it loose, I would've realized that looking like a model wasn't effortless after all. Keeping it under control was gonna take work, or as my mom's ex-friend Dorinda once said, "It's painful to be beautiful," as she bopped me on the back of my head with a brush for squirming. Now that puberty had found me, I'd said, *Fine . . . you can change me from gremlin to the beautiful swan, Mrs. Puberty . . .* She'd oblige and all of a sudden, I'd be strutting down the block like Cady in *Mean Girls*.

But Mrs. Puberty was too caught up checking herself out in the mirror to wave the swan wand at me. It turned out, to wrangle the hair on (all parts of) my body, I needed a straightener, two types of brushes, mousse, a razor, a can of Nair, and a whole lotta help.

I was a greasy, nerdy girl with every inch of my mouth covered in metal. I had a mouth spreader, an internal headpiece (that if I laughed hard enough would unhinge and stab my inside cheek), and braces on every single tooth. Not to mention, I had braces for ten years.

That was all about to change. I knew heads would turn when I walked into class the first day of eighth grade.

They did.

I walked past the lockers with my nose turned up just a notch to showcase a "snooty" vibe, rocking a pair of ballet flats.

"SANTOS IS WEARING BALLET FLATS!"

Not only was I wearing flats, I had actually started to use tampons. I'd become a certified girlie girl, as evidenced by the framed photo on my wall of Emma Watson at MTV's *TRL* dressed in a red-and-yellow bellhop jacket with her midriff showing. Those eighth graders had no idea the level of transformation I'd gone through. And I had the confidence to prove it. *I dare you to ask me if I'm wearing tampons,* I thought. I had even purchased a tiny red thong that had a little gold heart attached to the string. Audrey was with me in spirit. Along with my clothing, I'd changed my decor too. I'd tossed out my baseball and football bedsheets and traded them for purple and pink ones. I got an L.L. Bean comforter that had little pom-poms in every square.

Oh, and my eyebrows were suddenly missing.

Another thing that came with my penny-smelling period was also related to my tootie. Excuse me—my vag.

I was even hornier. My vag was pulsing twenty-four seven, like she was dancing to an EDM song at her party that she hadn't invited me to. I wanted to scream at her, *Turn down the music—are you really that inconsiderate?*

I didn't know what to do. She'd already gotten me in trouble at the *Love & Basketball* sleepover, and I took her to brunch for some real talk on vacation with Mom and Stepdad after she'd wanted us to party together after they fell asleep. She'd broken our trust. I tried pushing a pillow between my legs, which was effective—momentarily.

Despite our history, we were sort of strangers. I didn't like looking at her, and in some ways, she didn't seem real. Like we existed in two different realities. She was too cool, too assertive. I mean, I acknowledged her when she needed attention—but for the most part, we lived separate lives.

The new femininity coursing through my veins increased my bond with my mom. We were two southern belles, talking shit on the front porch, sippin' our sweet teas. We had just finished discussing how we'd be "Ya-Ya Sisters for life" when I left to restraighten my hair in my bathroom. It looked like a bomb had gone off in there from my self-taught beautician schooling.

I looked at my boobs in the heavily powdered mirror through my "whatever" shirt. This was a new daily activity that I had acquired. I imagined them being touched. Only a short while prior, I had refused to look at them or to even acknowledge their existence. Now I smiled and greeted my boobs. They looked up and said, "Hey, girl," as I told them coyly, "Stop it." They weren't as bad as I'd thought they'd be. In fact, they needed me to do them a favor. I was text-flirting with a high school boy at the time, and I worked up the courage to ask him if he wanted to meet at the pool.

As soon as we sat down on the folding chairs, I looked at him, looked at my boobs, and said, "You can touch them if you want."

"Really?" He looked around. The pool was completely packed with parents who were also avid churchgoers. "Okay." He didn't exactly rub them or really do much of anything—he just put his hand on top of one boob and held it there, cupping it as if to comfort it. It felt all right—a little thrilling. It was calming my vag and vamping it up at the same time.

When he pulled his hand away, I immediately felt shame. I had no idea what had driven me on this mission. It was like I'd been sleepwalking, and the next thing I knew, I was there at the pool, tit in boy's hand. The blood drained from my face. The boobs whispered, "Do it again!" but I gave them a dirty look to pipe down.

"Thanks, Adam."

I texted my mom that I was done "swimming," and she picked me up from the pool. In the car, I told her what had happened. I tattled on myself yet again. This time was different, actually. I was *confiding* in her as a friend, and I knew she'd have my back.

"Elizabeth! I'm drivin' you straight home, and you're gonna be grounded for a week."

"A week?" *What happened to us being Ya-Ya Sisters?*

"You're too young for that shit," she said. I was floored. My BFF was not being very supportive.

I needed to consult someone else about the pool incident and all the pulsing that was going on downstairs. If Susan got that upset about a simple cupping, then I couldn't imagine the fire that would be ignited by my telling her that I wanted someone to do more. So I texted my step-cousin—who I *admired* a lot. Listen—she was only my cousin by marriage. She was a college girl, twenty-one, and I felt we were practically the same age because she understood my angst.

`I feel . . . funny . . . all the time . . .` I added a ":-\" to show my frustration. This was pre-emojis, and our phones were emotionless bricks.

`That's normal`, she replied.

I had to move the texting to a real phone conversation. It's a habit I still have and won't ever break. Call me old-fashioned. Via phone, I admitted everything, including the shame and my mom's obvious wrath.

"You know, you're coming to the age where you don't have to tell your parents everything," she said.

"Really?" I was genuinely shocked.

"Yeah. Sometimes, it's better if you don't. No need to worry them."

We hung up. I hadn't asked her everything I needed, so I texted, `So what do I do when I feel funny down there . . . ?`

Over the course of a few more texts, she pointed me in the direction of masturbation with the simple, cryptic message that the remote control would be my friend.

I looked at the hulking TV remote with a bajillion buttons and unidentified sticky stuff on the back. *I'll end up in the hospital if I go anywhere near that.* I then noticed the slimmer remote for my black-and-red three-piece stereo system that projected blue lights when it bumped music.

I knew what I had to do.

I blasted "Grind with Me" by Pretty Ricky, blue lights and all.

And I put my boom-box remote in my vagina.

I didn't have instructions—and even if my step-cousin had supplied them, I probably would have ignored them. So I just treated the remote like a tampon and slipped it into the opening of my little flaps. It wasn't going in. I tried pushing harder. It hurt. I didn't want to look—I was too embarrassed—so I just pushed the remote in harder and let out a yelp. I was definitely hitting bone. *My vag is made of bone?* Surely I would have known by now, since my vag had been with me for thirteen years. Surely.

Surely not.

I pulled the remote out and examined it. I turned it on its side. I tried again and managed to get it a third of the way in with a little bit of force.

Now what?

I lay on the bed with the remote sticking out of my vagina. I sat up, lit my Yankee Buttercream candle, worried it'd burn the house down, knocked three times as I thought of Kate Hudson holding the love fern (a happy thought that should satisfy my obsessive thinking's thirst), and lay back down. I tried picturing my hunky classmate and crush Paul Dylan dancing with me at the Valentine's Day dance—double first name, double cool. I imagined his sweaty hands holding my waist. His brown hair was coiffed perfectly, covering up his pimply forehead. But then I thought about him dumping[21] me for Brianna right after Lonestar's "I'm Already There" ended. A couple of weeks before, when I'd told Brianna I liked Paul Dylan and wanted to go to the Valentine's Day dance with him, she'd said that she would take him my notebook-paper invitation, and then when I confronted her after seeing them dance together, she airily insisted, "I never said I'd take your invitation. I told you *I* liked Paul Dylan." That memory really killed my lady-boner.

I pulled out the remote, gave it a sniff, and wiped it on the sheet. No one else needed to know. It was *my* remote. But it hadn't helped. Vag was still throbbing and now annoyed. "Honk honk, babe, are we gonna hang or what?" Then, from underneath a pom-pom on my comforter, I saw a tiny, fuzzy white ear sticking out—Lammy. Lammy was the stuffed lamb that Grandma Sally's best friend, Dorothy, had gifted me on the day of my birth. Lammy was my comfort object. Lammy has been with me throughout the years. Lammy also was the perfect shape and size to wedge between my crotch and my bed. I looked around the room for other viable options. Nada. I had no choice. Poor Lammy, so innocent.

I stuffed my friend between my legs and grinded against her. Guilt overcame me—yet the more I pushed against her beady eyes, the better it felt. As the sensation increased, I grinded harder. I came alive. The harder I grinded, the more white-girl-wasted Vag became. I was sweating when I tossed Lammy to the side. I wanted to cry out, "I'm sorry, Lammy!" Instead, I shoved my right hand down my day-of-the-week (Wednesday) Hanes and rubbed what was begging for it. I had to finish the deed. I rubbed so hard and so fast and came so hard and so fast

---

[21] We were dates for Valentine's Day! By middle school standards, that meant we were steady. One more dance and you better get out the promise ring!

that my little chicken legs locked in excitement and my body floated in the air. I convulsed back and forth like a bad spirit was being exorcised.

Vag finally passed out, but not without a throaty, "Oh my God I love you soooooo muuuuch!" That certainly was the best day of our lives. Afterward, I looked down and noticed a big wet spot on my bed. Oops. I wiped myself in the bathroom (Back to front? Who knows?), returned, and made my bed to cover up the crime scene. It didn't occur to me that a made bed was much more suspicious than a wet one—a clean room meant I was up to no good.

Honestly, I was shocked at how wet masturbating was. I'd envisioned more like a T-shirt cannon–style projectile. I thought I'd need a tube sock, or at the very least an ankle sock. Why did I think I needed a sock even though I had a vagina and not a penis? No one ever talked about female masturbation. I got all my info from teen movies. I was lucky my step-cousin gave me tips, because I didn't have any other guidance. I sure as hell couldn't talk to my friends about it. We all pretended that girls who masturbated were *dirty*.

I kept pretending at school, but in private, I became a chronic masturbator.

One time, I masturbated in the car waiting for my mom to get groceries.

One time, I masturbated in my middle school bathroom while skipping algebra.

One time, I *did* masturbate in the same hotel room that Mom and Stepdad were sleeping in while we were on vacation.

I had OCD! What do you want from me, people?

Also because I had OCD, I'd masturbate until I'd had three orgasms. My hand would chronically cramp.

I then wore out *The Notebook* DVD, mostly just playing the same two sex scenes on repeat until it was scratched and wouldn't work anymore. At first, I imagined Ryan Gosling lying on top of me in that barn, on the floor, my head on a red blanket, his rock-hard abs brushing against my soft body, but the ab brushing didn't produce the same sensation that I read on Rachel McAdams's face. I flipped onto my stomach and imagined doing what *Ryan* was doing instead. I'd think about him lifting up his body to put P in V, over and over again. BLASTOFF! *Okay, I really peed myself this time.* I mean, I was a filthy little animal. My arms grew weak from propping myself up, and I got carpet burn from being on the floor for so long.

My unrelenting horniness led me to discover the webcam. I had done just about everything I could think of to satisfy my urges and knew that if I rode Lammy any harder, we'd wind up in Wyoming. I walked by my mom's home office one afternoon and noticed the webcam. It was like it was illuminated in the dark. The webcam had been in my mom's office for several years, but I was seeing it as if for the first time. Given the fact that it had collected a fair amount of dust, I assumed she didn't need it anymore. It was old. Yellowish. Made by Logitech. I plugged it into the computer (which was made during the same era—around the time Ford invented the Model T) in my room. My parents had given me a desktop computer that I'd have to smack on the side to make it work. Maybe the smacking didn't actually help, but it felt like it did the trick.

I shut my door and fired up the internet. The spinning wheel of death appeared, and the tower let out a depressing noise, which meant it would be loading for the unforeseeable future.

Two days later, it had finally loaded. I logged on to Skype and created a new username, something that seemed more sophisticated and "euro-chic" than squeekyshoes666@hotmail.com, a name that spawned years of "Don't go near that Elizabeth Santos. She's a sinner and clearly can't spell." I decided on soffigirl.

I hit up a guy named Beau, or on Skype, Bowfoshow69, a former football dude I knew who attended a middle school nearby.

We exchanged a few *hi*s and *sup*s until I asked if he wanted to be shirtless. Beau, that suave devil, said, If U do it, 2.

I had him right where I wanted him.

I took off my shirt, wearing only a padded Victoria's Secret bra that I'd furtively grabbed from the top of the stack and paid for without trying on. I asked Beau if he wanted to show me his . . . 8==D?

He looked to the side with no expression and then reached into his gym shorts and pulled out his *OHMYGOD IS THAT WHAT THEY LOOK LIKE?*

It had just dawned on me that I hadn't ever seen a peen . . . Just Ryan Gosling's abs and chiseled lines I'd heard kids call *whispers* . . . cum gutters?

(.) (.)? he asked.

I took off my overpriced bra and placed it gingerly on the ground just as Rachel McAdams had.

Now what? We couldn't bump our bodies up against each other's. He started to touch his *ha-ha-ha-ha seriously, what am I even looking at? A guppy fish?*

I also touched my vag, which was, of course, clamoring for attention, which was hard for me to accept, seeing as I liked all eyes to be on me. *Here we go . . .* I started to feel like I was peeing again. And then I grinded against the chair while he did his own bizness. We both came and then immediately logged off.

It started as an exclusive one-on-one sexy time (Beau wasn't always avails when I needed him), but I quickly added more and more boys from the other school. I knew kids talked, and I didn't want my secret to spread through the halls of my own school. Not only was I getting some action, I was getting *major* action. I had set up a little business for myself. No actual money was exchanged. Transactions were simply (.)(.) for 8==D. (Pre-emojis.) Showing off my newly improved boobs allowed me to look at boys' bods. I'd finish dinner with my mom and stepdad and then head straight to my lair. Throw on a power suit—I was a businesswoman. It was my game, and I thought I was in control.

I wasn't in control.

What I didn't realize was that guys were messaging me like crazy because word had spread that I was "down." They had named me "The Webcam Girl." I never realized they would spin the narrative so fast. I never realized they'd say that I was slutty.

Slutty. A new term I would learn for *girls* who wanted it, even though the boys were very willing participants.

At lunch, some of the other girls at the table were talking about how their boyfriends wanted them to do on-camera stuff. The total consensus was—*ew, who like, even does that?* My eighth grade best friend, Marissa, looked disgusted. "I don't know why anyone would do that. Boys screenshot everything."

Wait, what?

Great. I'd had no idea that those sessions might live on into photographic, pornographic posterity. And I had no one to talk to about it. I had to keep my camming a dark secret.

Marissa continued. "Once it's out there, it's out there forever. You don't want to wind up like Paris Hilton."

I wished I could keep my hustle going, but I was too paranoid. I couldn't sleep. I was tapping on anything and everything to not be outed as "The Webcam Girl." I frantically opened and shut drawers, trying to picture Kate Hudson, but the good thought was being overshadowed by the image of me stripping in front of the camera. I looked at my Skype chats and saw a few h3LLo cutie or just

;-). I closed shop immediately. If I could have taken a baseball bat to the computer, I would have. I considered chucking my hefty desktop out the window. My persona was out there, and it wasn't fun anymore. I frantically texted every boy: **Please don't tell anyone.** Some ghosted me, and some responded with, **IDK what you're talking about. I have a GF.** *WHAT?* Chyeah—it was over, boys. I sat on my bed, trying to fake pray that I wouldn't be a slut anymore. *At least I'm not in school with any of them, so I'm fine.*

Then I was transferred to that same school the next fall. System overload.

Advice from a Thirteen-Year-Old on How to Be a Cam Girl

- First things first, tell your parents that you have a best friend who you desperately need to talk to at all times of the day and night. Move over, AOL Instant Messenger, Skype is so fetch right now.
- Get a good camera, preferably one by Logitech, because that's the only one I know.
- If you need to clean the camera, don't use your spit, because it will leave a streak, and boys will think you look like a kaleidoscope. This is not the seventies.
- Make sure to lock your door. THIS IS A MUST. CHECK THREE TIMES. You don't want to be mid–body roll when your parents walk in. Cam days will be over and so will your lyfe.
- Always cam with boys from different schools than yours. Word will spread rapid-fire, and you don't want to be in lunch when people discover your secret.
- Don't transfer.
- Don't get into the bizness unless you're committed to knowing the different boys and what they like. But it's all pretty much the same.
- Actually, on second thought, don't do any of this. And burn this list.

Chapter Thirteen

I DIDN'T COME OUT AS A DYKE, I CAME OUT AS A MEZZO-SOPRANO

Like all comedians, I have a theater past. Long before webcams, years before puberty or even my parents' divorce, I had been obsessed with America's favorite freckled redhead and not-yet-tragic star Lindsay Lohan. More specifically, Lindsay Lohan in *The Parent Trap*[22]. She could do British accents! She could play TWO characters! The versatility! Watching Lindsay play both Hallie Parker and Annie James on-screen gave me an itch to do one thing: act. I made up my mind during the two-hour-and-eight-minute run time that I, Elizabeth Santos, would become an actress. (The likes of which they'd never seen.)

When we got into the car after *The Parent Trap*, I took a deep breath.

"Mom, Dad . . . I want to be in the pictures," I proclaimed from the back seat.

"Honey, you already have five thousand extracurricular activities—we aren't addin' any more to your plate," my mom said—like adding the five thousand and first would be so crazy! Dad turned on the ignition.

"Who wants ice cream?" he asked.

---

[22] As an only child, I'd also dreamed that one day I'd go to camp, meet my twin, and march home to berate my parents. "THE JIG IS UP. YOU SEPARATED US AT BIRTH. I'VE HAD A TWIN— A.K.A. BEST FRIEND—ALL ALONG. HOW COULD YOU!" I'd only found God at camp, which was *way* less satisfying.

My acting career had apparently ended before it ever started.

Mom was right—I did have five thousand extracurriculars. Competitive jump roping, being president of my elementary school, practicing my Oscars acceptance speech in the mirror—the list went on and on. I played at least two sports a season—so the real issue was that my mom couldn't add shuttling me to "play practice" (as she called it) onto *her* plate.

It's not like my adoration of the biz came out of nowhere. I'd been slowly discovering my performative side through nights at the local outdoor amphitheater, the Starlight, giving a soliloquy to my mom about how I didn't need to clean my room because it was my space, and flipping on the TV to marvel at *Inside the Actors Studio* with James Lipton. I envisioned James Lipton going through the litany of his famous ten questions such as, "What is your favorite curse word?" and I'd chuckle, press one hand to my forehead out of "embarrassment," and say, "Titty twister." An overachieving student actor in the audience would scribble in their notepad, hanging on to every word I said. My road to stardom had been in the making (in my head) for a while.

So when I saw a poster taped up next to the cash register in a local gift shop, I had to bring it up again. Lindsay Lohan had just been in *Mean Girls* and was leap years ahead of me.

"Mom, look! They're having auditions for *A Christmas Carol*. Can I go?"

"Honey, you simply don't have time," she said as she grabbed a few Buddhas.

"I'll quit basketball. If I get cast, I'll march straight into Coach Elkins's classroom and tell her I'm hanging up my high-tops," I promised. "Yeah."

A few days later, we pulled up to an old brick building for my first theater audition at the Whole Backstage Theatre. There were tons of kids in the lobby. I grabbed the script (or the "sides," according to Julia Roberts), and my mom and I were ushered into a rehearsal room with chairs that lined the wall. We sat down next to other parents and kids, some of who were already practicing their lines—this clearly wasn't their first time.

"Your 'want' isn't clear, Christopher. What is your motivation?" one of the moms coached her son.

After an hour, it was finally my turn to read the final scene for the director, Mr. Brewer, and a few older ladies. I was clearly too old to be Tiny Tim, but every kid took a turn at it—it was an easy way to suss out who could act and who needed to never show their face again.

I took a moment and used my best method acting by remembering what it was like to be in the hospital with pneumonia. And how I had survived. Tiny Tim was a survivor, no doubt. I looked at the actor who was playing my father, Mr. Cratchit, and then belted out, "God bless us, everyone!" I said the line with so much intensity, I figured Mr. Brewer would shed a tear. He scribbled on a notepad and had his hand in front of his face, so we can't be sure he didn't.

I proudly sat in my chair next to my mom, who gave me a pat on the leg.

Mr. Brewer stood up and addressed the room. "Casting will be announced on our website at eight p.m. tonight. We so appreciate everyone coming in." I tried to make eye contact with him so he'd remember me. *"Eye contact is the mark of a good solider,"* as my dad would say. I had my handshake loaded by my side, ready to knock his socks off. But he was out the door before I could bat my eyelashes at him and give my best forties starlet: *Please pick me, sir—I know I can do it.*

The moment the car pulled back into our driveway, I darted to the home office. Mom's Wi-Fi was faster. I sat down at the computer, even though the amount of adrenaline coursing through my body could have propelled me through the ceiling. A ring of dust was left from the webcam, but I didn't have time to worry about that. Starting at four p.m., I kept refreshing the screen. Again. And again. Waiting with bated breath to see if the cast list had posted early. My mom forced me to have dinner in order to try to distract me, but I brought my food to the computer and sat again.

Eight p.m.

Nothing.

They were late.

Obviously.

Refresh.

panics

REFRESH.

panics

REFRESH!

panics

CAST LIST—*A CHRISTMAS CAROL*

OH MY GOD, YES!

I scrolled down . . . past Ebenezer Scrooge. I hovered over his name. I mean, it could happen . . . past the wife . . . *Too mature for me,* I thought. Past the Cratchit kids . . . *Okay, well, those parts are too big, even though I was better than that Christopher, who got Tiny Tim. I agree with his mom now—he didn't know what he "wanted."* I scrolled all the way to the bottom. My heart pounded. Chorus . . . I didn't see my name. *I didn't make it?*

SHIT.

Then—at the very bottom, almost off the screen—I saw . . . KIDS' CHORUS. And finally, I saw . . . ELIZABETH SANTOS.

I let out a huge scream and started pumping my fists in the air.

I got cast.

I GOT CAST!!!

I printed out the cast list and held the dainty piece of paper like it was an ancient artifact as I went into my bedroom. I fell asleep, cuddled up next to my prized possession. Okay, maybe not[23].

As promised, the next day I planned to tell my basketball coach / math teacher that I was quitting. My mom was shocked that I was actually quitting and thought that once again, someone had eaten her daughter. I assured her that the actress inside me was ready to come out into the world. I prepared a passionate monologue that I practiced in my shower and went over and over in my head, as water dripped down my face dramatically. *I've found a new love . . . you've taught me valuable lessons. It's time I pursued a new path, Coach Elkins.*

I went up to Coach after class. She was standing behind her desk and rolling up a wad of tests.

"Miss Santos, you need me?" she grunted.

"Yes . . . thank you for taking the time out of your *busy* schedule," I said as I placed my hand on my heart.

She grumpily gestured toward me and then put her hands on her hips like, *Get on with it.* Her beady eyes stared straight into my soul.

"I've decided in the interest of one's time—*and yours,* of course—and to not overextend oneself, I should resign from the art of hooping this calendar year."

I donned an oversize scarf and big glasses and was planning my "exit, pursued by a bear" when she said, "Sounds good, Santos." She turned off the

---

[23] Okay, maybe yes.

overhead projector. The old-school kind where the images were grainy and you had to squint or you would miss an entire math lesson.

If Elizabeth has one math teacher with outdated equipment, how many Bs will she get until she breaks the projector in a rage?

"If it's tough for you to keep the team going," I continued as she walked away, "I can at least complete fall training until you find a replacement."

"I think we've got it from here. Thanks, Santos."

I wanted to say, *Didn't you hear me? I said I'm not playing basketball this year, you numbnut!* But she grabbed her protractor and left the room. To be fair, I was pretty bad at basketball. I sat on the bench ~~most~~ all games, and in fact, I was equally bad at math. I always failed in front of Coach Elkins. And between you and me . . . come closer . . . closer . . . good. Listen, she was a total lez. If it hadn't been for her Bible-thumping heart; JFK haircut; the tucked-in, collared shirt; nails filed to the bone. She was as conservative as they come, but instead of the higher the hair, the closer to God, she'd clearly read the wrong memo.

Anyway, I wanted her to beg me to stay! To tell me that the team needed me—that she needed me.

She didn't need me.

The afternoon of the first rehearsal, I pulled up to the old brick building and was welcomed by a few queens and ancient people. Community theater was in a league of its own. You will never see anyone more dedicated than the hundreds of people involved in a community theater. And you better believe they are just as good as the guys and gals on "the Broadway."

Sure, the costumes were pulled from dusty closets, and casting choices were based primarily on who could hover near the high notes, but that was part of the je ne sais quoi. It was all about the passion, baby. The directors had never set foot on a Broadway stage. Hamburg, maybe, or the West End (there was one old biddy who wouldn't shut up about it)—but the Broadway, never. Not unless you're talking about Broadway Road in Winfield, Alabama. In between rehearsal breaks, I overheard one of them say, "When I worked with Liam Nissan—no, no, Liam *Nissan* from Boaz, Alabama. Not to be confused with the *Nissan* car family either . . ."

And that confidence is almost as important as a résumé.

My mom got a taste of it when she joined me for my *Christmas Carol* costume fitting. The fitting consisted of each actor parading out onstage wearing their costume, and the director and their staff, who were sitting in the audience, assessing it.

An actor named Tom walked out onstage and stood there while the gaggle of older women and men assessed his midthigh coat and ruffled shirt straight out of *The Scarlet Pimpernel*. Tom was in finance, but by the looks of his turned-out foot—otherwise known as the bevel—only to pay the bills. By night, he paid his debts to Bernadette Peters.

The head of the theater, Dot Moore, screamed from the back, "It's supposed to be 1843, Carl, not 1792!" A man—Carl, I presumed—with a clipboard and a measuring tape draped around his neck shuffled Tom back offstage.

My mom leaned over and whispered, "How does she know that?" with sheer awe.

I smiled a metal grin. Well, that's just community theater for ya! *And everyone knows men's jackets got shorter after the French Revolution, Mom.*

Everything else in my life stopped mattering once I started rehearsals for *A Christmas Carol*. If my mom was a minute late to pick me up from school, I'd say, "MOM! I cannot be late to rehearsal! Don't you know? Fifteen minutes early is on time, and on time is late, and late means you're dead. Do you want me to be dead, *Mom*?"

I breathed in the dusty air and cozied up to my new friends, who were in their midtwenties. I realized they were much cooler than my thirteen-year-old friends, who were obsessed with gel pens and glitter lip gloss.

After three months of rehearsal, I invited Mom and Stepdad—and, coyly, a few friends from my class.

"Want to hang out tonight?" Marissa asked.

"I can't; I'm in a play. I'm an actress now . . ."

"Do you want me to come to your play?"

"If you'd like." I turned to leave, then turned back. "Actually, that would be wonderful! I'll tell Susan to send for you."

It's true that I gave up basketball to walk onstage with five other teens and sing "Christmas Is Christmas" for one measure and then going mute, just miming the song as Bob Cratchit talked to Scrooge in his shop. I opened and closed my mouth proudly and smiled so broadly that the last row of the audience must have been blinded by the reflection of the stage lights off my braces.

Then it came time for my bow. I proudly walked down to center stage with the other teens and bent my body, nose to knee. *THIS is what it was all for.*

I came out of the ~~stage door~~ lobby doors, where Mom and Stepdad presented me with a bouquet of roses. *I would have preferred you throw them at my feet during my curtain call, but this will do.* Mom hugged me and said I was by far the best chorus member. I had the "it" factor.

"Mom, that's insane!"

. . .

"But at what moment did this dawn on you?"

She explained her theory, and my ego had grown to the size of a small child, Tiny Tim even, as we all got into the car, and I knew a monster had been created.

Chapter Fourteen

ARABIAN NIGHTS

After a few shows, I told myself I was outgrowing community theater and realized that, if I wanted to keep pursuing my musical theater *career*, it was time for the big stuff: High. School. Theater.

I was also ready to get the hell out of the County School—a combo of middle and high school grades out in the middle of farm country. The main purpose of the school was to filter students into vocational schools, and I had been banished to that district because I lived outside city limits by less than a mile.

At the County School, they paddled students. My English teacher / the men's baseball coach would wax his long wooden paddle in the mornings and hang it up in the front of the classroom.

"Remember, kids, mine has holes in it. Cuts down on airflow so I give a nice swat. Now, who didn't read *The Giver* last night?"

I'd hear a good whack from a different teacher/coach delivering punishment in the hall, and I'd wince.

"Are you gonna let them paddle me?" I'd asked my mom.

"I don't think so . . ."

"You don't *think* so?"

Those Podunk ~~hallways~~ trailers don't need further mention. The teachers could gladly hoist up their paddles with holes, and I could gladly get out of there. The only thing that really mattered to me was my undying affection for my friend Marissa, but I knew she would choose the Lord over me. Her family belonged to the Holiness church, which is like Pentecostal times infinity. Once she was saved (which, by the urgency of the hands that pressed on her, was going to happen very soon), we wouldn't get to hang out anymore, because she would have to give up everything immoral—including makeup, jewelry, and cutting her hair. (Why the Great Almighty would care if a woman was sporting a nice, midlength hairdo was beyond me. He must have had a thing against Mandy Moore's beachy waves.)

I'd had it with the small potatoes. I was ready for the big potatoes. I convinced my mom to let me transfer to Arab High School for my sophomore year. It was the closest I could get to a magnet school[24].

The summer before I enrolled, I took it upon myself to arrange an introduction between myself and the musical theater teacher, Michael Fernsby. Fernsby was very proud of the program he had created.

"I marched right into the superintendent's office and told him I wanted fifty grand for my first production. What do you think he said?" Fernsby asked me as I stood in the theater classroom. His lips curled into a smirk.

"He said . . . yes?"

"Of course he said yes!" He looked up to the side as if he were back there that day. He continued to go on about his program for a solid forty-five minutes, with no breaks for air. His productions would, he said, cost him anywhere from $25,000 to $75,000—and they were all paid for by donations from parents and the school board. "Sometimes I swear we could have a production in New York if we could finance it . . ."

After almost an hour, he told me, "Oh yes. You were going to sing. I have about five minutes left, so let's make this quick. Much to do!"

"About nothing? Eh?" I thought if I could make him laugh, I'd definitely be in.

Silence.

I sang the iconic *42nd Street* song "I Only Have Eyes for You" to show my versatility and maturity as a fifteen-year-old. I made sure to hit the E-flat—because hitting a E-flat meant that I had talent. Mr. Fernsby and I shook hands, and he said he looked forward to having me.

"I think you might be a mezzo-soprano."

"Really?" I lamented. "I've always been an alto."

---

[24] If by magnet school you mean, not at all—then, yes, it was a magnet school.

"We'll work on your mix. Plus, strictly between you and me, you can't have a career as an alto. See you in a few weeks!" And he turned on a dime and went into his office (which was attached to the classroom with a one-way mirror like an interrogation room). I tried to peek in. Nothing.

With one foot in the theatrical door, I started my first day at Arab High School with "Arabian Nights" playing in the background. Seriously. The marching band was practicing the song from *Aladdin* when I hopped out of my mom's Acura.

After my tenth new school, this would be my last transfer.

I figured Arab couldn't be worse than dancing on bleachers that were nestled into cow shit. Plus, Fernsby wouldn't confide in just anyone like that—would he? The only thing I had to deal with now was my webcam reputation.

Okay, yeah, that was in the back of my mind twenty-four seven when I first got there. When I attended football games, I made sure to never walk past the student section. I didn't want people to stare at me and yell, "Hey! There's that webcam girl!" In fact, I wouldn't sit in the student section for the first few months. If I saw Bowfoshow69 or any of the other boys at lunch, I avoided eye contact and held my breath, trying to think of a damn positive image, until they passed me. I even considered not auditioning for the musical, because I didn't want more people at school to know me. But I coped like I had in the past with mistakes—and that was by sticking to my OCD routines. I figured doing so would ward off any hate, even if it meant having thoughts bouncing around in my brain for seven periods, and holding my breath until I felt nauseous.

Eventually a sucky girl by the name of Tara Fernell passive-aggressively told me at a party, "People are talking about you. That you did stuff." It was like the veil had been lifted. I cried myself to sleep for a month, then burned the webcam in the backyard while saying a hex from *The Crucible*. As I watched the toxic smoke float to the heavens, I took an oath that I'd take the shame to the grave while I fulfilled my destiny as a musical theater star.

You'd think that, in a town like Arab, the theater kids would be subjects for bullying and torture.

Wrong.

We were the cool kids. Okay, not all of us, but no one really bothered us, and we stayed in our lane. For a town that valued football so much, our team was *garbáge*. Most games were 0-49, and that was not too bad an ass whoopin'.

Thank God I went out on a high note in seventh grade on the Broncos. The boys in my class would support the players by painting themselves blue, only to lead us all back to a random field to drink at halftime because we didn't want to be seen with the loser jocks. Bottom line: parents were very happy to support the arts because it meant they had a real shot at their child being a star, which was not happening on the football field.

I was counting on theater to provide me with the tight-knit social circle that I craved. If community theater was about the community, then high school theater was about hierarchy. It was cutthroat and political, a society at war.

In order to survive high school, I needed to associate myself with the most talented people. I made friends with the monarch of the hierarchy. Her name was Anna. I idolized Anna. I had seen her perform as Sophie in *Mamma Mia!* the spring before and had an actor crush on her.

"You were sooo good," I brownnosed. "I mean, wow. One day I hope to be as good as you."

"Aww, you're so sweet. Tell me: What do you think about me singing 'Don't Walk Away' from *Xanadu* for my audition for *Little Shop* this fall? Too much?"

"Never! That's the perfect choice. You can practice for me if you want . . ."

"OMG, please! Come to my house tonight. Actually, just come home with me after school. You don't drive yet, do you?"

I didn't. Fifteen-year-old here, and I had just booked a session with a seventeen-year-old. I didn't know the musical *Xanadu*, but it didn't matter. I sneaked into the computer lab and googled the Tony Awards clip so I could act like I knew what I was talking about that afternoon.

She belted out "Don't Walk Away" in front of me and her mom as I ate popcorn and told her she would be a shoo-in for the role of Audrey.

"I don't know," she said. "Elise is pretty good. And never count Makayla[25] out."

I knew that Anna would get cast as Audrey. And deep down she knew it, too, but she was always challenging herself.

---

[25] Makayla was a ball-busting, southern Miley Cyrus who sounded like how a bug would sound if it sang. My friendship with her was short-lived because I kissed her ex-boyfriend, who dumped *her*, so fair, but who she had stolen from me TBH, so fair my ass, and she drove me to a park, made me get out of the car, and told me, "YOU ARE DISHONEST AND DESERVE TO BURN. WE WILL NEVER BE FRIENDS." She let me back in the car but blocked my number en route to my house.

She was the kind of girl who knew the entire musical theater catalog, Golden Age (presixties), megamusicals (*Les Mis*, *Secret Garden*, etc., duh), Sondheim—everything. I spent every waking minute at her house. Hoping she'd sing. Jealous of how well she could sing. She was a young Kerry Butler. (I only knew who that was because Anna taught me: Butler played Audrey in the revival of *Little Shop of Horrors*, thank you.) Anna only had musical DVDs, and we'd sit in her house and watch them together.

"You've never heard of *MOULIN ROUGE*?"

"Why do all these songs sound so familiar?"

"You're so funny," she'd say.

Or we'd just flip through her collection, discussing the merits of each performance.

"I love Sutton Foster," I'd say.

"Yes. I can see why you'd say that . . . but see how she plays the same character in both *Thoroughly Modern Millie* and *The Drowsy Chaperone*? But she can sing, no doubt about it."

I'd never thought of it that way. I was putting in my 10,000 hours.

Tristan, another transfer student with an impressive set of pipes, was equally talented. Tristan and Anna became friends, because talented people hang out with other talented people. I was the sidekick, just like LeFou, they'd say. I watched as the two of them sang together, wishing I could belt like them but happy to have a front-row seat to their brilliance. The three of us became inseparable. Not to mention, as a sophomore, I loved that I was friends with a senior! I felt protected. *I dare you to try me! I'm best friends with the star of the Arab musical theater program!* During pep rallies, I'd walk into the gym and make my way to the senior section, leaving my fellow sophomores behind. Tristan stood in his scarf and loafers, and Anna wore her pastel dress.

A few weeks later, auditions were held, and Anna and Tristan got cast as Audrey and Seymour, respectively, in *Little Shop*. I got cast in the chorus.

"That's really amazing, Elizabeth. You're a transfer. Transfers never get cast their first year," she told me with a twinkle in her eye. I wanted to point out that Tristan, a transfer, got the lead, but I would never disagree with her.

Tristan and Anna practiced every day. When it came time to audition for smaller roles, Tristan and Anna helped me prepare so I could knock it out of the park. Hell hath no fury like a kid auditioning for one line in a play. It was a dog-eat-dog world out there, and those in my way were wearing Milk-Bone underpants. They pumped me up, and I landed the part of Mrs. Luce.

Obviously, I had other interests besides musical theater.

Obviously . . .

. . .

Like every single other teen girl I knew, I had a tattered copy of the emo-riffic *Twilight* novels. Each of us was pining over our own otherworldly creature—werewolves, vampires—and nothing was what it seemed to be. Love knew no bounds.

For a while, I wanted a bloodsucking vampire to come to my bedroom in the middle of the night and stare at me with intense eye contact until I fell asleep (only me—not him, because he was a vampire).

Accompanying my moody reading was my moody music. I would crank up the tunes with lyrics such as, "DO YOU KNOW WHAT IT FEELS LIIIIIIKE BEING ALONE!"

I really did know what it felt like. Middle school had been lame. Being judged by a hundred classmates is terrifying, and trying to figure out where you fit into the social strata while also managing a significant physical metamorphosis was the toughest gauntlet I'd ever had to run. Coming to a new school had provided a bit of a reset, but middle school had left me off-kilter. In high school, I turned to musical drama and alt-rock to feed my inner turmoil.

Swoops my greasy hair to the side, covering one of my eyes.

What's more dramatic than emo attitude and cat eyeliner?

Um, nothing?

As far as I could tell, alt-rock was about escaping the problems of humanity, burning everything to the ground, getting the girl, and running to a beach. It fed my teenage need for intensity. Everything that those emo band members were going through seemed to be what I was going through. Because all the lyrics were vague enough to attach my life to them.

And that's when I was introduced to *Spring Awakening*. *Spring Awakening*: the angsty teen musical set in the 1800s but with music by Duncan Sheik, so it sounded like a really sad rock concert. With lyrics like "IT'S THE BITCH OF LIVING!" and "TOTALLY FUCKED!" it was the perfect combination for an emo-rrific lover and musical theater nerd. I would blast the music in my room, jumping off chairs like they did in the musical. I became so obsessed that I begged my mom to take me to New York City to see it live.

She got us front-row seats, a.k.a. the splash zone, and Jonathan Groff, "Groff Sauce," spat all over my face. It was so good that we went back at the end of the week after seeing Sutton Foster in *Young Frankenstein*, which—Anna, shut the fuck up (sorry! I didn't mean to overstep), don't ever talk shit about Sutton again[26].

Every day after school, I'd race to Anna's house, and we'd sit in her living room, singing show tunes and laughing together. Then something I hadn't foreseen started to happen. The more Tristan belted out Seymour's lyrics, the more envious I grew. *I* wanted to be Seymour. And maybe I wanted to be singing with Anna. I felt a sense of rage I hadn't encountered since Carly Simon with my babysitter Audrey. I kept shoving that emotion down as the rehearsals progressed. How was I to compete with Mr. Disney / Wears Loafers and a Scarf Like He's from New York City?

Soon, Anna and Tristan started developing a "showmance"—the very predictable phenomenon where the leads in a production fall for each other. Showmances are—point-blank—not worth it. Everyone knows they never pan out, yet the leads always fall for each other and risk ruining everyone else's lives because of it. Selfish.

I mean, it wouldn't be called *drama* without the drama. Tristan and Anna started hanging out alone—and when they decided to include me, I could cut their chemistry with a knife. I grew more and more jealous by the day. I did the only thing I knew how to do—I became a certified possessive bitch. I'd tell Anna that she was hurting me by being with him. I'd get moody when I didn't get my way. I was short with her when I knew she'd been texting him. I became the definition of passive-aggressive. I'd do everything in my power to make her feel just as bad as I felt; it seemed fair. *Little Shop* was both the happiest time of my life, because I had found a community to accept and support me, and also the saddest.

I was very emotional. I'd routinely pen letters to ~~my friends~~ Anna when we'd fight, declaring things like, "I apologize for my behavior and hope you'll talk to me." I'd fold my letter into the perfect paper dragon origami, write the recipient's

---

[26] She played the same character.

name (still Anna) on it, and hand it to them (Anna) during choir. Only to check up in person (Anna) the next day to make sure they (Anna) had read it. My vulnerability was amplified by listening to the bands I loved: Paramore, the Rocket Summer, Secondhand Serenade.

Anna and Tristan delivered the final blow: they went to prom together. I was shattered. I yelled at her in the car for treating me horribly.

"How could you do this to me?" I pleaded. "This is bullshit. You don't even like him."

"Elizabeth, I do . . . I just . . ."

"You're a bitch, Anna. You always have been, and you always will be. And you're not that talented."

Anna looked down, unable to speak.

And then I said it. The words that you can never take back.

"I hate you."

I managed to find a senior looking for a last-minute prom date just so I could go spy on them—some ginger kid whose family was loaded. I went over to his *Southern Living* home, and I knew no one as I smiled on the spiral staircase with the ten other girls. I huffed through dinner with all the couples. I stewed on the drive there in the limo. And when it came time to take our prom photo, I said, "Let's make this quick."

A few hours in, "Get Low" by Lil Jon & the East Side Boyz finished. As the sweat cooled off our bods from grinding (we were given a warning that if we sang the "till the sweat drop down my balls (my balls)" lyrics, we'd be sent to detention the following week—unity in numbers works wonders, my friends), "The Reason" by Hoobastank started to play. I held my date close while staring at Anna and Tristan slow-dancing together. "I'm not a perfect person," echoed around the civic center as I tried to make eye contact. After the song, Anna came up to talk to me. I walked straight past her, grabbed my coat and my date, and hopped back in the limo.

A couple of weeks later, I went over to Anna's house and walked up to her front door. I rang the doorbell. Instead of Anna coming out, it was her mom, Joyce. She stepped outside and closed the door, leaving a slight crack.

"You can't see her anymore," she said as she folded her arms and stood in her entryway. I tried to peer through the crack, but Anna was nowhere to be found.

"Will I ever be able to see her?" I asked, trying not to cry.

"Give it time. Maybe you can be friends one day. But your relationship has become unhealthy."

I was broken. What I needed was a blunt den mother to pull me aside and say, *Honey, you're gaaaay! And you're also being a bitch.* But unfortunately, I didn't have one of those.

I know it sounds very high school, and it *was* very high school—because it was high school. I didn't understand it at the time, but I was experiencing a full-fledged hormonal crush. An unrequited love that I couldn't classify. It was beyond the close friendships I'd had and the admiration I'd felt for so many women in my life. I was desperately infatuated.

I was also being obsessive. Those two can coexist. My obsessive behavior pushed Anna away to the point of no return, and that had nothing to do with being queer. It blew up in my face like Jamie and Cathy's marriage in *The Last Five Years.*

I also realized again, I did not do well in trios. In fact, I hated them.

To make matters worse, I was now on my own again. I had once been deemed The Webcam Girl and managed to shed that identity. Now I was the obsessive, crazy girl, which wasn't much better. The problems were changing and amalgamating into different issues. I had to get my ducks in a row—stat. To make matters double worse, the get out of jail free card of moving was not even an option. No more Korea. No more escape plan. No more nothing. I was stuck in Arab, Alabama. Population 8,340.

And I still had two years left of high school.

And I was still hurtinggggg.

Leaves goodbye letter on table. Curtain closes.

Chapter Fifteen

EVERY 15 MINUTES

With Anna a million miles away (emotionally), and with an opening for a new best friend, Emma was the perfect candidate. I knew that if Emma had my back, I'd be protected—because no one messed with Emma Baker. She was the most liked girl in my grade, an ex–Arab Knights cheerleader who left the squad and was *so* over it. As junior year rolled on, she would invite me to her house, and eventually group sleepovers became one-on-one sleepovers.

Emma had the same affection for emo that I did. We would blast emo anthems on the way to house parties. Emma, with her very straightened red hair and Mercedes-Benz, had surprising emotional depth. I always wanted to ride with her in her car. Alone. So we could listen to the Rocket Summer, duh! Now leave me alone!

Junior year, I also became an acolyte—the Episcopalian version of an altar boy. I was still not religious. But the opportunity was enticing. I got to carry the cross down the aisle like the saint I thought I was. All eyes were on me. I'd lead the way, and the reverend would follow behind me because, for those twelve feet, I ran shit. I got to sit with the reverend at the altar and look down at all my disciples. However, holding the cross was a rotating task. So when someone else—Eddie, the disaster of a human who carried the cross like a main dish at Thanksgiving, for example—would get the honor, I'd be jealous. I was a jealous person, if that's not already clear. Envy was my kryptonite. I've reined it in—and frankly, now, antidepressants are helpin' a girl out. I thought the jealousy I felt as an acolyte would be my only cross to bear. I didn't know a high school program would soon spark an even more intense episode of jealousy.

"What are they doing?" I asked in homeroom after noticing that the administration had roped off the front of the school with yellow tape.

"Every 15 Minutes," Emma said.

"It's a drunk-driving reenactment program," Savannah Hunt added, "to teach us that every fifteen minutes, a person is killed by a drunk driver—they're gonna do a big scene in the front of the school, and then they're gonna fake kill off some of our classmates. It's supposed to be a secret, but everyone knows."

Hanging out with Emma had also opened the door to the other popular kids in my grade: Suttles, Jacqueline, Savannah Holt, and Savannah Hunt. The Savannahs both had a last name starting with *H* and were both blonde with matching puffy jackets. It got confusing. It is confusing now. Let's move on. We'd all meet up in the high school parking lot after hours, where Chappy Johnson and the wannabe band (Colton, Randall, and Wyatt) would flail their arms listening to Dave Matthews Band. We'd all watch while sitting on top of our cars. After that, we'd head over to Savannah's house (you could never be certain which one) to discuss how Suttles and Randall broke up for the thirteenth time and to promise that we had her back when the boys called her Sluttles.

High school in rural Small Town, USA, can be defined by three things: drinking in the high school parking lot, drinking in a field, or drinking in a cemetery (um, no thanks). Oh, when you were a teenager, you didn't get trashed in a field listening to Flo Rida? You didn't drive down winding roads until all the streetlights vanished only to park about a mile away from the destination and continue on foot through fields until you spotted a fire in the distance—praying it was the party you were looking for and not a group of hillbillies waiting to attack you? What did you do? Go to house parties? How NORMAL!

I digress. Savannah *Hunt* continued the convo about the future manslaughter of my classmates, but then it quickly turned political.

"If Arab wasn't considering selling liquor in its gas stations, then we wouldn't have to do this shit." Remember, we lived in a dry town.

"I hardly think that's the reason, Savannah," I said.

We often fought about politics. She would bring up the Lord or some prolife argument, and I'd respond with, "Oh, I'm sorry, I can't hear you over the chanting from Obama supporters."

"Actually, drunk-driving deaths happen every eleven minutes—" began Ishaan, the only Other student at Arab High.

"Oh my God—no one cares, Ishaan!" Savannah interrupted. They had beef.

Our teacher, Coach Young (didn't coach, but it was the South, so that's what we called a lot of teachers), noticed things heating up and started to make jokes to try to lighten the mood. Coach Young had an unconventional approach to teaching, was "cool," and quoted *The Office* like he was the brains behind the hit TV show.

"Who do they pick? For the Every 15 Minutes thing?" I asked Emma.

She shrugged.

"They've already picked everyone," Savannah *Holt* told me.

Coach Young chimed in. "Waz crackin', class? Enough about that nonsense. Who wants to learn about World War II?"

Colton took off his shirt and swung it around in acceptance.

"I like your enthusiasm, Colton!"

"Who's in the drunk-driving scene?" I whispered.

"Some of the theater kids," Savannah Holt said.

That's funny. I'm a theater kid.

I wasn't able to pay attention to Coach Young trying to teach us how World War II related to *The Office*, because I was racking my brain to figure out why I didn't already know about the reenactment.

Who in the fuck got picked? I mean—maybe I just didn't get notified. I could have somehow missed that email.

All of a sudden, the fire alarm sounded, and Coach Young froze in his tracks.

"Oh no! There *must* be an *emergency*. Students! Why don't we check what's going on *outside*?" If he had winked any harder, he would have put an eye out.

We all got up and shuffled outside. In front of the school was a banged-up car, with several students trying to get out. They were coughing as if there were fire, but the air was clear. *At least have smoke?* The school had managed to also get the entire fire department and police force to assist in the demonstration. The officials all stood in formation, watching. Then I saw them: Makayla, Rodney, Elise—and Meredith! *Meredith* didn't even get cast in big roles! Makayla lay dead in the road with ketchup on her face.

I rolled my eyes.

"Help! Somebody!" Rodney cried out as he clutched Makayla's limp body. A half-empty bottle of Aristocrat—*it's possibly the best vodka in the world!*—rolled out onto the concrete. A cop picked it up.

Some of my classmates actually seemed shocked. I wasn't.

Why didn't I get picked?

"Now, students, this is what happens when you drink and drive. You kill your friends. And then YOU go to jail for manslaughter. For life." He put handcuffs around Rodney's wrists, forcing Rodney to let go of Makayla's limp hand.

COME ON.

After the principal explained that we were taking part in the Every 15 Minutes program, we went inside.

I was seething.

Why didn't I get picked?

As I passed by the theater room and saw Makayla, Rodney, Meredith, and Elise cleaning up and laughing, I stopped dead in my tracks.

Fernsby.

Fernsby had picked.

Does Fernsby not think I'm talented enough?

I went to Coach Allen's class and sat down grumpily. He was wheeling in a portable TV because it was easier for ~~us~~ him to digest *1984* by watching the film than by reading the book. We had gotten through ten minutes of the movie when the classroom door opened. A bright light (the daylight from the hallway) illuminated the room. Had heaven's gate opened to help the dead students? Oh no! It's the GRIM REAPER?! Wait, that doesn't make sense.

"Close the door, butt munch!" Colton said.

The door closed.

Now, in the darkness, there stood, at five four, in all his horror, the Grim Reaper, who had picked up his cloak from Walmart.

He walked over to Whitmore—arguably the most popular boy in my grade—and ushered him out of class. Then he handed Coach Allen a slip of paper. Coach Allen flipped on the lights—the reaper should have recoiled from the light, but nothing. *I would have, at least.*

Coach Allen read the paper aloud. "On November twelfth, Whitmore Hankins was killed by a drunk driver. His friend Colton was driving." He looked at Colton, who gulped. "Whitmore was just a year and a half short of graduating from high school. He was an active member of the football team and an A student. He is survived by his mom, Rita, and his stepdad, Rick. A moment of silence for Whitmore."

Silence.

Coach Allen crumpled up the paper and put it into his pocket. He turned the TV back on. As the movie flickered to life, so did my temper. The jealousy was overtaking me, but I was trying not to show it. With perfect timing, the film version of *1984* intoned, "If you want to keep a secret, you must also hide it from yourself."

Another five minutes went by, and then the door opened again. Whitmore came back into the classroom with white paint on his face. He sat silently in the back of the room.

Oh, so they're just picking the popular kids.

"Yeah, they're picking the popular kids, I think," Savannah Holt said to me during lunch.

Did she hear my thoughtcrime?

"Why?" I asked. *You know why, Santos.*

"I dunno. I think they had to get nominated by a teacher. And tonight, after everyone's killed, they're going to do a huge funeral, and all the parents are going to show up."

"A FUNERAL?" I nearly threw up my school pizza.

One by one, more popular kids were pulled out of class by the five-four Grim Reaper, and then the kids would return with white paint on their faces. The rule was that, once they "died," we couldn't talk to them. Because they were "dead." All my friends were picked. Except for Jacqueline—because, frankly, she has a face that blends, and I think people thought she had moved away years before.

And then it happened. The one person who I didn't want to die.

Emma.

My friendship with Emma had grown over the year. When Emma and I weren't together, I'd play emo songs in my bedroom, recounting every moment we'd spent together. Her smiling back at me as we drove down the road. Her red hair waving in the wind as her side bangs fell in front of one eye. Waiting on her as she pulled up next to me in our assigned parking spots so we could walk in together. The lyrics were something like, "I can't live to see another day until I see your smiling face. I'm sixteen, but I'll jump off a bridge if you don't choose me!"

I lay on my bedroom floor, letting my eyes well up and a single tear fall down, hitting the carpet. I'd imagine being best friends forever. At dances, I'd request "Fall for You" and hope guys wouldn't ask Emma to dance, so I could dance with her . . . because she was my best friend! Why couldn't we dance together? But of course, guys always asked her to dance.

The Grim Reaper pulled Emma from chem class, and my heart ached the moment she packed up her North Face backpack and walked out of the room. Only she didn't return like the rest of the students. She'd been pulled near the end of the period. Distraught, I walked up to my chem teacher, who was a short, toad-looking man with a pencil mustache. His MO? He hated everyone.

"This whole Grim Reaper thing is weird, right?" I said as I handed in my lab homework.

"It won't solve the problem, and it's frankly disruptive. How do they expect me to teach periodic properties with my door opening up all day?"

My thoughts exactly, sir.

Emma and I didn't have any other classes together for the rest of the day, and I tried to wait at our lockers, but she was nowhere to be found. At first, I was envious about her getting to be involved—but now that she was gone, I was grief-stricken. It felt real. So real that I started to write her a letter.

"Dear Emma," I began in sixth period. I scratched it out. Too formal. Then I threw my Spanish book on top of the note so that Miss Gomez wouldn't dock me for not paying attention in class again.

"You're Spanish, Sophia; I'm only trying to *ayudarte*!" Miss Gomez said. Her actual name was Miss Taylor, but she changed it to put herself in the "world."

"*Quizás. Lo siento*, Miss Gomez." I liked saying *quizás*, even when it didn't make sense, because it sounded like "ass." He-he. I continued my note.

"Hey, Em," I wrote. *EM?* I'd never called her Em in my life.

"Hey, Emma," I wrote. Better. I began to write her a long letter explaining how even though I knew she wasn't dead, it felt like the world ended with her being fake-dead. And I was really imagining her being dead—which scared the living crap out of me. And I might have PTSD.

After reading the two-page letter, with scribbles and words crossed out, I copied it freehand onto fresh loose-leaf paper. I held my hand steady so I didn't get inkblots everywhere. It had to be perfect, not because of my OCD, but because she was perfect.

Because she was "dead," I couldn't give it to her even if I bumped into her in the hallway. The Every 15 Minutes kids weren't allowed to talk to us. They could, however, talk to each other, which was annoying. I saw her laughing with Whitmore in between sixth and seventh periods.

Great. Here I am being distraught about your death—and yet you can laugh with Whitmore like everything is okay?

I couldn't shake the dread. It was coursing through my veins like a horrible poison.

The principal came onto the speaker.

"Students, please head to the gymnasium for a special assembly."

We all shuffled in. They had set up photos of all our classmates around one casket as we were handed funeral pamphlets. I opened my pamphlet. All the students who had been taken away by the Grim Reaper were listed—and there was her name, three-fourths of the way down the page.

"Emma Baker. Survived by her mom, Tina; her father, Ken; her sister, Valerie; and her brother, Barnett."

I then saw Emma's parents being ushered in, crying, dressed in black. Ken was consoling Tina, who clearly wasn't ready for her kid to die. Then all the dead kids filed in and sat in the front row, watching as each parent got up and gave a eulogy.

It was the worst day of my life.

After the assembly, I spotted Emma, who was hugging her parents and wiping away the white paint. I walked up to her and touched her arm.

"Hi, Soph!" She jumped into my arms, hugging me tight. As much as I hated the name Sophie, I loved when Emma called me "Soph." It almost made me want to change my name.

I had my hand in my pocket, ready to deliver the letter.

"I, um, that was rough, right?" I asked as my eyes shifted.

"Yeah!" she agreed as she wiped away a tear. "But it's silly. It's only pretend."

Her parents walked away, and I stood there, frozen. *Do I give her the letter now?*

"I wrote this when you were dead," I said. *I guess now works.*

"Ahhh, Soph. Thanks!"

That night, she invited me over. Emma truly was my perfect emo soul mate. The letter had really touched her, and we were both so grateful she was alive.

Eulogy to My Friendship with Emma

At the end of our junior year, Emma started dating a twenty-three-year-old, Wilbur. I understand now that their relationship was gross and illegal in most states where this story didn't take place. All I can say is that I did not think it was creepy at the time, and I was envious. (Emma's parents were aware and tolerant of the relationship.)

We were over at Wilbur's house one night with his friend Elmer, also twenty-three, and we were all tipsy from Mike's Hard Lemonades when we started to play Truth or Dare. They asked Emma first, "Truth or dare?"

"Ummm, dare?"

Wilbur looked at us and said, "I dare y'all to make out." *Make out?* I had never kissed a girl before. I'd like to be clear, I do not condone men asking girls, teenage girls, to kiss one another for their entertainment. He was, however, asking me to kiss *Emma*, which couldn't be that bad, and that's how it went down.

I looked at Emma, who giggled and said, "Okay, whatever," like it was no big deal.

She looked at me and I looked at her and we leaned in. When our lips touched, my insides exploded. I didn't look down because I knew my intestines were on the floor because they had busted out of my body. What I thought would be a quick peck turned into a lip-locked affair to remember. All I could think was, *She's a really good kisser* . . . and then she pulled away. *Wait. No . . . why?*

"That was hot, ladies," Wilbur said.

"Okay, y'all's turn!" Elmer said.

Yeah, how about we make out again? I think we would all like that, right?

"Uh . . . I d-don't know!" she stammered. "I dare you to run around naked, Wilbur."

Boring.

We continued to play, taking shots and doing dares on the level of prank phone calls. I was completely distracted. I wanted to kiss Emma again, as a friend, but I didn't dare ask. Eventually, we paired off and retired to our respective rooms.

Elmer tried to dry mouth me with his cracked lips and put his hairy beer body on top of mine. I lay still to give him the hint he wasn't getting any. He rolled over and passed out. I stared at the ceiling, thinking about what was going on in Wilbur and Emma's bedroom. Curious to know if they were having sex. Imagining they were having sex. Thinking about *Emma* having sex. Imagining her face, not unlike Rachel McAdams in *The Notebook*, in a sea of pillows.

The next day, I told Emma, "That was fun! We should have a double date again."

Listen, I needed to do what it took.

"Yeah, girl! Sounds good!" she said as she dropped me off at home.

I watched as her black Mercedes-Benz drove up my gravel driveway. I couldn't wait. I thought about the kiss happening again. Again, as a friend. We had gotten really close, and I thought it was important to grow in our relationship. Since Emma was a very sought-after gal, and Wilbur took a lot of her attention, I had to wait four weeks.

I was about to burst through my skin again when we were right back where we started 720 hours later.

"So . . . shall we Truth or Dare, boys?" I asked coyly.

"Sure!" they said.

For ten rounds, they didn't ask us to kiss. *Are you fucking serious? Isn't that what you fucking like?*

My eyes were nearly rolling in the back of my head when finally Elmer came to my rescue.

"Hey . . . y'all should kiss."

"I guess . . . I don't know . . . what do you think?" I tucked my hair behind my ear and looked like the damsel in distress I was.

"Sure, whatever, Elmer, ha-ha," Emma said.

"Topless," Wilbur added.

I looked at Emma. I mean, I wanted to, but I wasn't sure either of us was ready for that. This was a completely different level. Right when I was about to ask if she was cool with going topless, she took off her shirt. I looked at her body. Her red hair falling down and wrapping around her nipples like Poison Ivy from *Batman and Robin*.

She lay down, and I got on top of her. My knees accidentally hit hers, and I tried to position myself.

"Sorry!" I said.

I looked at her. I had seen her a million times, but never this close. I pressed my lips to hers, and we kissed again. The lip locking was longer this time, and our bodies pressed against each other was confusing and comfortable at the same time.

And then right as we got into it, we stopped. I awkwardly sat up on the couch and tried to move away without knocking her breathtaking kneecaps this time. We both got dressed in silence.

The guys were stunned. Judging by their silence, they thought it was hot too.

"So . . . want to go in the hot tub?" Elmer said as he dropped his beer.

As we sat in the hot tub and Wilbur put his arm around Emma, I couldn't stop imagining myself in his place.

After that second time with Wilbur and Elmer, whenever I spent the night at Emma's place, I'd ask her if she wanted to make out.

"Okay. Sure," she'd say.

We'd make out in her bed for a while and then laugh, and she'd roll over and go to sleep. I'd roll over to the other side. Feeling crazy. I'd stare at the back of her red head, yearning to pet it. I wanted to cry, scream, laugh. Ten thousand emotions were going through my body. And yet, I still couldn't figure out why. Was I supposed to know? Sure, most people would. But we're talking about someone who believed in Santa Claus until thirteen. My entire concept of reality was skewed from the jump.

Somewhere along the way, that girl Tara Fernell who'd called me out about my webcam browser history had gotten upset that I was close with *her best friend* Emma. I knew she was upset because when she would pass me in the hallway, she'd hit me with her shoulder. Or when I'd go to parties, she'd take the beer I had just opened for myself and chug it. I wasn't sure what I was supposed to do about it. Report to a high school official that I was being bullied at a party where there was underage drinking? I officially had a new bully.

Tara jamming her shoulder into mine didn't stop me from trying to get closer to Emma.

Word got around that we had made out, but I didn't care. Our make-out sessions meant that she thought I was cool enough to make out with. She didn't give a shit either. I overheard her say, "Yeah . . . so what?" And my heart fluttered. It sank when I later found out she'd kissed other girls too . . . even Tara. On the one hand, I couldn't believe I wasn't the only one. Truth or Dare was our game! On the other hand, it was cool she didn't care what people thought. Unbeknownst to her . . . and me . . . she was a gateway kiss to the long road that led me toward lesboville.

Chapter Sixteen

AND THE WINNER IS . . .

You know how most kids go through phases? Like, one day they're your little poet, and the next thing you know, they've put a rod through their nose and are wearing JNCO jeans with safety pins down the side? Or they were your little scientist, and you used to stay up all night making volcanoes with them for the science fair, and now the only thing they experiment with is meth and play video games?

One day, when I came down the stairs, my dad looked up at me and asked, "What happened to my little girl?"

I walked past him, looked back, and said, "She's dead."

My drug? Victory bouquets. My new phase? I turned into a full-on pageant queen.

Many years before, when I was about nine, I'd been sitting with Grandma Sally while she was wrapping her golden-blonde hair in foam sponge hair rollers. Putting her hair in rollers was her nightly activity. Even if she was just planning to garden her green tomatoes in the yard the next day, she made damn well sure that she would be ready for church or a funeral at a moment's notice. She was the youngest of eight children—and, at this point, her siblings were dropping like flies. That night years ago sitting with my grandma wasn't any ordinary night—in fact, it was a special occasion, because the Miss Mississippi Pageant was on. In the South, first place is God, second place is football, and third (although Grandma Sally would beg to differ) is pageants.

We sat in my grandparents' Wiggins, Mississippi, living room. Mom was on the couch, Grandma Sally was in her recliner, and Papa had been exiled to the kitchen. I had outrun my grandpa to his own recliner, which was a pretty bratty thing to do, seeing as he'd had two complete knee and hip replacements by that point.

Mom, Grandma Sally, and I sat in silence, with only the cicadas chirping outside, as the pageant started.

At the beginning of a pageant, previous winners would do a celebratory walk. The Walk of Champions. The lively host called out the year they were crowned and also the women's names, one by one, "1975 Miss Mississippi, Mollie Magee!" and so on and so forth. Former queens now in their fifties and sixties would come out and hit the bevel, as if they'd never gotten over the thrill of getting the crown. One seventy-four-year-old (1945) even drove her electric wheelchair down to center stage and made sure to use her cane to turn out her foot. The crowd rose to their feet and cheered. 1945 was known to not be a quitter.

And then my grandma, who was still putting in the rollers, pulled the bobby pin out of her mouth and froze. She started to squint at the screen.

"1977 Miss Mississippi, Mary Donnelly!" An attractive, blonde, Barbra Streisand–resembling woman paraded to the front of the stage. She had the kind of presence that everyone reacted to like, *Ooooh, it's Mary Donnelly! Mary Donnelly! Ooooh!* My grandma pointed at the TV as if she were summoning a lightning bolt.

"Here she comes—Miss I Don't Lay Off the Doughnuts."

"Grandma!"

"Twenty-five years, Mother. Twenty-five years," my mom said wearily.

I stared at Mary Donnelly. I didn't see any extra doughnut weight.

"You should've won, Susan. She only sang! You sang *and* danced! How many people can do both?"

"A lot of people, Mother."

In preparation for the Miss Mississippi Pageant, my mom would dance for ten hours a week, practice walking with her knees together while my grandma Sally studied her every movement, and she'd count her calories religiously to fit into her one-piece coral DeWeese bathing suit. Even then, my grandma Sally didn't think my mom took it seriously enough. When my mom chopped off all her hair in rebellion after her six hundredth pageant, Grandma Sally threatened to kick her out of the house. And that was where the animosity was rooted.

Grandma Sally mumbled a few "well, she's a bitch" and "what a waste of money" as I shimmied out of the recliner and plopped next to my mom to lay my head in her lap.

Proof that she actually won some pageants, and it wasn't a waste of money at the time!

I looked at my mom, who gave me a weary half smile and opened up another book, *How to Move to Mexico.*

Why would anyone want to put on a tight, bejeweled dress and hair spray that you wouldn't be able to brush out for weeks? It was chaos. It was cutthroat. It was not my cup of cornflakes. From that moment, I knew that I wanted nothing to do with beauty pageants.

Mom never wanted me to enter pageants either. In fact, she tried to steer me away from them for fear of PTSD from "the bevel." Seeing as I *chose* to wear a Dillard's tee that said "Nasty Boy" almost exclusively for a five-year time period, she was relieved that she never had anything to worry about.

So, when I was seventeen, in a local boutique called something like "Holy Art and Towels," and Mom noticed a flyer announcing "The Junior Miss

Registration Early Enrollment," I almost smacked her when she *suggested that I submit myself.*

"You *hate* pageants," I said. This time it was *me* wondering if someone had eaten *Susan.*

"It's a *scholarship program*, Elizabeth. It's not like the pageants I endured."

My mind wandered—because the way she said *"endured"* sounded like *manure.*

"Scholarship program" is a lipstick-on-a-pig way of saying *pageant.*

"You can put that money toward college," she added.

"I thought you were going to pay for college?" I asked. Spoiled or not, I did need to confirm.

"Doesn't mean you can't help. And if you go to pricey New York, pageants have to become your side gig."

This from the woman who used to be scolded on the way home from yet another pageant where she didn't win. She would laugh with Papa as Grandma Sally wailed through her tears, "You don't even care! All that money. You are so ungrateful."

Yeah, I'm good on Junior Miss.

I refused for a few weeks by immediately deleting any email from my mom with the letters *J* or *M*, but she kept up the chase. She assured me that I wouldn't have to wear floor-length dresses or be judged on my "look."

"The Junior Miss scholarship program is for smart girls—overachievers," she told me.

She had said the O-word. *Damn, Susan. You know how to manipulate the hell out of me.*

So that was that. I just needed to trust my mom.

Grandma Sally had passed a few years prior, or I would have called to tell her the news. On second thought, my sudden reversal would have given her a heart attack. Still, both my mom and I knew that, somewhere, she was shaking her fists and saying, "Susan! Watch her knees, and Elizabeth, shoulders back and—"

I signed up and didn't tell a soul. I might have embraced my Kim K. side in middle school (we both loved stripping for the camera), but I was still not a pageant girl. Sorry, Grandma. I didn't need the school to know that The Webcam Girl was vying for Miss Congeniality.

The day I signed up, I got an email that said, ELIZABETH! I'M SO EXCITED TO MEET YOU! MANDATORY MEETING AT THE FRANKLIN BAPTIST CHURCH ON WEDNESDAY. SEE YOU THERE. MRS. FAYE DAVENPORT.

Clearly someone needed to tell Mrs. Faye Davenport that she didn't have to shout. Also, CHURCH?

"Honey, it's just where they're havin' the meetin'. You know everyone's religious here."

Exactly. Um, earth to Susan? Do you not remember the Baptist camp? I'll walk straight into the dunking booth if you don't watch out.

I rolled up to Franklin Baptist Church. Waiting outside for the arrival of all the contestants was the head of Marshall County's Junior Miss Pageant, Mrs. Faye Davenport. (I had googled her.) She was a stumpy woman who wore novelty earrings and a choker of pearls so tight that I thought if she unclasped them, her head would fall off. She had a spiked and frosted haircut, and honestly, she was a direct replica of Professor Umbridge, if the professor had had a side gig as a debutante. I could tell by the glimmer in Mrs. Davenport's eye that she would go to great lengths to make me a lady.

"So nice to meet you, Elizabeth!" she said, giving me a hug. "All the other girls are inside. I'll be there in a second, hun."

I walked into the bible study room. *Praise be.* I noticed only three other contestants. I had expected preppy Vincyard Vines dresses, a Longchamp purse draped across a dainty Reese Witherspoon type. Instead, the first contestant had been attacked by her makeup (the makeup won), and it had created a flesh-colored ring around the neck of her monogrammed T-shirt. The second contestant had a cute blonde bob, but when she turned around, there were butterfly clips in there that she must've gotten on middle school trips to the mall store Icing. And finally, there was Darma—which I knew was her name because the back of her camouflage jacket had DARMA shellacked on it.

My grandma would have a field day with this bunch.

A moment later, I realized that since so few girls were competing, I could probably win. Then Faye Davenport walked into the room, beaming.

"Welcome to the annual Junior Miss program!" she announced. She did a little jig and then clapped. We all followed suit. I saw her try to mask her disappointment as she surveyed the motley crew.

"Y'all can call me Mrs. Faye. This is gonna be our best year yet!"

According to Mrs. Faye, the pageant was about celebrating girls for who they were! It was meant to encourage us to dream big and develop leadership skills and "maybe even become closer to God—but I can't really say that." The competition was broken up into five categories—because this was, after all, a competition, *ma'am*. Scholastics, Interview, Talent, Self-Expression, and Fitness. Whoever got the highest average out of all five won. Simple as that.

The following is an exact replica from FD's Junior Miss handbook and has NOT been embellished. The original font was Comic Sans—which I will spare you.

2008–2009 FAYE DAVENPORT'S GUIDE TO WINNING JUNIOR MISS

SCHOLASTICS: 25%

A Junior Miss maintains a high grade-point average. GOOD GIRLS HAVE GOOD GRADES. ☺

Duh, done and dusted.

INTERVIEW: 25%

LADIES! MOST IMPORTANT! PLEASE SEE SAMPLE QUESTIONS BELOW. The interview takes place a few days prior, and you will be interviewed by a panel, including potentially a CELEBRITY!

You are going to Mars—what three things will you take with you?

My DVD of The Notebook, Lammy, and Ritter Sport. I want to give it a go with Lammy in zero gravity, and I'm a foodie.

How do you feel about Junior Misses not being given a crown but a medallion?

I think it's OUTRAGEOUS and whosever idea it was should be sent to jail.

Do you think that secular music can be glorifying to God?

Depends if you think He'd be a fan of "the stanky legg."

TALENT: 20%

SHOW OFF YOUR SKILLS! PLEASE MAKE SURE TO HAVE ACT APPROVED BY ME. Singing, dancing, prayer recitation, let God lead you—just, once again, nothing too risqué. NO SOULJA BOY OR BATON TWIRLING!

A contestant took out an audience member's eye, and it was the talk of the town for years. Don't be the talk of the town . . .

SELF-EXPRESSION: 15%

KNOW YOUR STANCE ON CURRENT ISSUES! YOU WILL BE ASKED A QUESTION ONSTAGE.

Good answer: "I subscribe to the good Baptist God for everything."

Bad answer: "Gay marriage is good!"

FITNESS: 15%

YOU WILL LEARN AN EXERCISE ROUTINE FROM PAST WINNER JULIE JONES AND PERFORM IN FRONT OF THE JUDGES DURING THE LIVE SHOW.

Start practicing the Presidential Fitness Test's sit and reach.

That night, I flipped through the packet and realized I had to memorize the names of government leaders; Richard Shelby and Jeff Sessions along with Kay Ivey were at the top of the list. In the back was a color-coded schedule. *We have practice every single night?* I threw the handbook across the room. It landed with a thud against my dresser and opened to the last page.

The winner receives $2,500.

In cold, hard cash.

I looked up YouTube videos of former winners like Julie Jones. All of them had medallions on, engraved with "AJM" for "Alabama Junior Miss." They were all happy. Smart. Talented. *Winners.*

The next day, I went back to Franklin Baptist Church, hugged Mrs. Faye Davenport, and told her, "I prayed about you last night."

It. Is. On.

By the end of three weeks, I had learned to walk in heels (my mom looked at my knees after dinner), I could recite famous past Junior Misses (Diane Sawyer, thank you), and I knew how to answer, "How would you describe the color red to a blind person?" (Faye Davenport said this was the top question last year during the interview portion.) I knew the American motto (In God We Trust), and I knew my "stance" on the morning-after pill (wait till marriage—why would you kill a baby?). I could even recite the names of Jeff Sessions's grandchildren, which was largely thanks to a one-on-one session with Mrs. Faye, who made me write out their names with a mysterious quill that would etch their names into the back of my hand in my own blood as if by magic. Maybe kidding, maybe not.

With my bloody hand wrapped in gauze, I was ready to be a pageant queen.

The interview took place in a stuffy room at the local chamber of commerce. I shifted in my seat, a big, tufted leather armchair. I stared at the two women and one man who—by the looks of them—must have worked for Fox News. One *did* work for the Weather Channel, which meant he was the celebrity! The women each had large, perfect teeth and a soft, polite smile that seemed to say something like, *I might've killed my husband, but you'll never know.* The interviewers drilled me with questions. I gave my best Junior Miss responses:

"If you were a kitchen appliance, what would you be?"

"A refrigerator—because it has many drawers and compartments, and each fulfills a different duty. I am multifaceted, as well. And I'm able to compartmentalize my life, which is how I get all ten of my extracurriculars done."

"Do you think secular music can be glorifying to God?"

"I think that depends on if the person listening to the music glorifies God. And if so, then yes, secular music glorifies God. I mean, think of Dolly Parton."

"What's your favorite book?"

"*The Greatest Generation* by Tom Brokaw—because, after all, my grandparents are my heroes and part of the greatest generation."

It killed.

I mean, I leaned into the Republican shit *hard*. But I was in it to win it, and admitting that I was an Obama "Yes We Can" freak would have gone over about as well as eating a tuna salad sandwich in front of a school of fish.

A few days before the competition, my friends from school found out that I was competing for the MEDALLION of Junior Miss—because word always gets out in a small town. Also my headshot, with me vibing, "I'm destined to win, honey," was in the local paper along with the photos of the other three contestants. I was mortified that my secret was out. The truth was that I was actually starting to enjoy myself—and I didn't want any of the kids at school to know that. I was impressing people, who'd "ooo" and "aww" over my eloquent answers as a seventeen-year-old. I could work a room. I liked being in the spotlight.

I was accessing a side of me that, up until now, I'd thought was locked away in a metal box, that only a lover would be able to let out: my glam side. Instead, Faye Davenport turned out to be the key. I was comfortable in flats, but in heels, I was one kick-ass dynamo. And I felt pretty. Like, really pretty. And who doesn't want to feel pretty? The night before the competition, I tried on my green satin dress and gold heels, and my mom put Grandma Sally's pearls around my neck. I looked into the mirror as my hair fell to one side, and I could feel my grandma saying, *Mary Donnelly who? Give 'em hell!*

The next night, my parents came backstage with flowers and cards and told me to "break a leg." By that time, my dad had relocated to Alabama. He had remarried a woman, my now stepmom, Deb—which is like the most stepmom name ever! I'm thankful for Deb, but I'm mostly thankful that she still talks to me because when they started dating, I vetted her with a dating quiz. I gave her a C because she didn't know what a drag bunt was. Sorry, Deb. Both Dad and Mom liked being overinvolved in my life—which meant they had to reluctantly spend time together. The four of them sat in the front row of a quite desolate auditorium. Fortunately, Darma had brought her entire family from the backwoods. They hooted and hollered and draped their camouflage jackets and deer carcasses over empty seats.

As the auditorium continued to not fill up, I stood in the wings, practicing the opening choreography with the other contestants. I had done the work; I'd prepped for the talent portion by watching Sutton Foster's performance on *CBS This Morning* on YouTube the night before and stretched for the fitness portion by having one of the girls push my face down to my legs. And then I felt a tinge of something familiar. My competitive spirit. *It's game time.* The field was ready to go, and I was going to tackle them all. *You're going down, girls.*

"A Dream Is a Wish Your Heart Makes" by the Disney Channel Circle of Stars came over the auditorium speaker as the four of us hit the stage. For three minutes, I jazz-squared, fanned my arms, and (in a PG manner) shook my booty to empower the women who had come before me and those who would eventually come after. The smile I had been painting on my face during rehearsals and dropping behind Faye Davenport's back was genuine this time. As all the contestants gracefully tapped hands in the waltz-like move, I winked and said to each of them, "You go, girl!" And finally, as the spotlights illuminated each of us, we linked arms for the final moment—and I swear, a tear rolled down my cheek.

Move the fuck over, Diane Sawyer; there's a new girl in town.

The competition quickly was in full swing, and there was no time to process my feelings. The spotlights dimmed, and I quickly pranced offstage for a costume change into my Talent outfit.

Being the little schemer I was, I knew that I could sing anything I wanted for the competition—but while I was at it, why not show Mr. Fernsby that I was the perfect pick for Millie in our upcoming production of *Thoroughly Modern Millie*? I knew that Mr. Fernsby was considering a lowerclassman. *How dare he!* I belted "Not for the Life of Me" like I was singing for my life.

It did not help because he wasn't even in the audience, and I ended up getting the part of Muzzy instead. But for one minute and thirty seconds, the role was mine—and I swear that somewhere in New York, Sutton Foster herself was bobbing her head in appreciation.

I didn't have time to watch the other contestants, but I had already seen Darma demonstrate "how to gut a moose" to the tune of "O Holy Night," and I didn't need to see that twice.

Meanwhile, I was busy reading over my note cards of possible answers to Self-Expression. "Presidential terms should be limited unless Republican." I returned to the stage like I was in *America's Next Top Model*. I catwalked down and stood next to my fellow contestants, giving full God face. When my turn came, a member of the panel read out my question.

"It's important to encourage women to be themselves. What would you say to those looking up to you?"

Really? That's it? "Be yourself—but be good, godly, and generous." (What I really wanted to say was, *Let your freak flag fly, weirdos!*)

A quick change and we were in our Nike shorts, tennis shoes, and lime-green Junior Miss tees for the Fitness portion. It went fine. I was able to fake being fit, and I was way more coordinated than most in the bunch (except for Darma).

Finally, at the end of the competition, we all came back onstage for the closing dance and to hit our marks. Before the host announced the winner, I thought about how butt-hurt I would be if I didn't win. I had performed well. I was good at this. I realized that I wanted to win more than I wanted to move to New York. *I might actually be good at scholarship programs.*

"And the winner of the 2008 Junior Miss Marshall County is . . ."

My heart raced.

"ELIZABETH SANTOS!"

SEE? I TOLD YOU. I mean—WAIT! WHAT? I WON? I actually WON!

They gave me a victory bouquet and a medal, and I paraded around the stage like a true champion. My mom yelled, "Yahoo!" My dad called out, "Way to go, kiddo!" And I beamed like the pageant queen I was.

The only other time in my life I have held a bouquet of flowers was years later, at a wedding reception in 2017, when I pushed the groom's sister out of the way to catch the bouquet. Yes, by then I was a full-on, raging dyke—but competition is competition, baby. And maybe the "open bar" had been open for five hours. Anyhoo, back to Junior Miss.

Faye Davenport congratulated me and told my parents and me that she'd circle back with details for the next round of preparation the following week.

"We're gonna spend a lot of time together!"

Wait . . . Mrs. Faye! What do you mean? But she was already out the door.

In the week following my triumph, my name was in the paper—along with a huge photo spread. *Behold! Victory is mine!*

Taken in a basement at an older man named Herman's house.

A phone call and encyclopedia-thick handbook of more rules later, I learned that we were now in the big leagues—and Mrs. Faye was desperate to hold a candle to the city girls.

I was off to Montgomery—home of Alabama Shakespeare Festival and racism!

The girls competing at the county level had been, for lack of a better term, off-brand contestants—me included. Most of us had signed up out of boredom, had been forced to do it, or were simply delusional. That stage had been our own little misfit island. In contrast, the girls at state level had been preparing since *birth*. Their parents had spent thousands on piano lessons and smeared Vaseline on their kids' baby teeth to ease the effort of fake-smiling for long periods of time and had weekly etiquette lessons in Miss Carlotta's tearoom.

I was a small fish in a big pond, and that pond was frequented by prothonotary warblers. For ten days, I was on my own in Montgomery, living off an unrealistic caviar dream. I was ~~living~~ thriving in a host family's *mansion* with a fellow participant who was definitely in the Vaseline-since-baby-teeth category.

Contestants weren't allowed to contact home for fear of stoking stage-parent hysteria. Snail mail was the only way to communicate. That wasn't a problem for me because I'd already moved on. The host family was my new family. They were the only people I cared about for those ten days. *Are you my mother?*

This bonding with strangers was encouraged by the organization, which hosted events like a daddy/daughter party, where we hung out with our host dads and sang karaoke. After I wrote home, "I had the most wonderful time with my new dad," the return letter started with, "You only have one dad, Elizabeth. And that's me!"

We even posed for a family portrait. For legal reasons, I can't include it in this book, but let's say it looks like an ad for "We're Republicans—but just look at our diverse family with the mixed-race daughter we've adopted!" Still, I liked my host family. They were very sweet—sweet as Lipton sweet tea. Shout-out to my encouraging host mom, Tammy. She was high society. A Daughters of the American Revolution type. A player in the game of life. She'd stay up late with me as I'd pluck on the piano. She'd clap along and reward me with cheese and prosciutto on toothpicks—which I'd eat with one pinkie up. It felt like a crash course in being rich, southern, and white.

In between rehearsals, our itinerary included spending a week learning more about Alabama's rich history, like touring the Montgomery Cow MOOseum dressed in our Sunday best.

When we weren't being groomed as future Republicans, we were rehearsing our tight little bums off. The dance instructor, Stephanie, was an honest-to-goodness Olympian who only showed us the steps twice. That was it. "Ask a friend if you don't know them! We're moving on!" Despite how difficult the routine was, I found myself drawn to Stephanie. She moved her body so beautifully and used "space" to create "art."

Of course, I barely had time to admire her—because, in a pas de bourrée, we were already onto the next portion: Pure Barre fitness. Stephanie had actual visible ab muscles. I was impressed until I noticed that most of the other girls had abs too. Before then, I'd never even known anyone who had anything approaching abs. If I bent down, though, my fat roll looked like an ab.

At State, we had to do crunches and those godforsaken Six Inches. The finale of the routine was a somersault that ended with us squatting, holding one leg in midair, and stretching it out. I knew I was in trouble when my leg was visibly shaking at only half bent.

"Do NOT ask me for help, Marshall County. Figure it out." I rolled over into a plank, with sweat dripping off my face, and collapsed the moment she turned to another contestant.

NO ONE CAN DO THIS, STEPHANIE! I popped my head up.

Everyone could do this.

I had one week to get it down, but I needed a full year.

Ten days passed in the blink of an eye, and game time was once again upon me.

The competition was a two-day event. This time, Montgomery's megachurch hosting the competition was packed. People brought confetti cannons and custom handheld fans with contestants' faces printed on them. Each contestant had her own cheer section with her parents waiting to reunite with her. They weren't allowed to come backstage, but a text from my mom was all I needed to put me in the right mindset.

We're here, honey! Knock 'em dead! (And get that money.)

The State competition felt like living inside an Olay commercial. The blue spotlights! The girl power! Upbeat, positive music! An announcer resembling John Candy came on the sound system: "Ladies and gentlemen, welcome to Junior Miss!" You'd have thought we were at a Jonas Brothers concert, what with all the fanfare and screams.

All contestants came out to a Taylor Swift song for the opening number, and when it was my turn to hit the mic, I said in an extra-animated and projected voice, "Elizabeth Santos, Marshall County, contestant number ten!"

I made my way through the various portions without major incident. Mr. Fernsby wasn't in attendance for my encore rendition of "Not for the Life of Me," but who says I couldn't slip the performance DVD in his mailbox?

Everything seemed to be going my way until we got to Fitness. Despite the Olympian's daily sessions, practicing with my housemate during trips to the cow museum, and yelling at my abs to "SHOW THYSELVES, GODDAMMIT," I knew there was no way. I thought back to the dancers in community theater who'd told me that "flailing" would trick anyone into thinking I was performing

at a high level, and I figured the same tactic would apply here. We all hit the stage again in our lululemon yoga pants and matching pink sneakers. I watched as all the other girls landed their somersaults correctly, effortlessly—with grace, even—with their cheer sections applauding and letting out *thank God!*s after they nailed it.

"Contestant number ten!" the announcer shouted.

I ran to the front of the stage with my hands on my hips. The music pulsed. I did the beauty squats (normal squats, but you give a lot of face) and then the plank, followed by the side plank that I held while doing a body roll. I went back to the plank and did mountain climbers. And then it was time for the big shebang—the grand finale to my solo. I stood up, attempted a somersault, but started to lose momentum as it came time to use my "abs." I went to grab my leg but didn't quite make it—and instead fell directly onto my ass. There was an audible "OOOF" that carried through the auditorium and was loudly echoed by my dad. The Taylor Swift music pulsed behind me. I quickly grabbed my leg to show I was flexible, then hopped up, kicked my legs to my butt like a cheerleader, and scurried back into place, smiling the entire time. I returned for the closing number, and as I said, "Marshall County! Contestant number ten!" I held out hope that it wouldn't be the last time I announced my name onstage. I knew—deep down inside—that I would not be medallioned.

I was correct.

The hosts didn't call my number for the top eight, so my journey had ended. However, I did find out that I'd placed in the Self-Expression category (okay, werk). Still, I was bummed. Backstage, everyone told me they thought I'd had a fighting chance, including Faye Davenport, who was livid that I hadn't placed. "Fitness is only fifteen percent! They always leave out the county girls," she snarled. I think ass planting—in front of 6,341 people, to be exact—had put the nail in the coffin. But sure, maybe it was big-city snobbery.

I packed up my stuff and said goodbye to my host mom, Tammy, giving her a tight squeeze. *Pinkies up!*

On the drive home, I talked my mom's ear off about how . . . I'd had the time of my life as a Junior Miss. Let's cut the shit. A *pageant* girl. If there were colorful lights and Donny and Marie look-alikes hosting, then it was a pageant. Also, the point of pageants is to win money . . . so . . . case closed.

And I'd loved it.

Did I google more competitions to see if I could redeem myself? Yes. Did I realize you actually needed abs to win Miss America or any of the other pageants, which I knew I would never have? Yes. Not to mention it was a "YEARLONG COMMITMENT"?

"Yes, honey. Those girls are serious," my mom said.

No, thanks. I needed to get ready for college. Too bad, because I really would have liked to redeem the ass planting.

However, my status as a former State Junior Miss contestant made another group of women happy. Know what I'm talking about? If you think you do, just turn to the next page.

Chapter Seventeen

IT'S A RUSH!

The first time I was in the middle of two hundred girls was a mix of abject terror and fantasy fulfilled. I was shoulder to shoulder with beautiful women, packed together like sardines in a can. The anxiety and frenzy was palpable, and I felt my body vibrating with the potential of a new experience. I noticed this one particularly stunning woman. The type you read about in magazines. Her dress was the perfect amount of tight, hugging her hourglass figure oh so perfectly. After staring a beat too long, I looked away, nervous she'd caught me in the act. I definitely didn't belong there. I surveyed the women around me who were dressed to the nines, waiting for the opportunity to make a lasting impression. If we succeeded, it would mean we'd be in each other's lives forever. It was the first time I had gone this far down South—and I knew it would be my new happy place.

No, I wasn't at a lesbian bar—I was in the middle of sorority recruitment, a.k.a. "rush."

Freshly eighteen, I'd just moved into my University of Alabama dorm the night before. Roll Tide Roll.

I had gotten rejected from every school I applied to up north. NYU, Boston College, Northwestern, Harvard (although I did get an interview; *how do ya like me now?*)—even Boston University wouldn't give me a second look. I had my heart set on going to school in New York and pursuing my acting career. I tried to tell my school counselor that I wanted to go to an East Coast university, but she didn't know how to help me.

"I don't know how to help you," she said.

That's your job, I thought. "Here are the universities I am applying to. Do you know what would make my application stand out?"

"No one at Arab ever wants to go to a school that isn't Alabama or Auburn. Most students opt for community college first. Have you tried googling?"

Yes, moron, which is why I'm here with you. I didn't have time for the runaround.

In the hallway, between classes, I went up to my senior English teacher, still Coach Allen, who thought my papers were snarky (I relied solely on Ayn Rand references to seem smart).

"Coach Allen," I said, "what kind of college-application essay will make me stand out?"

"What if you don't write one at all? That will send a message," he said and let out a howl of laughter. Then he fist-bumped me and high-fived a football player as he left.

Alabama it was.

I wouldn't dare go to Auburn, the College of Agriculture. I wasn't a state-school girl, but—and I mean this with the utmost respect, y'all—I knew better than to set foot in that cow town. Did the CEO of Apple go there? Yes. Do I think slightly less of him because of it? Also yes.

Buck, a die-hard 'Bama fan, told me it would be a grave mistake if I didn't choose THE University of Alabama.

I applied to UA (by which I mean I filled in my social security number and answered a security question), and within two minutes, I had my acceptance letter. It was essentially the Staples Easy Button of universities.

It wasn't New York, but I was officially going to college.

Since I was going to go to a southern school, Mom thought it would be a great idea for me to join a sorority, seeing as she had been a Delta Gamma at Mississippi State in the seventies. And Junior Miss had pleasantly surprised me. I trusted my mom yet again, who was the Old Mill grits of the South. (That means queen bee.)

At first I'd said, "I don't want to pay for my friends."

"You pay to eat at the house, Elizabeth. I don't know why you're resistant! My best friends were my sorority sisters."

"Who?" I asked. As far as I knew, all her best friends were the Key West Lesbians.

"Well . . . I don't talk to them now, but that's not the point."

No matter—she and I had our work cut out for us if I was going to rush.

Basically, at any university with a thriving Greek scene, sorority houses scouted their recruits a lot like Nick Saban recruits his players. Roll Tide! Most girls who'll make it into a house have been wined and dined for an entire calendar year before they get to campus. Roll Tide!

"Find out if they have Delta Gamma at Alabama! You're a legacy!" Mom happily said.

"I'm a what?"

A *legacy* is the nepotism of sororities. It's also the only time that nepotism did ever—or will ever—work for me. (Unless you count getting a research grant or driving an M1 Abrams tank.)

As it turned out, UA didn't have a Delta Gamma chapter. But nepotism's roommate came to my rescue. Mom's college roommate, Stacey, had a daughter, Mary Catherine, who happened to be the chair of rush at a top sorority on campus, Gamma Alpha Beta, so Mom arranged for us to meet. We brought my résumé, listing every single extracurricular and including my "special skills." Mom and Stacey caught up. An hour later, Mary Catherine came down the stairs in an oversize sweatshirt that hung loose on her slender frame, with her ponytail barely held together by a string. She cradled a mug close to her body, as if for warmth. She drank coffee at seven p.m. She was superhuman. I had to keep my jaw from dropping to the floor.

"This is Elizabeth—or is it Sophie?" Stacey asked, confused.

"Sophie's fine," I answered.

"Sophie Santos. Her mom is my best friend from college, Susan." She grabbed my mom's hand in a comforting way, as if my mom were dying. "Sophie's rushing this fall."

"It's not a big deal. You'll be fine," Mary Catherine said and shrugged. She took seconds to look over my résumé, and then—without a word—disappeared back up the carpeted staircase.

We spent thirty seconds talking about rush. And—little did I know—that was all it took to get me "in" with the women of Gamma Alpha Beta at the University of Alabama.

I signed up for rush online.

"Do you wanna go by Sophie or Elizabeth at school?" Mom asked. "Please pick one. You're confusing everyone. Hell, you're even confusing me."

"Uh . . . Sophie? Sophie Santos seems cool."

"Too late. Already done."

Thus, my new persona was born. I received my "Greek Chic" packet. It had a glossy finish that smelled like "my daddy paid for it." A Brooks Brothers shirt flew out when I opened the first page. It made Faye Davenport's handbook look like shootin' cans in the backyard. Faye Davenport wore plastic novelty jewelry. These girls wore David Yurman 18k-gold bracelets also given to them by their daddies.

"Welcome to the University of Alabama fall recruitment! We're so happy you've decided to join us! **Full disclosure: no one is guaranteed a spot. You cannot sue or take legal action if it doesn't work out. But we hope it does.** Most importantly, BE YOURSELF. There will be ten days of rush. You will need ten different outfits. Preferably something that doesn't make you look poor.[27]"

"Day One and Two, Tea Parties: wear a sundress. Dress like you're going to a wedding, but a spring wedding." (The "tea parties" were where sisters would size up their recruits—which is apt, because most of them are in the Tea Party now.)

"Day Three, Philanthropy Day: wear something casual, like a T-shirt. But not a regular T-shirt. A blouse T-shirt." ('Cause kids with cancer care about the type of T-shirt one wears.)

I continued to scan the list. How did they all get their foundation to look like it was tattooed onto their skin? I needed to glow up fast, and we didn't have much time. Mom and I rushed to Parisian—the knockoff of Belk, which was the knockoff of Dillard's—and gathered all my new school items. This was the most intense school list I had ever seen. After spending all of my first-semester

---

[27] Fine, they didn't explicitly say that, but when the recommendations for those dresses are Lilly Pulitzer, Ann Taylor, and anything from Saks, then I'm gonna assume.

tuition on dresses and also purchasing an insurance package for my new accessories, I was ready.

It was a sweltering hot August morning in Tuscaloosa, Alabama. I wore my best sleeveless sundress, strappiest sandals, and biggest frozen smile. My three layers of foundation were rapidly melting. I couldn't touch my face or I'd risk ruining the smoky eye that I had worked so hard to achieve. Plastered mascara clumped my eyelashes together. Through all that, my heavily dressed-up eyes were hyperfocused on what lay ahead. The campus was deadly silent, and I was smack-dab in the middle of a pack of young debutantes, all looking similarly sweaty in their Sunday best, staring at the brass doorknobs of an imposing house.

Sorority Row at the University of Alabama consisted of twenty Colonial-style mansions on the edge of campus, each with fifty rushees waiting at its doors, arranged in a triangular formation. Every door had a "Rho Chi" (a leader) standing sentinel.

I was one of two thousand girls (*you heard that right—two thousand*) hoping to be invited to join one of the twenty sororities at the University of Alabama.

We'd been waiting for five minutes, sweating and praying they'd *open the goddamn doors*. I was about to go full villager-with-a-pitchfork on their asses. I kept ever so gently bending my knees, hoping to not pass out. I didn't want to be a liability. I'd rather bounce around looking like I had to pee than cause a scene by fainting.

Then, finally, my Rho Chi's face turned from stoic to widely grinning, still dead behind the eyes. She militaristically walked up to the doors and knocked three times. The doors swung open in front of me and revealed two-hundred-plus young women dressed in brightly colored sundresses blocking the doorway, set up like they were in a massive cheerleading pyramid, perched like owls behind one another at ascending heights. There was just a sea of hands extended in every direction and clapping in time. The women's smiles were as petrifying as the Grinch, and they functioned like wound-up dolls. *Is this the hellmouth?* They ~~chanted~~ screamed so loudly, it almost busted my eardrums, a song to the tune of "The Bunny Hop."

"I'm a Gamma Alpha Beta, yes it's true! We're the classiest of girls, and we sure want you!"

I heard different chants being sung, overlapping one another. The sound of four thousand women singing rattled the entire campus—you'd think we were under attack.

"Oh, Mu Mu! Makes me wanna go, cuckoo for you, you!"

"If you're a Kappa Tau, then you'll sure be wowed!"

"B-E-T-A, we are the gals you'll appreciate!"

It was harrowing. Then, all at once, the chants ended in unison, and the girls went from chanting to HIGH-PITCHED SHOUTING: "COME INSIDE! COME INSIDE! COME INSIDE! WELCOME! WELCOME! WELCOME!!!"

Just when I thought the screaming couldn't get any louder, the decibel level grew one final time. I felt the ground shake and one by one, their hands touched my back as they pushed me along. A spunky girl escorted me into the never-ending dining room. The screaming turned into chatter around me as we were all paired off. "Mae" was emblazoned on her name tag in perfect golden embossing. She fired a few generic questions at me such as, "Where are you from?" "What are you majoring in?" "What's your natural hair color?" I answered with rehearsed lines that I thought would win her over: "I'm from Arab, but I moved around a lot." "Business, with a minor in *political science*." And "Just look at my head, girl."

A blonde sister came to Mae's side. She looked like she should have the song "Poor Unfortunate Souls" from *The Little Mermaid* underscoring her every entrance. Hot Ursula sized me up and kept staring at my badge. Mae filled her in. "We were just talkin' about how Sophie's hair is naturally brown."

"It is?"

"Yeah," I offered. "Never dyed it once. Can you believe it?" I was trying to lighten the mood.

Hot Ursula kept looking me up and down. It had only been thirty seconds, and I was certain I had shit the bed. *Am I not pretty enough? Was the brown-hair thing weird? We all think this conversation blows, right?*

"And you grew up in a town called Arab? Like the Middle East?" she asked archly.

"I did, HA-HA—noooo, not the Middle East. I'm not from Arab anyway; I'm also not Arab. I mean—"

Before I knew it, the chanting had begun again from all around me, interrupting their interrogation. Some of the girls in the house had started the song to cue everyone else. The sexy sea witch disappeared into a sea of blonde, and Mae put her hand on my back again. I was shown out through a tunnel of bobbing heads once more. Mae passed me along to another girl, who passed me along to another, who gently, politely, but firmly kicked my ass to the curb escorted me to the front door. I took my place next to one girl who looked like she was in ecstasy, but the larger group stood with dazed expressions, and—one by one—the girls from the sorority snaked back into formation.

"We're sad to see you go! Our parting won't be long—that we know! We're the girls of GAB, the best on campus, just you wait and see. We're classy sweetie pies. Until we see you again . . . Bye-bye! Bye-bye! Bye-bye!" the women yelled from the house. Then the doors slammed shut with a loud BANG.

My fellow rushees and I kept smiling like someone was about to take a group picture. No photo was taken. I wanted to ask, *Did anyone else think that was fucking psychotic?* But before I knew it, we were already moving, silently, to the next house.

I did this over and over again for the next two days.

I dialed my mom the following afternoon after still being confused by my experience at Gamma Alpha.

"I don't know, Mom. It's kinda fun, but I don't think I clicked with any of the girls at Gamma Alpha. They kept staring at my dress and seemed a little standoffish. Not sure Parisian was the best choice . . ."

"That seems really odd. Let me talk to Stacey. At least put them down as one of your top choices so you can go to the house again. What's wrong with Parisian? I love Parisian."

"Fine, Mom. And nothing, Parisian is great."

I decided to get a second opinion. I got the scoop from the other rushees at lunch. We were seated according to alphabetical order, which put me next to Coach Saban's daughter and her lackey, Scholten.

"Iota Chi is called 'I ought to be high.' So unless you're a druggie, stay clear."

"Yes, stay clear," Scholten echoed.

"Got it . . ." I thought about the girl who had interviewed me and remembered that she did seem very alert.

"Psi Alphas don't know how to apply foundation. Delta Kappas are old money and look like ornate sculptures," she continued.

I tried to make little notes on my card without them seeing.

"I'm picking Tri Mu . . . there's no other choice in my opinion," Saban continued.

"Yes, there's no other choice," Scholten said, fawning over Saban. By her enthusiasm, Scholten didn't seem the type to get into Tri Mu, but I didn't want to speak out of turn.

"What about Gamma Alpha Beta?" I asked. *And while you're here, Parisian Inc. . . .*

"I mean, they have the best grades on campus, but I think they're overrated."

Normally when people said something was "overrated," it meant it was rated the best. I decided to take my chances. Plus, they had "Alpha" in the name.

That night, the rushees filed into a tiny computer lab in a basement to pick our top eight houses.

The whole process felt torturous. Having to pick favorites was not great for someone with OCD. The thought that I might accidentally forget to select the house I wanted was paralyzing. What if I hit "Send" too early?

The world was full of hazards.

I decided against Iota Chi, Psi Alpha, and Delta Kappa. And since I had accidentally blurted out, *"I was an equestrian,"* out of nervousness to a Sigma Sigma sister and didn't want to keep up the hoax for the next four years, I left them off the list. I decided to give Gamma Alpha Beta another shot. Sitting in the computer lab, I stared at the checked black box next to Gamma Alpha Beta. I looked away from the computer, closed my eyes, and turned back with one eye opened to assure myself that the check mark was still next to Gamma Alpha Beta, which seemed smaller this time. I did that three more times.

The next morning, we all shuffled back to Sorority Row. My group was on the corner next to Sigma Sigma. *Puts on wig and big sunglasses.* The Rho Chis gave out our name cards with all the houses we would visit that day. If a house was not on your card, you were not being considered for that house any longer. There were no redos, no changes, no nothing. Every decision was final. Hence why I stayed in the computer lab for two hours. I was handed my card and quickly noticed Gamma Alpha Beta had made it. I made a celebratory "yes" gesture, yanking my fist to my side in one sharp motion.

There were shrieks and cries of "oh my gawd!" But those were almost drowned out by painful sobbing. Being "dropped" in the first round was a harsh reality for young women who had waited their entire lives to rush the sorority of their dreams—only to be thrown out like a bag of garbage. The Rho Chis made it known that they were there to console—but that if anyone seemed at risk of self-harm, authorities would be called.

A girl dropped out of rush that day and transferred to Ole Miss.

I nervously returned to GAB, where the sisters who were majoring in theater fluttered around me, discussing *Spring Awakening* and praising my existence. Mary Catherine even came over and introduced me to the president. I felt special, and this felt like an entirely different house than it had on my first visit.

Despite my upswing, I started to hear rumors that girls I had rushed with had been placed on suicide watch already. I was deeply distressed by what I knew was an extremely serious situation—and at the same time amused that anyone would take rushing so seriously.

I returned to my dorm, where I sat in the lounge and gave the deets to Ryan and Frank—my dorm adviser and his buddy.

"Are you kidding? Killing yourself over a cult? That's a systemic problem within our university. The Greek system must be stopped," Ryan said.

I'd been accepted into a real hippie-dippie liberal program called the Blount Scholars Program, pronounced "Blunt." We were even called the Blountees, pronounced "Bluntee." And we may have made a small green figurine our mascot. It would have been insane *not* to.

The application requirement was to "take a blank piece of paper and make your mark upon it, so to speak. You may write, tear, draw, color, fold—anything you like except a photo collage (which doesn't rule out either photography or collages)." I drew myself hanging out by a tree in pencil. It worked.

The perk of being in ~~Blount~~ Blunt was that it had its own dormitory, and classes were held within the dorm. We never had to leave that building. *Talk about a cult, Ryan, but okay.* The three of us—Ryan, Frank, and myself—had already established a routine of sitting in the lobby, drinking Red Bull, and shooting the shit. They both wore Birkenstocks and were self-proclaimed anarchists who thought I was "too good" to be rushing.

"Come on, Soph—you're one of us," Ryan said. He had decided that I was part of the wolf pack within a day of meeting me. Judging by his wolverine sideburns that he had clearly committed to since he could first grow facial hair—once he decided something, that was that.

"I am," I said, "but . . . I'm also one of them." I thought about the theater girls and me singing "Mama Who Bore Me" together earlier.

"Nah . . . you'll just *become* one of them," Ryan replied.

Frank gave him a gentle pat on the arm, like, *Let's get out of here.*

"You're gonna forget about Sophocles and Nicholas Carr," said Ryan as Frank shooed him up the steps. I hadn't even started classes yet, but it seemed like a big deal.

I sat there alone for a moment. Mary Catherine had blown smoke up my ass like I was a rack of ribs, and I liked it. *And so what if I'm paying for my friends?* I was so tired of having to make impression after impression and give handshake after handshake. Being part of sorority life was like CliffsNotes—it was the literal playbook of how to make friends. And college was scary as fuck. Was I really supposed to believe that Wolverine and his sidekick were going to protect me?

My mom pinged me via text. *How'd it go today, honey?*

So much better. I met the president!

She sent back three hearts.

Over the next eight days, my list of houses narrowed, and as I continued to get to know the sisters at Gamma Alpha Beta, I kept an open mind. That is until Philanthropy Day, where Pi Chi was discussing the charity it donated to. I proudly told a sister at Pi Chi, "I had pneumonia as a child, so I feel like I can relate to the kids you support at St. Jude's!"

Understandably, Pi Chi dropped me the next day.

No matter. I had made it to the end of the week, and Gamma Alpha Beta remained on my card right in time for Preference Day, as a little blood spilled out from my ears. Preference Day, or Pref Day, was the grand finale. A farewell for some. Now it was the houses' turn to impress us.

Day Ten: Wear a black dress.

I stood with about ten girls in front of Gamma Alpha, the Rho Chis standing sentinel once more. They knocked on the door, and the doors opened—but instead of bursting open like before, they opened gently to reveal all the Gamma

Alpha Beta sisters wearing black, dressed like they were in mourning. Each held a white tulip and a candle.

A short girl with a very cute bob ushered me inside and sat me down on a cheap-looking ottoman that probably cost more than my mom's entire house.

"We're happy you're here, Sophie."

"Me too."

"Are you having any thoughts right now?" she asked.

"I can't believe this amazing time is almost over," I said.

And that I'll be able to hear again . . .

She nodded. Then she brought me into a room where the other girls were waiting. They all sang a quiet song about their mascot, the lute, and read out of a large, old, dusty book. I wouldn't have been surprised if they had taken out a ceremonial knife and started sacrificing people. But when the readings ended, we all left the room unscathed.

I didn't sleep the night before Bid Day. The Blunt boys, Ryan and Frank, had insisted on showing me clips of cult documentaries and told me how ballsy it'd be if I just didn't show up to the final day. I stared anxiously at the ceiling until dawn.

The unlucky recruits who were not chosen by any houses at all were called the night before Bid Day so that they didn't have to show up to the stadium only to leave sister-less. Ryan was on high alert in case anyone in his dorm got the fateful call.

In the morning, he knocked on my door.

"You okay, Soph?" he asked through the crack.

"I'm fine, yeah. About to head out."

"Ah. I was kinda hoping you got the call. Not that I wanted you on suicide watch. Good luck."

I gave myself one more look in the mirror. This was my last day as a civilian.

I approached Bryant-Denny Stadium. My parents had driven three hours to get there and were waiting outside the stadium for my arrival into sisterhood—right in front of the sorority houses. The moment before I walked in, I gave one last look at the Gamma Alpha Beta house and then shifted my eyes forward. I climbed the stairs and walked to the bleachers. A representative from each sorority stood in front of us. I sat with my fellow rushees.

"You will be given your Bid Day card. Do *not* open it. Please place it underneath your bums," said a Rho Chi whom I'd never met until that day.

My own Rho Chi handed me my card. I held it in my hand and then quickly put it under my butt.

"On the count of three, you're going to open your bid. This will be your new house. Your new sisters."

I bounced my legs like I had to pee.

"One . . . two . . ."

Girls squealed.

"Three!"

I grabbed my card from under my butt and instantly forgot how to open an envelope. Screams and pops of confetti were erupting on all sides of me. When I finally managed to rip my envelope open, my eyes glazed over. I saw "Alpha Xi . . . Omicron?" *I didn't even rush Alpha Xi—what the hell is this?*

"You got into GAMMA ALPHA BETA?" a random girl screamed in my face. I looked at the card again and saw that it said, "The Alpha Xi Omicron chapter of Gamma Alpha Beta"! I jumped up and down and screamed and held a girl I never spoke to again. She only got into the makeup-flawed Psi Alpha. *Ha-ha, sorry, bitch.* The transformation had already started.

"Gamma Alpha Betas—we're up first!"

All the new members of Gamma Alpha Beta lined up and then raced out from Bryant-Denny toward the mansion that would now be my home. I was beaming! Crying! Cry-beaming! My parents, in a sea of proud parents, were waving and smiling, and the letters etched onto the house were welcoming me in.

I was greeted by hundreds of smiling and slightly drunk sisters. The house was serving hors d'oeuvres, and I grabbed the tiniest sandwich. An older sister approached me and my parents, who were giving me a tight squeeze on both sides.

"Congrats! Welcome to Gamma Alpha Beta!" she said.

Wasn't. Kidding.

"Thank you! It's good to be . . . home. I'm so excited!" I said.

"Now, where are you from?" she asked, all giddy.

"I'm from Arab," I said in a way like, I *know, I know—the town's name is weird.*

She took me in for a moment.

"Oh. So you're from another country . . ."

"No. Arab, Alabama."

"Uh-huh." Her gaze shifted to someone else. "CLAIRE! CONGRATS, GIRL!" She ran away in an instant.

I frowned, then shook it off and laughed about it with my parents. I didn't realize I had just sold my little brown gay soul.

How to Be a Sorority Girl, or The Guide to Being Ladylike, Abridged!

These are real things I was told by my pledge trainer and have NOT been embellished.

1. Never smoke. If a lady must smoke, then she must do it sitting down, with her legs crossed. If caught smoking, you'll be charged a fine.

2. Never dance on a raised platform (this includes stairs). Iota Chis and random Psi Alphas dance on stairs. GABs do not.

3. GABs must maintain a 3.0 GPA. Even if you fall into a deep depression or become ill and must leave campus, GABs always maintain a 3.0 GPA. If you drop below a 3.0, you'll be brought to Standards[28] and charged a fine.

4. Never wear headphones while walking around campus—you'll miss out on saying hello to your sisters. Always be alert! If a junior says hey and you miss it, you'll be brought to Standards.

5. Never breathe near a sister's boyfriend. Don't be a "Sarah Beth."

6. Be mindful of SHIRLEY—the sorority's imagined version of Big Brother. Shirley is always around and can, at any time, ask you to refrain from what you are doing if it is, indeed, unladylike. (See this list for examples.) Shirley always has the final say. Surely you won't upset Shirley!

7. Do not come to dinner with wet hair. In fact, do not come to

---

[28] Standards is a friendly safe haven to discuss behavioral issues and is not meant to embarrass the Gamma Alpha Betas, even though the point is that we will be reprimanding you for violating any of the 1,035 rules.

dinner at all if you are late (even if it's because you had a study group).

8. Always stand when the housemother arrives. The housemother is the official hostess with the mostess!

9. Never "shack" at a fraternity house, even though you will be going there twice a week and the goal is to set you up on dates. Furthermore, do not make out with your dates, even though we are going to have you both "bump." You'll learn about bumping in person because we can't (for legal reasons) write about its existence.

10. Never wear scrunchies. We shouldn't have to explain why.

Chapter Eighteen

MATTHEWS, OLIVERS, AND FOUNTAINS

On a brisk October evening, I signed my name in blood, drank from the cup of the goddess Hera, and buried my body in the ashes of former sisters. I officially pledged Gamma Alpha Beta, a.k.a. Grades and Babes. *Screams, "Ain't a Beta? Don't be a hata!"* Fine, not exactly—but after $3,500 a semester in dues (*ah, this is what Ryan meant*), it felt like I had given up a kidney. Not to mention the mandatory rush traditions:

- The soul-crushing, two-month-long initiation process, which included "signing parties" (otherwise known as memorizing all 272 sisters' names and their respective hometowns).

"Susanna Thompson, Florence, Alabama," I said as I gave the older sister a piece of paper for her to initial.

"It's *Susan Thomas*, Florence, Alabama. Are you dumb?" She shoved the paper back in my face.

- Learning the entire history of the organization while also never focusing *too* hard on the handbook on the quad, for fear of fucking up Rule Number Four[29].

---

[29] See previous chapter! By this time in the book, I'm a sorority girl, and I don't have time to help you read this book NOR do I want to baby you LMAO!

- The three-hour initiation ceremony where we all wore white dresses, white ankle socks, and no makeup or jewelry (major Holiness vibes). We all held candles and sang a cappella.

That was just the tip of the iceberg.

I would have preferred the ashes.

Nevertheless, I was officially a sister, and I followed their lead on everything. By providing me sisterhood, teaching me leadership skills, and helping me get a good education, Gamma Alpha Beta was setting me up to be a bona fide southern belle. At first, assimilation seemed pretty simple. I could pray with them at dinner, and being forced to keep a study log was not that hard, and not having bare feet at dinner was honestly a pro health tip. The payoff was dope. I was surrounded by some of the most driven women I'd ever met—women who were triple majoring in accounting, premed, and prelaw. But over time, something became clear. The goal of all GABs during our four undergraduate years at Alabama was to become a successful, bright young woman. And being a successful woman boiled down to one thing, one simple task.

We were in the dining hall, having lunch, when an older sister mentioned it like it was the most normal thing in the world.

"After all, the whole Greek system calls our sorority 'the ones you want to marry'!"

"Wait. Seriously? Why?" I laughed.

"Because we're all wife material! Look around! We're smart, talented, and we look great in oil canvas portraits . . . KIDDING!"

She wasn't.

I looked around and quickly realized I had been too busy trying to learn her frickin' name (which I didn't have the darndest clue of) to notice.

She was right: everyone was fixated on getting married, getting what I would learn was their *MRS degree*. Their "Missus" degree. The goal was to be engaged by the age of twenty-two—which, honestly, was a touch too old according to the panic on the faces of the "older girls." Girls would be devastated if they didn't get engaged by senior year for a celebratory candlelight ceremony. It was just like Fight Club, and there were no rules in the pursuit of the first candlelight ceremony of the year. And don't get me started if a sophomore got engaged before a senior. The bloodbath!

For those who are interested . . . fifty-seven out of seventy-one of my pledge-class sisters are now married. Eleven out of the fourteen didn't make it to the initiation ceremony, and then there were two who got kicked out. Even the one other lesbian who has since come out is married now.

Hell, just to snag a good seat at the football games, you had to secure a date with a fraternity brother. The promise of a front-row seat in Bryant-Denny Stadium would make any woman punch a fellow sister. The fraternities, and only the male fraternities, blocked off the best part of the student section, a rule that had been written into the student government's constitution—much to the annoyance of the rest of the student body. The plebes (the rest of the student body) had to get to the stadium ten hours before kickoff if they wanted a shot at not being in the nosebleeds. Meanwhile, the frats would show up drunk, full, and with dates on their arms five minutes before kickoff with the perfect view. It was like a precursor to redlining districts and getting their women in line.

At first, I thought the whole thing was stupid. I thought I could just focus on the leadership stuff and ignore all the marriage talk. But I watched as sisters basked in the attention of their relationships and possible engagements. They got to go to formals in New Orleans with their soon-to-be husbands (the men were the only ones allowed to throw overnight parties). And then I witnessed my first candlelight ceremony. We sat in a circle as Charlene discussed the elaborate proposal her now-fiancé had planned a gondola ride in Italy with his pledge brother secretly tagging along so he could snap the best photo. He fell into the river, and it was the best part. As each girl, one by one, hugged her, they all stood up and chanted her name as she ascended the steps to retire to her room.

I had to make a choice, and a choice I did make. Operation: Sophie Gets Her MRS Degree began. I didn't want to be the only one without a ring on my finger by senior year, and I genuinely thought the way into a frat guy's beer-soaked heart was by showing my lady pearl. Lucky for me, I had my first swap to look forward to, and they were swarming with my gentleman callers.

Swaps were the holy grail of being a sorority girl. They were what all our parents' money funded (sorry, Mom and Dad). Why were they the highlight of my Tuesdays and Thursdays and sometimes Fridays? Because each swap was a party with a fraternity and that party had a theme. We got to get tore up from the floor up, clad in some handcrafted costume. I spent most Mondays and Wednesdays browsing the Michaels aisles for paint, fabric, and a flower crown.

Our themes included Angels and Devils, BET vs. MTV (great choice for a white sorority; I opted to be the Moon Man), and Cowboys and Indians (again, totally not problematic). Gamma Alpha Beta swapped with only the best fraternities—and out of the goodness of our hearts, sometimes the freshmen were forced to swap with fraternities that we pitied. Sorry, Nu Epsilon Phi.

My first swap, I was in for a rude awakening. We all gathered at the house. I was wearing a Pocahontas dress that I had made out of a large, long-sleeve T-shirt. I'd cut fringe at the bottom, glued beads all over, and tied a leather belt around the waist to give it that "Pocahontas in college" vibe. I wore a headband with one feather poking out, and I'd spent more hours on it than the tree porcupine. Because I had brown skin and long, dark hair, and because of the attention I'd get from the girls, I thought wearing a Native American costume was a great idea.

2010 MTV Awards
University of Alabama

"You look just like Pocahontas!" the girls would tell me on their trips to Disney World and send me a photo of some actor dressed in the costume.

"THIS IS YOU, SOPH!"

Get me tipsy on mystery punch and I'd bust out "Colors of the Wind," much to everyone's amusement. Nothing was off-limits.

This is exactly where so many political scandals begin.

We all walked over to the frat house and down into the big, dark basement that had seen one too many swaps. If the room could talk, she wouldn't, because she was probably too busy chain-smoking cigarettes, terrified for what was to come. She was wrecked. A gooey film was caked onto the floor, and my moccasins (yes, I wore moccasins) stuck to it with each step. The walls and the floor had been painted black, and the only light came from our teeth and the words *Roll Tide* in neon paint.

Immediately, the pledge trainers started lining up the freshmen single file. The older fraternity and sorority members formed a giant circle in the middle of the room, much like at a middle school dance. I, however, was not break-dancing solo like I had in middle school. The freshman girls' line and boys' line approached the circle from opposite sides. I couldn't see anything in front of me, but I could hear people laughing. When I reached the middle of the huge circle, the pledge trainer turned me around to face her, my back to the middle of the circle. I caught a glimpse of the frat trainer doing the same to the boy a few feet away.

"You're gonna bump in a sec, okay, girl?"

"What's bump?" I screamed over T-Pain's auto-tuned riffing on the speakers.

"You're gonna walk backward, and then you're gonna 'bump' into the guy pledge, who's also walking backward."

". . . And then what?"

"And then he's gonna do something that his pledge trainers told him to do. It's all in good fun, though, okay? Don't be scared." I saw her look above my head as she made eye contact with someone I couldn't see. "He's gonna be your date for the evening."

My date? My . . . *date.*

"Here we go!" She gave me a gentle push, and I slowly walked backward. I felt lost in time. *What on earth is going to happen to me?* I had heard of bumping, but only in myths and by way of eavesdropping at house dinners. Some pledge sisters who were privy to info chose to stand in the corner with their arms crossed because their boyfriends were in different frats and would be upset. And there were the girls who'd gotten out of it because "God." Not me. As scary as it was, I wanted the sisters to know I was fully committed. I closed my eyes until I felt my butt graze against another butt. I turned around.

The pledge got on one knee and chugged a beer in front of me, crushed it on his head, and picked me up and lightly set me back on my feet.

MY date.

I have a date.

We walked over to the keg together, and I looked him up and down. He was sporting the same pledge uniform as the rest of his brothers: green tucked-in polo, stained Wrangler jeans, and Velcro Reeboks. I was scrambling to find something sexy to say about his Velcro footwear when he walked off. *Wait a minute, I thought you were my date!*

I stood at the keg and watched the same bumping happen to more of my pledge class.[30] Some of the bumping dares included motorboating, dangling from the rafters and wrapping their legs around the sisters, or light humping.

Yet all I got was a beer splattered on me and a date who ran for the hills. WTF?

As the semester dragged on, I discovered I liked bumping. I always hoped one of the pledge bros would show his undying affection for me, but I didn't even get a motorboat. They'd take one look at me, and the pledge trainer would say, "Give her a hug," or the pledge would say, "Oh, man—really?" and that would be that.

As problematic as I see it now, as a doe-eyed eighteen-year-old, I wanted to be too legit to quit. I had to go full throttle to impress the older girls. Plus, it was a moment of physical contact with someone. And it was how most of my sisters found their boyfriends turned fiancés.

After a few failed attempts at being wooed, I started to get calculating.

The way I saw it, the best way to get in with the hotties would be to hang out at swaps with sisters who had boyfriends from high school. Their boyfriends had brothers who were single, so my strategy was guaranteed to put me into a situation with a solid couple and an eligible bachelor. I'd hang on the arms of my sisters as we drank the mystery punch—expired orange juice, Hawaiian Punch, Malibu coconut rum, and mostly Everclear—and talked about our majors and our love of Burberry.

"This is Sophie—she's my new sister!" a platinum-blonde Brittany would tell her boyfriend, Timmy, who'd nudge his friend, Matthew.

I'd give future bae Matt puppy eyes. *Thanks, sis,* I'd think.

"Cool." Matt would nod, his cup held close to his nose.

"She's my sister, and she's grrreat," Brittany would say, trying to egg him on.

"Nice," Matt often said unenthusiastically.

I'd pretend that I wasn't expecting her to say such a nice thing. Then she'd whisper to her boyfriend—who, like clockwork, would whisk her away—and

---

[30] Bumping, it turned out, was the main reason why older sisters liked going to swaps. Because it was free tickets to a good show. Better than the Broadway.

I'd stand there awkwardly with Matt. "Matthews" were cookie-cutter; there was nothing special about them, except that most of them became VPs of banks, yet all the guys took them under their wings, and all the girls wanted to date them.

Matt would fill the silence with, "So you're a Gamma Alpha Beta?" which was obvious, because at swaps, there was only one fraternity and one sorority. And then, pretty quickly, another frat guy would hook his arm around Matthew's neck, dragging him away, and another girl would lock eyes with him. I attempted and failed many times to hook up with a Matthew. Sometimes I'd get the conversation to advance to "where'd you grow up?" only to be cock-blocked by a "Sarah Beth." Matthews and Sarah Beths usually ended up together.

Matthews, I'd come to learn, only wanted girls from their hometowns. *Easier to plan the wedding, I suppose.*

Then there were the "Olivers," who were nice enough but not quite as popular. They were shy and often ran around during the swaps doing servile stuff for their older brothers, like chiseling the paint off the floor or dumping more Everclear into the huge cooler.

"What do you got there?" I'd ask.

"Uh . . . vodka . . . I think," the Oliver would squeak out before running away under the watchful gaze of an older dude across the room. To be fair, the fraternities' initiation process was nuclear. In their identical outfits, they were constantly sweating, and every once in a while, someone would have their arm in a sling. I'd ask Oliver if he needed a hand, and he'd frantically shout, "I CAN'T TALK ABOUT IT!"

Olivers were almost always too uptight to land.

And finally, I identified a "Fountain." Fountains were in their own category. Fountain was the guy who'd barely made the cut. Maybe his dad had been in the same frat, or maybe they got his numbers mixed up with someone else's and he'd sneaked in. Fountains were try-hards. I did feel for them because one of the reasons I'd sneaked in myself was that some of the girls had thought I was Greek (as in from Greece). Fountains were too eager and too into me—right in my wheelhouse.

"I grew up in Arab," I'd say.

"ARAB? No waaaay. My cousin lives off Blue Jay Road," he'd say and shuffle backward for a minute.

"Yeah, I know that road . . ." My eyes would wander, and I'd spot an Oliver tying an older brother's shoe. I hated that Fountain knew Arab.

Out of the corner of my eye, I could see Fountain giving me a big grin. He'd move his face back into my line of sight. By the time everyone else had paired off and the three-piece Guns N' Roses cover band was packing up, I knew I was out of options. And just like that, Fountain and I would go back to his room in the fraternity house.

"Freshmen don't usually get to live in the house, but the guys must like me," he said.

The room was a closet, and there was a sign that said JANITOR. *They don't like you; they love you.*

I normally wanted to go directly to: +

We had upgraded to real emojis.

Swapping spit just didn't do much for me, so I wanted to cut right to the chase. At the time, I also thought I wasn't much of a foreplay person. Truthfully, I didn't think women could enjoy foreplay. I had overheard a few sisters say when discussing the deed, "We're really there for them . . ." or "Oh my God . . . he went down on you? That actually happens?" or "Saving myself for marriage, bless up."

I'd lie there in the perfect oil-canvas pose until he was done flailing, as I clutched my pearls I had strung together from Michaels, and then—knowing that I had accomplished what I had set out to do—I'd wait for him to ask me out on a date.

Want to go to the game with me on Saturday? he texted the following day. I'd accomplished my mission. My sisters would be so proud.

My first date was with a guy whose name was actually Fountain. It was Game Day at Alabama. Game Day was more sacrosanct than church on Easter and holier than the Catholic church on Ash Wednesday.

It was also an excuse to get hammered at ten a.m. That Saturday morning, I woke up in my dorm room at Blunt, hopped in the shower while drinking a mimosa, and then, after avoiding eye contact with Frank and Ryan, who were over me at this point, I hit the quad, which was like the tailgating equivalent of glamping. Then I headed to the sorority house for the fanfare.

I was wearing a Free People black romper (that I'd had no business buying because it was way out of my budget), my four-inch heels (including pageants, game days were the longest I'd ever stood in heels), and I got a blowout (again, that I couldn't afford). I looked like an Alabama hound dog trying to be a French poodle.

The house had been transformed seemingly overnight. Only a few hours before, the dining hall had been adorned with glow sticks and forgotten beer cans. But on Game Day, it was like a royal wedding with ascots and funny hats, but the fascinators were made out of houndstooth, and instead of the queen, we were all there to pay our respects to Bear Bryant and celebrate the ascension of Nick Saban.

All the girls and alumnae were now in their best red, white, or black dresses, with their Burberry coats and Tory Burch handbags—*Sara, I saw you puke in that purse last night.* The alumnae walked around, introducing themselves as we tried to impress them. I gave a little curtsy and some alum would exclaim, "Now, where are *you* from?"

"Arab!"

"Oh, wow . . ." She'd take a microscopic bite of her finger sandwich while I tried to swallow the entire one whole.

". . . ALABAMA!" I clarified while choking.

She had already walked away.

I met up with some of my pledge class in the ornate living room, where we didn't actually sit because the furniture was too expensive and an older sister had claimed the only sittable couch.

After saying hello and goodbye to everyone, I walked over to Omega Sigma Pi, also known as OSP or Old Southern Pride.

The OSP house was overrun with frat bros, both current students and alumni. The alumni all looked like some version of Tucker Carlson—clean-cut, boyish hair, with a little softness to their chins. Everyone held a Solo cup of beer. I met up with Fountain in the dining hall, where the brothers had set up a buffet-style lunch.

"You look so beautiful," he said.

He had swapped out his pledge outfit for their game-day pledge outfit: khakis, a red tie, and a blazer. Still identical. Still horrific. His older fraternity brothers got to dress to impress in their Vineyard Vines red vests, North Face puffy jackets, or their Brooks Brothers suits. Although Fountain was wearing the same thing as the seventy other pledges, he still stuck out like a sore thumb.

He was red in the face, with a few pimples that could only be described as the final Eagle Scout badge.

"Thanks," I finally said.

It felt nice to hear, but I found myself scanning the room for a Matthew and found one in the corner with his entire family—and Sarah Beth! She pointed to her ring finger and laughed. *That was fast . . . I'm starting to think that Sarah Beths really get shit done.*

There was also an Oliver up on a stepladder, hanging the frat's banner, with an older brother unnailing the other side so it dropped.

"What the hell, dumbass? You didn't nail it in enough!" the older brother said, cackling, and made Oliver hold a plank position on his elbows for punishment.

Fountain and I ate our buffet alone because he didn't really have friends, and—being an innocent, doe-eyed GAB—I wasn't friends with any of the older girls who were there. "Rule Number Twelve: Say hi, but then get lost." I was wishing I had stuck with my friends, who—judging by the Facebook duck-face photos—were clearly having a much better time together back at the sorority house. FOMO was real.

Fountain was a die-hard Omega Sigma Pi. His father was an Omega Sigma Pi. His grandfather was an Omega Sigma Pi. And now Fountain was an Omega Sigma Pi. The joy on his face over just being part of Game Day at the frat was like a kid's on Christmas morning. I had not heard of Omega Sigma Pi before this, so I wasn't really sure about the prestige. Then again, I hadn't heard of Gamma Alpha Beta until a few months before rush.

Fountain was explaining that their most notable event was an annual "Old South Parade."

"Old South?" I asked with a bowl of gumbo in front of me.

"You don't know Old South?" Fountain's face was now as red as an apple. "It's a parade! We march around campus dressed in Confederate uniforms, with our dates dressed in antebellum dresses."

And this is what I can look forward to if we continue to date?

He pointed to the photos lined up around the dining hall. I had somehow missed them upon walking in.

"Hey, Fountain! You're an Omega Sigma Pi now!" An older fraternity brother tousled his hair and laughed like he couldn't believe it himself.

I began to feel bad for Fountain. We left for the game and awkwardly stood for three and a half hours of football. Standing in four-inch heels on bleachers is a skill I never mastered.

I had entirely lost my love of football during my years of high school theater mania, but then in college, I experienced the phenomenon that is . . . the man . . . the myth . . . the seventh wonder of the world . . . Paul "Bear" Bryant. In that moment, my tackle-loving former self rose from the dead.

The marching band had been playing "My Dixieland Delight" when they suddenly went quiet. A rumbling filled the 101,000-person stadium. And then "Requiem for a Tower" played on the sound system with different words projecting on the jumbotron, words such as "Intensity!" "Passion!" or "Guts!" As the music amplified, I fell into a trance. Then Paul "Bear" Bryant's photo appeared on-screen. I recognized his face from staying up late watching football documentaries with Papa. His image was accompanied by his low, southern drawl: "I'd like for the people to think of me as a winna, 'cause I ain't never been anythin' but a winna."

"ROLL TIDE TILL I DIE!" I screamed and feverishly shook my red-and-white pom-pom in the air. Now I knew why people sold their first male child to get season passes. With every tackle, I realized that we were dominating. The Process. Built by Bama. A Goddamn Dynasty. I witnessed the first national championship under the head coach Nick Saban. Nick Saban[31], if you're reading this, I love you too.

Fountain and I hung out a few times after that, but his only topics of conversation were how much beer he could drink and his love of Robert E. Lee.

You do realize the South won't *rise again—and that that's a good thing?*

"I can't believe they canceled the Old South Parade this year! Some idiots on campus seem to think it's racist. It was a total accident that we stopped in front of the Black fraternity. There was traffic. God."

. . .

As the year went on and I attended more swaps, I stopped answering Fountain's texts. And yes, the incident in front of the Black fraternity is a true story.

---

[31] In 2020, Nick Saban led the Black Lives Matter parade at UA, and I swear I saw the sky open up and God touch his forehead.

In the pursuit of finding my gentleman caller, I also was drawn to cozying up to the older girls. I specifically wanted to be around Mary Catherine, my mom's college roommate's daughter, who had gotten me into the sorority. She walked into the room as if a book could be balanced on her head, and she sat like a regal Victorian empress. She could do no wrong. Much to my dismay, she was elusive. I often wondered if she was just off drinking her coffee in that oversize sweatshirt, with her ponytail loosely thrown together. When I'd see her on campus, I'd duck behind a building so she didn't spot me. It was hard being in her presence, and I seemed to lose my words around her.

I had gotten close to the pledge-class trainer, Quinn, and despite protocol, she invited me out for drinks.

"If you can get into Gallettes, we'll be there tonight."

"I can definitely get into Gallettes."

"Ha-ha-ha, okay, suuuure," and she grabbed a snack from the snack room and went upstairs to the sleeping quarters. I grabbed a few snacks and headed out, back toward my dorm.

Gallettes was a bar that was notorious for ID'ing people, and I didn't exactly have one yet. Because I was eighteen.

I really didn't want to miss out on the opportunity to spend time with ~~Quinn~~ Mary Catherine. I begrudgingly texted Fountain, who did have a fake ID. I showed up and was let in through the back door by Mr. Old South himself. I quickly ditched Fountain in the sea of people and looked through the crowd for Quinn and her posse. I weaved in and out of drunk frat bros and sorority girls, to the tune of a one-man band covering Sugarland's "Something More," and then I spotted her.

Mary Catherine. Her Burberry coat snugged her body and her Pandora bracelet flashed as I noticed in the same hand was a yellow hammer cocktail. She held the cocktail close to her body, as if to cool her down in the crowded, sweaty bar.

Mary Catherine the saint drinks? She's too holier-than-thou!

"FRESHMAN!" Quinn said and turned and looked at me. The rest of the seven juniors also turned and gave me an intimidating stare. As freshmen, we weren't allowed to be at Gallettes, but I had been given a hall pass that could be taken away.

I went up to the bar and ordered a few shots to impress the older girls, mainly Mary Catherine, but when I turned around with a fistful of Slippery Nipple shots, she was nowhere, so I passed them out to the girls who remained and Fountain, who was harder to lose than I'd hoped.

I then noticed Mary Catherine crying in the corner. One of the girls walked over and tried to console her. I found out that Mary Catherine and her boyfriend had broken up, and my heart inexplicably flickered[32].

With Slippery Nipple liquid courage, I decided to walk up to her. Who cared that I was a freshman? I wanted her to know, as a sister and potential new best friend, that I was there for her.

"Hey, Mary Catherine."

"Hi," Mary Catherine said, barely audible.

"I, uh, I'm sorry about . . ."

"It's fine." She looked above me, like she was searching for someone else.

"Do you want a drink? I'll get you something."

"No, I'm good."

"Thanks for getting me into Gamma Alpha Beta. I love it. It's the best thing that's ever happened to me!" I enunciated my words to try to seem sober.

"You're welcome."

And then she was enveloped by the group of older sisters, and Mary Catherine, Quinn, and the rest of them left the bar. I stood there alone. Eighteen. Happy I finally got to talk to the woman of few words, Mary Catherine.

I was totally in awe of the older sisters. I wanted to do everything to impress them and meet their expectations. But the sorority wasn't my only influence. I still had a tenuous finger on the pulse of liberalism. The Blunt classes like Pathological Man and Reading Comics interested me, and I became particularly close with one professor, Dr. Schwab. We'd have lunch and coffee and talk about all things anarchy. He was a former CIA agent and a lover of Saint Augustine, the bishop/philosopher.

"You're a good thinker, Sophie. I really liked your paper on Plato's *Republic* and the *Apology*." He patted his western tie confidently.

---

[32] At the time, I thought this was an amazing opportunity to get praise from the older girls, spend quality time with them. Now I realize . . . well, we all know what I realize.

Then why did you give me a B?

"Keep going. You have good intuition."

"Thanks," I said as I sipped my coffee.

"You should take another one of my classes on Cuba during the Cold War."

I felt dumb. I was sitting in front of this genius man in my oversize sorority-letter shirt that fell past my Nike running shorts and a full face of makeup, hoping my sisters wouldn't see us and conclude I was a Democrat.

I loved Dr. Schwab as a mentor. Part of me wanted to ask him, *I look ridiculous, right? Like I should go change out of this getup?* But I didn't. I had to stick with the agenda: Operation: Sophie Gets Her MRS Degree.

Between the sorority's demands and Blunt, it was getting hard to juggle everything. I was used to the clown act, but college, I was learning, was an entire three-ring circus. Beep-beep.

Catherines the Greats

As a freshman, I was assigned a big sister. She was the person I'd go to if I had problems or needed additional support. Mine was a dud, a devoted Christian, and I couldn't be bothered. I think we can all agree I had had enough religion in my life. But my grand-big was not a dud. Her name was Catherine. She loved rock climbing, and I would find myself at the rock-climbing gym, bouldering, and after falling on my tail, I would just watch her climb up effortlessly. Not to be confused with Mary Catherine but both wonderful, nonetheless. When I became a sophomore, it was time to be assigned a little. I found myself drawn to a freshman named Katherine, with a *K*. She had the same meerkat-esque quality that Mary Catherine and Catherine had and had the most symmetrical face I've ever seen. I *had* to be friends with her.

I started to ask Katherine with a *K* to spend time with me and my grand-big, Catherine (with a *C*). I'd also invite Mary Catherine, but she would respectfully decline. Katherine and Catherine would boulder, and then I'd grab us lunch (salads for them, burger for me) for us to eat outside the gym. I'd have given up my career to go live in a commune with the two of them. Of course, I couldn't say that, and they were both occupied by dating brothers on the Alabama football team. I couldn't compete.

No matter—Katherine picked me to be her big. Cue the "All I Do Is Win" track. On the big/little reveal, I was happily sandwiched between my two beautiful C/Katherine friends, wishing I could stay there forever. My actual big was at church, so she didn't make the photo op.

Chapter Nineteen

BAMBI AND THE HUNT FOR THE RIGHT D*CK

As the search for my future ex-husband continued into sophomore year, I plowed through men like I was some sort of tilling machine. But the encounters were not the kind of steamy sex I had hoped for, and I started to think that if they ever put the kind of tepid sex I was having on television, the human race would die out. Judging by the number of men I was adding to my list of conquests, you'd think I would proudly flaunt the number. Instead, it felt like a hollow victory.

I was with a group of my sorority sisters when one of them told me, "You just haven't found the right dick yet."

"How will I know?"

"Girl, you'll KNOW." She shivered, and her eyes glazed over like she was experiencing an exorcism.

I recognized that look, but the sex I was currently having couldn't hold a candle to the orgasms Lammy and I had achieved.

Frances, my sister and now roommate, who I lived with in an on-campus house, shouted, "At least you're having sex, Sophie! I'm still a fucking virgin!"

I would happily have given her some of my men. On second thought, I didn't want her to be ruined by bad sex too.

I had to keep up the pursuit of the D. But I was so tired!

That's when I met Hudson. Hudson and I were in student government, another outlet I'd found for my competitive spirit. We were both elected as SGA senators and loved saying it.

"Hi, Senator Argyle."

"Hi, Senator Santos."

"Ready for our first meeting?" I asked.

"Yes, although . . ." He leaned closer to me. "The head of Senate is such a bitch, right?"

"Totally! OMG!" I whisper-yelled.

At this point in my college experience, I'd started leaning a little further right. My Greek environment started to shape my thoughts. Hudson and I linked arms and walked into the meeting, where we valiantly upheld our Greek Alabama traditions against the scruffy liberal kids who wanted things like coed dorms and to get rid of fraternity block-seating privileges at football games.

He had a really sweet, pouty face; swoopy hair; and a shady yet relentlessly positive personality. He was a brother at Delta Upsilon, a.k.a. Drugs Unlimited—because pot and any drug literally imaginable could always be had at their parties.

"Nice tie, Argyle. Crimson. How original. Bold, even."

"At least I'm not wearing a tweed sweater jacket, Sophie. It's eighty degrees, and your makeup is running."

We were perfect for each other. He'd hold my hair as I vomited, and I'd rub his back after he did shrooms. We represented our caste in student government, but privately, we questioned Greek life together. At times, we'd look at each other and say, "This is wack, right?"

Hudson had been arrested for weed possession after getting pulled over for speeding, the first weed-fueled high-speed chase I'd heard of. Even though he was on probation, the idea of being without something to smoke was just preposterous to him, so he bought a pack of "Spice" at a local gas station.

At the time, we didn't know much about the designer drugs that were being legally sold at smoke shops, gas stations, and bodegas across the country. No one we knew had turned into a face-eating zombie from bath salts. Spice was a mix of herbs and chemicals that looked pretty similar to low-grade weed. It was sold in a metallic pouch with professional branding.

We went to his room at the frat house, where Hudson held up the little psychedelic baggie. He was very proud and excited. I was skeptical. I surveyed his Don't Tread on Me flag. My eyes wandered down to his *Golden Girls* box set. His frat brother Sam sat on the couch.

"I don't want you to get arrested again," I told Hudson.

"I got this at a gas station," he said. "It just hit the market."

My fears started to fade. *How bad can it be if gas stations are selling it out in the open?*

Hella bad.

As soon as I took my first hit, the room started flipping. I was out of control, writhing on the bed, and couldn't even lift my head. Sam ran over and shoved the orange soda he was drinking in my face, as if he could heal me with a sip.

Hudson tried to calm me down. "Just breathe, Sophie! You're okay! Sit up! Sit up!"

I can't! The room keeps flipping on its side every time I try to sit up, I said—but only in my head, since I couldn't actually form the words.

The high lasted for only about ten seconds, but every second felt like a century.

I slowly and shakily sat up in the bed. Hudson held me up while Sam sat with a relieved look on his face. I'm sure he was afraid their frat would be kicked off campus if there was, ya know, a dead girl found in the house.

Even with the dodgy drug use, though, I knew Hudson was from my planet. I wasn't sure which one that was, but we were speaking the same language.

Hudson invited me to his formal in . . . you guessed it . . . NOLA! We had barely started to stroll down Bourbon Street when he excitedly said to me, "Let's go to a strip club!"

"Ugh! Really, Hudson?" Now that I was a classy GAB, I was *so* not into the idea of watching a girl dance around naked.

"Come on, it'll be fun."

We looked up the best strip club in New Orleans on Yelp—because we were classy—and walked into a place that was straight out of a James Bond movie. Men in three-piece suits, women walking around in Armani undergarments. I was impressed by how clean the place seemed. I'd heard frat boys talk about strip clubs and how you had to be careful where you walked because of the vomit and semen splattered everywhere. "Better pack your black light."

Not here. The floors were marble, and the hostess had a French accent. We clearly couldn't afford to be there. I decided to pretend I was married and sneaking around on my husband. I imagined my wedding ring was in my pocket, and I kept my head down so I wouldn't be recognized.

I went to the ATM and got out a few twenties, then tucked the cash into my bra. As I looked at my receipt, I discovered that it was the type of place where the name on the building didn't match the credit card statement. *Dorothy, you ain't in Kansas no more!*

We sat down on a crescent-shaped lounge settee in front of a table with a long golden pole that shot up to the ceiling. All of a sudden, the Katy Perry hit shifted to a sultry song. A petite redhead with a pear-shaped body stepped out in vinyl platform heels and started to wrap her leg around the pole. Her red hair looked like a wig, but it was perfectly positioned. Her body shone in the spotlight. There was suddenly a shift in my downstairs. It was the same sensation I'd had back in Arab, making out with Emma. It made me uncomfortable.

"Hey—how long do you want to be here, Hudson?" I asked with my eyes fully locked onto the woman before me.

"I don't know, Soph! We have all the time in the world!" he said with a smile. "Can we get two Jägerbombs and two Maker's Mark and Sprites?" he asked a waitress who had cozied herself up next to us.

I turned around and found my face practically in her breasts. I jumped, then gave her a nod like, *Yeah, all good,* as I looked down at the carpet.

When I looked up, the redhead wasn't on the pole anymore but was crawling toward me. I pointed at Hudson like, *Do him!*

She shook her head.

I pointed again, more emphatically. *No, really—do himmmm.*

She shook her head even more intensely—NO.

Everything's okay, Soph. Just breathe. Just breathe—she's just gonna say hi and then be on her merry way.

She sat up and unclasped her bra and threw it down in front of me. Her perfect boobs glistened. Both nipples were pierced with diamond-encrusted bars. In a heartbeat, she was within an inch of my nose.

"Can I motorboat you?" she asked.

I finally got my voice back. "No, no, no. I'm okay; Hudson wants—"

"OMG, DO HER!" he screamed in a high-pitched voice.

Where the fuck did that come from?

"Come on, it'll be fun," the ~~stripper~~ hardworking professional woman whispered into my ear.

Fuck.

She put her head in between my boobs and motorboated me. I froze, half-excited and half-confused. *What the hell is this anyway? Like, why is it called motorboating? Is her nose supposed to be the water and my boobs are the oars?* The men around us hooted and hollered. She glided back to the pole like a minx, and I grabbed the whole wad of crinkled cash out of my romper and threw it onto the stage. Too much? Don't care. The lights shifted to signal her song was over, and she gathered my money and walked off the stage.

"That was awesome! She's gorgeous," Hudson said.

"I'm gonna go to the bathroom." I got up out of my chair and walked past an older gentleman with a cigar who was for sure Sean Connery. Sean nodded at me. *Yes, sir, I know we all saw that. Thank you for embarrassing me.*

I sat down on the toilet, collecting my thoughts as the stream of pee exited my body, when I heard a voice—the same gravelly voice that had been in my ear just moments before. I quickly flushed and opened the door. There she was. The petite redhead. Her body was even better offstage, even with the fluorescent lights and the clumps of body glitter that had moved because of her sweat. She was freshening her makeup.

"Hey," I said.

"Hi, cutie."

I cleared my throat as drunk women pushed past me. "I've . . . I've never done that before."

"Mm-hmm," she said as she put on her lipstick.

"What's your name?" I asked as I washed my hands slowly.

"Bambi."

Like the Disney deer?

"And yours?" she asked, seeming interested. Or maybe she didn't give a shit—I had no clue.

"Sophie."

"Oh, like *Sophie's Choice*."

Touché.

"Well, would love to do it again sometime," I said. *What am I saying?*

"Here, take my number," she said. She grabbed my phone from my front pocket, put in her digits, and walked out.

I came back from the bathroom, and Hudson got up.

"Hey, babe, we're leaving."

"Wait—why?" I asked.

"Because the drinks are so expensive, and a bunch of the guys are at another bar." He handed me my coat and fixed his thinning, swoopy hair in front of me.

I tried searching for Bambi as we rushed out and saw her talking to a table on the far side of the room. We were out the door before I could say goodbye.

Later that night, back in the hotel room, Hudson tried to make his moves, but I told him I was "tired," and he rolled over to sleep. The strip club had been so exciting, and since Hudson was unconscious, I figured I'd just go back by myself. The night was young. We were in New Orleans! I contemplated actually texting Bambi.

So am I just gonna straight-up text a stripper?

Like, what does this mean?

I guess it means that I want to be friends with a stripper.

I typed in the words, *Hi, this is Sophie*, and quickly sent the text. I put down my phone and closed my eyes. Pretty sure GABs shouldn't be texting strippers.

Buzz, buzz.

`Hi, Sophie.` 😊

The eagle has landed.

`Hey! When do you work again?` I asked.

`Tomorrow night.` 😊

Now I *did* have to convince Hudson.

The next afternoon, we were walking down Bourbon Street drinking Hand Grenades.

"Hey, so . . . after the formal, can we hang out at the"—*looks around*—"strip club again?"

"You wanna go back to that place?" he asked.

"Yeah. I liked the vibe."

"No . . . it sucked. None of the girls was that cute," he said.

You literally called her gorgeous . . .

"Do you remember what it was called?" I prodded.

"No idea. 'Sup, Sam!" Sam was approaching with his date. "Let's go get wasted!" Everyone raised their Hand Grenades in the air like some salute, except for me. I had begun frantically searching locations on my phone. I looked up strip club after strip club to no avail. *What if the place doesn't exist, and we just got caught in some space-time continuum?*

I did one last search and found it! Top Shelf Only. Now the problem was how I was gonna get back there.

After dinner for two hours, the frat's formal for four hours, drinks for three (yes, I was counting), and an eternity of doing other things besides being at Top Shelf Only, I knew what I had to do. *I'm gonna sneak out while Hudson's sleeping.*

I left the hotel room, very drunk—too drunk to be solo—and walked for fifteen minutes to my destination.

"ID?" the bouncer asked.

Yes, yes. Here, here.

I gave him my fake, which was a Louisiana ID that I'd found on the ground at Gallettes. My guardian legal adult's name was Antoinette Bordeaux, and she had my back for a year. She looked like she was on meth, which worked in my favor because most of the time, the bouncers would think I'd just had a really rough night before the picture was taken. That, or it was so pathetic, they found it amusing. I didn't question Antoinette's powers.

I walked in and began immediately searching for my baby deer. After nothing short of looking under the lounge chairs and businessmen's feet, I sat down defeatedly at a table. A different girl walked out onstage, but I didn't want her. I wanted Bambi. The club felt seedier tonight. It had lost its effervescence. I got an overpriced Maker's Mark and Sprite—and as I sat there casing the joint, a bouncer noticed me being shifty and came over.

"Yo, you good?" he asked.

"Yeah. I'm just looking for somebody." *Okay, don't say that if you don't want to seem shady.*

He gave me a look like, *Care to share with the class?*

"Um, her name is Bambi? She works here, I think."

"She's getting ready. She'll be up at three a.m."

"Thanks."

It was one a.m. *Guess I'm waiting.* I waited and tried not to fall asleep as more and more girls came onto the table. I shooed them away. I was a one-woman girl. At three a.m., I finally saw her. At another table. A table that was full.

I watched from afar as she danced on the table and motorboated another girl.

I thought that was our *thing—but whatevs.*

She then scooted off to the bathroom. I quickly got up, ~~walked~~ ran to the bathroom door, and took a deep breath. I pushed the door open, keeping my head down to act discreet, until I "saw" her.

"Heyyy, Bambi! Oh my God, this is crazy. You're here," I said, convinced I was completely fooling her.

"Hi, sweetie," she said. She gave me a very tight hug. She was barely clothed. T.O.: Thong. Only.

"Are you having a good night at work?"

"It's—ugh, whatever. I have to be up early for school, so I'm trying to get through it."

"Sure, sure. I get that . . . I'm in school too," I said. "So anyway," I began again. "We should hang out."

"Do you want a room?" she asked.

A room? Alone time. Cool. Maybe she'll do the thing again, and then we'll just talk!

"I mean, sure? How much are they?"

"There's pricing in the menus. If you want one, just tell the bouncer," she continued. "I have to run, though. Bye, girl."

I grabbed a menu from the bouncer.

"VIP ROOMS starting at $500."

Five hundred dollars?

How the hell was I going to get $500? *I mean, I can think of one way?* I looked at the pole and did a little shimmy. The gentleman next to me furrowed his brow in confusion. *I guess the money maker is not going to be making the money.*

I texted her. **Hey, Bambi. I can't really afford the VIP room. Do you just want to hang out?**

She didn't respond.

I texted her again.

Sorry, I wrote. **It's just that I'd love to see you, but I'm a poor college student.**

No response.

Okay, I'm gonna head out, I texted after ten minutes, hoping she'd beg me to stay.

Silence. After a few more texts, unrequited on her end and slightly borderline obsessive on my end, I left. I sneaked back into my hotel room and slid into bed close to dawn. Hudson put his arm around me. A few hours later, I got a text.

Hi. Yeah. I need to make money. So what you're asking isn't fair to me.

I decided to not respond, as I was too embarrassed for ~~wasting her time~~ obsessively texting her. And disrespecting her profession.

"YOU GOT A STRIPPER'S NUMBER?" Frances screamed and guffawed back at the ramshackle house we'd rented with our other sister, Mary. "HA-HA-HA-HA."

Mary was also laughing and shaking her head, but not really paying attention because *The Bachelor* was on.

"Yeah, I did. Look at me now."

"You're so crazy, Sophie." Frances just kept staring at me, busting into laughter.

"I think it's fucking awesome," I said, trying to puff out my chest.

"Yeah. I mean, it is, I guess. But BAMBI? Her name was BAMBI?" Frances's wide eyes grew wider.

I don't make fun of your name, Frances GERTRUDE.

Frances broadcast the news to our entire friend group via text moments later. My sister Madison backed me up and said she was jealous. *Thank you, Madison.* My friend Presley thought it must be a violation of GAB rules.

A stripper? Why the hell did you want a stripper's number? Did you tell Hudson? Presley asked. She sent the emoji with an eyebrow raised.

It must have slipped my mind, I texted. *Night, y'all.*

Things with Hudson weren't exactly hanky-panky anyway. Go figure. He made a point to call it out on our return from New Orleans.

"Why aren't we having sex?" he asked.

"We are . . . we do," I said, stunned by the question.

We don't.

"We barely ever have sex," he said.

He looked like a lost puppy.

"I don't know! We're busy!"

"We're in our sexual prime!" he said. "We should be having sex every day!"

"Okay, you're right. But not tonight—we both have class at nine," I said.

I rolled over and stared at my iPhone. I liked Hudson, and I didn't understand why I didn't want to have sex with him. I thought about the other guys I had slept with and shuddered. Lawson put it in and passed out, Hunter came as soon as I touched him, Tex was okay, but his ex-girlfriend caught us in the middle of the act and snapped a picture of my naked body, so that killed the mood—it made sense that I hadn't really been into them. But Hudson was amazing; he was like a *brother* to me. I counted the guys I had slept with. Twenty-five. Twenty-five guys—a pretty impressive number—and yet, clearly, I still just hadn't found the right . . . *dick* yet.

I knew if I didn't find the right dick soon, I wouldn't be getting that MRS degree. I didn't understand why sex was so important. We loved spending time together, but that wasn't enough for Mr. Sexual Prime. We decided to part ways.

Eight years later, I was in New York, flipping through Twitter, when I saw a post by Hudson that was something like DON'T YOU PEOPLE WANT FREE HEALTH CARE? It stopped me dead in my scrolling. Seeing Hudson's name in my feed was a blast from the past. I read the tweet again and felt a wave of joy. *Is Hudson a scruffy liberal now?*

I stalked him more. He still had the same doofy grin and floppy hair. I scrolled to other tweets. "Gay rights are human rights, you idiots!"

Wait.

HE CAN'T BE . . .

There he was at Pride, holding a flag under a rainbow with the same pouty face I had noticed years before.

He is.

Chapter Twenty

ROCK BOTTOM

Had I known that wearing my Dorothy costume every day for a year would put me in the middle of my very own twister, I would have burned it. *Dorothy—that she-devil—cursed me!*

On April 11, 2011, an EF4 tornado hit the University of Alabama. With that storm, my anxiety rose from the twirling cloud like a villain in a superhero movie. In this case, my anxiety villain showed up as a demented Dorothy in a ripped gingham dress who exclaimed, "I'm here, you fuck. What now? And guess what, Toto's dead."

Two hours before the tornado hit, I was skipping around campus, feeling invincible hell, I was even known to stop and text in the middle of the street while cars went around me.

Thirty minutes before, I was thinking about going skydiving with a bottle of Jack in my hand. Ke$ha approved, so why not?

And then, ten minutes before, I was now in class, and a fellow classmate piped up that he had been checking the radar on his phone.

"Hey, y'all—it looks pretty bad! I think we should get under our desks."

"I think we're okay," my professor said. "So as we were saying, Nick Carr says that the internet is rotting our brains . . ."

Then the sirens sounded. I was still calm. The professor kept lecturing. And unbeknownst to all of us, we had five minutes to go.

Two minutes before, the same student had turned up the livestream so loud, it drowned out the professor, and a normally calm meteorologist named James Spann shakily announced, "Everyone take cover! It's coming right now!"

I suddenly forgot how to run and managed to bang my knee on the table as we all raced into the hallway.

We put book bags on our heads and lay down on the ground.

Pure silence.

I heard some rustling but mainly just my heartbeat, which was now extraordinarily loud. After a few minutes, the meteorologist came back on the livestream and said it was over.

That wasn't bad. Maybe we'll get to go home early!

"That's it for today, class. I'll see you on Friday—"

I almost fell over running back to the classroom for my stuff, threw my binder (bursting with loose paper and candy wrappers) into my backpack, and skipped out the door.

Out of the building—despite it being an overcast sky—everything looked fine. I was midway across the quad when I heard students yelling.

"HOLY SHIT! THIRTEENTH STREET IS GONE!"

And . . .

"SOME OF SORORITY ROW TOO!"

I immediately started running toward the Gamma Alpha house with my backpack bouncing up and down on my butt. My group text started blowing up.

`Is Mary okay?`

`HAS ANYONE HEARD FROM MARY?` Frances texted.

`I'm okay`, Mary replied. `I was asleep.`

`Presley?`

`Present.`

`Madison.`

`I'm studying!!!`

`Good we're all here,` Frances remarked.

`Hey, guys. I'm fine. Just so you know . . . ,` I texted.

`Haha. Okay-good to know, Soph`, Frances said.

I got to Sorority Row and saw members of other sororities clearly disoriented. Some were holding each other, crying.

The tornado's 5.9-mile path created wreckage in only a matter of minutes. It killed six students and took fifty-three other lives. It destroyed all of the town's main strip. It ripped our university to shreds. And later cost $100 million to clean up. It was shocking to see death come out of nowhere, make a frightening appearance, and leave my community devastated in its wake.

I joined a group of people who were visiting the site where the tornado had touched down. We walked around to survey the damage—power lines down in the middle of the street, businesses crushed by trees, car glass scattered—shocked, confused, and anguished. It was a war zone. The entire town was reeling. I later found out that the tornado had come so close to my rental house that it missed us by only one street. As Mary slept upstairs.

I called my mom, freaking out. "How the fuck are students dead? People don't die that young!"

"Yes, honey. It can happen."

"I could die?" I asked, genuinely surprised.

"Yes. You will one day—but hopefully, it won't be for a very long time."

"Right."

Much like Santa Claus, I was behind on the whole "death" thing too.

Two days later, school was canceled for the semester, and three days later, Frances and Mary moved out. I had planned to stay on campus to take summer classes and get my shit together. The first night, I was alone, and I felt the walls closing in. I jumped under the covers and tried to breathe. My throat felt like it was closing up.

I immediately dialed my mom's number again.

"I think I'm having a panic attack."

"Okay, honey. What are your symptoms?"

"I feel really anxious and afraid to be alone," I said.

"Here's what you're gonna do. Go down to the urgent care and see if they can assess you."

I was very familiar with the university's urgent care. During my freshman year, I had every illness imaginable—strep throat, bronchitis, hangovers, swine flu. Yes, I got swine flu my first week after rush, which may or may not have been because I was making out with everyone I could. Pre-COVID, preawareness. The clinic had my chart ready to go at all times, to their annoyance. The nurse practitioner sized me up and prescribed a little yellow magic pill—Klonopin.

"This should help," she said. "You're not alone, ya know."

That was the thing. I realized I hadn't really been alone in a long time. And I'd never been alone for an extended amount of time. I had never slept in a house alone before, and I was planning to stay alone for a whole three months.

I'd avoided being alone at all costs. If my mom went out of town, I went over to a friend's. I had roommates in college. I had over two hundred sisters. I, Sophie Elizabeth Santos, was never alone. That night, I decided to keep the trend going and drove over to stay at my friend and sorority sister's apartment.

I called my mom again the next morning.

"Mom, I don't think I can stay in my house all summer."

"Come home, honey. It's okay."

My mom had relocated to Kansas City for a new nursing job. She and Buck were on thin ice, because of his continuous infatuation with something that rhymes with "thorn." His thorn infatuation might not have been such a problem by itself, but he also didn't have a job. Instead, he spent my mom's money on beer and cigars while watching thorn at all hours of the day and night. No one messes with my mom's money. I thought about telling my mom, *Told you so*, but it wasn't satisfying seeing her get duped.

Mom had also just helped my sorority sister Madison get an internship at her hospital, and Madison was going to be staying with my mom all summer.

"Madison's drivin' here tomorra," my mom told me. "Follow her to Kansas City and you'll both stay here."

"Okay," I said and hung up the phone.

I followed Madison from Alabama to Kansas City in my burnt-orange Chevy Cavalier, a.k.a. the baby carrot. We weren't ten minutes outside of Tuscaloosa when I started texting her that we had to pull over—every time a semitruck or even a Mini Cooper would drive past me, I felt frozen with panic. Plus, I kept closing my eyes—which I do not recommend when you're behind the wheel. The fifth time I asked to pull over, we found ourselves on a tiny dirt road and both got out of our cars.

"Soph, what is going on?" Madison asked. "We can't pull over every five minutes."

"I'm sorry. Driving is a lot to handle right now!" I didn't want to say I was terrified that a semi was going to hit me and splatter my guts all over I-55 North. *Death is looming, Madison. He's right behind us.*

I hadn't taken the Klonopin that day.

The label said, "May cause dizziness while driving." I needed one less thing to worry about.

"It's an eleven-hour drive, Soph. Let's go, or at this rate, it'll take us two weeks."

Two weeks sounded okay to me, just so long as I arrived there alive. I got back in my car and gripped the wheel for dear life for the rest of the trip.

We pulled over six more times, and I walked into my mom's house twenty hours later.

Two days after my arrival back home, I went to a nurse practitioner in Kansas City. When I told him I was having trouble breathing and felt anxious, he prescribed me beta-blockers, a medicine that's regularly used to treat hypertension. I had a gut feeling that I shouldn't take beta-blockers. But I filled the prescription, hoping to stop—or at least slow—the panic attacks.

I was right about the beta-blockers.

The very next day, I was supposed to be leaving to go back south for the Bonnaroo Music and Arts Festival. My mom had helped with airfare and made me swear that under no circumstances would I bail. I'd been planning to live out my sweaty dreams working the festival.

The car arrived at five a.m. to take me to the airport. But I had taken the beta-blocker, and I could barely lift my head off the couch.

"Mom, I can't go. I literally can't get into the car." Every time I stood up, the room would start spinning.

"Fine! Go back to bed!" she said, having completely lost her patience in an instant.

I ran into her room, hid under the covers, and cried until I fell asleep. Suddenly, normal, everyday events did not feel so normal. I didn't want to get in the car. If I got into the car, I was convinced another driver would commit suicide by crashing into me. I didn't want to go to a music festival because I was certain that a terrorist bomb would take me out with the crowd. I didn't want to leave the house for any reason for fear of an active shooter—or worse, that a guy who thought I looked funny would knife me, leaving me to bleed out and die. The world had become a very scary place.

I tried leaving the house to grab the mail, and when my mom saw me not graze the first step, I told her what was going on inside my head.

Up until this point, my ego had been so big that I thought I couldn't die. And once I realized I could die, my own mortality paralyzed me. The tornado had me convinced that death was creeping just around every corner. I was petrified.

"Sorry, Soph—or actually, I'm not?" Death would say before he broke my neck over his leg.

My mom decided that I should go to an outpatient psychiatric program for two weeks. Eight hours a day, with constant monitoring and therapy to help me get my life together. I heard her over the phone, talking to my dad. "Ben. She's really bad. It's even worse than I had imagined." I pulled the covers up over my head to drown out the embarrassment, hoping that Madison either didn't hear or was already at her internship.

A day after I couldn't leave the house for Bonnaroo, a van picked me up to take me to the outpatient program. It was humiliating. How could someone who had been raised with such confidence be suddenly scared to drive or even to set foot in a Target without thinking the building was going to collapse on top of her? Only a week prior, I had been sitting in the sorority house, laughing at the photos we had taken at the spring formal. Now I sat in the van with two other nervous-looking people and stared out the window.

We pulled up to the hospital. I was expecting a *One Flew over the Cuckoo's Nest*–type building, but it looked modern. We walked inside, and they sat me down at a table and had me fill out some paperwork. After I signed a few pieces of paper, a security guard patted me down and made me remove anything sharp from my body.

"We'll need your keys."

Why? So I don't shank you?

Yep.

"Can I use the restroom?" I asked.

The security guard took out his walkie-talkie and said, "Code yellow. Santos restroom."

He walked me to the restroom and stood outside. I closed the door. I opened it again.

"There's no lock," I said.

"I know. No one's coming in. That's why I'm here."

After I unsuccessfully tried to think up a way to escape, the security guard escorted me to a bigger room that resembled a conference room, where there were about ten people already sitting down.

"Hi! Sophie! Welcome!" a counselor said as I walked in. "I'm Jennifer!"

I scanned the group to identify anyone who was normal, like me of course, because there was nothing wrong with me and everyone else was crazy. They all seemed older. There was a guy in his forties, who looked fine—pretty boring. There was a short woman with spiky red hair who seemed okay, but she had definitely seen some shit. She had been in the van with me. There was also a girl who was rhythmically knocking her fists against her head. I pegged her as someone to avoid.

I chose a seat close to Jennifer, figuring she must be the most normal out of the group. "We have a new face today," Jennifer said like she was my friend. "Please make her feel comfortable. Now, let's go around the room and have each of you share what you'd like to work on *today*."

Everyone took turns telling the group their areas of focus: "anger" or "not being too hard on myself" or "don't repetitively pet the ceramic goose, Fred, on the way out the door." When it was my turn, I didn't have anything to say.

"Hi, I'm Sophie." I waited. Silence.

I thought that they'd all say, *Hi, Sophie*, in unison, but they all just stared at me, except for the girl knocking her fists.

"I'm working on . . . I guess what I want to work on . . . is staying calm?"

Jennifer smiled encouragingly. "Great job."

Okay, I think I'm done here.

"For this session, we will spend two hours using cognitive behavioral therapy—otherwise known as CBT," Jennifer continued.

After two hours of weird meditation like imagining my arm is lifeless to suggest "I'm in control" and spotting five things in the room to ground me, I went into the cafeteria, and that's when I saw patients in tear-away clothes.

"Inpatients," the woman with the spiky red hair said, nudging me. "Cuckoo!" She laughed.

I nodded and tried not to laugh.

"I'm Ruby. Come sit with me, kid."

I followed her to the back of the cafeteria. She introduced me to everyone as they all went around introducing themselves. One guy had tattoos all over his arms and a cigarette tucked behind his ear. He'd also been in the van with me.

"This is Jeff," she said, gesturing to a guy at the table.

He nodded. "Hey, kid," he said gruffly.

"Nice to meet you all," I said. I sat and I dug into my brick-like lasagna.

The last part of the day was a meeting with my psychiatrist, who didn't spend more than fifteen minutes with me before he said, "Here's your scrip."

I looked at it.

"Lexapro and Klonopin?" I asked.

"Yep. We're going to ease you up to twenty mg of Lexapro over the course of two weeks. If you have any reactions, let me know."

I didn't think I was going to be MEDICATED! The Klonopin and the beta-blockers seemed like one-offs to get me through a rough patch. What the flying fuck? This is the real deal. Do they not know who I am? I am . . . ! I am . . . !

Fuck.

"Next!" he yelled as Ruby came in briskly and sat down in the same chair as me so fast, I bounced out from her taking my spot.

On the van ride home, I pressed my forehead against the window again. *God, Madison's gonna think I'm fucking crazy. And what if she tells everyone in the group chat? I'm done for.*

I walked back into the house, and my mom gave me a big hug.

"How'd it go, honey?"

"Fine."

I walked upstairs and knocked on Madison's door. She told me to come in.

"Hey . . . I'm back." I looked down and tried not to act like I was a complete nutcase. I kept my face blank, my arms on each side straight as a board, and talked extremely slowly.

"Oh! Cool, girl! I'm just studying HIPAA compliance. I met Dr. Blumenthal today. He's so awesome."

"That's cool," I said.

"How'd it go?"

"Fine."

I left it at that and Madison, bless her, did too.

For the next nine days, I got up, met the van outside, and went to the hospital. I was pleasantly happy to open the door and see Ruby and Jeff sitting in their seats. I attended group therapy, where we talked about our feelings and how to manage them.

"The anxiety is making you feel like the world is crashing all around you—when in reality, everything is okay," Jennifer told me.

"But what if I'm in a plane and the pilot decides to nose-dive into a cow farm?" I asked.

"I can't say you will or won't ever be on a plane that has issues, but it's *normal* to get onto a plane. You aren't putting yourself in danger by doing what is routine."

"I see," I said. "I guess that makes sense."

And I got close to Jeff and Ruby, which meant I was able to ask the question that had been on my mind since I started. We sat near a tree while Jeff puffed on his cigarette.

"Why didn't you all say my name after I said, *'Hi, I'm Sophie*?" I asked.

"Why would we? This ain't AA," Ruby pointed out. "Ain't that right, Jeff?" Jeff let out a guttural laugh.

"I'm sorry, I didn't mean to offend."

"You didn't. But you'll offend me if you stay here longer than two weeks. You've got a good spirit about you, kid," he said.

I had regular meetings with my psychiatrist, where I asked him repeatedly, "Will the medication affect my sex drive?" To which he replied, "Most likely." I became friends with the people I'd deemed not normal—even the fist girl, who, once her medication was sorted out, was a badass lady.

Normal. What was normal anyway? Anxiety—it turned out—didn't discriminate. I had gone into the hospital expecting to be surrounded by looney tunes—and it turned out that we were all looney tunes, including me. I'd been diagnosed with generalized anxiety disorder, depression, and they said I was suffering from PTSD from the tornado. They got a lot right but missed the OCD. I decided to choose my battles, because I was currently battling the terrorists in my mind.

I felt that my issues were much more complex than that. I started to spiral. This manic episode made me look at the past two years in a different light. For two years, TWO YEARS, I had been obsessed with trying to become "the one you want to marry." I was nineteen and felt incredibly conflicted over the idea of marriage. When I went on a date with a guy, I'd immediately start trying to decide whether I could imagine us having kids two years down the road. And the answer was irrevocably *no thanks*. Before the sorority, I had never imagined my wedding, had never fantasized about a husband or the path to getting myself one. I'd never envisioned a dress and a bouquet.

I forced excitement when a sister would exclaim, "This is for my vision board!" opening Martha Stewart's *Weddings* magazine to the tissue-paper section. I was only jealous of the *attention* when a note was placed in the hallway reading, WE HAVE ANOTHER CANDLELIGHT TONIGHT! MEET AT THE HOUSE AT FIVE P.M.! DON'T BE LATE!

"OMG, who got engaged? I want a ring and a candlelight ceremony!" Frances would whine while I wondered when I'd finally find someone who made me feel that way.

Fail!

I poured my competitive energy into desperately trying to climb my way up the student government ladder. I worked tirelessly, coming up with legislation such as "Here's a meal program that takes all the leftover meals students don't eat and gives them to students in need" to prove that I should be elected. And I slept with tons of boat shoes who thought I was just using them to get a vote. I mean, they weren't wrong. But who cared?

My sorority sisters—that's who cared.

"We know you're just sleeping around to get ahead."

Fail again!

I'd been brought to Standards multiple times for my grades. In my two years at the University of Alabama, I had changed my major seven times: business with a minor in politics, then economics, next accounting, then I created my OWN major with the New College that involved going to the Cannes Film Festival, followed by financial planning, then Arabic (why not embrace my destiny?), and finally a double major in English and history. Turns out, you can't party every night, vie for student government domination, and still be a straight-A student. You can only have two out of the three things. It's like the triangular assessment or whatever.

Literal fail!

I was wearing heels to football games. I was spending thousands on T-SHIRTS FOR SWAPS. I'd found myself saying conservative things like, "Well it's so-and-so's fault if they're poor. People should work harder." I had completely lost myself in it and had no idea who I was anymore. I couldn't carry on. As much as I tried, it was like fitting a very large block into a circle, and I had jammed it in there, but it was all cracked and broken. My inner chameleon had changed so drastically that I didn't recognize the person in the mirror—and I hit rock bottom. And to make matters even worse, I replayed this realization three times over.

Being forced to talk about my anxiety made me realize that it didn't start with the tornado—it manifested in different ways. The anxiety had been there when I was six and ran down the stairs to see my mom, and it had been there when I was on the couch at my dad's place in Fort Hood. And when I compulsively watched *Harry Potter* to make sure my mom didn't die and checked the stove like a detective so that tiny insects didn't turn it on. It had *always* been there—and now I was at least able to name it.

Besides the doors with no locks that I kept discovering, I started to get over the stigma of my daily trip to the hospital. I became friends with the van driver. I was practically high-fiving the lunch ladies as I grabbed my nondescript food item.

As the days waned, I started to feel sadness that I'd be leaving.

I also started feeling better. It was probably due to the Lexapro, but I no longer felt death was nipping at my heels.

"You're gonna do great!" Jennifer assured me. "You have nothing to worry about. You killed it."

On my final day in the program, a new patient arrived. A man who had two kids and a good job.

"I'm here because I, well, I don't know. One day I was driving to work, and I was scared someone would hit me and I'd . . . yeah."

"Anyone have any advice?" Jennifer asked.

I smiled at him and nodded to Ruby.

I walked out of the clinic, and this time my mom was waiting there to pick me up. I looked at the van as Ruby and Jeff got in.

"Thanks!" I yelled.

"Go! Go! You've got your entire life ahead of you," Ruby shouted back. She and her spiky red hair got in the van as I headed back home with Mom.

PHASE THREE

"The Final Phase That Isn't a Phase"

Are you scared the lights will show how gay you are?

—Gabe, 2012

Chapter Twenty-One

SUMMER-CAMP GAY

My first experience hooking up with a queer woman was at a summer camp at Wellesley College[33]. Women's college: the place where *all* gay young women go to lose their lesbian virginity or chop off their hair. Or both.

A few months into my happy pills, I showed up at Wellesley with two shiny suitcases, beaming as I took in the crunchy, artsy, granola-y, anthropology major's paradise in all its glory. At the time, I didn't know that Wellesley was a notorious breeding ground for the future Fran Lebowitzes of the world. I simply planned to lose myself in the beautiful ponds and woods and gaze at the ancient-seeming nineteenth-century architecture. But then again, I also didn't know yet that Birkenstocks were certified lesbian footwear, and I'd been wearing them since I could ~~walk~~ waddle.

I had been offered a teaching position at an educational summer program hosted by the university. Unlike the other counselors, I was not majoring in education, nor did I have a passion for it. Fresh off a stint in a mental hospital, I was not what you'd call a promising candidate. That's not to say I didn't mind helping the youths. I thought kids were *fine*. Then again, *That restaurant was fine* means, *We're never going there again. I think dogs are fine* means, *Keep that*

---

[33] Here are the top lesbian colleges, a.k.a. the Holy Trinity. If you hook up with someone while you're at one of these, then you're gay for life. I don't make the rules.
The Holy Trinity:
1. Wellesley (I'm biased)
2. Mount Holyoke
3. Smith
Honorable Mentions: Barnard & Bryn Mawr

mongrel away from me. Realizing I needed to keep my trap shut, I decided to tell the interviewer that kids were "great." Apparently, that was enough to land me the job.

The politics of the University of Alabama and the nonstop "how will I find a suitable gentleman caller by my twenty-second birthday" lifestyle had gotten to be too much. And I had always been curious about New England. I was obsessed with the song "Boston," which actually featured the lyrics, "I think I'll go to Boston. I think I'll start a new life." So that's what I decided I'd do. I'd start a new life—if only for a summer.

It turned out that I'd taken a job with an elitist program that attracted the wealthiest kids from across the globe. In one class, I had Shoshana, an Upper West Side daddy's-princess type who was only eleven years old but whose earrings cost more than my rent. And then there was an actual princess from Jordan, whose pencil box cost more than my life. We weren't exactly making s'mores and singing about God around a campfire.

It was an enriching experience for the children of parents who summered in Milan and thought classes in the summer, with day trips to ring the bell on Wall Street, was camp. To sum up the program in a nutshell: we were forbidden to call it a "camp." It was a "summer program." Because *camp* is for poor people or Baptists! It was a C-A-M-P with a steep price tag, and I'm very excited to get that off my chest now.

I was to teach theater and commercial marketing and advertising—which, despite having had seven majors, I had never taken. I felt like an imposter. Enter David Summergrad, the program's head of curriculum, who would become a dear friend of mine and remain so for years until his untimely passing. David was a fierce educator, an unabashed liberal activist, and a mentor to thousands. That was the thing about David—no matter how many thousands he taught and inspired, he made you feel like the one. That first day in the curriculum office, he quickly advised me to lean on my strengths.

"What are you good at?"

"Theater . . ."

"Okay, so you're a storyteller!"

"Maybe?"

"You are! Why don't you have your class create commercials? We're a hands-on facility here, so any sort of project will go over quite well."

"That's brilliant, David!" I said, scribbling in my notebook.

"Now, what's the analytic component to your curriculum?" he asked as he leaned back in his chair.

"Well, I feel like commercials have a way of brainwashing. You know how they do beautiful cinematic commercials, like in the forest, with string lights hanging, and it feels like it's a festival for wood nymphs, LOL, and people are sending off balloons in like, a commune, and then you find out it's for Absolut fucking vodka?"

"I do."

"Sorry for my language."

"That's all right. I'm rarely offended." He continued to beam.

"I could pause it and have the kids try and figure out what the commercial is even for?"

"I think you're on it, Sophie."

He had a twinkle in his eyes, like a proud dad. I looked down at his red Converse and then back up to his soft goatee, his encouraging smile.

"Thanks, David!"

"You should really be thanking yourself. You're smart. You'll be great."

Class went off without a hitch, and the kids loved creating commercials as well as trying to spot which commercials were pulling the wool over the sheep's eyes. The students picked apart the ethics of product placement, and I realized that I had assembled a troupe of future Steven Pinkers.

I learned as much as my students that summer, discovering a shocking world that existed outside of Greek life. I saw people with blue hair, people with tattoos. My colleagues wore whatever they wanted: bomber jackets, trash bags, and was that the forbidden item known as a scrunchie?! *Opens up sorority handbook and screams.*

As always, I adapted. I bought a pair of bright-orange Supras—the ones that Bieber liked. Humiliating, but it was a start.

I hooked up with our IT guy, a Harvard undergrad—and with every thrust, I felt my IQ grow. The only fraternity he belonged to was Mark Zuckerberg's praise group. I made friends with a crew of people who only knew Martha Stewart as an ex-con and a friend of Snoop Dogg.

We'd all go skinny-dipping in the pond, and I'd splash around naked, unafraid of being brought to Standards for a reprimand. Sure, I got Lyme disease[34], but if it took a diseased tick for me to realize that I'd been suffering from emotional asphyxiation, then so be it.

Everything I had been told at UA was getting thrown out the window (including the handbook). I was being reprogrammed, my software overridden by a system update: Mac OS X Mountain Lion—just kidding, it was me.

And it turned out—I loved my students, and I really loved teaching.

I had one student who was a mini me: hair parted like a butt crack, suffering from crippling OCD. She wouldn't touch anything or anyone and washed her hands constantly. We'd sit and talk about it.

"I know my OCD is holding me back," she said.

"At least you recognize that it's hindering your ability to have fun! That's a great step!"

She smiled as she wrung her hands.

I hated how torn up she was, but at least she was figuring it out that early! I wanted to tell her of my trips to the mental hospital but figured it wasn't appropriate. On the last day of the session, right before she got into her car, she gave me a big hug in front of her mom. Not going to lie, that was a powerful moment.

Thanks to the kids and my colleagues with blue hair, I knew what I had to do. I Skyped my closest sorority sisters and told them, "With a heavy heart, I've decided to leave Alabama and transfer," then waited for the wailing to commence. They all blinked at me for a moment and then began to fill me in on one of our sisters' boyfriends.

Must be a weak Wi-Fi signal.

"Did you hear me?" I asked. "I'm transferring."

Momentary stares were followed by Madison declaring, "It's not like you're dead! Anyway, so how's Chad? Oh! And Frances, aren't you going to Paris soon?"

Okay. You're still living in my mom's house, Madison. Show some respect.

Back at the beginning of freshman year, Ryan and Frank had warned me that joining a sorority meant I was buying friends, but I didn't think my purchase would be voided the moment I stopped paying dues. I sent out a mass text to Gamma Alpha Beta: *Dear girls, I can't believe I'm saying this, but I have decided that it's best for me to move on to a*

---

[34] They caught it in time, and I'm fine. I think. Would love for a doctor to confirm.

new chapter. Not a different sorority chapter (I WOULD NEVER) but a new chapter in life. I am going to be transferring this fall . . . to live out my dreams in the theater . . . etc., etc., YOLO!

A few hours later, I got three responses saying, *Aww! Will miss ya, Soph!* ♥

Maybe they're crying on the other end and they don't have the strength to tell me. Regardless, the chains were breaking. I was like a middle-aged woman leaving her husband as she shouts, "I'M TAKING CONTROL OF MY OWN LIFE, DAMMIT! I don't know who I am, but I'm about to find out!"

It was the freest I'd ever felt. On the last day of camp, I packed my bags, said my goodbyes to my Harvard boyfriend, and boarded a plane back to Kansas City. Then I started counting down the days until I could return to Wellesley. I was an adult obsessed with summer camp. For the next ten months, I was chomping at the bit to go back.

I was also chomping because I was snorting a lot of cocaine.

I had enrolled in the theater department at a local college and landed a role in a production about the Industrial Revolution where my only line was, "Hi, honey, how's inventing coming?" I was on my way! That is, until I met Mitchell, a wannabe beatnik poet / performing arts certificate program dropout who'd moved back home. He wore white V-neck tees and wayfarer glasses, with his hair gelled like he was straight out of the fifties. I should have known that a hipster in Kansas City was probably too good to be true.

He was a thirty-year-old man. I was twenty. And yet I moved in with Mitchell after knowing him for only a few weeks and lived in his house, where I thought I'd spend the rest of my days.[35]

Nights were spent dripping sweat, performing monologues from Eugene O'Neill's *Long Day's Journey into Night* in my underwear, while he coached me, equally sweaty, with a cigarette hanging out of his mouth. He stared into my soul as I grabbed his face after the scene and gave a primal scream at the top of my lungs. We'd do coke off each other's bodies while *Boogie Nights* played in the background. We showed up to jazz clubs dressed as June Carter and Johnny Cash, looking for his drug dealer at three a.m.

---

[35] Textbook. Lesbian.

My love was . . . a poet. A writer. A heroin addict?! *That would have been good to know before I got hooked on him, but okay, fine, we can totally get past the heroin stuff!*

We didn't get past the heroin stuff.

I came home one day to find him painting the wall with his own blood. From what I could make out, it said, "I am who I am, and no man is the man."

Deep, Mitchell.

Despite concerning Manson parallels, *he* was the one to end it with *me*. He was writing messages in his own blood, but I had my own insurmountable problem: I had gotten too clingy. I cried for months, dialing him, begging him to reconsider.

"I'm an addict, Sophie! As soon as I'm better, we can try again," he said lifelessly.

I promised him that as he got better, I would too. "I'll work on my clinginess!" I didn't know why we couldn't make it.

I found out on Easter that he'd overdosed and been rushed to the hospital and that his girlfriend was by his side the entire time. That didn't make any sense—because *I* was his girlfriend. I went to *our home* to pick up my stuff, and I asked him if he loved me. He said, "No." *Well, you are an addict—so maybe you don't know what you're saying . . .*

I asked him to repeat himself.

He said, "Please go."

I hit rock bottom AGAIN. So much so that I got kicked off an airplane on my twenty-first birthday for accidentally mixing Klonopin with gin and sweet vermouth. *No one wanted to tell me not to mix liquor with Klonopin?* Slam! Back to outpatient treatment. After another two weeks of group therapy and not being diagnosed with OCD yet again, it was time for summer camp! Cue the fun-house music.

I was advised that Wellesley would be a good distraction from "my break" with Mitchell (there was still hope!). I walked back onto the campus, this time with more weathered baggage, and the doves sang with sore throats.

I just want to have a normal, good, easy summer.

I couldn't wait to reunite with my crew from the previous year. We all put in requests to be on the same staff together, so we'd have the same nights on and off duty. I liked my East Coast friends. We thought the same politically, which was refreshing. Though I'd had a crazy year, I thought our bond was unbreakable. And this year, I was a veteran teacher, practically a pro. What could possibly go wrong?

Upon arrival, we had our big introductory meeting. The staffers went around the room, saying where they went to college and choosing a descriptive adjective to attach to their names: Handsome Henry! Mischievous Melvin! Sparkling Sophie!

I clung to my clique—Awesome Ava! Soaring Sarah! and Cavernous Charles!—so that everyone knew that we were friends, with a capital *F* for Flawless. I had reserved us seats and called them over. Somewhere close to the end of introductions, we all turned toward a girl wearing a flamboyant floral dress and bright-purple eyeliner that caught the light.

"I'm Glamorous Gabriella, 'Gabe.' I'm majoring in education at Mount Holyoke."

Gabe had a type of energy I wasn't used to. I couldn't pinpoint it. After realizing I had been staring, I gave her a tight smile and turned back to my friend Ava. My stomach fluttered, but I wrote it off as hunger. When Gabe's plastic orange lanyard flipped around, I saw that she was assigned to A staff. The same as us. The meeting ended, and my friends and I rushed off for family dinner and sake bombs. *Ah, just like old times.*

The next morning, we welcomed the kids, and the program went into full swing. I was still a day adviser, which meant that I took care of the Boston locals, commuters who arrived in the morning and left in the early evening. Like in most elitist programs, the *camp* always reserved some spaces for scholarship kids. Being a day adviser was less responsibility, which hurt my pride. Come on! I was a veteran. I was desperate to show I could handle a one a.m. call to action to help crying girls deal with boy drama. Because I had my own boy drama and I could relate to being in love with someone who couldn't see the good thing in front of him.

All my friends were residential advisers, and that meant I saw them less. But Gabe was a fellow day adviser. We bonded over being exiled to the land of the weird locals. I found myself really wanting to get to know her. She, too, came from an immigrant family, and I felt like she understood me in a way my sorority sisters hadn't. The more time we spent together, the more I wanted to seek her advice. She was funny, a good listener, and unafraid to call me on my *Sophie bullshit.*

"My mom wants me to graduate in four years," I complained.

"That sounds like a pretty good plan," she said.

"But it's so hard!"

She laughed and patted my back. "It's really not. Want to walk together?" she asked. "We're teaching in the same building."

We made the long journey to the other side of campus.

We walked in tandem, and I felt her force field inching closer to mine. It was different from any other female friendship I'd had. Most of the time, I found myself pouring my heart and soul into girls who, if I were lucky, would give me 80 percent back. But Gabe? Gabe would slow down the car so I could jump in and flee a crime scene.

I had started hooking up with another IT expert shortly after we'd arrived on campus. Since my hookup the previous summer had been with the IT technician, I figured going geek had worked once, so why not do it again?

In the middle of the night, after he'd leave, I'd text Gabe.

You awake?

Mm-hmm . . . just finished my nightly progress notes. This kid Travis won't stop being mean to the girls, so I'm going to have to go to the head of the program tomorrow.

That sucks, I wrote. *Ugh. Why you gotta be mean, Travis!*

I know! We need to build strong girls and not let these boys think they can get away with this shit at this young of an age.

I put the phone down on my hard plastic bed and drifted into her head for a moment. Wondering if she was getting ready for bed or just staring at her phone.

Okay, I'm going to go to sleep . . . , she said to no response. *Good night.*

Again, no response from me.

I wanted to text back, but I couldn't bring myself to. Why was saying good night to my friend so fucking hard?

The next morning, I couldn't wait to see her again. I rushed out of the room, almost forgetting everything I needed for the day. I was also rushing because I was going to be late, and being on time was the number one unbreakable rule at this *camp*. I was almost out of breath when I got to the outdoor amphitheater, where we met the day kids.

"It was eight when I walked up, Charles. Just letting you know."

He gave me an annoyed look, and I could tell he was marking me late.

"Morning!" Gabe said, giving me a weird look, like, *Why are you sweating?*

"Morning!" I said back. "Good luck today."

"Thanks. You—"

"Okay, bye!" I said and charged past her. "Sup, Danielle! Ready for cake baking today?" I asked a student and sat on the opposite side of the steps. Danielle was secretly taking Cupcake Baking 101, even though her parents had signed her up for Stock Market 101. It was choppy waters to traverse. As I sat down, I looked over at Gabe, and we briefly made eye contact.

It was hard to focus on teaching that day. Luckily, I had a prodigy, Flavia, who knew how to use Final Cut Pro, a video-editing software, and could teach the other students. This was especially helpful because I didn't know how to use it. What admin don't know won't hurt 'em.

My head was fuzzy. I was supposed to be teaching these future marketing professionals the dangers of brainwashing the masses, but I kept thinking about Gabe's smile. She had razor-sharp canines that were revealed when she shook her head, like, *Sophie, come on.* I wanted them to puncture me. She had a septum piercing that she'd tuck into her nose—but then at night, when the kids weren't around, she'd pull it out. I thought about her tucking it into her nose and out of her nose. And then back again. Her big, red-rimmed glasses made her brown eyes pop. I melted when I thought about her speaking Spanish to fellow Latino counselors.

"Sophie? I think we're done for the day," Flavia said, tapping me on the shoulder. She was thirteen years old and about two feet shorter than me.

"Oh! Sorry, guys. Have fun during lunch!"

"Bye, Soph!" They all got up in unison and walked out, leaving me to come to terms with my ever-growing problem.

It certainly was a problem. I couldn't figure out what Gabe's deal was. I mean, I had heard that she might have dated women, but that was her business. It wasn't mine. And I couldn't confirm it, so it was like her gayness didn't exist. Plus, it didn't matter if she had dated women—because I wasn't gay. I just liked her company. Who cared if I was thinking about her twenty-four seven? And imagining what she was doing at every waking moment? And ~~sometimes~~ always hoping I'd accidentally stumble into her by the pond between classes?

During lunch, I saw her talking to another counselor, a hand on her arm. Were they sharing a moment?

That night, as I was wrapping up a night game of Quidditch on the quad, I spotted Gabe coming my way. I'm not sure if it's possible to look forward to seeing someone and dreading their presence at the same time, but that's how I felt. I tried to hide behind a broomstick, to no avail. Her floral skirt moved with the soft swaying of her hips, and I found myself noticing her curves. The moonlight reflected off the fresh purple streak in her hair. By the time she reached me, my stomach had dropped like I was on one of those free-fall amusement park rides. I think they're called WHY DOES THIS RIDE EXIST? ALL IT DOES IS DROP YOU TWO HUNDRED FEET! Watching Gabe was excruciating, disorienting, and exhilarating.

"We're going to Andi's room—wanna come?" she asked.

"Uhhh, I think I was going to hang with Ava." I checked my texts, which were completely empty. "On second thought, how 'bout I'll just hop out when she texts."

Back at Andi's dorm room, Andi began giving Gabe advice.

"Look at these texts she sent me! They're entire books. My ex-girlfriend is a nightmare," Gabe said.

"EX-GIRLFRIEND" reverberated in my head like a cannon had blasted.

Andi grabbed the phone. "Yeah, dude. Tell your girlfriend, 'Bye, bitch.'"

I shifted in my seat. The word *girlfriend* was being thrown around very loosely. Too loosely.

"She wants to get back together, but I can't handle her crazy episodes."

My mind was swirling in *"she"* and *"her"*s, and I wanted the whole conversation to slow down. Something about the way they were all talking so candidly and confidently made me excited and petrified. Once I got my voice back, I said, "You have a . . . *girlfriend?*"

"Yeah," she said and paused. "I mean. Not anymore. I don't know . . ." She turned to Andi. "Am I dating this ho?"

"Does it matter, man? She sucks. She's dragging you down."

They went back and forth, going over the pros and cons of her botched relationship—and I sat there, transfixed. If she really was a . . . *(says extremely fast)* . . . lesbian . . . then there was a chance that whatever I was feeling for her might be more than friendship. And if that was the case . . . I was totally fucked.

I tried to chime in.

"I mean, is she treating you right?" I asked.

"No. She's literally the worst."

"Then there's your answer."

"I guess I'm single, then," she said.

I wiped the sweat off my brow. Phew. I had engaged, done my part, and I was not gonna ask any more questions. Ever.

Ava finally texted me hours later, **hey. the sake place closed down, so we just stayed in.**

Nothing. Is. The. Same.

I texted the IT boy to hang out immediately. Hooking up with him allowed me to let off some of my pent-up energy through a lot of bumpy, boney, bad sex—but just seeing Gabe across the lawn stirred more feeling in me than the sum total of all the weeks I'd spent with him.

As the days dragged on, Gabe and I would dance around topics and flirt, but I kept trying to keep our relationship squarely in the friend zone.

"What did you use to do with your girlfriend?" I asked.

"Watch movies, drive around with the windows rolled down, go to dinner. Normal stuff."

"Sounds pretty normal," I said, pondering the normalcy.

In addition to acting like a child around Gabe, I was also acting like a literal child. I thought it was cool to befriend the students—because if they liked me, then I'd be the coolest counselor. I hadn't yet kicked my habit of wanting to be the best and most liked. We'd laugh together and put glue on our hands and peel it off just like eighth graders did. Except I wasn't an eighth grader—I was a fully grown adult. Other counselors did the same thing but still managed to maintain boundaries. After all, these kids were still kids, and we had to discipline them.

"I don't think you're taking this seriously enough," the head of the program said during a routine check-in. "You can't be friends with these kids."

"Oh, I'm not! I'm just listening to them." *And also have opinions on the beef between Josh and Jackie . . . and am totally gonna accept their friend requests on Facebook.*

"You're late every single day."

Only by one minute, because Cavernous Charles, my friend, *is a spineless prick.*

"And you're hosting the variety show, but you keep writing yourself into skits?"

"I thought I made a more believable Katniss!"

"I don't think you're reliable, Sophie. I can't in good faith have you come back here next summer. Finish out the season, but I think this will be it."

All right, Stewart. Like you've never arrived one minute late to anything. And who gave you the right to be so judgy?

Not being invited back really was a blow. And how could Cavernous Charles tell on me like that? So much for my fucking friend group. Ava and Sarah were completely ignoring me. When I asked Sarah why they'd been ghosting me all summer, Sarah said, "We're just different people, Sophie."

"Can you elaborate?"

"It's just—sometimes you're so immature. You can't be friends with eighth graders."

"You were literally laughing with them and playing with glue too!" I said. "And that girl Alice is Facebook friends with Chola from Brazil and Skypes with her family during the off-season. I thought that's what we did here."

"None of that matters. Can we just be adults?"

"Ava? Care to share your thoughts?" I asked, as she had yet to say a. Single. Word.

"I mean, you did get kicked off an airplane after you visited me in Boston."

I told you that in confidence!

I didn't know how I'd make it through the rest of *camp.* The glue that had held my friendships together had become less sticky. Much like the glue on my hands from playing the glue game. Every day that remained became a countdown to my last. And last but not least, I was struggling to identify if I was a lesbian.

Then intercession happened. According to the *camp's* website, intercession was a brief period between the first session and the second session. The kids left, staffers regrouped, and then the new kids came in the following day. It was also the time we let off steam and fucked our fellow counselors. It was the dramatic crescendo of the summer. And I, personally, was ready to burn it all to the ground.

One of the local counselors secured a Harvard frat house for the party. Thirty or so of us cranked up "Danza Kuduro" by Don Omar, busted out the Solo cups, and started to dance the kuduro! My cocktail of choice those days was vodka and Crystal Light—a sophisticated recipe I'd mastered behind those stately pillars of the South.

I had been hanging out with a few random people while my friends hung out together, avoiding my every move. I had my own agenda of avoiding someone else: Gabe.

I'd do typical teen shit like brush past her while avoiding eye contact or look at her from across the room, only to look down once she returned my gaze. But finishing my third vodka / Raspberry Ice™, I found my confidence. I summoned my best cool-guy tone "Hey, let's get out of here."

We both stumbled out the door, down the steps, and then the world went brown-ish.

I came to fifteen seconds later, in a gravel parking lot, fully going down on her. I believe it was the pain of my knees scraping against the gravel that made me come to my senses, or maybe it was the fact that I was having sex with a woman for the first time in my life. Once I figured out what I was attempting to do, I panicked, jumped up, and started to yell whatever came into my brain.

"Oh my God! Uh. Uh. I'm not gay!"

I was furiously picking the pieces of gravel out of my knees. My legs and hands were scraped, practically bloody, and I was in full panic mode.

Gabe calmly got to her feet and dusted off her butt.

"Here, let me help you—"

"We've been gone too long!" I screamed. "People are gonna notice!" *Or maybe the volume of my yelling will draw their attention.*

"It's fine, Sophie. Who cares?"

"I care! People are gonna think I'm gay—which I'm not!" Literally. Wipes. Mouth.

I wish I could go back in time to this moment and tell myself that it is not chill to tell a girl—whom you'd ignored for weeks and then led into a parking lot, where you attempted to CPR-style resuscitate her vagina back to life—that you're not gay. I left Gabe behind in that parking lot. I ran back to the party, pretending I was just coming back from a smoke break. My heart raced, and my head pounded. I was paranoid. *Everyone knows. Everyone knows. Everyone knows* was running through my head in a panicked loop. I was as guilty as someone on a procedural who had just murdered someone. Or worse! *Law & Order: Special Homophobia Unit.* I tried to hide the scrapes and cuts—convinced that the logical jump anyone would make would be that I had just drunkenly had sex with a woman.

Just act normal! I told myself. Then I saw the IT guy across the room. I went over and stuck my tongue down his throat and initiated a very slobbery make out. Nothing says *I'm not a lesbian* like swapping spit with a boy in front of everyone.

Meanwhile, Gabe must have walked herself back in from the parking lot, because she stopped dead in her tracks. I knew what I was doing was wrong, but I didn't have the courage to stop, so I kept tying tongues until I saw out of the corner of my eye that she had walked away.

The next day, I went back to avoiding Gabe. The new kids arrived, and we counselors nursed our hangovers while trying to be decent human beings. It was all about the kids, after all! I was convinced that the only two people who knew about our parking-lot tryst were Gabe and me.

But this "program" was a camp, after all. Everyone knew.

It turned out that the gravel parking lot wasn't just a random gravel parking lot—it was the fraternity house's parking lot, just a few feet away from the party. I was outed.

That didn't stop me from being a major dick. When I saw Gabe, I ignored her. When I folded and started to talk to her again, I said, "We can talk as long as you know I'm not gay." I didn't want anyone to see us together—because then the rumors would be true. The noise of the uncertainty grew louder in my head, and I was taking an express train into my personal hell.

The problem was that, no matter what I did to distance myself, I could feel her all around me. Her force field had completely intertwined with mine, and I couldn't shake her energy, no matter how hard I begged whoever was upstairs. Certainly not God—He had failed me one too many times. After a few days of spiraling that felt like months, I invited her to my dorm room.

"Please don't tell anyone you're coming," I said as I barely left a crack in the door for her to walk on through.

"Okay, Sophie."

We sat on my bed in the dark.

"Do you want to turn the lights on?" she asked.

"No!"

"Are you scared the lights will show how gay you are?"

I felt way too sober for this. She took off her bra, and her boobs were *Venus de Milo* marble sculptures. Only the faintest light from the moon came in, but I could see them clearly. I'd only ever seen my high school friend Emma's boobs—but they had been like cheesecake bites on a plate that she'd brought out for her boyfriend. Instead, these boobs were intended for me. They were welcoming me. I wanted to press my face to them. I just wanted them. I'd never been so turned on in my life by just staring at someone's naked body. As she gingerly caressed my body like it was covered in oil—extra-virgin—I melted into the sheets. We were sliding around together like two amoebas. Every kiss felt like one thousand wondrous nights. Every touch felt like an electric shock to my core. With each deep breath, I was floating to the heavens.

At the same time, I felt so much shame. I was fresh off a disastrous relationship with a drug addict, my friends had turned me in like Judas, and I didn't want to give them another reason to think I was unhinged. I imagined the disgust of my sorority sisters, the explanation I'd have to give to my parents, and though I was a fan of the Key West Lesbians, I wanted only to be an ally. I thought that if I allowed myself to actually, ya know, have an orgasm, that would mean I was crossing the threshold into certified gaydom. After we'd rolled around in the bed for an hour, she got up, got dressed, and left.

We did this a handful of times.

Sometimes I'd sleep with the IT guy immediately after Gabe had wrung me out like a sponge, to try to fuck the gay away. I'm sure he knew something was up—the whole camp knew (again, I wore Bieber's favorite shoes that only teenage boys and pop stars wore)—and was equally confused.

My stomach was in knots all the time, and I was beginning to wonder if I had a cr . . . cru . . . crush.

I was entering lesbian puberty.

When you start down the long path toward realizing you're gay, it's like going through Puberty 2.0. No one can prepare you for it. I was still under the impression that if I hadn't realized I was gay when I exclusively wore cargo shorts, or in my teens making out with Emma, or when I considered purchasing a room to be alone with Bambi, then I wasn't gay! You can't go through puberty in your twenties, right? It's inconceivable!

And yet, I couldn't sleep. I was horny twenty-four seven. It was like a light switch had been turned on, and there was no way of turning it off again. Tootie was back, dammit, only this time it was Tootie 2.0.

Gabe had gone from one shitty ex-girlfriend to a new shitty hookup. I'd invite her to go skinny-dipping with other staff members, only to ignore her the entire time. We'd sext each other in staff meetings, but once it got hot and heavy, I'd hit her with, "I'm not gay." I'd say her name on the quad only to turn around and walk in the opposite direction. Gabe took it all in stride. She was incredibly patient with me and treated me like a delicate little bird who'd been wounded. I wouldn't have been surprised if she left this baby bird in a shoebox to die, but she didn't.

Weeks went by, and Gabe and I circled each other. It was a cat-and-mouse game, and it exhausted us both. In the end, I just wanted to go home like a sad kid who had a bad time at camp.

The summer was drawing to a close, and I had signed up to stay after the session was over to help pack up the classrooms. Gabe decided to hang back too. I wish I could say that I took that time to get my shit together and that we spent the next few weeks packing up camp by day and sharing my dorm room bed by night. Unfortunately, I came down with the flu and ended up leaving the day the program ended. Gabe went back to Mount Holyoke, and I went back to Kansas City.

Oh—and Stewart, I was late a lot because I was busy trying to come to terms with my sexuality, so thank you for understanding!

My mom was furious upon my return because she was still hung up on the Mitchell debacle, even though—unbeknownst to her—I was now hung up on Gabe. She gave me one last chance to get a college degree. She told me that she was moving back to Mississippi to get away from Buck and their failing marriage, to start a new job, and to start a new life of her own.

"I'm going to be teachin' at the University of Southern Mississippi. I think they might have a BFA program—but I really don't care! All I know is you better not flunk out again." Turns out, if you do coke every single night, you won't show up to class—and even when you do, the teacher will notice you're strung out. "And you're gonna live with me—I sure ain't paying for another apartment."

I was on thin fucking ice.

Turns out again, they did have a BFA program. I really needed to do well in school this time, or I'd either become a coke dealer with a face tattoo or have to look for a new family. I moved to Hattiesburg, Mississippi, with my mom and started college for the third and final time. Driving down the highway in my Chevy Buick, windows rolled down, blasting "Boyfriend" (Bieber again), I was excited for a new chapter. In high school, I was the obsessive webcam girl, at Alabama I was the girl who slept with people to get ahead, and this summer, I was a childish prick! But new university! New me! That lesbian hookup was just a summer fling, and those feelings were history, baby! I'd left them behind in Boston and was ready to go back to my ordinary, extremely hetero life.

I had just gotten settled at school when some new classmates and I went to a local pub. A woman walked in. She was the lezziest lesbian I had ever seen: greasy hair, chipped nail polish, huge glasses, a beanie drooped over her bleached-blonde hair, and a ring of keys attached to her black Hot Topic belt. "Dream Weaver" instantly started playing in my head. A spotlight seemed to follow her movement. I watched her hug every single patron and the bartender. It was déjà vu all over again, and I had to face the music that I—well, I had a lot to figure out.

I know it's shocking, but Gabe and I are still friends. Trust me—I don't understand how either. But they were the catalyst into my dykedom, and we've felt connected ever since. That summer changed my life—and despite my being a shithead, was validating and reforming for them too. Just like I've evolved from the girl who, after going down on a queer person, shouted "I'M NOT GAY" over my shoulder while running in the opposite direction, Gabe has also gone on their own journey. Gabe recently came out as trans. When we discussed their journey on the phone, I literally teared up and told them, "I'm crying while looking at my neon pothos," at which we laughed and said in unison, "So gay." Also, Gabe wants everyone to know, "you're welcome" for making me gay.

Chapter Twenty-Two

PUBERTY, PART II: THE SECOND COMING

Seeing that mysterious woman at the bar brought questions about my sexuality back like Jason in a horror film—unwanted yet inescapable.

I started having dreams about the mysterious woman. *Who is she?* My nipples had become rock-hard daggers, so I started wearing extra-padded sports bras to cover up my weapons. It didn't help. I looked like I had cones on my breasts. Even the smell of a woman's hair made me want to suck it all up like a vacuum. I was miserable. I was like a lost cat just wanting someone to take her in and tell her everything was going to be okay.

All I could think was, *WHAT DID GABE DO TO ME?* I'd curse Gabe's name to the gods.

My mom had prepared me beautifully for my OG puberty. The growing pains. The frank discussions about periods. The birthing videos. I think the *Spice World* birthing scene was my favorite part, if I'm being honest. But no one prepared me for Lesbian Puberty, a.k.a. Unwanted Puberty, a.k.a. The Second Coming.

Again, we think of teenage boys as disgusting human beings who'd be better off left in their rooms until they turn twenty-five. I can confirm that a lesbian in Puberty 2.0 is even more intense. In fact, multiply that shit by one hundred. That is lesbian puberty. It's sticky. It's wet. It's tiring. And it's hell. Or at least mine was.

Lesbian puberty is baffling and hard to navigate if you're not even sure that you're gay. I realized that I needed to talk to someone, but I wasn't sure who could help me, who I could trust. The best idea I had was to consult someone who had been at the bar when the mystery woman had arrived. A few days after the encounter and the onset of my deranged state, I decided to message my friend Marcos with what I thought was a discreet text.

Marcos! It's Sophie. Had fun a few nights ago.

Me too! Got a little drunk near the end, Marcos responded.

Oh no, I thought. *Did I get drunk and make a fool of myself in front of the girl I'm not-so-sure-if-I'm-crushing-on-because-I-can't-just-admit-it-yet?*

He texted again, *Hope I didn't do anything too weird!*

Oh, thank God. It wasn't me he was referring to.

I stared at his two texts, contemplating if I should hit the "Eject" button on my investigation. I could act like I meant to text another Marcos and bury myself under my floorboards, never to be seen or heard from again. I kept staring at the phone.

What's up, Sophie?

Nothing! Making sure you got home all right. Lies! By the way, I continued. *Who was that girl you were with?*

Which one? Mila? Why?

Mila . . . Her name is . . . Mila.

No reason. Thought she was cool.

A moment passed with no response from Marcos.

What's her deal? I wrote.

She's a lesbian. Ha-ha! Why?

HA-HA! WHY?

I shut off my phone, wanting to die; pulled the covers over my head; and tried to fall asleep. Except that I couldn't go to sleep. I lay in my bed thinking of Mila. I hadn't even spoken to her yet and was imagining the kids we'd have, trying to convince her to take a road trip in the Tacoma truck I imagined she owned all the way up to New York City with me.

Total. Lesbian. Behavior.

I closed my eyes and relived my kiss with Gabe. Her long hair swishing around, her beautiful vampire teeth. I tried kissing the air. It took only ten seconds of envisioning her and I felt the same peeing sensation I'd felt years before. *Yep, I either wet the bed or—* I wanted to kiss a girl again so desperately. *I could visit Gabe.* Fat chance. I would have to apologize for the whole "I'm not gay!" thing.

Like an unwanted blast from the past, Tootie 2.0 reemerged a changed woman and said, "Sup, dude. You smoke?"

NOOOOOOOOOO! It was starting again.

I opened up my computer, closed the blinds, lit a candle (this time a prayer candle with Biggie on it), and went on YouTube.

I typed in an obvious choice—"lesbian make out"—and hit "Enter."

I scrolled to a thumbnail that had two women grabbing each other's butts on a bed. Seemed appropriate and a great way to ease into things. The video started out with potential. Svetlana and Olga played with each other's hair. Laughing. Giggling. And if it weren't for the microscopic bodies and the Russian accents, it was practically Gabe and me. But then it took a dark turn. They leaned in to kiss but missed each other's mouths and started kissing their eyeballs. And then wiggled their tongues at each other like snakes. They scraped their long, ten-inch nails alongside each other's cheeks and purred like leopards, just before they got to the climax of the scene—which was slapping each other's butts.

"He-he-he-he! Oh, Svetlana! Play it like a timpani, he-he-he!"

I was offended. I'd expected it'd be two cute girls, makin' out in a car or something. Tootie 2.0 shook her head and said, "Yeah, bro. That search was never gonna work." *Well, we can't all be as smart as you, Tootie 2.0!* Instead, I had stumbled across "lesbian porn." "Should never see the light of day" porn. "Made for and by men" porn. "I Hate This" Porn.

Simply typing in "lesbians kissing" did not return the results I wanted. It returned the results intended for a middle-aged man who still used Axe body spray, wore sweatpants with stains, and took women on a date to Golden Corral.

I decided I had to be smarter with my word choice. I googled: "real live lesbians." The results were even worse. Then it hit me like a drag queen's beaded purse on the dance floor. When I was in high school, I had watched a lot of teenage soaps like *Beverly Hills, 90210* and *Gossip Girl.* I suddenly remembered a pivotal scene from a magical show called *The O.C.* with Mischa Barton and Olivia Wilde. Cue "California" by Phantom Planet. Mila looked just like Olivia Wilde! I typed in the words "Olivia Wilde" into the search engine and hit "Enter"—but not before my mom knocked on my door.

"Liz? You in there?"

I slammed my laptop shut, inadvertently pinching my finger. I stifled a yelp and managed to get out an "uh-huh."

"I'm gonna take a nap," she called through the door.

"Okay, sounds good." I heard her lingering outside my door.

"Can I come in?"

"I'm also trying to take a nap," I said. My mom loved naps—she'd respect me wanting to take one too.

"Okay, honey. Sorry to bother you."

When I was sure she had gone, I quietly reopened the computer and kissed my red, swollen index finger. Then I got out of bed to find something else I needed: headphones.

I plugged in the headphones. A few videos had come up, but not the one I wanted. I switched to IMDb and searched "Olivia Wilde," scrolled through her list of credits, and found her *O.C.* character name: Alex. Confetti time! I went back to YouTube, and there it was: "Marissa and Alex Kiss 2X12." California, here I cum.

EXT. BEACH—NIGHT

Marissa and Alex sit on a blanket and stare at the ocean. An emo beach band à la Ryan Cabrera plays in the background. They stare at the tide as it inches closer. Alex looks at Marissa longingly.

ALEX

The tide just turned.

Alex looks at Marissa, leans in, and kisses her with intense passion.

They kissed as if to symbolize that the tide turning was Marissa turning full fucking lez. At this point, I was so horny that I managed to get Tootie 2.0 baked before the forty-eight-second clip ended—injured index finger lifted to help the circulation and all.

The beauty of YouTube is, once you finish one clip, another plays instantly. Pandora's lesbian box had officially been opened. I discovered "Callie and Arizona" from *Grey's Anatomy*. And then "Callie and Erica" and then "Callie and Penny." And that led me to *Imagine Me & You* and Lena Headey and Piper

Perabo rolling around (too quickly for my taste) in the flower bed, which led me to *But I'm a Cheerleader*, where Natasha Lyonne and Clea DuVall hooked up at conversion therapy camp. And then finally, to Gillian Anderson as Scully slamming a door. My eyes glazed over as I went through a Rolodex of lesbian film and television—my new porn. *Orange Is the New Black.* Idina Menzel and Tracie Thoms singing "Take Me or Leave Me." *Orange Is the New Black.* There was no stopping me. It would be a few weeks before I discovered lesbian vloggers.

Then I met Shane no last name needed—from *The L Word.* The entire world tilted on its axis. Shane is the epitome of androgyny. A modern-day Joan Jett but sad. A sad puppy Joan Jett. Who only smolders and has sex. I stumbled on a video titled, "The L Word Shane & Carmen." I had no idea who Carmen was, but she had a tattoo that wrapped around her body from her butt to her lower back and worked in a recording studio, which worked for me. The fifteen-minute staring contest between them was enough to satisfy my needs.[36] Then they traipsed throughout the house, bumping into things and kissing while a slow beat underscored their antics. The beat was accompanied by a woman whispering, "Shane, Shane, Shane," "Carmen, Carmen, Carmen." Very nineties and pre-ASMR. I watched one video on repeat for hours—and from then on, I was in a deep and very committed relationship with Shane from *The L Word,* which is ironic because she doesn't commit to anyone.

I'd go to class sore, my underwear spoiled from my all-day sordid affair. You'd think from my disheveled appearance and hair sticking in every direction, I was in a new and very steamy relationship. The truth is that I was in a relationship with myself, and I was in the honeymoon phase.

The chronic masturbator *extraordinaire* was back again.

Months went by. I successfully finished *The L Word* and finished myself. My body had turned into putty. Tootie 2.0 was in the corner silently swaying as she hotboxed my room.

My mom took me out to lunch one afternoon, and on our way home, we were singing at the top of our lungs to Adam Levine—a heartthrob to every suburban mom—when she suddenly turned the music down.

"Honey, when are you gonna stop diddlin' yourself to *The L Word* and get yourself a *real* woman?"

---

[36] Lesbians love long gazing, as waves lash against a sea cliff beneath their feet.

I was horrified. Actually, *horrified* doesn't begin to capture how much I wanted to die. I could hear Adam Levine faintly crooning, "Payphone . . ." in the background.

I was surprised. I hadn't even tattled on myself this time. *How does she know?*

"What are you talking about?" I snapped.

"Come on, honey. You've been holed up in that room for months." There was a tenderness to her voice that was tinged with concern.

Does the house smell? I wondered, panicked. *Is this like the time I shaved my pubes in the guest shower at my dad's house, and my dad sternly said that I needed to start picking up after myself?*

"I'm working on it," I mumbled. It's kind of hard to say I was *"working on it"* when the only thing I was working on was my relationship with Tootie 2.0—but I had nothing else to say. We sat silently, with the exception of Adam Levine's wails, for the rest of the ride home.

She knew. She knew that I was potentially, probably . . . somewhat bi? Bi! Of course! Maybe I was bi. Either way, my mom knew. I was definitely not straight, and in a car to the tune of Adam Levine's "Payphone" was how I was outed by my mother.

Marcos had sent me Mila's number, and she'd agreed to meet with me at the college café. The café reeked of patchouli and microwave lentil curry, and the owner played the White Stripes on repeat. I sat clutching my coffee cup. Checking my phone again. Putting it into the other pocket. Wiping my palms on my legs. Staring at the door. I was fiddling with the coffee cup sleeve, pretending to be hella invested in its position on the cup, when I heard the door ping open. The White Stripes's "Ball and Biscuit" started to play as Mila walked in. She came over and sat down across from me. The electricity of that moment made me feel like stealing a 1969 Dodge Charger Daytona and driving it off the top of the Tokyo Skytree at 150 miles per hour.

"Hi, Mila," I said.

"Hey, sorry I'm a little late. My car wouldn't start, so I had to borrow the truck." I spotted a small two-seater pickup through the window. Her beanie was pulled down over her ears, and I noticed she had tattoos etched in random places. Some, if not most of them, looked unfinished. Those unfinished tattoos were the most attractive thing I had ever seen.

"Thanks for meeting me," I said.

"No problem!" she said. Then she very politely gave me that "you brought me here, so please speak" look.

"I guess I'll start," I croaked. "Um. I heard you might be gay."

And I think I might be gay?

"Um. A *lesbian*," I continued. "Heh. You know. I guess *you* don't know, but I've been having these feelings . . . not feelings exactly," I said, faltering, "but I hooked up—with a girl, I think? I mean, I did. Definitely." And then the word vomit, all in a rush. "Yeah. I hooked up with a girl, and I can't stop thinking about other girls, and I don't understand what's going on. And I'm not sure why this is happening so late in my life? I heard you might be gay."

Mila laughed. I couldn't believe I had just unloaded that onto a stranger, a woman whose tattoos I was aching to trace with my tongue. *Maybe*, if I played my cards right.

"I see," she said. "And I am."

The needle caught in the groove, and Jack White's voice skipped in time with my heart.

"I just thought you were supposed to figure it out in middle school—or high school, even? But *now*? I'm twenty-one!"

She chuckled. "As a *twenty-seven-year-old*, I have to say, twenty-one is not that old . . . but there's no timetable. A lot of gay women discover it later in life."

Though I didn't know it at the time, there's never been a truer statement. *Late-blooming lesbians*, they're called. Sometimes they don't realize until after being married to men. Wanda Sykes, my mom's best friend from college, my mom's other best friend from work. The list goes on.

And that was exactly what was happening to me. *Or is it, really?* I sat in the chair and scanned the coffee shop, wondering if other people could tell I might be gay. I tugged at my clothes. It was like I had been hit with a gay brick, one wrapped in flannel with REI sewn on the front. I remembered when a coworker had asked if I was a lesbian and how I'd thought she needed to be fired for coming up with the idea . . . My kid self proudly wearing Birkenstocks complete with my knock-around pair, an at-home pair, and a dress pair. And—*cue Mitski playing in the background*—my irrevocably and most definitely, completely over-the-top, could not bear to be a minute apart, intense friendships with girls throughout the years.

Nahhhh, those couldn't have been signs.

"You should come out with my girlfriend and me," she continued.

CLOSE THE GATES! LOCK THE DOORS! IT'S OVER. GIRLFRIEND? I THOUGHT MILA AND I WOULD DATE FOREVER.

That. Stung.

"Sure, I'd like that," I replied. I didn't like it, but I had no choice.

"We go out a lot, so I'll text you."

Great. Not only was it becoming clearer that I was gay, I had also fumbled the ball on the first lesbian I had laid eyes on post-Gabe. Shane, of course, wasn't able to reciprocate.

When it was time to go, Mila gave me a big hug. We walked out together and then she got into her *actual* Toyota Tacoma.

Chapter Twenty-Three

CONVERTING TO LESBIANISM

After giving one more guy a *Twilight*-caliber performance of head, during which he asked me point-blank if I was gay, I realized it was time to hang up the pursuit of *the perfect d*ck*. I did give it the good old college try. At three universities and twenty-six penises, thank you. But still. I was officially not going to be the one you wanted to marry. In fact, I was going to be the one your parents warned you about.

I converted to lesbianism. It became my religion.

The first task I needed to tackle now that I was a stone-cold butch was to cut my hair. I needed to cut it fast. No one was going to notice I was into women unless I had signifiers. Wearing a flannel shirt would have been easier—but I wanted a full transformation. And to be honest, straight women have been appropriating the flannel-shirt look for far too long, so I couldn't be certain it would work to my advantage.

I scheduled an appointment with my mother's hairstylist, Colleen. Colleen worked at Kitty's Bold Designs. The main hairstyles at that salon were "May I please speak to your manager?" and "I'm fifteen, and I'm in a beauty pageant."

I met with Colleen, whose dirty-blonde hair was cut into razor-sharp edges that framed her face with black roots splaying on top like a spider plant. Like if Rachel in *Friends* had loved punk-rock concerts, whiskey neat, and hated Ross. Colleen wore hoop earrings and washed-denim jeans that were embellished with rhinestones. She was a bedazzled lady who didn't know who she was, which was why she was the perfect person to help out an equally unknowledgeable person. We were kindred spirits. I plopped into the chair, and Colleen asked what I wanted.

"Please chop it off," I said and made a chopping motion in the direction of my extremely long hair.

Colleen asked me to repeat myself, and I said once more, "Please chop it off."

She asked me to show her exactly how short as she held the scissors to my collarbone. I raised her hand up higher, to just above my chin.

She lowered her hand.

I raised it once more. Even higher. Hoping the scissors would graze her.

"Are you sure?" she mumbled, like God would smite her.

"As God is my witness."

I watched her look around the room for backup. All the other women and their clients shook their heads.

"You're on your own, sister," a woman sitting under a hooded dryer said from behind a glossy magazine.

I'd had long hair for most of my life. My last haircut above my shoulders had been in second grade, and the less said about that the better. After that, I insisted on only ever getting one inch carefully *trimmed*. My hair was the only thing, looks-wise, that I felt I had going for me. It was my signature. From third grade until that moment at Kitty's, I'd scrutinize what the stylists were doing—nothing short of using a magnifying glass like Sherlock Holmes to make sure they didn't take off more than the one inch I had specifically requested. So it came as a surprise that Colleen wasn't into it. Aren't you into these types of thangs? Bold cuts? Kitty's BOLD Designs, my ass.

When she asked me one final time, I said, "If you don't chop off my hair, I'll do it myself, and yes, this is a Britney Spears quote." I didn't want to be rude to the woman, but I had to debut as a stud, and I needed to get this done—stat.

She put her hands up in surrender. She mentioned something about Samson's locks, and I smiled and reassured her that I would be okay, "but the ground might shake a little."

When people have hair down to their asses—which mine was—and want it cut short, the hairdresser usually puts the hair in a ponytail before they chop it off. But because my hair was so thick, "my girl" (as my mom would say) had to do more. She put my hair in tight *pigtails* and gave me a firm nod. I held my breath as she started to ~~cut~~ saw through the first. After a few slow and hard clamps, she held up the now-detached hair and placed it gingerly on the table in front of me.

The hair cried out, "Why would you do this to me?"

"For sex," I told it.

Colleen continued on. She clamped down hard, really put her back into it, and after a *snap* that almost knocked her off her feet, she then placed that one on the table too. I looked in the mirror in silent disbelief. My brave face must have disappeared because she croaked, "Oh, now, shit—don't tell me that you're already regrettin' it?"

"Nope," I said to mask my bewilderment.

I tried to tuck the remaining hair behind my ears, but it fell into my face again. *She's only just begun. That was just to chop it off, Soph.* In my best Scissor Sisters's voice I thought, *Fire up the straightener, throw on some mousse, and let's let this woman get to work!* Colleen went to town finessin' and stylin' my hair. The initial deed was done and so was her worry. She was singing to herself while doing little snips here and there and shaping it around my face. After she blow-dried my hair in record time, I looked in the mirror once more. What used to be a flowing mane of Kim K. realness now resembled the brunette version of Kelly Clarkson's *Thankful* album cover.

The woman with the magazine lowered it ever so slightly to get a glimpse, then quickly put it back to cover her face once more.

Jesus, take the wheel, 'cause this ain't it.

I wanted a *dyke* haircut. A *Shane* (from the beginning of the series) haircut. A "desperate for vertical smile" haircut. But in my mind, I couldn't just march into a southern salon and say, *Please give me the dykiest, leztastic, lezzified, "get me some sapphic loving" 'do.*

I ended up with Kitty's bold "May I please speak to your manager?" cut. I looked like an assistant at the local chamber of commerce. Even a bowl cut would have been better.

I managed to appear less gay than when I first sat down.

And my mom had been right in keeping me from cutting my hair off for so many years.

Despite the disaster at the salon, Operation: Sophie Becomes So Gay She's Stoned to Death was in full swing. I needed to piece together an ensemble that matched my new 'tude.

I'd blazed through *The L Word* and quickly found BBC Three's *Lip Service*. My relationship with Shane had been unhealthy, but I was ready to do things right. I moved on to Frankie, who had the same shaggy (but blonde) hair and a beautiful British accent. I binged, but at a much slower and more methodical pace.

I had assembled a few photos of my growing team of lesbian avengers: Shane, Frankie, and I went so far as to add Katy Perry's assistant, because I had discovered through Tumblr[37] that she was a lesbian.

I sneaked into my mom's room to see if she had a Carhartt jacket or something else butch I could put over my dainty elephant crop top. Mom had taken a job as a researcher, so she'd transitioned to working from home most days. While she'd been a Chico's devotee, at home she was always clad in loungewear, which was typically a Columbia men's Bahama shirt and scrubs from the nineties. I tried on a Bahama shirt.

It wasn't quite what I was looking for.

Combined with my "momager" haircut, I was slipping further from gay. I kept looking through Mom's clothes. Chico's, Talbots, black leggings. I struck out—until I saw the stained alpine flannel shirt that had belonged to Ex-Stepdad. I held it up in front of me and slouched with one hand in my pocket, visualizing an entire outfit until I realized that my mom would be pretty upset if I started wearing her ex-husband's shirt. I brought it into my own room so she wasn't tempted to set it ablaze.

I dug through the piles of clothes on my floor. Items that had once given me so much joy now struck me as horribly girlie. Items that I had purchased just a month before looked off and wrong. I threw them around the room in disgust. Clothes hanging off the lampshade, the back of the chair, the front of the TV. My room was in total chaos. I didn't have the time to give this wardrobe the Icelandic send-off, with a lit bow and arrow burning at the center, that I'd given my tomboy clothes.

---

[37] A blogging site that also served as porn for lesbians.

I stood there sweating, trying to think of the one thing that was universal in lesbianism.

It clicked.

I needed a beanie. (Cue the choir of singing angels.)

I already owned one that I had never worn. I had gotten it in New York because I was cold, but it was wool, black, and had pilling on it. I told myself that it was the best ticket to dykedom a girl could buy. I continued to tear apart my room, looking in every corner to see if I could find it. On my hands and knees, going through my closet, I remembered I'd dropped it and accidentally kicked it under the bed. I lay flat, staring at the dust, and—in the back corner—I saw a black ball. It was either a tiny demon that would kill me or my now most-prized possession. I reached out, praying nothing would bite me, and grabbed it. Unbitten, I got up, wiped off the dust, pulled the cap down over my haircut, and looked in the mirror.

At least it covered my hair.

With the beanie, something had changed. I felt closer to my goal. But I was still wearing my crop top, skinny jeans, and my David Yurman ring. A ring I'd begged for after I joined the sorority, and one my mom had gone to great lengths to procure.

But now, with the beanie on my head, I stared at the ring. I twisted the ring on my finger, back and forth.

The ring has to go.

I knew it in my heart. No raging-bull dyke would be caught dead in a sparkly David Yurman ring. No matter the sentimental value. I took it off and put it on the bedside table.

I turned to my nails. They were painted a deep, dark purple—which, I decided, was a fine color for a dyke. But I needed to look grungy. Mila looked grungy.

I started chipping away at the paint. The nail polish fell to the ground in tiny pieces. That would have to do until I could save up for my own unfinished tattoo.

I sized myself up like I was on *Project Runway*. "The hair—she could make it work, as long as she sews the beanie to her head. The nails—fine. But the overall look is a bit of a mess." I needed a unifying element. *Eyeliner.* I raced into the bathroom and peeked into my plastic Ziploc baggie . . . There was an eyeliner pencil covered in shimmery eye shadow. I drew a dark, thick line on my upper eyelid. Move over Avril Lavigne. Sk8er boi here.

I laced up my winter boots and prepared to debut my look. Despite the birds chirping and the Mississippi sun beaming down through my curtains, my impression was that lesbians dressed for winter 365 days of the year. It never dawned on me that most of my lesbian icons were just dressing for the New England winter. I practiced walking in a burly way down the hallway, the way I'd seen Frankie from *Lip Service* walk, like she was always carrying twelve duffel bags. If only I owned pants with a rise that hit lower than my navel. Unfortunately, unlike all the girls I wanted to dress like, I had curves. No matter, I was well underway.

In 2012, I'd traded in my MRS degree for my BFA in theater—my Bad Fucking Actor degree. Because my mom's voice kept ringing in my ears (*"This is your last fuckin' chance"*) and because she was my roommate, I kicked it into high gear. My first day in Hattiesburg, I walked into the theater building, made a beeline for the chair's office, and proclaimed, "I'd like to enroll in the BFA program—can we make this happen?"

He responded with, "I mean, can you sit down first?"

I sat.

Dr. Warrick was new to the theater department, too, and had barely unpacked his boxes before being accosted, an only-child move for sure. Little did he know that I would write a paper in his class about how Edward de Vere, seventeenth Earl of Oxford, was really Shakespeare—and thus this only-child move was definitely on brand for me.

"You're my adviser," I continued as he tried to find his computer.

"I am? Interesting. Sounds good to me."

A beat.

"What do you think about this space? It's obnoxious, right?" he asked me.

"Your office?" I looked around at the big glass window to his left and the yawning space between his desk and my seat. "You're the chair of the department. It *should* be obnoxious."

"Fair. Ahhh, here we go. Here's the course manual. Now, where's my computer?" He had found the paper guide tucked in between *Tartuffe* and a crumpled poster of the Clash.

"And here are my course requests," I said, handing him the sheet before he could grab a blank one. I had spent three years in college and had nothing to show for it, so I was not wasting any more time. And now yours truly was paying for college, so it changed my perspective.

"I googled that I needed Meisner, Intro to Acting, and Theater History," I told him.

He kept flipping through the manual.

"So what do you need me for exactly? If you are certain of the classes?" he asked.

"Can you get me into them?"

"I can try."

"You're the chair."

"Fair," he said with a tiny nod.

Dr. Warrick got me into all three classes so I could qualify to audition for the BFA program the following semester. Otherwise I wouldn't have been able to audition for an entire year, and I was not about to take seven years to graduate college. Six was plenty. I left his office feeling even more determined than I had been that morning.

Over the next weeks, the theater students told me that, every semester, the professors encouraged us to put on our own showcase. Putting on a showcase was scary. By casting yourself in the role of your choice, you could easily look like a narcissist. Like, if I said, *I'm going to play Hamlet*, it meant that I thought I was good enough to play Hamlet.[38] But I needed a meaty role that would give me decent stage time in order to get noticed.

Now that I had converted, I had become obsessed with lesbian theater. YouTube was just the beginning. Most of the time, I would skim through a play and skip to the make-out scenes. *In the Wake* by Lisa Kron and even *The Children's Hour* gave me some titillation. However, I noticed the running trend. Lesbian plays were always steeped in trauma. They were always about some eighteenth-century romance where the ingenue falls in love on her wedding day with a trouser-woman, who has somehow escaped marrying. They fall in love in two days' time (by a pond, no less), gaze into each other's eyes for hours until they explode—and then the husband finds out and has the trouser-woman shipped off to Australia.

I couldn't relate to that—couldn't see myself wandering about near the seaside with water thrashing against a cliff. Nothing in the sapphic dramatic oeuvre made sense to me until a professor handed me a play called *Stop Kiss*.

I'd quickly made a habit of grabbing coffee, lunch, or a spare moment with my professors. I'd eat whatever vegan food Robin Carr had in her mini fridge as a way to bond—"try the banana pudding . . . it's rawwww"—as she dragged her words, humming every syllable. I'd join Dr. Warrick anytime I caught him dining alone at the restaurant where I waited tables and order us both heavily discounted shots of Don Julio 1942. But the one who was my soul sister was Monica Hayes. She must've known I was at least the "+" in the LGBTQ+ community, because *Stop Kiss* was the first play she suggested I read. We were in her office, and I noticed she had gotten a haircut.

"The bangs really suit you, Monica."

"Thank you! I wasn't sure, but I think I'm pulling them off," she said with a smirk as her crystal-blue eyes dazzled. "Talk to me. You're thinking of doing a showcase?"

"Yes, but I haven't quite decided what I'll perform," I said. I was being coy, but I also literally had no clue. I just knew it needed to be about modern-day trouser-women.

---

[38] I'd rather not say if I think I'm good enough—"O, that this too, too solid flesh would melt, Thaw and resolve itself into a dew!"

"Have you heard of the play *Stop Kiss*? It's about a lesbian couple who—"

"No! But I would LOVE to hear about it."

She riffled through the books on her bookshelf and handed me her copy.

"Let the words take you away," she said as she stared out the window wistfully.

I started reading it the minute I walked out of her office, while I was still in the hall. It's about two women, Callie and Sara, who don't even know if they're gay but fall in love. They kiss for the first time in a park, and then one of the women is beaten because of it. Never mind the beatdown—there was a kiss!

Did I pick *Stop Kiss* to get into the BFA program? Yes. Did I also pick it because I hadn't kissed a girl since August 8, 2012, at two p.m., and I needed it to happen—even if it was pretend? Double yes.

I needed to find my Callie / scene partner / lover. It couldn't be just anyone. It had to be the best actress in my class. Choosing the best actress meant I had taste. I wanted to kiss a girl who was really talented and who would make me look good. Elizabeth McCoy was the coolest undergrad actress. Her nickname was Freckled Porcelain, but don't be fooled: she'd give you a beatdown with Shakespearean insults, leave you begging for mercy.

"Villain, I have done thy mother." Drops mic.

I approached her in the greenroom one afternoon.

"I found this great play, and I think you'd be perfect to star opposite me."

"What's it about?"

"Two women fall in love, but on the night they kiss, one of them is beaten in a hate crime."

"That's awful. Yet riveting. It's modern, yeah?"

"Yeah. At one point, I'm in a coma, on life support. It's *great* material."

"You know, that sounds great. I'm tired of playing the ingenue, especially in shows set in the 1800s. I'd like to show what I can do with something modern. Something with depth and maturity."

Look at us both being conniving . . .

"Let's give 'em a hell of a show," I said and high-fived her.

So the play was chosen. The actresses were cast. My friend Robert agreed to direct. He loved the play, and he wasn't creepy about it. We rehearsed everything but the kiss. No need to practice it. "You both know how to kiss, I'm assuming," Robert would say nonchalantly.

"Yep," Elizabeth said confidently.

"Chyeah, duh!" I tugged at my clothes. *This is really happening. Can I do this? Am I a* freak *for doing this?*

We invited everyone. The professors (naturally), Elizabeth's friends (I was new and didn't have a lot of friends yet), and my parents. I don't think a coming out is necessary after inviting your parents to watch you suck face onstage with a girl—but then again, I was an actor.

The play ends with the kiss, but Robert wanted to do an inverted version—where we start with the kiss and work our way backward. It's set in New York, and the last scene takes place just after the characters have left Henrietta Hudson.[39] We started with banter.

"Do you wait in line or on line?" Sara said.

"I wait in line, but also on line," Callie said.

Everyone was laughing at our lines, and the energy was palpable. It felt like everyone knew what was coming. And if they didn't, they were about to find out.

Sara said, "Okay, fine. You wait in line. I wait on." Then, just like that, Callie (a.k.a. Elizabeth) planted one on Sara (a.k.a. me).

We locked lips. The room stopped for a moment. I could feel the heat from the stage lights hit my face. I shut out the thought of my parents watching and just enjoyed it.

I pulled away.

"You just did that," I said.

"I did," Elizabeth responded.

It was so quiet that you could hear the audience members breathe. My heart was beating out of my chest.

"Nice," I said and laughed. The room laughed. We broke the tension. We tried to kiss again but bumped heads per the script. Finally, Elizabeth said, "Try again." We leaned in, kissed, and the lights went down. AND SCENE. I had kissed a girl in public. In front of my parents. I was alive.

I'd found some lesbian YouTube inspiration, transformed my look, and orchestrated an entire showcase just so I could kiss a woman. I was well on my way to mastering lesbianism. After the showcase, I managed to get my hands on a leather jacket, oversize sunglasses, and even started smoking! With the sorority

---

[39] A bar I am oh too familiar with now.

far behind me, I was even getting better at remembering not to cross my legs but always to manspread instead.

Mila made good on her promise and invited me to go out with her and her girlfriend. She had a friend she wanted to introduce me to. Mila, being twenty-eight, hung out predominantly with people who were in their late twenties or early thirties. Her friend Caroline was twenty-nine and was willing to give a younger woman a shot. We met up at a dive bar near the university called The End Is Near! It was a bar that had toilets for barstools and those toilets had many functions, including conveniently containing any barf at the end of the night.

And while I would discover that Hattiesburg was queer AF, just like the rest of the world, lesbian bars didn't exist, so a sports bar was the next best thing.

They looked up as I commenced my carrying-twelve-duffel-bags walk.

"There's the baby dyke!"[40] Mila and her friends shouted. I mouthed a *Shut up!* that screamed, *Please say it louder!* I wasn't embarrassed around them. I felt cool.

There weren't many words exchanged between Caroline and me. Just casual arm touching and heated foosball matches. Even though she was my hookup, that didn't stop me from playing like it was the world championship. I didn't spare her feelings. We went back to her house that same night. It was my first time since Gabe, and we couldn't get to the bed fast enough. I had moved past hiding behind women's legs and finally was ready to be in between them.

Mostly.

I had an erotic fantasy that Caroline, as the savvier lesbian, was going to tell me what to do as our bodies meshed together.

"You're really bad at this," she said with a grimace as I tried to kiss her body.

That was not the kind of "telling me what to do" I had envisioned.

The next day, out on her front porch, she leaned in to kiss me goodbye, and I backed away. Big mistake.

She furrowed her brow.

"I don't want people to know that . . ." I hesitated. I looked around at the empty street.

"What?" she asked coldly.

"That I'm gay?"

---

[40] Baby dyke. A newly awakened individual or an older butch who's extremely small!

This was a pretty close repetition of the move I'd used on Gabe—only this time it wasn't met with warm, gentle acceptance. It was met with harshness and disappointment.

I stood there on Caroline's porch and looked at her. Really looked at her. She was fully present in her body. She wasn't confused about what had happened in the bedroom—except maybe my attempt at *circular* tongue movement. And she certainly didn't have any time for my confused bullshit.

"I'd like to see you again," I quickly said to lighten the mood.

"Then you're going to have to kiss me in public."

I thought about it for a moment. That felt like a big price to pay. I tried to give her baby-dyke eyes, like, *Come on . . . I'm just a little deer. I'm still learning* . . . I leaned in and kissed her while looking over her shoulder, which she noticed and asked, "What is your problem?"

From then on, Caroline pretty much hated me—and yet, she continued to hang out with me. She'd invite me to her place but tell me I was bad at sex, and we'd get into stupid, drunken arguments.

"I love you," I'd say.

"What the fuck is wrong with you!"

One night, we were at The End Is Near! and she sat next to me at the bar, just barely putting up with me. Her eyes wandered. I was a few shots in when I said, "I want a tattoo."

She scoffed. "Okay? So get one."

"I want one right now."

I had known for a while that I wanted a tattoo. And all the dykes had them.

Caroline killed her beer and got up from the bar. "Let's go, then." We sat in her car, and I googled tattoo parlors.

We found the only tattoo parlor open on a Sunday at two a.m. in Hattiesburg. We walked inside. It was exactly how you'd think it would be. Dingy, with an old, salty dog sitting by himself, smoking a cigarette, and watching reruns of *WrestleMania*.

"What can I help you with?" he asked while "Argh" and "Give it to me!" rang out in the background.

"I'd like to get a tattoo," I said as Caroline perused the design books.

"I know. What tattoo do you want?" the old man grumpily asked.

Two a.m. clientele meant one of two things, annoying or drunk, and I was both.

I drew out the design and handed it to him. He looked it over and said that it'd cost sixty dollars. "She can come with you into the back, if you want," he added. I looked at Caroline as he and I headed back, and she followed. Caroline held my arm as the man scribbled—and I mean *scribbled*—onto my wrist. My lesbian initiation was complete.

The next morning, I woke up with a headache, rolled over, and noticed the bandage on my wrist. I unwrapped the bandage and saw what was intended to be a cursive tattoo: *Believe*.

Did I pick this because Justin Bieber's album had just come out? I plead the fifth.

Caroline and I ended things a week later.

Two weeks later, I got another tattoo. It upstaged the previous one. It was misspelled. I asked for the Dumbledore quote on my side, and what I got was: "Happiness can be found in the darkest of times, if one rembers to turn on the light."

Four months later, I got into the BFA program.

How to Be a Lesbian, or
The Guide to Being a Dyke, Abridged!

These are real things I was told by a drag king and have NOT been embellished.

1. Smoking is the only way you'll pick up chicks. Develop the habit, and fast. Strike up a convo with the strike of a match! Feel free to hunch over, spread out like a man, and act like you have grit.

2. Don't be concerned when you start to feel undying affection for Rachel Weisz. The spit-in-mouth scene is all you need to know. I mean, what will she do next?

3. GABs, a.k.a. Gay-Ass Bitches, must balance a level of success with trips to Fire Island, Provincetown, etc. If you aren't having fun, then you will be questioned by the group.

4. Wear big headphones on public transportation and bob your head like you know good music. People respect that shit. If a girl says, "Hey," take a few extra beats before looking up to make it seem like you didn't hear her.

5. Don't be afraid to hook up with your entire friend group. That's just the way of lesbian life, and no one will judge you (except maybe your ex, who's sleeping with your other ex).

6. Be mindful of LANE. LANE is the Woker-than-Thou Dyke, is always around, and can, at any time, expound on why what you're doing is showing your internalized homophobia that you weren't even aware you had because you're just trying to figure it out.

7.   Wet hair is hot. Have you seen Kristen Stewart? So are undercuts, shaved heads, and well, really, any girl's hair is hot.

8.   Respect your first gay den mother, a.k.a. lesbian spirit guide. That's Girl Code 101. They gave you your gay card, and they can take your gay card away. Don't be a dick. For a concrete example of how to be a dick, see Chapter Twenty-Five.

9.   It's okay to shack up at a hookup's place. In fact, move in right away.

10. Be prepared to spend long nights staring into your girlfriend's eyes and crying about the number one thing lesbians hold dearest: communicating.

11. Your ex might sleep on your couch for a while. This is normal.

12. Get really good at pool.

13. Never let someone call your girlfriend your "sister." If they do, say, "Yes, she's my sister," kiss her on the mouth (maybe with tongue), and then ask, "Any questions?"

14. Don't glom on to the first person who's nice to you in a bar. It never works out. No one likes anyone who's desperate.

15. Purchase nail clippers. We shouldn't have to explain why.

Chapter Twenty-Four

CHRISTIAN MINGLE

While I was getting my acting BFA, Mom figured I was back on track and moved to Alabama for a new job, and I stayed in the house with roommates under the age of fifty-five. I also landed a boutique talent agent from the New Orleans circuit who'd send me out every few months. Things were looking up. I'd drive two hours for two-minute auditions, trek back for another two hours, only to find out I had not booked it the moment I pulled into the driveway, grinning because I was in the biz regardless. The big time.

My first agent was a real Estelle Leonard type who would tell me that theater acting was a waste of my time and hers. And that I was wasting my time going to class.

"You'll never make it in this town if you pull some theater shit."

She knows we're in New Orleans, right?

"Gotcha, Angelique," I said as I packed away my playbills on my bookshelf, not wanting "Spider-Man: Turn Off the Dark" to distract me.

My first audition was for a commercial for Christian Mingle, the Christian internet dating app, and Angelique told me that it would be improvised.

"Just be you—except none of that Arthur Miller shit."

"Yes, no Arthur Miller shit."

She'd never seen me perform, so she had nothing to go by, but I knew better than to pull the "theater shit" because I had a hunch that Angelique had ~~spies~~ other clients who'd tattle on me.

Christian Mingle? Pshhh. Talk about a cakewalk! I was good with the Christians. According to Grand Oaks Baptist Assembly, I was still saved. There was no proof to the contrary. Anyway, I was an actor! It was my job to play different characters. #GodFreak

The day of the audition, I drove the 112 miles, pulled up to the casting office, and walked inside. There were about five actors waiting in a small room with a sign-up table at the front. The door on the other side of the room had a sign that said, QUIET PLEASE: CASTING IN PROGRESS.

A casting assistant greeted me as I approached the sign-up table.

"Hello. Sign your name next to your time slot and wait for it to be called. We're bringing you in pairs," she said and went inside.

Dammit, pairs?

I didn't like having to audition with another person. I was and am a very Nervous Nellie. I'd work myself up for about a week before any audition, barely sleeping and having a bout of IBS, GERD, and overactive bladder combined. My acting coaches have told me that eventually the stage fright and audition jitters will cease. That has never been the case. I've now done hundreds of auditions and countless shows onstage, and the anxiety before takeoff has never gone away. However, despite the amount of stress I put my body through, there's always a soft landing, and I walk away feeling like I've accomplished what I set out to do, happy until the next audition hits my inbox. The one time I wasn't nervous, I botched the audition. Literally forgot my words while the accompanist played the note over and over again to a full theater of casting directors. Ever since, I've deemed my nuclear anxiety a good thing.

After I signed my name, I put my game face on. Despite my insides imploding, I was going to act like it was a wonderful opportunity to work alongside a fellow actor. *Be malleable.*

I set down the pen, turned, smiled at the room, unsure of who would be joining me, and sat down like a Victorian lady, legs crossed at the ankle. After about a five-minute wait, they called my name and the name of another actor, Shonda, and we sauntered in to see three overtly cheery personalities sitting behind a large table. They grinned and made direct eye contact with both me and Shonda.

"Hi, Sophie! Hi, Shonda!"

I smiled, scanned the room, and said, "Hi," in a way that said, *I'm approachable, castable, and easy to work with.* That's when I noticed the woman behind the camera taping the audition. She had a boyish frame, messy short hair, and her long, buttoned-down shirt hung over her body. Androgynous and noncommittal and a photographer—like the love of my life, Shane. My heart started racing.

"Okay, girls, so we're gonna ask you a few questions, and we want you to just say whatever comes to mind," the male casting director said. His sweater vest and round glasses screamed, *I know talent!*

"Sophie, we'll start with you."

"Awesome, sounds great," I said again in a casual tone that said I was *approachable, castable, and easy to work with.*

"So, like, who's your crush?" the woman casting director asked as if we'd spent the night before sharing a bottle of red wine while playing Fuck, Marry, Kill. I froze. Then laughed. The casting team laughed. I glanced at the Shane look-alike. And then back to the less-smiling table. And then back to Shane. Their smiles were fading. I had to make a decision quick.

Maybe I can say Jake Gyllenhaal. No. Gross. Absolutely not. I don't think he's hot IMHO, and I cannot tell a lie! Chris Evans? Even worse. Acting has to be rooted in the emotional truth, according to Stanislavski.

Alas, actor though I might have been, I was still very deep into lesbian puberty, and puberty was about to win the fight against my better judgment. I made drop-dead eye contact with Shane, and—before I could stop myself—I said in Darth Vader slow motion, "Shane from *The L Word.*"

The slow motion continued. I laughed long and hard and deep, like I had really been approachable, castable, and easy to work with. Shonda's eyes slowly grew large, and she microscopically cocked her head back like, *Bitch, are you crazy? You know this is* Christian *Mingle, right?*

My eyes said, *Ha-ha-ha-ha, I know, but we're all inclusive because gay rights are human rights! Episcopalians have a gay archbishop!*

The casting team shuffled their papers and looked down. One cleared their throat. The other scratched his head. Shane kept her little head behind the camera, as was her job.

"And you, Shonda?" the casting woman slowly asked. "Who's your crush?"

Shonda responded with, "Alex Trebek!"

Immediately, the slow motion stopped. The casting office and reality were back. They were putty in her hands.

"Really? Ha! He's so old!" the woman said.

"Yes, but I think older men are sexy. What can I say? I'm no ageist."

"I LOVE ALEX TOO!" the woman said, banging the table.

I tried to smile, but I knew I had blown it big-time. *Know your fucking audience, Sophie.* I walked out with my tail between my legs, got into the car, and drove the two hours in silence out of sheer self-punishment. I replayed the scene over and over in my head, in sets of three no less, while holding my breath.

"How'd it go?" Angelique asked.

"Fine! I think it's a warm-up for the next one, though."

"I hate those biblical fucks anyway."

Hitting on photographers wasn't exactly working out. I needed to change course or I was gonna be single forever. I didn't think chasing after an MRS degree was a problem anymore now that I was a lesbian. But maybe I needed to hold back during a casting session.

I still didn't know what I was doing in the lady department. After Caroline, I dated a grad school student for a few weeks, but I didn't feel the spark. She accompanied me to my Halloween party, and we dressed as Tricia and Nicky from *Orange Is the New Black*. I loved our couples costume, but that was about it. She was way too into plants. Not in the normal, "decorating the apartment with ferns" way lesbians are into plants. She was passionately interested in morphology—the study of the evolution and development of plant leaves, roots, and stems. I mean, give me a fucking break.

Then there were the countless girls who I wished were gay but who I'd discover were straight after a couple of months flirt-texting. All those years in the South hadn't exactly honed my gaydar. I longed for a relationship. One night while celebrating the opening of *Top Girls* by Caryl Churchill at the local pub, I spotted a group of sporty lesbians hanging out at a nearby booth. I kept making eye contact with one of them. As the night wound down and my castmates all headed home, my friend Hope said, "You coming, Soph? Last chance to ride with me, or you're on your own."

"I think I'm gonna hang back."

She deadpanned, "You're so weird," and left. I approached the sporty lesbians, full of confidence. A very butchy woman invited me to sit at their table. The butch had just broken up with her ex, and I spent the next hour downing shots, roughhousing with them, and arm wrestling. The next thing I knew, I woke up in an unfamiliar bed the following morning. I looked over and saw the butch woman's bleach-blonde fade on the pillow next to me. I officially had been Top Girled.

I shimmied out of the bed, very confused, and walked around the strange house. A dog barked as I entered the living room.

"Shhhh! Please keep your voice down, sir, I'm begging you," I whispered. I never understood how to talk to dogs.

As I looked around the room, I tried to piece together the night. *Where the fuck am I? And how did I . . . ? Oh yes . . . did we do Jameson shots? And I remember some car ride? And the make-out session standing with our heads out of the roof of the SUV on the highway?* I walked into the kitchen, and there was another woman I didn't recognize making breakfast. I tried to sneak away, but the floorboard creaked.

"Just in time, Sophie!" she said.

"Hi. I'm so sorry—I didn't mean to bother you."

"No! Sit—I'm almost done with breakfast, and everyone else is passed out. Someone needs to eat this feast."

I sat down at the round kitchen table. *Who is this person?*

"Have fun last night?" she asked.

"Yes? Seems like it . . ." I looked toward the bedroom.

"Glad I could pick you guys up. No one was in any condition to drive. Here, eat up." She offered me a huge stack of pancakes. "I'm Blair," she added while I put the entire stack into my mouth. She had frizzy ginger hair that looked like Ms. Frizzle's from *The Magic School Bus*, and it seemed like things could get stuck in there.

"Really nice to meet you—or, I guess, see you again . . . ," I said through bites. We both laughed. After I downed the pancakes, drank a shit ton of water, and mainlined Gatorade, Blair drove me home.

"Sorry to put you out. This is ungodly nice of you."

"Dude, I really don't mind! Anytime!"

I held on to my head and tried to smile graciously and not throw up.

"So what's your story, Sophie? Where are you from?"

"Ha-ha, that's complicated," I said. *Okay . . . sketchy answer . . .* "But I go to college in town. I'm a theater major." I waited for her to make fun of me.

"Shut the front door! Girl! I work at the Alabama Shakespeare Festival during the summer!"

"You shut the front door, girl! I've never seen a show there, but I've always wanted to."

"Wait—if you're in theater, then you must know Amelia Rose?" she gossiped.

"I mean, kind of . . ." Amelia Rose sucked, but I didn't want to bash her in front of my new best friend.

"God, I hate that bitch," she snapped.

"I'm so fucking glad you said that, because I also hate that bitch."

Amelia Rose was a theater minor but was always singing. Always. Like, we get it.

As Blair pulled up to my house, I stayed for a second. I didn't really want to get out. My roommates were straight, and I was having the best gay-ass time I had had since the lesbian fairy ignited Tootie 2.0.

"I like you, Sophie. You should hang out with us more. Come over for a football game."

"Hell yeah! Roll Tide!"

"Get the fuck out of my car! GEAUX Tigers! I can't believe I just became friends with a Bama fan," she added with a smile. "Don't fuck this up, Bama." She drove away and waved as she turned the corner.

Blair became my den mother. My lesbian spirit guide. The blonde butch was nice, but her nicest act was staying asleep and connecting me to Blair, who I hung out with constantly. Not to mention, the butch had already gotten back together with her ex. I'd drive over to Blair's house, where she'd cook me meals and we'd chat about all things gay while her redneck girlfriend grumpily watched duck hunting. Blair and I would go into their bedroom and watch her *Gilmore Girls* DVD box sets. She'd invite me over for crawfish boils during the LSU games, just so long as I didn't show up in crimson or so much as *think* the words *Roll Tide*.

I, of course, did both.

I juggled hanging out with my theater friends and scooting over to Blair's. It worked out in my favor because, most of the time, my theater friends went to bed early to be fresh for class the next day, and I'd head over to Blair's. For once I was able to juggle having fun and having a good GPA. Probably because I was a lesbian.

"You wanna go out?" I'd ask Hope at the end of the day.

"Sophie, are you kidding me? We have Suzuki class tomorrow."

Suzuki was a sweaty, cruel acting technique where you were supposed to let out your animalistic side. We'd do the "Tomorrow" speech from *Macbeth* as we held . . . you guessed it . . . six inches and our teacher slapped a bamboo stick on the ground to make us do a crunch and then back into the workout that has followed me my entire life—Six Inches. Hangovers did not mix well with physical torture, although I successfully prevailed.

One night, Blair mentioned that her friend Rylee was in town. I told Blair I'd come through after rehearsal. When I arrived at her house, I spotted Rylee sipping on a beer with her other hand in her pocket. She had chin-length black hair, oval glasses, and a soft yet tough demeanor. She wore an Arctic Monkeys tank top and a beanie that covered most of her hair. She kept razzing Blair, who I'd never seen keel over like that before.

"Really, Blair, you're gonna get another dog? So you can be the only one to take care of it?"

"I don't know. I guess not. Shut up, Rylee!" she'd say as if she wanted her to keep talking.

Blair always shut down her girlfriend, Cris—not that Cris often tried to speak. But not Rylee. We were halfway through watching *Summer Heights High* when Rylee got up and grabbed a cigarette from her back pocket.

"I'll join ya," I said.

Blair waved us off. "Love that y'all are killing yourselves!" she shouted.

I followed Rylee, who lit my cigarette when we were outside. I had mysteriously lost my lighter.

"So, what—are you a theater geek? Blair tells me you guys bond over . . . musicals."

"I mean, yeah. What's it to you?"

"It's not," she said. She kept sucking in her cigarette with one hand stuffed in her pocket like it was glued there.

I scanned her body. Clarks boots. Hunched over like she was carrying twelve duffel bags. Definitely from my tribe. "Says the woman wearing the Arctic Monkeys T-shirt. Didn't they stop being cool like—I dunno—ten years ago?"

"Fuck you! Alex Turner is genius."

"Subjective, but sure."

"I'm going to show you their Glastonbury Festival show. And when you fall in love with them, you'll owe me."

"Is that so? I'd like to think I don't owe anyone anything," I said and dragged on my cigarette. I had now put my hand in my pocket too.

Rylee quickly looked to the side. She was officially on the defense. She puffed on her cig again.

"So if you're in theater, then you know Amelia Rose. I went to high school with her."

"Don't you dare ever put me in her camp. I should walk away right now."

"Then do." It took her a hair too long to smile. But finally, I saw her smirk. I was having a successful organic flirt. A real flirt.

"All right, well . . . shall we?" I let her go first, hoping she would hold the door open for me, but she went right in and didn't look back.

I stomped out my cigarette and followed her back inside. As the evening pressed on, we continued to all razz each other—only this time, it was me taking shots at Rylee.

"I was there in the crowd," Rylee said. Her eyes glazed over as the beatnik lead singer crooned onstage.

"Didn't realize you had a crush on a dude," I teased, pointing at the lead singer. He looked like my ex-boyfriend.

She jerked her head back and gave me the middle finger.

After Rylee passed out on the couch and then got up to go in the guest bedroom, Blair and I stayed up a little longer.

"God, isn't she great?" Blair whispered.

"Yeah, she really is . . ." I dreamily stared off.

"Between you and me, I've always been in love with her," she said.

My dreamlike state stopped. Everything halted.

"What? What about Cris?"

"I mean—yeah, I love Cris, but Rylee's my best friend. And I don't know . . . she gets me in a way Crystal never will."

I mean, that made sense. Crystal was practically a mute and behaved like a husband who lived on a farm. The only words she seemed to know were, "Feed me, woman." Commence caveman sounds.

"I don't think Rylee's gay anyway," Blair continued, also in a dreamlike state. *Are we talking about the same fucking dyke I was just with?* "Please don't tell anyone that I ever said anything, *ever*."

Just like that, she got up and went to bed.

Well, this blows. My perfect flirt was clearly someone else's perfect flirt. I had a decision to make. Do I fuck up my relationship with Blair and go after someone she's in love with, even though she's in a *four-year* relationship? Or do I let Rylee go? *It was a five-minute conversation about nothing. Literally nothing. I'll find someone else eventually. But wait . . . that's selfish of Blair! She's in a relationship. It shouldn't fucking matter. She doesn't own the rights to Rylee!*

It did matter. That's Girl Code 101. You don't sleep with someone's current crush (unless you have permission; we don't have time here to discuss the art of poly). Blair had stated her case and done it before I could let her know that I was digging Rylee too. Apparently, Blair had her own code: anybody she found attractive was off-limits to Sophie. But Blair had taken me under her wing. We'd broken bread! I was a member of the House of Blair. There was no way in hell I could backstab my den mother—even though I had already made up my mind that I would.

Two days later, I got a call from Mom that Papa had passed away unexpectedly. He was the life of the party. He made me proud to be southern. He was my buddy, and I thought he was going to live forever.

I pictured him only a few weeks prior, lowering his fake tooth retainer to scare me; recounting the first time he saw Showtime's *Shameless*, "That's the damnedest thing I've ever seen, have you seen that shit?"; dancing as he walked around the house to get from one room to the other; taunting that he was gonna give me a jar of his "goosel" (the skin under his neck) so I could have a piece of him forever.

I wish he had.

At his funeral, the priest said, "If you wanted to know anything going on in the parish, all you had to do was call up Bobby Rouse. He had the skinny on everybody." What a little gossip queen.

I made a Facebook post about how I'd lost him (and despite this maybe being a lame thing, it did help me grieve). Rylee saw it and messaged me.

`Hey, I'm really sorry to hear about your grandpa. If there's anything I can do, let me know.`

`Thanks, I appreciate it,` I typed back.

Her profile picture popped up in the corner showing that she had read it. I thought for a moment and typed some more.

`I'd love some company tonight. If you want to watch the Alabama/Auburn game with me at The End is Near!` Yeah, I used my grandpa's death as an excuse to spend time with a girl, but it wasn't like he was coming back.

I met Rylee that evening. She had already gotten us a booth. I walked up and took a seat next to her.

"You know what I hate more than theater?" she asked as she continued to stare at the TV that was showing the game highlights.

"What?"

"Alabama football."

"Then go? Door's right there," I said. She got up. *Oh, shit.*

"No, thanks," she said. "I'm just gonna get us some drinks to ease the pain."

"That's what I thought!" I shouted as she disappeared behind the wall separating the booths and the bar.

"How you feeling, by the way?" she asked when she returned.

"I'm okay. Actually, I'm not—but thanks," I said.

She had lost someone close to her, too, and she knew a lot about grief. I was stunned that she opened up about it. I didn't know how to console her, and she didn't want to be consoled.

"It's okay, really," she said. During the commercial, a song played that made her perk up. "Wow, he used to love this song."

"Oh, wow. That's crazy," I said.

"I'd tell him it's on, but he's dead."

My face felt like a frying pan had just hit it.

"I'm kidding! I mean—I'm not, but lighten up." I knew then that I was dealing with a truly one-of-a-kind gal.

Alabama ended up losing to Auburn in the Iron Bowl (the biggest rivalry in sports), 28 to 34. Known as "The Kick Six," it has since gone down as one of the worst losses in Alabama and sports history. Rylee smiled and screamed at the TV, "OH MY GOD, they ran it back . . . they fucking ran it back. Did you even see that?"

I had seen. I had seen the Alabama kicker line up to do the game-winning fifty-seven-yard field goal. I had seen the ball look like it was going to go between the goalposts. I had seen the ball fall short. I had seen the ball fall into the hands of an Auburn player. And I had seen the Auburn player run it back for the hundred-yard touchdown while the game clock went to 0:00. I have yet to watch it since—and I won't—but in that moment, I had seen it.

What a shitty way to end the shittiest day.

"Hey, seriously, it's not a big deal," she said later in the car. "You guys will get them next year. Sorry if I was too harsh. I know you had a rough day," she added as we pulled up to my house.

"You know what could turn it around?" I asked and eyed the front door. Being with her made me feel like I was gaining swagger.

Without saying a word, she turned off the ignition, grabbed her backpack off the back seat, and looked at me.

"Are you coming?" she asked.

We walked into the house, dropped our bags, and went horizontal for the next few hours. The only thing that could make this worse than Blair finding out about Rylee and me was the discovery that Rylee lived seven hours and twenty-eight minutes away. And she was going back the very next day.

"DALLAS? Ya should've led with that!" I told her the next morning in between make-out sessions.

"You didn't ask."

"So now what?" I asked as she got her stuff together.

She shrugged, and I watched her drive away. I dialed her after she had been gone for twenty minutes.

"Hello?"

"Hi. It's Sophie."

"Yes?"

"Just wanted to see if that Prius was working like it should."

"It is, thanks."

We talked her whole drive—all seven hours and twenty-eight minutes to be exact. From then on, I'd call her, and we'd talk on the phone for hours.

"Sophie, get off the floor. What are you even doing?" Hope spotted me on our rehearsal break lying in the middle of the hallway with my iPhone glued to my ear.

I'd wave my hand to shut her up, because I didn't want to interrupt Rylee.

Things started getting complicated when she visited Hattiesburg and didn't want anyone, least of all Blair, to know we were seeing each other. I had my reasons, but I didn't understand hers. I'd wait for hours until she texted when the coast was clear so we could spend time alone. It didn't feel great to be someone's secret. After about two months of "talking," I decided to break the news to Blair. I felt guilty for going behind her back. Blair had just made me another plate of her homemade étouffée when I asked her to sit.

"Blair, I need to talk to you."

"Everything all right?" she asked.

I didn't know how to break it to her that the love of her life *even though she had a girlfriend* was becoming the new love of my life.

"Um, so Rylee . . ."

"What about her?"

"We're sort of. I mean, I don't know. We probably aren't. But . . ."

Blair's face became stone-cold. She stood up. "I think Cris and I are gonna run some errands, so we'll have to hang later, Sophie."

"Blair, I'm sorry. I don't really know how it happened."

"Yeah, you do." She turned and went into her bedroom. I was left alone, really unsure of the future of my friendship with Blair. I tried calling Rylee that evening, but she didn't respond. I called again. No response. By the fifth ring, she picked up but was silent on the other line.

"Rylee?"

More silence.

"Rylee, are you okay? Talk to me."

"What the fuck did you say to Blair?" Rylee said, seething.

"I told her that I liked you." *I actually didn't even get that out, but whatever.*

"Why would you ever do that, Sophie? That was really fucked up. What's going on between us is private."

"Okay, I know—but we're hanging out."

"And it's no one's business."

"Aren't you gay?"

"It's no one's business what I may or may not be."

That stung. I knew she was reserved, but I hadn't really dealt with someone who was closeted before. Except for me, when I was rejecting poor Gabe and avoiding kissing Caroline in public. However, the double standard didn't occur to me at the time. I was finally comfortably out in my community, and I wanted a real relationship with Rylee.

Blair was pissed that I had stolen her imaginary girlfriend, and Rylee was pissed because I had outed her to Blair. I proceeded to plead to Rylee for the next three hours, promising that I would make it up to her and that I would never tell anyone else—which was the first of many promises I did not keep.

Chapter Twenty-Five

THIS IS THE SHIT I DIDN'T WANT TO WRITE

A lot of writers talk about how they were fucked over by that one shitty lover or partner and raise their fists like, *HA-HA-HA, sucker—now everyone knows what you did to me, you piece of shit. Congratulations, this chapter is dedicated to YOU.* It's certainly a freeing feeling to be able to complain to a national audience about the one who fucked you up so badly that you needed to move to another city and start over. I'm happy to report that I also get to talk about that person. I'm unhappy to report that that person also happens to be me.

Rylee and I were not the match in heaven I thought we were, despite ~~dating~~ the fact that I strung her along for almost two years. The long distance sucked, her being in the closet sucked, and I, frankly, sucked. She'd asked me not to tell anyone we were dating, so naturally, I told everyone. I had clearly already told Blair, I told my mom, and I told the entire theater department.

"I'm taken, so I can definitely relate to this *relationship* scene, Monica, thank you."

I was over the moon to be in love and to be with someone who liked spending time with me, every third weekend out of the month and sometimes fourth. But she had explicitly asked me to keep our 'ship a secret, and I had explicitly promised. We had no chance.

I started a vicious cycle of clinging to our relationship and trying to burn it to the ground, which I called Sophie's Choices. Rylee and I would fight about me not prioritizing her, I'd lie and say she was the priority even though she'd started to take a back seat to my career and everything in Hattiesburg. And then after we'd go back and forth on the phone for about three hours while I was at a college party, no less, my friend Hope would finally say something like, "Sophie, you're at my house—get off the fucking phone." I would work out my intimacy issues like I was Shane from *The L Word*. No one could tell me what to do.

And, class . . . what did Shane do to work through her intimacy issues? She cheated. She literally left Carmen—WHO HAS A TATTOO WRAPPED AROUND HER BOD LIKE A SERPENT AND IS THE MOST LOYAL WOMAN ALIVE—at the altar to fuck off with Cherie Jaffe, an unavailable woman who would never leave her husband and her Bel Air houses and "trips to Paris." As awful as that may sound, that's how I behaved. My new sexuality gave me confidence. Overconfidence. I was the hottest shit in a small town—and no one could change my mind.

I had created this version of what I thought gay should be, and I tried to play out my fuck-boy fantasy like I was on some goddamn TV show. Except these were real people with emotions, not characters. By the time I graduated, I had spun so many lies that I'm surprised Rylee didn't get a face full of spiderwebs every time she walked through my door. That's because I managed to cover my tracks. I went to ridiculous lengths to not upset anyone who knew about my cheating. Without telling me, my roommate moved her boyfriend and his three dogs in to my house—and because she knew about my cheating, I felt I had to let her. I even gave them the master bedroom.

I do want to be clear. I did love Rylee. She helped me understand what first love is about. I loved holding her hand while we rode around in her Prius with the windows rolled down, singing her favorite song: "Everywhere" by Fleetwood Mac. Thinking of her saying "ole girl" still makes me laugh. The time we slept on an air mattress in her best friend Troy's living room and had garbage-fire-smelling sex, laughing when Troy's boyfriend came out to grab water, caught one whiff, and retreated. For the first time in a relationship, I thought about our future together.

At the same time, I also wasn't ready for that kind of commitment. Rylee was evolving, slowly coming out of the closet, but I was evolving too. When I thought about the future, I started to believe mine was in New York.

These thoughts were all inside me having a complicated debate.

"Sophie's not in it for the long haul; she needs to let the woman go," said Worry.

"My thoughts exactly! She's being selfish!" said Conscience, slamming the table.

"She's in college—*let her have fun. Who cares! No one actually marries the person they date in college,"* said the voice I ultimately listened to—No Fucks. She'd clearly been talking to Tootie 2.0.

Rylee was settled in a career, and I wanted to go out and explore. I felt like the world revolved around me, and—despite our fundamental differences—I wouldn't let Rylee go.

It does feel odd to acknowledge that, during my shithole years, I was well on my way at school. I got cast every semester. I also did professional theater during the summers. I even got twenty callbacks at a theater conference whose most revered theater was in Branson, MO, doing *The Lost Colony* reenactments. However, one of the white girls in my program said in response to all the attention, "She only got twenty callbacks because she's ethnically ambiguous."

My friend Brittany Butler—the nicest person to ever grace this earth, yet no pushover—overheard the twat and stood up for me in the Starbucks where the twat worked: "Sophie didn't get callbacks because of her RACE; she got callbacks because she's talented. Oh, and I'd like my latte redone—it's cold. Thanks."

Thank you, Brittany, for going to bat for me, and rest in power, diva. I love and miss you.

But also, Brittany, it did have something to do with my race. I *was* called back for being the one person who could pass as Native American in a sea of white people. One callback, they made me roll up my sleeves to look at the sturdiness of my arms as three white women hovered around me for a half an hour. Another callback, they wanted to test if I could fill the room with a Native American chant ('cause of course I must know how to do that). And because I can't get away from the Christians, another callback was as Moses's wife for Sight & Sound, a theater that exclusively produces Bible stories. When they asked me about my feelings about God during the callback, a question that threw me off, I muttered, "I mean, yeah, He's cool." I hadn't exactly been practicing, and Faye Davenport's handbook was long gone at this point. The casting director quickly and politely ushered me out the door without asking to see my interpretation of Zipporah.

Despite the twenty callbacks, none of the roles seemed right, and I didn't want to be performing in Branson, MO, for the rest of my dying days. My professor Robin Carr used her vegan powers and nominated me for the diversity spot as an acting intern at a theater festival in the famous *Berkshires*. The place where Broadway actors go to do a stint in the woody pines as their summer vacation. And where James Taylor was born. And where the white people of New York go to live out their *Dirty Dancing* fantasies. This time I was happy to be the diversity kid because, while all the other interns paid for their spots, that shit was free for me.

A week before I graduated (with honors—to my parents' surprise), I broke the news that I was leaving the South to Rylee, who vehemently expressed that if I went, we wouldn't make it as a couple.

"Come on! That's nonsense. I'll come stay with you in Dallas once the summer's over." She could tell that wasn't the case. Probably because I had bought a one-way ticket to the Berkshires.

I rolled up to the internship housing, and—with a gust of wind—I was immediately greeted with thousands of pages of sheet music hitting me in the face. It was full of people who went to schools like Boston Conservatory, Emerson, and even NYU Tisch. TISCH? The famous theater school that had not accepted *moi*?

I considered myself a musical theater performer too. But the leads at USM, including myself, smoked pot, cigs, and wore leather jackets. We were bad to the bone. I thought all actors were like us. The first night at the internship, as my fellow interns and I were hanging out sober, I went to smoke a cigarette and noticed no one else was smoking. I asked my roommate Liv.

"Maybe Caitlin does? But doubtful," she responded. And then she touched her neck softly. "Their voices."

"Ah."

I quit cold turkey. I was thrown into ten-hour days, so there really was little time for anything outside of the program. Music classes, rehearsal, yoga, and learning the choreo to *Sister Act II*'s finale. This was the real deal. And in the meantime, I had developed a bond with my roommates in less than twenty-four hours, and we nicknamed ourselves "Xanadu"—much to the annoyance of the other interns.

I had been in Massachusetts for about forty-eight hours when I went on a run with some of the guys. Yes, this was weird because I didn't run—but I also didn't eat healthy or do Israeli Gaga dancing before the internship, and I was suddenly letting the music take me across the floor.

On my run, Rylee sent me a text about how what I really wanted was for the guys to run through me. She had no idea that I'd cheated on her, but the text was harsh. I wasn't sleeping with, or interested in sleeping with, men at all. I sent her nothing short of a dissertation in return, and she sent one back, and when I didn't respond to her (because I'd gone in to rehearsal without resolving anything), she sent an even angrier one. She felt blown off. With so many things to distract me, I felt, for the first time, that I could let her go.

My main distraction from Rylee was one of the interns. At the opening party for the season, I saw Jillian from across the room, winked, and then looked away like James Dean. I patted myself on the back for that one. She had a beautiful voice and, oftentimes, made it known by singing a touch too loudly in warm-ups. The night of the party, I came back to my room, and she was there talking to my bunkmate and friend, Piper.

"How do you two know each other?" I asked Piper once Jillian left the room.

"We started hanging out the other day after practicing Cole Porter for the elderly."

That's weird, because you only hang out with Xanadu, and I've never heard you mention her. I shouldn't have been surprised—there were only ten acting interns.

As Jillian and Piper got closer, it was clear she was being initiated into Xanadu. On the way to class, scanning a casting announcement for a new production, Jillian would casually drop hints like, "She's not my type or *my type,* y'know what I mean?"

I did know what she meant. And Rylee was causing me so much stress that I started to confide in Jillian about it.

"She told me that I should let the boys run right through me," I said, holding up the text.

"I mean, that's fucked up."

I called Rylee to tell her I wanted a break. Not to break up but a break—to give us both space. I tried to state my case, which wasn't coming out like I had planned it in the shower. (Granted, there were thirty people living in the house, which was like being back at the sorority house, but not at all, and because I was scared of catching a disease, I wore a bathing suit in the shower and splashed water on my body like I was about to be shipped off to war. So I didn't really get to think it through.)

"I think we should take a break . . . I need space."

"Are you fucking KIDDING me, Sophie? You're fucking me over again?" She shouted about how I was giving up.

I walked back into the room, collapsed on the floor, and cried my eyeballs out as Xanadu circled around me and helped me onto my feet. I felt so much pain. And then I dried my tears and grabbed a pack of cigarettes. Fuck the vocal pipes.

Cue the blues rock track.

I spotted Jillian in the kitchen as I grabbed a bottle of Jack. Pulling my hoodie over my head, I asked her to join me.

"You know, it's probably for the best, Soph," she said genuinely. "She was causing you so much stress."

I caused her plenty too, but sure.

"I mean, we've been fighting since the moment I got here. I know I'm never available. But we're busy! You know how busy we are."

Jillian nodded sagely. "Do you really want to be fight-texting your . . . girl-friend . . . ex, whatever you want to say . . . with the only fifteen-minute break you have?"

I didn't. I might have not been putting in the effort, but there honestly wasn't any time. I could barely think, I was so busy. And when I wasn't busy, I wanted to enjoy the program to the fullest, and also talk to Jillian.

I puffed on a pack of Marlboro Lights as we lamented some more. We chatted about musical theater, which was honest-to-god refreshing because she knew about the existence of the Tony Awards. In fact, she even knew more than I did.

"Have you heard of *Waitress*, the new Sara Bareilles musical?"

"Have I heard of *Waitress* . . . Sophie. I already have tickets to the world premiere at the American Repertory Theater. You're so late to this."

What I didn't tell Jillian was that I had also broken it off with Rylee because I wanted to have guilt-free sex with her, which we did against the wall of the internship building that night.

And then again in her car the next day.

And then in the theater parking lot.

And then during our lunch break back at her mom's house, which happened to only be about forty-five minutes away.

So did I stop talking to Rylee officially that day and ride off into the sunset with Jillian?

Uh, no.

The following morning, after calling off my relationship a mere ten hours earlier and after having Pompeii-explosion sex with *Jillian*, I called *Rylee*, telling her I was a wreck. Because it had hit me that I was now without the person who had been my rock for the past two years. I was in a completely different time zone, girlfriendless, and away from everything I knew. The thrill of sex with Jillian had worn off, and I had to face the fact that I was alone and I missed Rylee. I still hadn't coped with being alone. I turned off "Ex's and Oh's" by Elle King and blasted Miley Cyrus's *Bangerz* album instead. (Which is still one of the best breakup albums of all time, and I highly recommend it.)

Except I didn't face the music, because Jillian was right there in my corner. Always. A burst of energy and life—and, not to mention, a completely sure-of-herself individual. Before I left for the internship, I had been in Texas at Rylee's place, avoiding her neighbors because we didn't want them to question our "friendship."

My fling with Jillian could be a wide-in-the-open romance. I mean, if it wasn't for the fact that everyone knew I was already in a relationship.

And a new and even nastier phase of Sophie's Choices had begun.

The Asshole Phase.

I'd have Mitski-soundtrack-level sex with Jillian, and then maybe fifteen minutes later, I'd go behind the house, call Rylee, and tell her how much I missed her and how much I was still in love with her. I'd see Jillian smiling at me through the kitchen window, and I'd duck behind the bushes and lower my voice.

"Who was that?" Jillian'd ask when I returned with leaves in my hair—which she'd pick out.

"Um, Rylee . . . she's . . . ya know. Really in a bad spot." *I'm also in a bad spot.*

"Okay," she'd say, perplexed.

"Hey, it's not like that with her," I'd say. And then, "I'm falling for you."

Jillian would sleep in my bed that night, and I'd hug her while reading texts from Rylee and telling Rylee how much I was still in love with her.

Then, the following morning in our Gaga dancing workshop, not to be confused with Lady Gaga, the ethereal teacher would say, "There's a little ball of light. That light is energy. Let it travel through your fingertips and down into your body and let it move you through the space." And she'd turn on Tove Lo's

"Habits" (the remix), and I'd move through the space and somehow end up near Jillian, with our balls of light touching as our bodies convulsed. I'd throw myself onto the ground, almost crying, and then pick myself up. Stare at her and then move away slowly with every bone in my foot touching the ground as I walked back to my imaginary box.

For two months, I actively pursued both of them. Rylee would write me love letters, including a letter about how she finally came out to her family. I'd read them secretly outside and then go to stash them away—only to notice that Jillian had picked up my side of the room, folded all my clothes, and written a note that said, *If your room is tidier, you will be happier.*

I thought I could keep it under wraps, but I started becoming more distracted, texting Rylee under the table while Jillian went to the bathroom.

I carried on this behavior for four months. I thought I was going to combust in the middle of Tanglewood, Massachusetts, and turn the trees into ash.

Jillian started to call me out for using her and wasting her time. We'd break it off, only to circle each other during rehearsal and then kiss passionately in the rain like we were in Showtime's *The Affair*.

During a long weekend, Xanadu went to Jillian's beach house, and Piper—my closest friend at the time—gave me the advice I didn't want to hear. "Just choose, Sophie. You can't date two people at the same time. It's not fair. And you know that."

It had become embarrassing. Even Jillian's mother knew that I was two-timing her daughter. She'd try to have a nice conversation with me, but through her pursed lips, I could tell she wanted to either slap me or hope I'd magically drown.

I stared at the ocean. I knew dating two people wasn't right, but secretly, I got off on it. It gave me a sense of power I hadn't had before. I was a womanizer—and for a brief moment in history, I liked it.

After the summer ended, when Jillian was back at college in Ohio and I was in New York, I convinced her to give me one more chance (there had been a lot). I planned a huge trip where I'd come down to see her at school, spend the weekend, and we'd start our long-distance relationship. Yes, another long-distance relationship that was, also, seven hours and twenty-eight minutes. A few days later, a friend invited me to the opening night of her Broadway play, and I told Jillian I needed to push the trip back by a day so I could go. I told her that it wasn't that big of a deal. She didn't seem to feel the same.

I went to the play to network, and the only thing I gained was a net loss of good karma. My friend left early, and the star was surrounded by her agents the entire time.

"I'm not sure you're going to like what I have to say when you get here, Sophie," Jillian told me as I was boarding the plane the following morning.

I refused to listen, telling her, "Stop!" and "I'm so excited to see you."

She broke up with me the moment I got off the plane. I deserved it and should have totally seen it coming, but I still felt blindsided. I hated her. Really hated her. But wanted her. I cried and screamed and hugged her legs, begging her to change her mind. Nothing worked. She was over it. In a desperate move, I begged her to have sex with me—which, after I'd pleaded for three hours, she did. It was manipulative and not okay.

On the way back to the airport to drop me off thirty-six hours later (we couldn't find an earlier flight out), she said, "You're a good friend, but you're a shitty person to date."

My ego was bruised, and her ending things was devastating. Even though I knew I hadn't treated her well, it took me a long time to get over.

I mean, really.

Have you ever just sat in your shit, knowing you are truly the worst human in the world?

Have you ever dated two people thinking, *Hmm . . . I think I can get away with this.*

I'm truly embarrassed by all of it. When Jillian and I broke up, if you can even call it that, I sent her a voice recording reading an apology letter to her that was humiliating and performative and ended with a fucking sonnet. I sounded like I was auditioning for *August: Osage County*, not actually trying to win back a woman who had given me a thousand chances. I kept saying over and over how I truly understood why she had walked away, but . . . no, I didn't.

I didn't, because when Jillian called it off in Ohio, I sought comfort in Rylee and told her only half the truth of what I had done. For a few months, we half-heartedly tried to piece things together, but it was clear that our relationship was over.

Those years might be over, but even a few months ago, I had a nightmare about my behavior during that time. I've had to spend countless hours of therapy with my therapist, Ellen, who will relive it with me as many times as I need to.

I've had to work to come to the realization that the person I once was is not who I am now. And I owe my life to Ellen, who doesn't judge me, even on the days I judge myself.

My dad used to say that when he was in high school, he was the one dads didn't want their daughters dating. He always worried that I'd find a guy who had his MO, but I don't think he anticipated that it might be the other way around.

I often think back to my dad and how he lost my mom. He's since moved on to someone else, and Mom will often say that she doesn't understand why he treats his new wife better than he treated her.

"He never wore his wedding ring, and now he never takes it off."

I hate to say that I understand my dad's behavior. You shouldn't have to treat women poorly to not do it again, but once they walk away, it changes your perspective.

Like him, I left a bad situation of my own making, wanting to be better in my relationships. I was a dingbat and a selfish person for a long time. I'm still working every day not to be. I have made mistakes since, and I will probably continue to make mistakes, but over time, they've gotten smaller and easier to recognize.

I hate this is in the book.

Lessons I've Learned from My Shane Years

- You can't text someone an insane number of times to get them to talk back to you. That would mean a restraining order.
- You will lose all your friendships if you choose someone from that friend group and fuck them over.
- Going to Tibet to pay your debts is not a good way to parse out the way you've hurt people.
- Therapy, however, is a great way to figure out how you've failed in the past, and it's even cheaper (depending).
- Being a cool lesbian doesn't equate to being a womanizer.
- Don't date two people at the same time.
- Shane is a character on television.
- I hate this is in the book.

Chapter Twenty-Six

A GIRL HAS NO DOOR

Career-wise, the summer in the Berkshires had been pivotal. I had been cast as a lead, where I got to dress in 1905 drag and perform with real Broadway actors. We had the opportunity to make connections to the New York scene. My music director, a bigwig at Juilliard, became a mentor. If I was in hell personally, I was in heaven professionally.

Shortly before the end of the program, I rubbed shoulders with an old-school Broadway actress who invited me and a few others to watch her perform at a cabaret with the band the Skivvies. The woman looked incredible! I will NOT say *for her age*, because I certainly don't look as good as she did, even at thirty years younger.

When I got back to the intern house, I couldn't stop thinking about the performance, and I sent her a message over Facebook wanting to ~~network like hell~~ grab coffee and said, You were amazing, and I'd love to get together once I get settled in NYC. (I had no official plans to move to the city.) She messaged me back and asked if I liked cats. Naturally, I told her yes . . . even though I neither liked them nor hated them. They were fine.

Great! Want to cat-sit for me for a few months? she asked. After waiting the appropriate amount of time,[41] I said, Sure! When?

How's next week?

I had a quick dinner with my Juilliard mentor, Deb, who was a New York legend. She was no bullshit, would tell you when you're flat, and wouldn't kiss

---

[41] A good three to four minutes is fair.

your ass. If Deb thought you had it, though—buckle up. I told her I was debating between New York and LA, and she stopped me in the middle of my sentence. "Kid, why would you *ever* want to live in LA when you can live in New York?" And then, "You gonna eat or what?" She had a point. I scrapped my tentative plans to head to LA, packed my bags, and moved to the Big Apple.

Mom flew up and we rode the Amtrak together to New York. She stayed for twenty-four hours just so she could be there when I became a city girl.

This time, my bags were better than the last trip but had seen some shit.

I moved in with the seasoned Broadway actress. *Whoever could it be, Sophie?* Well, I ain't sayin', but I'll leave you to imagine that maybe it was Liza Minnelli herself. The actress radiated old-timey Upper West Side, New York City! mystique. She was a wafer-thin person who apparently survived off sheer drive and talent. She would wrap herself in a blanket and walk as if she were floating and speak as if every word were from the *Grey Gardens* script.

I had barely gotten my bags in the door when she sultry-squeaked, "Thank you. Here's the keys. This is how you change the litter. I'm off to my summer home. Have fun!" The word *fun* had a special ring to it—as if she'd sung it. She had a way of speaking that was very low in timbre and yet squeaky. It was my favorite part about her. Before I could muster up a "thank you," her big hat disappeared behind the door.

Suddenly, I was alone. I surveyed the place. Her apartment looked like she'd furnished it with a prop from every play she'd ever been cast in. I walked into the office, which had a baby grand piano that I was certain Jonathan Larson himself had done a little ditty on.

Her bedroom was strictly velvet. Huge red curtains. A velvet settee for reclining while drinking Chianti. She had bolster pillows that I swung around like they were on my nipples. And round, tufted chartreuse ottomans at every turn, which I didn't dare touch. There was a four-poster bed so high that you had to get a running start to jump onto it. I'd lie there and think, *This bed will provide the right REM cycles for me to be on Broadway in less than a year. I'm sure of it.*

I looked out the window, down at all the tiny cars. The apartment smelled like what I'd expect an Upper West Side apartment to smell like: old money and cat piss.

I sat on the couch, Pip hopped up on me, and I wondered, *Is this what living in NYC feels like?* I had dreamed of it all my life—and here I was with two suitcases and a cat in my lap, ready to start my career in theater—short only a beret and a ukulele. I had made it! But it felt much sadder than I had expected. Lonely, even. I didn't really know anyone, and I was surrounded by a city full of people who clearly had bigger things to worry about than my arrival. I was forced to face my shortcomings. But I told myself to turn that frown upside down, because I was going to live in a real Broadway actress's home. And out of all the interns who Facebook messaged her (just me), she had chosen *me* to live in her home.

Sprinkled throughout the apartment, the Broadway actress had framed photos of herself from the time she was in the musical titled REDACTED and the one about CAN'T SAY! She only had canned lentil soup in the cupboard. I looked at her slender frame in a photograph at the opening of YOU'LL NEVER KNOW and thought, *Ah, yes. If I want to hit an A♭ note, then I needed to eat lentils and drink Italian red wine—I mean, Chianti—thank you, and have a troupe of cats.* Her three cats were underfoot at every turn. I think they could sense that I was lonely because they greeted me one by one and said, "Hey, kid. New York is tough—but you got this. Meow, meow."

I didn't got this.

I looked up a few auditions on Backstage.com, which I'd asked my mom to buy me a subscription to because I didn't have two pennies to my name. I went to a total of two open calls. At the first, I wasted my entire day staring at all the hopefuls in their pastel dresses but never got seen. At the second, I walked in confidently, smiling, so they'd know I was *approachable, castable, and easy to work with. The plunk of two chords and!*

"I'm high on the mountain—"

"Thank you."

I turned and left as the accompanist handed me my manila folder with the full thirty-two bars that I had craftily pasted together the night before.

I decided I was not cut out for musical theater. I wasn't going to be able to audition as much as I wanted to anyway, because first things first—I needed to find a job and my own apartment before the Broadway actress's summer house turned too cold.

Through a Xanadu friend, I met my soon-to-be roommate, Chandler, and he recommended me for a job at a restaurant. It was the kind of place that Patrick Bateman must have frequented. I walked through the golden door and waited next to the large metallic dinosaur commissioned from Alexander Calder himself. I surveyed the servers in their starched, white-as-cocaine aprons; red Vicious Trollop lipstick by MAC; and updos so tight, their eyebrows were on top of their heads. They marched in such organized formation, Dad would have approved.

I filled out the application, which included a fifty-question portion that was literally fashioned after the SATs; had a business-formal meeting with HR; and shadowed a militant server without pay for two nights. During the shadow, despite the server's hands being full of scalding-hot, $100 steaks, as a child guest attempted to walk past us, he pressed his body very hard against the nearest wall, grabbing me with him, to let the tiny human pass without us brushing shoulders.

Completely my vibe. Nevertheless, I needed a job.

Every once in a while, the Broadway actress would come back from her summer home and spend the night. If it happened to be on one of my few days off, we'd sit on the couch together and drink *Italian* wine, and she'd talk about the industry or colleagues.

"One time I was working with Patti . . ."

LuPone?

"And she was a mess!" (A mess meant a good thing.) "And Christian was there. God, I love Christian REDACTED. He's so talented," she cooed.

"You know Christian?" I squeaked like a schoolgirl. (I imagined I was on a first-name basis too.)

"Of course—do you?" she asked, genuinely curious.

"Not really, no. Met him one time."

If by *"met"* you count the brief moment at the stage door where he signed my *Playbill.*

The Broadway actress and I would talk for hours about her time onstage, and I related it to *my* experience onstage. After all, we had been at the same festival (even though my performance was in the lobby of the theater where she was onstage). I finally asked, "How do I make it?" *Tell me—I'M BEGGING YOU.*

"You're smart—you'll be fine," she told me.

Like street-smart? I didn't know Manhattan was a grid until last year.

I wanted more details—a road map, perhaps. The keys to the city! But I couldn't complain—just spending time with her was more than I ever thought

I'd accomplish. Half the battle of "making it," I learned, is affording it. I had to rethink my income completely. I was used to living comfortably on $300 a week in Mississippi. In New York, I needed to make $300 a night just to stay afloat. And to get an apartment in NYC, you had to have the first month's rent, the last month's rent, a deposit that equaled a month of rent, three golden shoes, an egg from a witch, and a magic elixir that restores youth.

I started an apartment search with Chandler and one of his a cappella band-mates from Cornell. I'd never met an actual Chandler, but the fact that I was going to be living in New York City with a Chandler meant that I was officially in the cast of *Friends*.

I still didn't know up from down, so I let Chandler take the lead on finding an apartment. He said he wanted three things: "To be near the 4/5/6, to have laundry in the building, and to have a mail center in the apartment." Those were very specific characteristics of a living space that I didn't particularly care about. I didn't know (or care) what the best train was, I didn't like doing laundry, and I never got mail (unless it was from debt collectors). And, as it turned out, achieving all three of Chandler's wishes was next to impossible in New York City. And who gets that much mail?

So ~~we~~ Chandler found an apartment on Wall Street. Wall Street. A place with no grocery stores, or usable sidewalks, or anything except the big Bull, which, last I checked, wasn't edible. Chandler wanted somewhere "safe," and Wall Street was very safe and desolate. After the closing bell rang, it was so desolate, it started to feel unsafe. The name of the building might as well have been "NO ONE LIVES HERE; WHAT ARE YOU DOING?" When people asked me where I lived, I'd say, "Wall Street," and ten out of ten would say, "Not where you work—where do you live?"

"Yes, Wall Street!"

"But . . . *why?*"

We had laundry! We had a mail center! It was near the 4/5/6 train! And bonus—we had a doorman named Alfred!

It was, however, only a one bedroom (with an office). "We'll convert it into three bedrooms," Chandler told me. I looked at the layout online, since I had yet to see it, and—because I didn't know how to read a blueprint—decided that fitting three bedrooms in there sounded possible.

"It's smallish . . . but everything's small in New York," he said.

I mean, I was excited! I had laundry! I had a doorman! Did I mention we had a mail center? I was living it UP. After signing the lease, I visited the apartment and realized that it was actually a *studio* with an office. Not a one bedroom—as Chandler, the salesman, had told me. A studio . . . with an office. Five hundred and fifty square feet. That's like a two-car garage, and both cars are Mini Coopers, and the doors hit the walls when opening, and the cars are actually fucking LEGOs. There were three of us. No matter—we ordered temporary walls and thought we'd cheated the system. What we didn't know was that temporary walls weren't like normal walls with drywall and stuff. They were basically made of thick card stock. I realized this fact as the company was installing them and I asked why they had brought over paper when we had ordered walls. They told me that the paper actually was the wall. I called another company, and they offered the very same product. The workers who eventually installed the "walls" also didn't build them all the way up to the celling.

"It's a fire hazard," they told me.

I also realized one other very important thing.

"There's no door," I pointed out.

"We can't add a door . . . it's a—" the worker began.

"Fire hazard," we both said at the same time.

"You got it," he confirmed as he continued to make the hole for where a curtain rod might go.

They put an L-shaped paper wall around the section of our apartment containing our only window. They left, and I was alone in the apartment. I sat on the floor in my sliver of a room. I could lie down in only one position or my body wouldn't fit. At least I had the window. *Shit—but the A/C is on the other side.* Two hours previously, I had been excited because I had Alfred, my doorman. Now I had a doorman and no door. I wondered whether I could trade Alfred for one. I loved him—I'd only just arrived and he was already giving me advice: orange juice is the key to good health, but I figured he'd agree that I should have a door.

To make matters worse—our third roommate played video games twenty-four seven. I know we had a third roommate only because I constantly heard "Ooof!" "Yes!" "Come on . . . come on. COME ON!" And joystick movements on the other side of the paper wall. When he wasn't playing video games, he was talking to his girlfriend. I didn't really want to hear him talk to his girlfriend while I tried to sleep or nap or do anything in my own ~~room~~ sliver. I wasn't sure if he existed, but our rent was always paid in full, so I'm going to assume he lived there.

Chandler constantly complained about having no windows in his office/bedroom, and the tenth time he mentioned it, I said, "If you complain one more time, I will move your stuff to my door-less room—and then, for a change, you will have no door, and I will have no windows!" That shut him up.

When I started making friends in the city, I would go over to their apartments and see that not only did they have doors, but they also had what passed for space in New York. *You mean you don't have to cook eggs in your roommate's room because your kitchen isn't part of your roommate's room?*

Everyone would nod like, *Are you okay, girl?*

Still, now that I'm a New Yorker and have learned to be blunt about subjects like rent, I will proudly say that my share of the rent was $1,110 a month—which granted me a third of a studio and no door—for my first year in the city. If that didn't make me a real New Yorker, then nothing would.

It also made me an idiot.

Chapter Twenty-Seven

MY VERY OWN KEY WEST LESBIANS

My first year living in New York can be summed up as "hands!" and "corner!" and "coming down!" All commands that I learned from the kitchen while working at the restaurant with military-style training. I lived at that restaurant—partly because I needed money and also because they were short-staffed and called on me constantly.

The managers would ~~text us~~ harass us incessantly.

I'll give you $200 if you work tonight, a preppy manager wrote me at three p.m. when I was waking up from a nap.

I have plans. How's 6-8 p.m.?

5-9? And leave at 9 p.m.?

Walking out the door with my street clothes on at 9 p.m. No exceptions, I replied.

Done! 😊

Every single food item had to be labeled in abbreviations as we took the guests' orders so the rest of the team could read it, in case one of us was captured by enemy servers from the restaurant across the street. I had to know the history of the building, down to the place the carpet was from. It was Fabrica, if you're wondering. And we needed to get a real shine on the saltshakers or the shift manager would have us drop and give them twenty.

I slugged through the long, arduous shifts, while rich assholes sloppily ate their sixty-dollar barbecue ribs and gulped their thirty-dollar glasses of wine.

If we were late, we were suspended. If we had stains on our shirts even after working doubles, we'd be sent home. Which, like—joke's on you! I got a night off. I'd smile until I checked my bank account, which was somehow negative again. If we were putting in an order and the chef asked us to run food, we were expected to drop everything for her, including the plate of food we were already carrying. I might have considered a military life once upon a time, but this was not for me. (Love you, Dad.)

However, the restaurant did afford me a solid group of friends, and we'd commiserate over drama and the servers who were shitty. Management might have treated us like peasants, but we considered ourselves the queen's court.

I was enjoying making money, spending time with my friends (including Chandler, whose wit and sense of adventure overshadowed his neuroses), and soaking in New York. But I spent most of my precious nights off dressed in all black, hanging out on the Lower East Side, hoping a girl would point at me, say "LESBIAN!" and then come home with me. No matter how good my Indiana-Jones-meets-Edward-Cullen look was, it rarely happened. I figured being in New York would make it so much easier to be gay. In between hearing about my gay friends' hookups, I kept asking myself, *Where are all the lesbians?*

I'm sure it's amazing, if you're a gay man, when you finally embrace your sexuality. The freedom. The choices. The all-you-can-eat buffet of boys all day, any day. I'm talking about the sex apps, baby. Grindr, Scruff, and if you're like some, My Disney Experience mobile app.

For whatever reason, lesbians get the short end of the stick with most everything, including the dating apps. When I first moved to NYC, we had *one*. It was called Her. Like the 2013 Joaquin Phoenix movie about an inanimate lover. Most single lesbians are forced to use straight apps like Tinder and Hinge. After seeing the same profile of a graphic-designer lesbian for two straight weeks, I decided to take my profile down from Hinge. If that lesbian was so great, then I was pretty sure I could find her in the coffee shop she was apparently five feet away from.

Listen—I get that dating on the apps is toxic for anyone—and I hear you, boys . . . it's only about appearance, and some men are mean and catty. But I'd love to experience that kind of any-time-of-day action. Just one day is all I ask! Plus, maybe I *do* want to know what it feels like to be rejected by a floating torso! Bite me.

I realized that I didn't have many choices, but I was desperate to hook up with someone. I was not yet over Jillian, and I needed a healthy way to cope. Sleeping with people you don't actually know but have just met on an app is *very* healthy.

At the same time, I'm very old skooL. I didn't want to meet my soul mate through a device that I also drunk-ordered food from. It wasn't my style. I often dreamed I'd run into my soul mate on the streets of New York—a real meet-cute—and have a lifelong love affair. Sadly, that hadn't happened yet. So I hopped on the apps and got to work. And what do you know? I got a small taste of the male hookup life.

Fancy Frolic

I matched with a woman named Elira. She was thirteen years my senior. A lawyer. She asked if I'd like to get lunch, and I replied, Lunch! How adult of us!

She responded, Why, yes—we are adults. ☺

I've had a mild fascination with older women over the years. Like what the gay men call a "daddy." There's something about a mom with kids taking me for a spin in her master bedroom overlooking her pool and then, after the adult romp, I help her pack her kids' lunches as we discuss her ex. That really gets me going.

I met Elira on the Upper West Side at a French restaurant. I always look up the menu before I meet for anything because I don't want to spend any time stressing about what to order while also stressing about making an impression. The menu for the French place, I noticed, had the frightening $$$$ classification.

I searched the restaurant name again to make sure, and—yep, $$$$ was correct. The menu was also in French.

I figured that, as a lawyer, Elira probably had money, and I decided to let her treat me before she officially offered. The restaurant was her choice, after all. I showed up in my vintage, thrift-shop coat and had the restaurant staff check it. I was meeting a lawyer—therefore, I must be upper class.

Elira was shorter than I had expected and not exactly like her picture. She seemed more tired, and now that I think of it, her photo did look like she was in undergrad. But she did have the same twinkle in her eyes that had made me interested in her in the first place. She wore pearls and a Cartier bracelet that I wanted her to choke me with later. Hey, a girl can dream.

"I'm paying," was one of the first things out of my new sugar mommy's mouth.

I nodded.

"I'll take the Chablis," I told the real live, in-the-flesh French waiter, motioning toward my glass.

"Right away, mademoiselle," he responded, making a grand gesture.

"And the salmon."

"Excellent choice, mademoiselle," he said with a full bow from head to toe.

"Salmon is the best. I once learned how to catch salmon in Japan," the lawyer offered.

I quickly rattled off my knowledge of salmon—which I hadn't learned overseas like her but in server training. I didn't really know what I was saying, but after discovering the menu was in French, I'd picked the salmon because it was the only thing I could identify. Regardless, it impressed her.

We discussed academia and law—where I used my Political Science 101 class to guide me.

I finished the meal with a *digestif.*

I couldn't go home with her right then, since she literally had to go back to work to defend white-collar criminals, so we penciled in a date for drinks the following night. I was disappointed that there was no afternoon booty call.

But the next night, we had drinks for only twenty minutes—just a formality—before she invited me back to her place.

Elira had a doorman too. She even had a door—a lot of them! With ornate brass doorknobs!

She had the entire apartment to herself. Not to mention—her apartment overlooked the city. It was *real* casual. She offered me a whiskey on the rocks, and I looked at the felt pennants laid out on her beveled glass dining room table.

Harvard, Stanford, and MIT.

"Where did you say you graduated from?" I asked suspiciously, as if she had killed somebody and taken their pennants.

"I forgot those were out. I'm sorry!"

She hadn't answered my question. Why are smart people embarrassed by academic achievement? I would have flaunted the fuck out of that shit had I been accepted to any one of those institutions. I'd be like (in my best Katharine Hepburn imitation), *What's that you ask? I couldn't hear you because I was thinking about that time I WENT TO HARVARD. Have you ever heard of HARVARD?*

Did I tell *you* that I landed an interview for Harvard—a fact that I casually drop into most conversations, even after finding out that almost everyone who applies to Harvard gets an interview.

Wearing Elira's robe, I looked over the New York City skyline and patted myself on the back for achieving high-class gaydom.

Starlight and My Very Own Eyeball Kiss

I swiped right on a woman named Starlight who could have been a model for Mugatu's fashion company, Derelicte—complete with a tiny dog. We started the night in Bushwick, the land of hipsters and graffiti tours. I showed up at a hazy bar that hadn't passed health codes in years. It was like a time warp back to the nineties. With everyone dressed like the cartoon character Doug.

I was early, but Starlight was already there with her dachshund, Meryl, who sat in her lap the entire time. Meryl was named after one of her grandmothers, and not the actress—who was "overrated" in Starlight's book. Yes, she'd seen the Taste of Streep Instagram, and it hadn't swayed her.

Starlight asked me questions about what I did (which was not much), where I lived (which was not much), and how I was liking New York (which was not much—because I couldn't afford more than dollar-slice 'za).

She took me back to her three-bedroom apartment, and we hung out with her roommates. It was like you'd expect. A bad date where the person takes you home to a crowded NYC apartment with boring strangers. I tried to be chill with her roommates as they dished over work and their annoying other roommate, Moon, who I think was also in the room with us. Then we all went out to a smoky dive bar, drank PBRs (I hoped she wouldn't drink too many because I couldn't afford it), smoked a joint inside like the rebels we were, and played pool. After three hours of friend hanging, we got back to her place. By then, I'd honestly forgotten hooking up was a part of the plan.

We started to make out, and she put her hands all over my face and kissed everywhere except my lips. I kept wanting to pipe up and say, *Hello! Hi! Miss? Yes, you. As much as I think it's so sweet of you to kiss my eyelids—and yes, I saw that video on YouTube too—I think I'm ready to do mouth-to-mouth now.*

But I didn't pipe up, and she didn't stop. I let the bad sex run its course.

When it was over, the problem was that I was very far from home here in . . . Bed-Stuy? Bushwick? Outer Mongolia? I had no idea where we'd ended up. And I didn't feel comfortable taking the train because it was two a.m., and I was high. An Uber was *sixty dollars! Who does a surge in the middle of the night on a random-ass Tuesday?* Just an hour before, I'd been afraid I wouldn't be able to pay for her two-dollar PBR.

So it looked like I was staying.

As she tucked herself into bed and rolled over, she said, "You can stay if you want," and fell asleep before I could say, "Are you sur—" She threw her arm over me, and I stared up at the ceiling. The next morning, she got ready for work, and we did an awkward goodbye.

We parted ways and never spoke again. My date with Starlight was pretty representative of the types of encounters I had with lesbians on the dating apps. I kept trying to use them, though, and would end each tiresome search by throwing my phone across the room. I had moved to New York City—the biggest city in the USA—but I kept seeing the same four women in my dating pool.

Kea

I was at the end of my rope when I matched—once again—with a girl on Tinder who invited me out. I really didn't want to go. I, like, *really* didn't want to. I had decided that I was over meeting strangers—and that I was an introvert after all. I took a test online that confirmed it, and I used that to prove to everyone that I needed alone time. "Sorry—can't go out. I'm an introvert, and I need to recharge alone."

Kea, a psychology doctoral student from Germany, said we *could* hang on Tuesday (which I'd suggested), but why not on Wednesday instead? That's when all the lesbians went to ladies' night at a little haven called The Woods.

When I first heard this, I thought maybe she was trying to make me go camping on our first date. But she meant a *bar* called The Woods. I'd always thought "ladies' night" was a thing that straight girls went to when they wanted to ditch their annoying boyfriends and dress up in ten-inch heels to make the boys jealous via social media while Outkast yelled, "Hey, ladies!" in the background. The Woods did not have your typical ladies' night.

I walked in and realized where all the lesbians had been hiding.

Kea introduced herself, and I misunderstood her name. I mumbled back something that roughly approximated her name, which she either didn't care about or didn't notice.

Kea and I kinda knew from the jump that we weren't into each other. For starters, she tried to pay for my drink, and I wanted to play the role of the charmer. The Woods had six-dollar beer/shot specials, which was exactly right for my bank account. Cheap and cut straight to the chase. They also had six-dollar pickle backs for anyone yearning to wake up extra dehydrated in the morning. But Kea was trying to out-top me, and I really wanted to work on my topping skills. That's not to say we didn't hook up—because we did—but we weren't a match.

I cried after she and I had sex. I wept silently to myself because I was still distraught over Jillian. I tried to hide it, but it seemed like Kea could tell when she handed me a tissue as she put away the double-sided dildo. *Cries more.* We agreed to be friends.

And thanks to connecting through the double-sided dildo, I had my first group of New York lesbian friends. Kea added me to her crew's WhatsApp group text, where we talked about how to find hotties. I was also relieved to discover that none of the women seemed to know how to say Kea's name. I asked my new New Zealand mate, Cherri, who said, "I say Key-A, but I've also heard Kay-ah."

"So . . . which one is it?" I asked.

"I don't know! It doesn't matter! Tomato, tomahto." She laughed it off. Also, her name was Cherri, like the fruit. Not *Cherri*. I put cherry emojis to remind me.

The girls I met through Kea were from all over the world. Bali! Italy! South Carolina! It was the World of Lesbians. They introduced me to parties held in secret, big Bushwick warehouses. One of the women was in a band, and we'd check out her live shows and dance to the punk beat while she plucked on a bass in the front row. I was living my best life. Everyone was smart as hell, and they partied like there was no tomorrow. They worked in cool jobs for start-ups and in film. One friend still attended Yale grad school and would travel down to the city just to party with us. I spent the better part of my first year and a half in NYC hanging out with and ultimately sleeping with these women. Ah, lesbians! Things got messy—as they do—once the group reached a critical mass of hooking up with each other and swapping girlfriends. I was slightly infatuated with a girl, Blake, who started hooking up with Kea.

I thought Blake was a tech dream. She was a start-up geek who had a chic way of wearing sweaters over button-downs and the most gorgeous pair of Blundstone work boots. She would call me out on my shit like it was no big deal (the cornerstone of my type) and tried to explain what Bitcoin was. I still have no idea what Bitcoin is. Despite us hooking up once or twice, she had just gotten out of a four-year relationship. Not to mention, she had driven across the country with her ex, who actually worked for Bitcoin, and who was somehow a lesbian Trump supporter who went viral for getting punched by a liberal. Blake wasn't ready for a new relationship, even though I thought that lesbians bounced from 'ship to 'ship.

I went out of town for a summer serving position and came back to find that Kea and Blake had become an item. Turned out she'd just been looking for a different 'ship. While I was away, Kea had advised me that with a little more time, Blake might come around—which meant the sitch double sucked.

I tried to stomach the betrayal, but it really stung. I decided to create a little distance and focus on my career instead.

Still, finding that group of friends had really helped me find myself. I had never experienced anything like it. With them, I attended dinner parties with a huge table of lesbians. I danced on the roof with Cherri, who'd never seen snow before, and we watched the sunrise together. For the first time in my life, I had a posse of lesbian women who had my back. My own Key West Lesbians.

Kea passed away in a freak accident only a year after we met. I had walked out of a bar after watching the last 2016 presidential debate, pressing my phone to my ear to hear what my friend Nikki was saying. I raced to her apartment to sit with that group of women. The first person I saw was Blake. I didn't know what to say. I hated how I felt. I had been so mad at Kea for dating the girl I was in love with, but that all seemed trivial now. Kea was gone. She had been a brilliant human being who had gifted me with a group that accepted me. She had been the glue for all the friendships. She had been the one who was building up the Brooklyn lesbian community. We sat in Kea's apartment for hours, mainly in silence and disbelief.

Late that night, I went back to my apartment, but no one was home. I was alone again. I sat in the dark for hours, trying to understand that Kea was gone. I was still mad and hurt—but more than anything, I wanted to see her again, to thank her for gifting me with my first solid group of queer friends. She always brought people together, even if the jury is still out on how to pronounce her name. It turned out that Tinder wasn't so bad after all.

Chapter Twenty-Eight

YOU CAN'T TELL ME WHAT TO DO—I'M THE PRESIDENT

If you're looking for the chapter that tells you about my big break on *SNL* and walking through the halls of 30 Rock, where I discover Lorne Michaels eats popcorn continuously, and a detailed account of that one pitch meeting where he didn't laugh at my idea to do a spoof of *Swan Lake* in which the other swans eat the feral baby in a bloody, contemporary dance, then this is the wrong book. I'm very sorry to disappoint if you've managed to get through me riding Lammy into the sunset, becoming a fake Christian, and my god-awful remote-control wedging story.

ALL FOR NO JUICE ABOUT THE BIZ?

However, if you are wondering about how a D-List? E-List? Not-Famous-Whatsoever-List person is still trying to make it and has had some small victories, or you're curious about Bravo's *Blind Date* reboot where—as a writer—I gave daters thought bubbles like, "Strawberry? More like straw-marry me!" as they relaxed in a hot tub, then this is about to get good! And who doesn't love hearing about an NBC writer who doesn't report to Rockefeller Center but rather the beloved second location, STAMFORD, CONNECTICUT?

This is where you say, "I do!"

In high school, I was at the annual convention for Junior Civitan, a student-led service club, waiting for the teen night crew committee to come by each hotel room to tell us it was time to go to bed. Despite having been elected the international president of the board, I still had to abide by the curfew—which I was more than happy to do. Miss Marshall County wasn't my only title, thank you.

Like clockwork at ten p.m., Thomas, who thought he was a head boy, swung by with his flashy lanyard and announced to me, "Hi, Elizabeth. As you know, it's now ten p.m., so from here on out, you can't leave the hotel room."

With a blank expression, I said, "You can't tell me what to do. I'm the president."

His eyes grew wide, and he recoiled like I had spit on him, then slapped him, and then poured bleach down his shirt. After a moment of holding his gaze until he was about to soil himself, I broke into laughter. I said, "Dude! I'm kidding! Of course, you got it."

He straightened his lanyard and cleared his throat.

"Right. Curfews apply to everyone, Elizabeth. Being president does not make you exempt."

"I know, Thomas; it was a joke. I'm well aware. I don't think I'm above it at all."

He turned on a dime and left.

Five minutes later, I received a call from our adult adviser, who scolded me for an hour about what a horrible example I was setting and really what a fucking disgusting human being I had to be to feel so entitled. It was a privilege to be president. A privilege that could be taken away.

Since I was graduating, I was about to pass the baton to the already elected president in twenty-four hours, but our adviser felt the need to threaten impeachment anyway. Despite crying my eyes out to my board (who only came over because I was flailing and howling) and convincing myself I had not made a joke—but had, in fact, shot Thomas (the weasel) square in the chest, I gathered my thoughts and made a decision.

It was in that moment that I knew I had to commit even harder in the future. Thank you for kick-starting my comedy career, Thomas Claire.

Dark humor always seemed to settle well with me. I remember when Jimmy Kimmel (who was known for his large-scale pranks) invited a kid to come onto his show to shoot a free throw for a chance to win $1 million. They played home footage of the kid practicing in his backyard for hours. He'd practiced ruthlessly to the point that there was no chance for him to have the slightest margin of error. It was a lock. As he went to shoot the ball in front of a live studio audience, Kimmel knocked the basketball out of the kid's hand and ripped up the check.

"It was so funny! You gotta watch it," I told my classmate.

"That sounds really fucked up, Sophie. Sounds like that kid really needs the money."

I didn't think I'd have a career in comedy, though. I was too much of a musical theater nerd to see past a future on Broadway. More importantly, for a long time, I didn't think I was "funny." I can see how things I've done in the past are funny, and with training, I've gotten to a point where I can confidently admit I have decent timing and am comfortable humiliating myself.

During teenage trips to NYC with Mom, in between geeking out at the Eugene O'Neill Theater, I led a double life. I started hanging out with my cousin Amber Nelson. The first show she invited me to was at the Upright Citizens Brigade Theatre. The show's name was *ASSSSCAT*, and it was the Sunday night improv show with, apparently, the best improvisers in the biz. It was no ordinary night. It happened to be a special drop-in show where Amy Poehler herself did thirty minutes of improv. As an audience member tried to take a picture of her, she mimed burning the camera.

When I walked back into the hotel room, I told Mom about the magic I had seen.

"They came up with everything on the spot, and AMY POEHLER was there!"

"Get out! AMY POEHLER?" Mom felt I had made it just by breathing her air. "Did you tell her you want to make it like her?"

I didn't have the heart to tell Mom that's not how it works . . . so I just waved it off with "yeah-huh" and "sure, yeah."

I continued to hang with Amber throughout the years in the basements of clubs and sit at shitty bar shows or in a random apartment where I'd have to scale the fire escape, while she did her tight five in Bushwick.

About a year before I graduated high school and hundreds of shows later, Amber and I were waiting for the L train, which was the biggest deal to me at the time. I was very familiar with the Jefferson stop and could even ride the subway to meet her, all by myself. She looked so cool in her thrift-shop pink coat and leather boots.

"I can't wait to move up here one day," I said as I beamed at the other thrifty grifters and as the train across the platform rattled through.

"You'll do great! But you should be flexible when you get here. You might think you know what you want to do, but that can all change. Just keep an open mind."

I wanted to respond with, *Tell that to my loose sheets of music,* but she was right.

After my first year living in New York, I hadn't booked anything, and I had a growing fear that the restaurant job was the best gig I'd land. I figured I should take matters into my own hands. I started making videos that I could cast myself in, which ultimately led me to get comedy training at the same theater where Amy Poehler burned the camera, UCB.

Getting into classes at UCB was impossible. You'd have an easier time donating an organ to a child in need. Spots filled up in less than a minute, so you had to sign up for notifications to come through on your phone via Twitter and have $400 at the ready to throw at your screen. I'd be in the middle of taking a table's order, feel my phone buzz, and walk away with no explanation, only to see that it was not for a UCB class but a GIF of Tina Belcher from Mom. I continued to be on high alert, until one fateful day, SKETCH 101 M/W/F flashed across my phone. I clicked the link and signed up in ten seconds, threw cash at the screen, and bam! I was in.

On my first day of class, my sketch teacher, Eric Cunningham, plopped down in a chair as sixteen of us sat around a table, eagerly anticipating the advice that would turn us into comedy geniuses. UCB's now-defunct training center had lined the halls with photos of all the house teams that'd started the careers of comedy greats like Kate McKinnon, Nick Kroll, Aubrey Plaza, Donald Glover—and oh yeah, Amy Poehler. And every time you walked past, you were reminded that one day, that could be you. *Future Childish Gambino, don't mind if I do!* Eric was a charming-looking guy who wore a purple sweater, Rachel Maddow glasses, and his hair stuck out from the top of his head like Jimmy Neutron. He had total dad vibes, and I'm so glad he owned it.

"Wazzup, guys! We're doin' it, we're doin' it!" He lifted his hands in the air to build up the excitement. We all cheered, and some slammed the table. He pushed his glasses up, clearly sorta embarrassed for inciting the inner fury of us and also slightly proud of himself.

"You're here because you want to learn the basics of sketch," Eric continued.

One class clown piped up and said, "Whoops, wrong class," and pretended to get out of his chair while we all stared at him until he crumpled.

Eric, not ever wanting to make even a mouse feel bad, said, "Ha-ha, yep, yep. Where was I?"

I waved at Eric to continue, even though he didn't see me.

Eric continued. "Best advice I can give you when starting to write sketch is this: if *you* find it funny, then at least one person thinks it's funny. Follow the funny."

Follow the funny.

I mean, sure—telling that to a room of people wanting to be the next Zach Galifianakis or Kate McKinnon might seem like a no-brainer. But at the time, it felt like precious advice.

We were tasked with writing one sketch by the next week, and by the end of the two-month session, we'd build to two sketches a week. I started following the funny and cultivating my own comedy petri dish.

I wrote a sketch called "The New Gaydar" about how since straight women were appropriating lesbian and queer culture, all the lesbians had to invent a new gaydar device. It was a vagina brooch. It's never graced the stage, but I was honing my voice. I kept taking swings. I wrote sketches every single night.

I lived at the ~~theater~~ cult, standing at the back wall, watching sketch show after sketch show, pounding LaCroixes and really imagining what it'd be like for me to perform there. Those beer-stained walls were my new drug.

I started to examine the world differently once I knew what "game" was. The repeatable funny thing. The positive side was that I was getting good. The negative side was that it was now hard for me to take anything seriously. Comedy ruined my life.

I'd write down any semblance of an idea in my server handbook when the managers weren't looking. Apologies to my now girlfriend, who has put all my "ideas" from the past several years into binders for me because I won't throw anything away. I know I haven't opened them—but I WILL soon. Promise.

At work one night, I casually said to a fellow server, "It's insane that this place is so militaristic, right? Like, no one's talking about how we're all acting like soldiers and slaves to a fucking restaurant. And not only that, but look at everyone here. We're literally in *American Psycho*. That guy in the Brooks Brothers shirt for sure killed his wife and is drinking a merlot, basking in the thought of it."

He responded with, "Did he really kill his wife?"

"No . . . he just looks like it. I was just fucking around."

The server marched away, realizing a manager was about to send us home for talking, which was also absurd—but WHATEVER. The idea went nowhere, but I wrote it down anyway.

Even theater was hard to take seriously. THEATER. My lifeblood. My very raison d'être.

At a Broadway production, the lead actor shouted out, "My dead, lifeless sister is dead!"

I whispered to my friend, "Hey, do you think she's really dead, or do you think the actress just likes saying the word *dead*?"

"Sophie, shut up," my friend said.

Even talking to my mom became funny for me. When visiting her, I asked if we could watch something besides marathons of *Law & Order: SVU*, and she, unaware, turned the channel to *NCIS*. Touché.

I even wrote *Duck Lake*, the *Swan Lake* spoof. Yes, it exists.

It was my second great awakening, only this time it was about comedy, not an overdue reckoning with my sexuality.

I realized that all my theater training could be repurposed to do parody sketches and to play with genres. And accents and archetypes. One afternoon, a few weeks shy of my completion of Sketch 201, Eric—my teacher and new favorite person—sent me an email. I felt my phone buzz in my apron at work and slipped into the broom closet to check the notification that had UNSOLICITED ADVICE in the subject line. I scanned the email and immediately saw the words *recommend* and *job* and *website*. I took a deep breath and forced myself to slowly read it from the top.

I want to recommend you for jobs, so GET A
WEBSITE. My mentor once told me that years ago,
and now I'm telling you. So. GET A WEBSITE. (We're
doin' it.)

I knew I had been in the broom closet for far too long, and table ten's food was probably dying at the pass, but I was ready to walk out of the restaurant that very moment. Sorry, folks, I'm about to make it. *Rips off apron.* JOBS? I could actually get a job doing COMEDY?

I had moved out of my Wall Street sliver and into a bona fide Bushwick apartment. That afternoon, I threw my new roommate, Barrett, twenty dollars and a bottle of wine to make me a website (he's a voice-over artist and totally gets it), and within a day I *got* a website. A really well-done website. A week later—and again, at work—I got an email from MTV asking me to join them for a brainstorming session. MTV! The home of *TRL* and *Ridiculousness* and *Ridiculousness*. I tried to play it cool and to not seem too eager—I did a lap around the restaurant and then raced back into the bathroom to email the producer back to confirm my attendance. I also wanted to run and find Eric wherever he was to scream, "I OWE YOU MY LIFE." I couldn't leave work, but I will say now, Eric, I owe you my life.

Later that day, the producer sent me my first contract, and I got to take off work for a week. *Actually takes off apron.*

My first day, I walked up to the utopian Viacom building and rode an escalator with one of the illuminated jumbotrons peeking over the top as Top 40 hits played. I was thirty minutes early, so I sat in the lobby until it was appropriate to let them know I had arrived. Twenty minutes later, I walked up to the front desk.

"ID?" the security guard asked.

"Oh! Yeah! Here you go." I gave her my driver's license.

"Which floor?"

"I'm not sure. I'm here for the brainstorming session for MTV. I'm a writer." She pressed a button.

"Hi, Miss Santos is here. Uh-huh. Okay, I'll send her up. Look into the camera." She snapped my picture and printed out a name tag that showed me as a blob that could be mistaken for the neighborhood night watch cartoon, but which I knew I would laminate nonetheless.

"You're all set. Floor REDACTED."

The automatic turnstile swiveled.

I hopped into the elevator, which was flashing more lights in purple, and blue, and green, as a bunch of people got in. Donning my classiest snapback, I was holding my backpack tightly. We shot up incredibly fast as more people got on and off. By the time we were about four floors away, I noticed it was just me and a tall, lanky guy with dirty-blond hair that was stuffed under a Patagonia hat. He was also clinging to the straps of his backpack.

"You here for that brainstorm team thing?" he asked.

"Yeah, you?"

"Yes, sir."

An assistant greeted us, and we were ushered into a big glass room that overlooked the now shuttered Guy Fieri's Guy's American Kitchen & Bar (who Eric has said is the hardest-working person in the world) and the former *New York Times* building (which, fun fact, is the reason why Times Square has its name, also from Eric). We swiveled in our chairs doing bits, rolling back and forth across the floor.

"Do you know what this is about?" I asked.

"No fucking clue."

"Me either, but I'll sign up for anything."

"I'd give my arm to be in a building like this," he added.

"Kidney, my body, my brain. Doesn't matter," I continued.

"I'm a sellout. I'll say it," he said.

"Always say it."

"And I like it. Let's admit it—we all like doing it," he continued.

We both grinned and continued to spin in our chairs like the Mad Tea Party ride at Disney World.

"I'm Sophie."

"John."

Apparently, either we were both very early or everyone else was late, but we had the room to ourselves for another half hour. I didn't know it at the time, but I had just met one of my most frequent collaborators and one of my best friends. Here we were, doing bits like two idiots who'd just smoked a bowl.

"Oh my God, is that New York City's John Trowbridge?" one of the writers said as they entered the room.

I furrowed my brow and turned to John. "I didn't know I was meeting someone so famous. Why didn't you mention this before?"

"Well, I didn't want you to treat me differently."

"And you knew I would have," I concluded.

As others filtered in, I realized I was in a room full of people who'd already had TV jobs. A guy who was Letterman's warm-up comic, another comic who'd had his own TV show on Fuse. John, who was a "New Face" at Just for Laughs in Montreal. And then there was me. A Sketch 201 student.

We all bonded over not knowing what we were there for and what we were about to do for the next week, as everyone cracked more jokes and swiveled in their chairs.

Two hours later, a very LA producer walked in and sat down.

"So, we're rebooting *TRL*," he said.

I tried to nod like I hadn't just been thinking about walking the same halls as Carson Daly moments prior.

"And we're also hoping to bring a version of our LA show *Ridiculousness* to New York with a new host."

Bam, there it is.

"We'd love for you all to come up with fun games that we could use. Or, if you're feeling frisky, even show ideas for the network."

At the time, I didn't realize that the $500 a day they were paying us—which is, unquestionably, a nice chunk of change—didn't begin to compare to the private-jet money people can actually make selling a TV show idea.

"Here's an idea to get ya goin' and something I think is hilarious, team," the producer continued while laughing to himself. "What if we got a vat of barf and made the contestant try to retrieve something from it. That would get a lot of views, right?"

We all smiled and nodded. "Oh yes, a vat of barf is such a funny and original idea, sir."

He patted the table.

"Okey dokey! I'll leave you all to it." Then I heard him mutter under his breath, "Barf, ha-ha. That's a good one."

After he left, we all agreed to put that down at the top of the brainstorming document and commenced talking about how barf would be the real BREAKTHROUGH MOMENT OF MODERN TV.

An hour later, we were told he was on a plane to LA, and we already had a different boss. And that's pretty much how my first paid week as a comedy writer went. I felt like I had made it. And we were all, in fact, really doin' it.

Chapter Twenty-Nine

I THINK I'M IN LOVE WITH YOU

I had only been dating Amy for three weeks when she left me to visit her family for Christmas. We had spent every moment together up until then. We hadn't spent one night apart. Not even when she had to work an hour away in the Bronx and she drove back in the middle of the night so we could curl up together. That was when I fully realized she wasn't just someone who let me keep my socks on during sex. I kissed her goodbye as she got into the car and headed to Jersey. She'd only been gone for a few minutes when I had an old and very familiar sensation. A panic. *What are the road conditions? Why didn't we check the forecast before? Did the Uber driver have nuts in the car—SHE'S ALLERGIC TO NUTS.* As soon as she left, I began to . . . ahem . . . blow up her phone.

Are you okay? I casually asked in my first message. Followed by, *You're not responding . . . did something happen?* And then:

AMY, WHY AREN'T YOU TEXTING ME??!!!!!????!!!!????!! The three thousand exclamation marks really cemented the fact that I was currently losing my mind.

Hiiiii, sorry, she responded. *I'm here! I fell asleep.*

From that moment on, I was panicked that every time Amy left the house, it would be her untimely demise. That a steel pipe would fly off the bed of a semitruck, leaving her lifeless body lying on the pavement with yellow police tape strung around the scene that would keep me from holding her lifeless body one last time.

Mom had come to the city to spend Christmas with me. I had been pacing the apartment, pale and terrified, ranting about how Amy was gonna die from the nuts that were potentially in the Uber driver's car, when she stopped me and said, "Honey, I think you're in love."

Cue the Jessica Simpson track.

Amy and I had met IRL. We were working on the same late-night show where she was the digital producer and I was a writer. Don't shit where you eat, they say! But it tastes good, I say!

On my first date with Amy, we went to a Spanish tapas and wine restaurant. When she suggested it, I quipped back, *Did you just pick that place because I'm Spanish?*

NO! OMG, sorry. We don't have to go there!

A moment.

Wait . . . are you joking?

I sent back the emoji sticking out its tongue. 😛

For the first time in my life, I was dating an Italian Jersey girl who pronounced the word *talk* as "tohwk." Fortunately, she didn't act like the people on *Jersey Shore*. I told her I thought all Jersey Italians loved GTL. And she told me she thought all southerners were simpleminded.

Good thing we met or neither of us would have ever known the truth.

When we sat down, she asked what kind of wine I'd like, and I said, "Something with minerality."

"Is that another joke?" She smiled.

"No, certain white wines, depending on their region, have minerality. Some taste like seashells."

She squinted her eyes. "Seashells? I don't believe you."

She was testing me, or at least she'd thrown out a challenge I'd created in my head. I decided I had to win. The server came over, and I puffed out my chest to ask, "When it comes to your white wines, do any have minerality to them?"

"Of course! The Vespaiolo is very nice. Tastes like seashells," she confirmed.

I winked at Amy.

"We'll sidebar and let you know."

Amy sat there with her mouth fully open. I took it upon myself to cash in on winning.

"See . . . it wasn't a joke. Do you like seashells?"

"I guess we're about to find out."

Our date lasted ten hours, and we ate at two restaurants that night. Two! I guess she had me at seashells?

Jury's still out on whether she always picks up on my sarcasm.

After gazing into each other's eyes over tapas and mineral wine for ten hours, I felt an "uh-oh!" sensation. I never took myself for someone who'd find "the one." *The one?* That shit's only written in screenplays. Our grandparents only feel that way because they thought they *had* to find the one.

"When you know, you know," people would say, and I'd nod like that didn't sound like total nonsense.

But with Amy, something clicked. She fit like a glove. The first time we kissed, the world felt like it stopped on its axis. I was in a tunnel with every sound and image that ever existed racing through my head.

Bare feet running on grass. A train whistle blowing. The wind in a tunnel. Water dripping. A real heart beating during surgery. An eye opening for the first time. A mouth gasping for air. A deer grazing. A Coke bottle being opened for the first time and hissing.

If that wasn't "you're the one" shit, then I don't know what is, but at the time, I still brushed it off because I was not, I repeat, not looking for anything serious.

Unfortunately, Amy was a bookish girl next door, and 1,000 percent my type.

It was shocking that she stuck around after she came home with me and got an up close and personal view of my gross-ass room. I had told her that I was "messy, but not that bad." In reality, clothes were everywhere—any visitor had to have Olympic gymnastics balance to get from Point A to Point B, like the floor was lava, and navigate exclusively by one-leg hopping between piles of paper, clothes, and unidentifiable items. And . . . I hadn't washed my sheets in a few years.

I know I know I know I know.

I know.

I'VE SINCE CHANGED. I own two sets of sheets that I rotate once a week, thanks to Amy.

But I hadn't washed my sheets because:

A) I didn't think it was a big deal?
B) I was lazy?
C) I didn't want to put on a fitted sheet by myself because I didn't know how.

All of the above are correct.

Amy bravely navigated the floor of lava all the way to my mattress—which was also on the floor.

The next morning, I woke up alone and in a blur. WTF? And what kind of assassin-level skills does she possess? Amy called to apologize and told me that she'd had to run home to change before work. I told *her* that I would personally wear the same clothes back to back after a first-time sexcapade, but that's JUST ME. She explained that *she* would have been embarrassed and had her own routine. If there's anything I could respect, it was a—albeit very strange to me—routine. I asked her to come over again and bring a change of clothes, and she did the very next night.

She didn't leave for six months.

We alternated between our apartments, but we couldn't stay apart. I have since found out that she would leave my apartment early in the morning, traveling the forty-five minutes back to her apartment so she could get ready for work in a bathroom where there was actually a shower curtain. Over time, she finally admitted she couldn't deal with my "chaotic and messy lifestyle," but only after we finally moved in together a year later.

During that blissful six months, my brain started inventing all sorts of nightmare scenarios. What if we fall asleep and Amy never wakes up? What if she gets poisoned by a self-proclaimed vigilante who mistakes her for their archnemesis? What if I have a nightmare and stab her with a kitchen knife?

It was a dangerous world, and I had to protect her at every cost, nothing short of Bubble Wrapping the apartment with her safe inside.

I was too embarrassed to tell Amy that she was about to die, but I also started sounding like a controlling asshole, so I had to decide if it was better to confess than annoy her until she left me. Especially because it started to get worse.

I started tracking her on Find My Friends because I wanted to know if she'd had a hit put out on her (she *is* Italian). Or I'd show up to brunch unannounced because I didn't want her to get roofied. You know. Casual things like that. She politely told me she would need me to stop doing these things, but only after showing me how it was impossible, given the position of her cup, that there was a roofie in it. Every time she'd come home, I'd kiss her face like she had just returned from war. *Is this what love is? I don't like this feeling one bit. Please do not sign me up.* I understand this was a very weird paranoia and a direct result of my OCD, but please—if you are feeling this way, speak up! A LITTLE LOUDER, PLEASE.

When it comes to dating, I'm not sure when a relationship makes the jump from "had fun last night 😊" to "I'm sorry I'm late for the fifth time, boss. Here's your schedule for today. Am I in trouble?" Almost immediately, the level of comfort between us was astounding. I literally texted her, `I want you to sock me in the face and make sure people ask about it.` WHO SAYS THAT SHIT? (For the record, Amy still won't do it.)

We boinked all night, every night. We once boinked in a dirty Manhattan Starbucks during my fifteen-minute lunch break. Starbucks in NYC aren't like Starbucks in the suburbs. They are there for anyone and everyone to take huge shits in between meetings and, frankly, are emergency shelters for the homeless to hang out in, since there's nowhere else for them to go. Looking at you, DeBlasio!

We both went into debt in the very first two months we dated. We blew *all* our money. Every night we'd either order in to refuel ourselves after life-altering sex or we'd go out. We'd find ourselves a cute little restaurant and take each other out on a date. Like how some people do weekly, or most do monthly, or on their anniversary. We had those dates nightly. I'm talking wine pairings. I'm talking walking into a five-star restaurant on a Tuesday and ordering the damn tasting menu. We each gained about twenty pounds and lost our minds. We took ourselves on trips! For our one-month anniversary, we decided we'd go upstate to live out our lesbian wet dream.

We went where everyone goes: Beacon, New York.

Ahhhh, Beacon. The streets. The cafés. The museums that have sterile bathrooms to have sex in!

I had somehow turned a "very responsible, never in debt, paid off student loans, would disinfect her electronics before she went to bed" type of person into a frivolous and carefree one. But she also turned this "non–sheet washing, wears underwear three days in a row, noncommittal" person into a kind and caring (cleaner) one.

And also a paranoid freak who thinks death is always looming.

I'm still working on that last part, but I wouldn't have my life any other way.

Chapter Thirty

ARCHIE ANDREWS AND THE QUEST OF ASCENDING INTO LESBIAN STARDOM TERRITORY

For the first time, both my personal and professional lives were #trending upward. John and I decided to write a two-man show that was a hypersexual reimagining of the hit CW show *Riverdale*, which was an already hypersexual reimagining of the Archie comics. We created a live episode and a Halloween special called *Riverdale Live* and *Riverdale Live: The Halloween Squirtacular*, respectively. The premise: gonorrhea was running amok at Riverdale High because all the horny teens couldn't stop sucking and f*cking, and Archie, the teenage hero who was cut like a thirty-five-year-old Thor, was going to save the town the best way he knew: through his acoustic music. If you're thinking, *Jesus, Sophie, I had no idea how filthy you were*, then I say, *Have you not been paying attention?*

John and I played all the characters (Archie; Veronica Lodge; Betty and Betty's teenage BDSM alter ego, Dark Betty; Archie's dad; Cheryl Blossom; and more), most in drag, and ran back and forth onstage while John narrated as Jughead in between scenes. We first performed at Barbra Streisand's famous The Duplex and then at the hip Brooklyn venue Union Hall. We had a one-page spread in *Time Out New York* and went on to perform in Philly, and finally, we got the chance to bring our sexy show to the iconic Edinburgh Festival Fringe in Scotland.

Riverdale Live had a steamy shower scene where Veronica yells at Archie for being poor, so to the Edinburgh Festival we went.

We were accepted at Edinburgh's oldest gay bar, the Planet, by a booker whose emails were written as if he were a spam robot. His name was Ned Cox, and he was delighted to have fellow Americans at the venue. I wired him 350 pounds to cover our fees and prayed to God that wasn't the last I heard from him and that my identity hadn't been stolen.

John and I showed up to the venue and were approached by a short man with stringy hair and a long face. This must be Ned. He knew nothing about our show. Let me rephrase. He knew we were coming. He had seen the posters. He'd even read some of the old Archie comics. But he was not prepared for the beloved satirical parody we were about to grace his stage with. And neither were the old gay Scot barflies who were having a pint while we rehearsed our lines about choosing "music or football" and how "high school is so hard, especially with cum gutters."

The stage wasn't a stage but a raised platform in the middle of the bar that could only fit one of us at a time. A woman who looked like Big Boo from *Orange Is the New Black* ran the lights for us. I assumed that both she and Ned were gay, only to learn, after the run of the show, that they were partners.

I mean, cool, love is love. And apparently, I still knew nothing.

We both had taken the red-eye and were running on fumes. We had one hour to rehearse, and then our first curtain was two hours later, at four p.m.—a perfect time, according to Ned, for a show. Because it was a bar, four p.m. meant happy hour. As Ned explained, "Fifty-fifty chance guests will be there for you instead of the three-pound shots . . . On second thought, maybe forty-sixty . . . heh." *So much for the premium slot.*

We rushed to drop our stuff off at the Airbnb, which was run by a Spanish man who wore a bathrobe the entire duration of our stay.

"He's definitely hiding a dead body," John said as we got into the cab.

"Yep, and we're next. Sorry to tell you, but you will have to protect me. As you know, I subscribe to traditional gender roles."

"Right, I'll grab my shotgun after the show."

Back at the venue, I got ready in the ~~greenroom~~ bathroom. The back of the door had the bill pasted on it. The lineup was as follows:

- A Diamond Diva: Europe's only dwarf drag act
- An Audience with a Transvestite: a happily married transvestite and his wife tell of their life
- A Queer Love of Dix: a Weimar cabaret (Kurt Weill/Brecht) set against a backdrop of Otto Dix paintings
- Bilbao Is Not in Spain: Dr. Woof (Britain's bearded drag) and performance artist Aletia Upstairs's burlesque
- Riverdale Live: a hypersexual reimagining of the teen drama The CW's *Riverdale.*

Four shows only, baby.

Ned also had a special one-night-only performance where he himself was a banana man (dressed in a banana suit) and talked about his life as a banana man with anecdotes starting with every letter from the alphabet.

John wanted to start the process to remove his citizenship on the spot.

"Can we wait to start the paperwork until after our four shows . . . ?"

"And then . . . he's out of here," he said.

I nodded.

At four o'clock, with about three people in seats, Ned gave us a thumbs-up and we were on. For a half hour, we performed our *Riverdale* parody to the old gays of Edinburgh, much to their amusement and bewilderment. For some reason, right as I was saying, "Who's with me, Bulldogs?" in a towel and spray-painted abs, my back went out, and I had to bite my lip to keep from yelping for the heavens.

It's stress, honey. You've been running around like crazy, my mom texted that night. Then, *And please turn off your phone, the bill is going up.*

Okay, thanks. Love you.

Love you too. Call me later.

After the show, Ned came up to us with the money bucket that he had passed around. A few coins clinked in the bottom.

"Great show, lads! Don't be discouraged. Three people is like fifty for the festival. That's a job well done."

Didn't have to tell us teen heartthrobs twice.

We bopped around that night and hit up a pub to celebrate as I gritted through the pain. *Is this what it feels like to be in your late twenties?*

The following performance, more people trickled in.

After another "Pie in the sky, Archie would climb through Betty's window, and it would look like some horny remix of *Clarissa Explains It All* and a long version of *Blue Is the Warmest Color*," a jovial couple from a village on the shore came up to us.

"Me husband's been waitin' to see this show fer ages. He wouldn't stop talkin' about it, would ya, Finlay?"

Finlay, red in the face, almost moved to tears, slipped us a fifty-pound note and waved us off like he couldn't speak.

A young Scottish teen came up to ask for a picture, which we later discovered on his Instagram page with an excited caption about how it was the world premiere.

And the old gay Scots suddenly found themselves audience members during their afternoon pints, like clockwork. I even caught them watching and nudging one another.

I called Amy to tell her about how we might just be onto something, to which she said, "God, you two are such idiots."

That night, we found ourselves at an Australian party where they tried to convince us to attend the Adelaide Festival by plying us with free drinks. We danced all night long to a cut, and I mean cut, European DJ who spun like a goddess, then went to a halal place and ordered a pizza with everything on it, and finally went back to our Airbnb and passed out on our shared full bed while watching *Misfits*.

For a week, we attended dumb theater, good theater, and bad theater; day drank; and performed *Riverdale* in a foreign country. I think Archie would have been proud, had his gonorrhea not gotten the best of him.

Back at home, I was dipping my toes in the stand-up circuit. I found it more fun to perform on gay-run shows. Obviously because I'm gay . . . but also because it felt nice to get up in front of a supportive community. One of the most supportive people was Tim Dunn, who gave me my first stage time during his show *Queerball*. I even got to do the *Best of Queerball* show at the former UCB Chelsea. Right where Amy Poehler performed. I did my own version of Jimmy Fallon's Thank You Notes, which were all gay-themed. "Thank you, nail clippers" was among my favorites. I was not only on my way as a writer but reinventing myself as a performer.

The more I performed around town, however, the more I realized that the shows were often run by gay men. Lovely men, but consistently gay *men*.

And the more I kept searching for shows led by queer women, the more I kept coming up short. I didn't want to fulfill my destiny as an angry lesbian, but I was certainly becoming one.

Growing up, when I'd have tantrums about something pissing me off, my mom used to say, "Honey, is it out of your control?"

"Yes . . ."

"Then don't give it one more ounce of your energy. You can only control what you can control. Ommmm . . . ommmm," she'd say as she gently pet my face. She'd clearly been learning from all her books throughout the years.

Could I control the fact that other people were hosting shows? *No.* What could I control, then? *I mean, I could do my own show . . . but . . . not really.* I hadn't been doing stand-up for more than six months, and I wasn't even allowing myself to call it stand-up yet.

"I do bits," I told someone who wanted to book me. "And sometimes musical comedy."

"So do you wanna do the show or not?"

But the problem with the industry was more than just the hosts. I was noticing that lesbians were left out of the narrative a lot. When we're written into the narrative, we're always being killed off like we like it or deserve it.

I decided to reach out to another queer comic who I'd seen murder the room every time she did a set.

I sent her a text that was like, `Hey, been doing a lot of comedy shows lately and it seems there aren't many or really any queer women hosts. We should do a show together?`

Now normally, if some half stranger were to send that to me, I'd brush it off as a psycho-alert. That's, like, a rule in comedy. Because doing a show takes chemistry and time. But I knew there was a hole in the market, and as a lesbian, I felt like I was running out of time. Death is always lurking.

A few months later, after mulling it over, she came back around and said, `Hey, I do want to sit down, actually.`

From there, we started what we deemed the next big variety show that Lily Tomlin would be saluting from the set of *Grace and Frankie*, *The Lesbian Agenda*!

Rule #1: Only queer women on the lineup, except for men who were raised by two moms.

Rule #2: We'd do agenda items that we wanted to accomplish like, "Get health clinics to put out a bowl of nail clippers to promote safe sex." This one was extremely important to me.

Rule #3: Rachel Weisz should be a central topic.

"Yeah, we'll start with one show, and then maybe we can do another and then, pie in the sky, it's a television show!"

I think she was surprised by my energy.

Luckily, it didn't scare her off, yet.

We got a few photos snapped, made a poster, the booker put it on Eventbrite, and bam! The show started selling out immediately, and we were already getting all kinds of press from *Time Out New York* and lesbian media. Clearly we weren't the only ones who wanted a space where lesbians and queer women could talk frankly about lesbian and queer stuff! I knew there was a need for it, and I was happy other people did too. Now we just had to do it. We bought matching Wildfang suits, which were a costly thing but totally worth it. We joked about them sponsoring us, in which they kindly tagged us on their 'gram.

The day before the show, as I picked out a fresh pair of kicks from Vans, my girlfriend gave me a kind of wistful smile.

"What's wrong?" I asked.

"Nothing at all. I feel like you're leveling up. Pretty cool."

I tied the laces and looked in the mirror. I did feel a tinge of something brewing.

As the night started, we put up a slideshow of queer celebrities—mainly photos of Rachel Weisz. I sang a song about how Rachel Weisz and I were going far in life, with my cohost interrupting to remind me that she's married to Daniel Craig. We had a lineup of incredible performers. All queer. All fierce. All excited to have a clubhouse for lesbians.

From there, the one-off show turned into every other month, and then we got the offer to do it monthly!

Things were heating up, and soon we were scouted by the acclaimed tech group Lesbians Who Tech.

The CEO messaged us both on Twitter: Lesbians Who Tech? Lesbian Agenda? Sounds like a match, huh?

She invited us to attend the conference. I had never seen so many high-profile lesbians: Kara Swisher, lesbians who were CFOs at Nike, Patagonia, even the senior adviser to President Obama.

I was on a hotel rooftop in Hell's Kitchen overlooking the city, as I was served the finest steak and rubbed shoulders with women who worked at Facebook and Goldman Sachs.

"Enough about me—what do you do?" one woman asked as she poured me more wine.

"Oh, I'm just a comedian." I shrugged, a little embarrassed.

"JUST? That's awesome!"

"I think NASA's more awesome, to be honest. You're actually doing something with a huge impact."

"No, I think what you're doing is having a bigger impact." She was incorrect.

The Lesbians Who Teched wouldn't let me downplay it and made me feel like I belonged. If this wasn't a full-circle, coming into my own, flat-out episode of *The L Word*, then I don't know what is.

The Lesbians Who Teched invited us to perform in San Francisco a few months later. We had taken some time off over the holidays but met up to work on a comedic dissertation about how lesbian the tech industry really is. Tech is a lesbian. For starters, Alexa, Siri, and GPS Woman are all practically "Bette" from *The L Word* with their condescending yet reassuring approach. And iPhones require touch and communication. Enough said.

It became clear that despite our great writing relationship, we didn't have the chemistry that could uphold a long-term show. She was a true stand-up, and I was a sketch/variety person. So after our performance, which was a roaring success, we walked to a café, dressed in our matching Wildfang suits, and decided to part ways. She gave me her blessing to continue *The Lesbian Agenda* on my own.

The show was really taking off, and I was scared shitless. What was I going to tell all our fans? Or the venue? Not to mention, I had never hosted a comedy show by myself, *not to mention* one that was selling out. There was no bad blood, but I was deeply sad and, for a moment, depressed. I found myself, again, in an airport, recovering from a breakup, this time a comedy breakup, freaking out to a friend, who reassured me.

"I think it's time for you to shine."

I heard my dad saying, *"So, soldier, you just gonna stand there or you gonna do something about it?"* He was very much still with us, but he had an Android, and I couldn't text him on the plane.

Amy happened to be a producer and told me she'd produce it for me.[42]

"What do you want out of the show? It's yours now. So what do YOU want?"

"I want it to be a talk show for lesbians. I want it to be like a *Daily Show* for lesbians, with correspondents . . . more segments, interspersed with other performers performing stand-up."

"What if we do a segment where you interview famous lesbians?" she asked.

"YES! Called Lesbian Icon?"

---

[42] Yes, because I am a lesbian, I also work with my girlfriend. #codependency

"Mm-hmm," she said. "Do you know any famous lesbians?"

"NO!"

Amy said she'd ask her boss at the time, Jamie Babbit. Jamie showed up, and I got to interview her at our fireside chat (a cardboard cutout of a fire), asking her about her start, directing *But I'm a Cheerleader*, and did a lightning round of questions called "Lez-Be-Honest" while the band the Veronicas played underneath us. It was full circle again.

From there, it grew. It was up to me to create the content, and I did fun things like a Woman on the Street, where I asked people of New York to name a famous lesbian. Answers were "Ellen," "Ellen's wife," and "ha-ha, no." We shot a music video based on my girlfriend and me being mistaken for sisters. And we had my good friend Jessica come on as the lesbian correspondent to search Miley Cyrus and Kaitlynn Carter's boat in Lake Como (very important 2019 news) to find out if there was an apartment lease on board. We booked notable lesbian personalities: the CEO of Lesbians Who Tech, the CEO of Wildfang (a full-circle moment), and the founder of Backstage Capital and the only Black woman to make the cover of *Fortune* magazine who wasn't an athlete, Arlan Hamilton.

We got invited to perform at the New York Comedy Festival and even performed at The Bell House.

And we took the show to LA.

And we pitched it as a TV show.

And we're still pitching it as a TV show.

The point is . . . it sucked having to regroup, but it was a blessing to get to flourish on my own—with the help of my wonderful girlfriend and talented producer/director, Amy, and a small group of people whom I'm forever indebted to.

I found purpose with that show. A voice. My voice. And even if it never goes anywhere else, I know that we created a community that, for a brief moment in time, knew their voices were heard.

Chapter Thirty-One

SWAN SONG

I'd pulled into a huge gravel parking lot with Amy and stared at the dozens of other cars already parked. Our rental car, an upgraded Cadillac (Enterprise's accident was our gain), hummed as we sat, ignition running. My heart was in my throat, and my hands were shaking as I turned off the radio. Amy put her hand on my leg and said, "We don't have to go in there until you're ready, babe."

My phone buzzed in my pocket. Through the windshield, I continued to look at the long walkway in front of us. My phone buzzed again.

"Babe?"

I looked up at Amy, who radiated goodness. I wanted to cry, looking at her perfect sparkling green eyes. *GOD!* You know how you want to squeeze your partner's face and also like put the peach fuzz from their butt cheek in your mouth?

"If that high school bully Tara pulls anything," she sternly said. *There's that Scorpio tail.* "If *anyone* pulls anything, we'll leave. Not a second warning. No one messes with my boobie."

I watched as an older, slightly rounder Colton hopped out of his minivan and started walking toward the building. He'd upgraded his Ford Mustang since the last time I'd seen him.

"Babe, you in there?" she asked.

It's a phrase Amy has said many times over the course of our relationship when I go silent. Sometimes my brain goes so fast that I can't get anything out, and I stand there with my mouth open like my RAM is in overdrive.

"Let's come up with a code word," I said.

"Sophie, stop," she said with a laugh. She'd heard this a million times.

"How's *Brexit*?"

"Brexit? No!"

I started crying.

"Why are you crying?"

"I don't know!"

I finally took out my phone.

I'm here! read the text from Emma, my best friend from high school. Followed by, *Well . . . lady, are you comin'?*

"Emma's here. Maybe we should go in," I told Amy.

"I'm right behind ya."

We were back in Alabama, about to walk into my ten-year high school reunion. I'd gotten along with people in high school, but I was a closeted pageant contestant then. How were they going to react now that I was showing up in rural Alabama with my New York girlfriend and my chinos?

I had told a few people in New York that I was traveling ~~home~~ back to a place I hadn't been since graduation. I wanted to know whether they had been to their reunions. Okay, fine, and *also* to see if I was batshit for entertaining the idea. I had just done a set in a fashion store in the middle of Bushwick and, afterward, gauged the temp from one of the comics who I was friendly with.

"I'm heading out to Alabama in two weeks."

"Whoa, dude. Why?"

"Going to my high school reunion?" I said.

"I can't believe you're doing that. I could never."

I softly asked another friend a few days later, "Did you go to your high school reunion?"

"Hell no. Fuck those people."

I wasn't exactly getting the response I'd hoped for. It's not like I had ever really looked forward to a reunion. I'm sentimental as hell, but a reunion with people I had grown so far from emotionally, geographically—and everything else? It felt like I'd evolved into a totally different person from the ~~Elizabeth~~ Sophie Santos they'd known. No, thank ye.

My high school class had started planning our reunion the moment we graduated. Literally. Every other year, I'd get a Facebook notification, SEVEN MORE YEARS! HOW WILL WE WAIT THAT LONG? Apparently, no one in Arab had anything better to do than count down the years until we'd all be together again. Years went by until, finally, I got a notification that we had to let the world's most active planning committee know if we were attending. The reunion was scheduled to take place in six months. Something kept telling me I should go. And by "something," I mean my manager, Jack.

"Whether it's fun or not, it'll be good material," he said.

Jack had, and has, a way of persuading me to jump off the ledge, which is something I am thankful for. Even though, that day, I was most certainly not giving thanks.

"It's all about the experience," he continued. "Gotta have something to put in that book of yours."

"Yeah, totally." *Cries self to sleep.*

I kept floating the idea with other folks, waiting for someone to forbid me to go. I told my therapist that I didn't want to fly.

"Have you been on a plane that's crashed before?" she asked.

"No." I knocked on wood three times as I answered. *Ugh, got me, Ellen.*

I asked my girlfriend, "Would you go to my reunion? *If* I wanted to go? Major if."

"If you wanted me to, then yes."

No one thought it was the worst idea of all time. I kept circling and circling it until finally Amy said, "Sophie—you clearly want to go, so stop asking everyone else for their opinion."

I bought the plane tickets the next day.

The day of our flight, I told Amy that I had lost my favorite hat.

I said in my best Grinch impression, "That's it! I'm not going!"

"It's already packed, Soph," she said and pushed me out the door.

It was worth a shot.

After everything—the flights, the money, the hours I spent in the mirror in a loop of looking away and looking back to try to ward off a possible plane crash—I still wanted to pull the plug.

Once Amy had finally coaxed me out of the rental car, she and I walked down the long gravel parking lot and rounded a corner to see a dozen of my former classmates standing together in a circle. I took a few steps backward. Amy squeezed my hand, I took a deep breath, and squeezed hers back.

"SANTOS!"

I'd have recognized that blunt, raspy voice from a deep sleep in a chamber locked in the ocean. My stomach dropped. It was Tara Fernell. She came charging toward me out of the circle in the same bulldozing fashion she once had.

This is it, I thought, *she'll punch me, and then Amy will carry me out, yelling* YOU HOMOPHOBES, *and we'll finally settle the lawsuit ten years from now, taking her for every last penny.*

Tara got right up in my face.

Just do it already.

"We're so blessed that you decided to come down to Alabama and spend time with us! I can't begin to describe how grateful we are that you chose to come here." She put her hand on her heart and then rubbed her cross.

Is she shitting me?

She gave me a bear hug, almost knocking the wind out of me.

Okay, now she'll shank me and let me bleed out in front of everyone?

She let go of me and moved on to someone else. I overheard her say, "God has really been with us this year."

Tara Fernell—a.k.a. the most terrifying bully of my youth—had welcomed me and said that the class was so *blessed* to have me celebrate with them. That *I* took the time out of *my* life to attend.

Am I in an alternate universe?

We'd barely made it a few more feet when I saw a woman with long red hair. She looked exactly the same. She had large and thick glasses on, and her outfits weren't so Hollister-esque, but that was her. Just as I remembered her. It was Emma.

"Hey, Soph!" Emma said with a deep exhale.

I gave her the biggest hug. I wanted to cry. I had missed her so much.

"This is my girlfriend, Amy," I told her, amazed that my two worlds were colliding. I waited anxiously for her response. *Please don't be homophobic. Please, God.*

"It's so wonderful to meet you, Amy."

She gave her a big hug, and I watched as two people who I had cared deeply about at different times in my life met.

I stood there watching them laugh and talk, as the world sort of slowed down. I didn't know whether to laugh or cry or punch myself for thinking there'd be any ill will toward us.

The group of us walked into the venue like a posse, got our name tags, and then went straight to the bar for our complimentary glass of Barefoot wine.

Okay—the jig is up, everyone! You can all tell me how you really feel about how lesbians are an abomination!

But it kept going and only got better.

"What are you doing?" a former classmate would ask at the bar.

"I just got hired to work on a TV show for Bravo," I'd casually reply.

"Holy shit! No way!"

"Yeah, it's cool." I feigned an incredible amount of nonchalance. I mean, it was cool, and it was a real fact that I casually dropped anytime someone approached the question of what I was doing.

I was about three drinks in when I started talking to Whitmore Hankins, who'd been the hottest and coolest student in school. He looked disheveled.

"I'm an accountant now," he said.

"That's fun!" I said, trying to force the conversation.

"I guess . . . is it?" He let out a laugh and looked to the side like he was having a crisis.

WTF is happening? How could Whitmore Hankins be unhappy with his life?

He ended up leaving the party early, because he and his very pregnant wife had to get back to their *other* kid. All my friends in New York could barely afford health insurance, while everyone in Northern Alabama had at least two—if not three—kids to get home to.

I sat down next to Savannah Hunt, who I used to go head-to-head with debating politics in history class. The Savannah I'd gotten into screaming matches with about Republicans vs. Democrats.

"Soph and I used to get in doggone fights! Ooooooohhhh, did we," she told Amy.

"Yeah, it was rough," I said with a chuckle.

"But I gotta say . . . you were right all along. I'll tell you what, my grandma is not happy about it, but I keep telling her, 'let me live my life!!!'" she cackled.

WTF IS ACTUALLY HAPPENING? WHAT HAPPENED TO ALL THE BAD PEOPLE I WAS SUPPOSED TO ENCOUNTER?

By this point, it was safe to say that I was on another level. Feeling myself to the tenth degree.

I gathered about ten people in the foyer of a modern warehouse building and ordered fifteen shots.

The bartender didn't say anything and started pouring. I pulled out the fancy credit card I had just gotten and hit it against my hand.

"How much?"

"Seventy dollars."

"Seventy dollars? That's fucking nothing. Here!" A publishing advance had just hit (for writing this book). Whoops.

"Hey, everybody! Grab your shit!" I said as people one by one grabbed shots off the bar. I brought one to Amy and to a few others hanging about.

"ALL RIGHT, EVERYONE! TO SOPHIE!" a guy shouted.

"TO SOPHIE!" everyone cheered, and we all tossed 'em back.

I had made Amy promise that we would leave early. She had said if anything happened, we were gone.

We were the last people to leave.

We even went to the after-party.

We hung back with my old group of friends, listening to country songs. As we departed, another girl came up to me. "I'm your biggest fan. I follow you on social media every day. Good luck, Soph. We're rootin' for you."

I had truly thought that people were carrying around some kind of hate for me. That I was weird. That being gay would be a huge blocker to anyone even thinking about looking in my direction. It couldn't have been further from the truth. And shame on me for thinking that. I had a fine high school experience as a "raging liberal, wears Obama shirt to school for a week" girl. So why would things have been so different now?

All I know is that—for the first time—I was the cool kid. And I loved it. Cool kid. Had money. Just booked my first TV writing gig. Had a BOOK DEAL. What I thought would be the worst night of my life, ever, turned out to be the best night of my life, ever. And something was different that night—for once in my life, I truly didn't care. I finally wasn't wasting all my energy on playing a role, on trying to fit in. I finally didn't give a rat's ass.

OMG! I didn't give a rat's ass!

DID YOU HEAR ME? I DIDN'T GIVE A GREASY, DIRTY, TRAIN-SCOURING RAT'S ASS. DO YOU KNOW HOW GOOD THAT FEELS?

Amy and I headed back to the Best Western, and the moment we got into the hotel room, I tackled her on the bed.

"DID YOU SEE THAT? I was the COOL KID!" I screamed, fist pumping, my legs wrapped around her waist.

"Yeah, Hot Stuff. Now get your pajamas on and get in bed."

She'd been a trouper. She didn't have to come with me back to Alabama, but she did—even though I would've bet my life that it was going to be an unpleasant experience for the both of us.

My heart raced the rest of the night. Probably from the tequila, but also most definitely from feeling like—for one night—I got to be the King of High School. And they had accepted me. They'd liked me even more than that person I'd tried so hard to be years before.

I love you, Arab High School.

But also, can you please change your name?

Chapter Thirty-Two

HOT TUB TIME!

My friend Meghan O'Neill—who, besides being talented at playing horrible white women, including in a highly acclaimed Lena Waithe film, is the bee's knees—called me up one day and was like, "Hey, you know that old show *Blind Date* with Roger Lodge?"

"Um, yaaah, are you going on a date with him or somethin'?" *Furiously googles* Blind Date.

"Yes, I am. And I'm also working on the reboot with Bravo," she said.

"Sleeping your way to the top, I love that about you."

"I love it about me too."

She asked if she could recommend me for the show.

"I mean, duh. I'll write for fucking Lucifer for that kinda cash."

"Great, 'cause I already did it, BABE."

"Thanks, BABE."

A writer's packet and a few weeks later, *Blind Date* offered me the job as a temporary hire to fill in for someone else while he went away for a comedy festival. I didn't get the job right away, but I was going to get four weeks of that cold hard NBC cash, a nice li'l credit, and a li'l badge that said NBCU, SOPHIE SANTOS.

At this point in time, my OCD was making a grand return, and I was struggling with a fear of getting blown up on the train. Ya know, how that always happens every time people ride to and from work? So my girlfriend took off work, rode with me to Grand Central, and handed me off to Meghan, who thought (at the time) that Amy was just being supportive on my big first day. My god, I truly owe my life to her.

Meghan and I boarded the Metro-North. An hour later, we arrived in Stamford, Connecticut, sans being blown to bits. Throw up the doves!

I was about to embark on my first staff writing gig.

Because it was a nonunion job, the production company insisted that we call ourselves "comedy producers." This was more frustrating than the camp/program distinction, and I've already put the scholarship program behind me. When will we just be able to call things what they are? I'm not legally allowed to say we were writing jokes, but you can watch the show and make that judgment call for yourself.

Day one, my butt had barely grazed the bottom of my chair when the show-runner did this thing I would come to love: he bounced in, and we immediately needed to know what he was talking about.

"HOLD ON TO YOUR BUTTS!" he announced to the room.

I figured it was an inside joke I wasn't privy to, but I laughed anyway.

"See . . . she thinks it's funny," he said. And then did a double take because he definitely didn't know who I was.

"HOLD ON TO YOUR . . . BUTTS?" he said again.

Meghan swiveled around to face him.

"Not working for ya, Brian?"

"I don't know . . . HOLD *ON TO* YOUR *BUTTS*," he repeated with different emphasis.

And then the other ~~writer~~ producer, Nick, and Meghan started shouting random sentences.

"Keep the car running!"

"Keep that butt glued to the seat!"

"Sexy time, get your tail in line!"

"BINGO!" and he walked out the door in his Yeezy Desert Rat 500s.

Ah, this is how he gets people to riff.

"Shit. I should've riffed," I said to Meghan.

"No, trust me. I didn't know that's how he wanted us to pitch jokes until, like, yesterday. He was referring to a joke we wrote for the sizzle reel a few days ago. He won't even remember coming in here."

For those who aren't familiar with the nineties phenomenon, *Blind Date* was a dating show that ran for five thousand episodes. It was like watching a date on Snapchat where there were filters and Bitmojis galore, with almost every single date ending with the pair in a hot tub, feeding each other strawberries and the man spraying whipped cream on the woman's ta-tas. They rebooted it. Back in the day, most of the daters were strippers, but this go-around, the producers wanted the show to be inclusive and diverse! Still strippers, but queer and people of color!

I was thrown into the deep end pretty immediately. We'd watch a rough cut of the dates to figure out what each of the daters' vibe was. So like, one dater was a nerdy HR rep, but when he got drunk, he'd get progressively more outgoing. So we called his drunk ego "Party Peter!" His Bitmoji would don a snapback and hold an overflowing beer and would get sloppier while having thought bubbles that said things like, "Let's turn up the heat so we can get in them sheets! 🍺👣"

Each date was about fifteen minutes, but the producers wanted a joke every fifteen seconds, and we had to come up with three or four options that the higher-ups could choose from. I'd walk in at ten a.m. and leave around eight p.m. or nine p.m. with Bitmojis and thought bubbles piling on top of me. #help. Then Meghan and I would trek back to New York for another two hours door-to-door, since I didn't live at Grand Central.

Fortunately, I love being tired. I thrive off it. Kate McKinnon was once asked, on a *Hollywood Reporter* roundtable, how her life had changed, and she responded, "Oh, I'm so tired." And that's the dream, right? I want to feel so crazed, I can't see the forest for the trees for the Bitmojis. Ya know?

The hours were long but the vibe of the ~~writers' room~~ room of typists with ideas was casual. We took breaks whenever we wanted, and Meghan would sometimes use those breaks to go swim at the Y, returning with sopping-wet hair. My friend Brendan, another writer, and I would go to get coffee a half hour away to come back to see that no one noticed we'd left. After a few weeks of writing copy for the new host, Nikki Glaser; generating one-liners; writing #fireemoji #HOTTUBTIME; and even creating a character called Lezzy the Lez, which never made it past graphics but was appreciated, we were all sat down by Brian, who said that not only was the guy I'd filled in for coming back, but we were all being invited to stay on. We popped some champagne, and I swear a Bitmoji jumped out.

All of us rode the train back to Grand Central together, with Brian reminiscing about the first time he met Kanye as we drank spiked seltzers, cheersing to our new adventure of a job that didn't have a defined end date.

The following Monday, I showed up to work, excited to have landed a full-time gig, to see all the producers scrambling. Men in suits were walking around the floor, poking their heads into our *comedy producer* room, nodding at all of us.

Brian huffed past our office and disappeared.

The word came down that Brian, our Yeezy-loving showrunner, had been sacked. We had all just gotten hired full-time, and he got sacked. What were the odds?

"That's it! We're all getting fired," Nick proclaimed.

"No one's saying that," Meghan said.

"I mean, to be fair, I've never known a new showrunner to come in and not clear out the entire room," Brendan said as he leaned back in his chair.

In that moment, Sam, the guy I'd replaced, walked in, fresh from his leave, and said, "Oh, hellooo! Heard we're all fired today! Talk about a hate crime!"

I didn't know what to think. On one hand, I was of course nervous. I really liked my job. I was good at it. And I loved the ~~writers' room~~ people probably working on tweets. But I hadn't expected to fill in longer than four weeks anyway . . . I only had begun planning my next two years the weekend prior. Then again . . . fuuuuck. No one wants to get fired. No one. And not from your first long-term gig.

After three long days of not swiveling in our chairs, and not being allowed to work, and discussing who we thought was getting fired first, the new showrunner walked in: K. P. Anderson.

K. P.'s a classy man who likes golfing and dad jokes. He was the creator of *The Soup* and now was the creator of my schedule.

Not gonna lie. It's intimidating when you have to convince a new showrunner to not fire you. Why shouldn't he? I mean, if a showrunner gets fired, that means things aren't working, which means the jokes aren't working. Thankfully, K. P. immediately reassured us that we were all staying, and he kept his word.

From that moment, the #PartyPeter vibe was gone. But we started to work like a well-oiled machine. We had weekly meetings and watched the rough cuts, pitched jokes as a group, and then would be assigned our own episodes. Then we'd have a real deadline, where we'd have to work alongside the editor to make sure our jokes were implemented. Finally, we had to present our date to K. P. and the execs in a grand showing. No sweat.

My date, Dan and Nadia, were hippies, and my god if they weren't straight out of *Napoleon Dynamite*. I worked all day with the editor, and around 11:00 p.m. I presented our cut.

I waited as they watched. There were chuckles here and there but mostly stares. K. P. smiled, but his eyes were fixed on the screen. Really studying it. I sat there, sweat starting to drip down my neck. After about two minutes of little to no chuckles, it dawned on me.

They hate it.

Another godawful twelve minutes later, and maybe one or two chuckles max, the editor said confidently, "And that's it!"

K. P. leaned back, closed his eyes for a moment, and then turned to me with a supportive smile. "Look, Sophie, it's funny. But you gotta let it breathe more. These two people are so funny by themselves, you don't even really need jokes."

He gave me a crash course on the new vision of the show in about twenty minutes. There were some notes that I didn't agree with, but overall, he was right. I had overcomplicated it.

"But nice work. Don't sweat it. Lee will help you out tomorrow."

Lee was his right-hand man and also former writer for *The Soup*. It felt like he'd been assigned to babysit me.

The next morning, Lee sat down with me and started stripping away all my jokes. I'd riff here and there, but for the most part, he showed me how to implement the style they wanted.

It was a lesson in poise. I mean, it's always humbling when someone shits on your ideas; it's helpful but it blows. And it doesn't matter that they don't love your material, but it does matter. After Lee was done, he turned the episode back over to me. And now I understood what K. P. and Lee wanted, so I was able to write in the voice of the show.

"Okay," I told the editor, "Nadia mentions a car crash, so let's have graphics put a Band-Aid on her face. And she specifically mentions she wants six-seven men, so let's have a ruler next to the drummer that they meet later on, measuring six seven." I had caught on.

One day, one of the other ~~writers~~ grown adults with LEGOs on their desks who was brought in during the reorganization, got assigned a lesbian date. I was partly fine with it because it showed we didn't discriminate, but I really wanted to have fun working on a queer date.

When we watched the cut, there were two women in a hot tub. Beside them, a frog Bitmoji appeared out of nowhere, drooling, and in a male voice said, "Kiss her." And if that opening line wasn't enough, once they did kiss, he appeared again and said, "Keep going."

It really punched me in the gut. I don't know who needs to hear this, but lesbians aren't here for your pleasure, guys. We aren't objects that you can just tell what to do. Also, why da fuck are we still dealing with this in the twenty-twenties? Also, I didn't realize frogs hung out at hot tubs. I really wanted to say something, but I was also scared because I didn't want to seem hard to work with. And I was making headway after the initial Dan and Nadia fiasco.

"It's demoralizing," I told Meghan. "It delegitimizes queer women. It's basically saying that our relationships are not real and are just for men to enjoy. We would never have a joke like that for any of the straight dates or the men's gay dates, so why would we make a joke like that for women?"

"I know, Soph. Maybe we can all talk to K. P. together," Meghan suggested.

Weeks went by, and I didn't know how to bring it up. But it kept eating at me. As the months wound down, we were all given our final days. The day before I left, I mustered the courage to walk into K. P.'s office.

"Hey, K. P.?"

"Heyyy, Soph. What's going on?"

He was always like a nice midwestern dad.

"I, um, wanted to talk to you about something that might be a little problematic and just wanted to draw your attention to it."

"Oh my God. Please, yes. Tell me."

"Well, the frog in the date between Gina and Lisa? Ya know, there's this horrible idea that lesbians are meant for men's pleasure, so when the frog tells them to kiss—"

"Say no more. I'm on it." He got up to walk out. "Actually, do say more. Sorry. Got ahead of myself." He sat back down.

"No, that was pretty much it. Besides me carrying the torch for lesbians, ha, I just think we're trying to reach a wider audience, and I can imagine a clip of that going viral on Twitter, ya know?"

"You're absolutely right. Thank you. Thank you for telling me."

A few months later, I found myself in sunny Los Angeles, and K. P. and I met up for coffee. I had just pitched my first TV show, and we were talking about how it had gone.

"Really good. I think it'll just come down to whether it's right for the network," I said.

"Just remember: no matter what, never compromise your vision. Don't let them turn it into something it's not. You know your show better than anyone else."

"Thanks, I'd love to think so!"

"Speaking of TV, how would you like to come back to *Blind Date* next year?" he said.

"Really? I'd love to."

"Yeah, yeah. Good, because I'd love to have you back. You know, what you said to me in my office that day really hit me. About the frog. I'm just an old white guy, and I'd never thought about it like that before. And I want to learn. We can really use someone with your perspective."

"Thank you. I'm glad I said something. I tried to hold my tongue but knew I'd be kicking myself if I didn't speak up."

And it was true. I almost didn't say something, but I couldn't sleep. And maybe I care too much, but I really wanted to help change the narrative about queer women, even if it was by getting two jokes taken out of a date show that I still haven't watched. Just kidding, I have and it's divine.

I left LA with my show being sent up the ladder at a network, with a job waiting for me in the fall, a goddamn television VETERAN—and then the pandemic happened. I think you can take a good guess at what went down.

Chapter Thirty-Three

ROCKEFELLER GAL

Okay fine, I lied. I have *walked* the golden halls of Rockefeller and have taken *a meeting—maybe two* there. Don't at me. There is no greater feeling.

The bustling.

The grandeur.

The confusion of all the winding corridors and elevators! *And where the fuck am I? How did I end up in what's basically a strip mall underground? Can anyone help me?*

My first time at 30 Rock, and my first time taking a professional comedy meeting ever, the third "looked in wardrobe for a Wes Anderson movie" security guard I encountered had to physically show me how to get through the turnstile by walking in the turnstile and out for me. I guess I was too nervous and forgot how basic devices worked.

I was set to meet with Lorne Michaels's company Broadway Video for what we in the industry call a "general." It's a casual conversation where they get to know you, get your hopes up, and then never speak to you again. Like dating, except almost exclusively they ghost you, even though you leave thinking you're soul mates.

After exiting the elevator and walking down the wrong hall, then finally finding the room, I arrived at the production company's suite. A very nice secretary greeted me by name and offered me a beverage, which I politely declined. I'm too much of a nervous wreck. Liquids go straight through me, so I need to dehydrate myself—but not too dehydrated so I don't pass out—before every meeting, or I'll be strategizing about asking to use the restroom instead of listening to the person who (I hope) is trying to help my career.

The producer met me in a huge glass room that overlooked the city. A few posters hung on the wall: *The Tonight Show Starring Jimmy Fallon*, *Late Night with Seth Meyers*, and Tina Fey's *30 Rock*.

The producer walked to the edge of the room and casually said, "This is a beautiful view, isn't it?"

"Well, it's . . . ?" I wanted to say *gorgeous*, but I couldn't see a damn thing. The overcast sky made it look like we were in a smoke bomb.

"It's terrible," he continued. "It's normally a beautiful view, but the weather sucks today. Too bad. Seriously, wish you could see it. It's something."

The view was shit, but I'd have rather been looking out at the shit from up there than from down below.

The meeting went well, and as I was leaving, he brought up the view again. "It's really a shame you missed it."

"Maybe another time," I said.

"Yeah! For sure."

And thus, we started dating.

Three years later, a lead in an NBC/Comcast commercial, and a lot of emailing back and forth, we continued to keep it casual.

Broadway Video cast me in an Audible Original *Hit Job* (no, they didn't pay me to say this—but I would love it if they did). And I got cast to do a few minor roles alongside Pete Davidson and Keke Palmer. This was the gig that got me my SAG card, so it was extra special and extra intense. The night before, I started to panic. I don't get starstruck, but the caliber of talent does mean you have to be on your A game. And I wanted to be on the A-ist of the game-ist.

My OCD had fully returned at this point. As in, I was *finally* diagnosed. I was literally diagnosed while writing this book. As it was my anxiety's MO, it manifested in a completely new and baffling way. I started to have this terrible fear that I would wet myself at any moment's notice. I have never been a bed wetter, not really into golden showers (although I'd probably give one if asked nicely), and am not a bed wetter now. Unless my girlfriend gingerly rolls me over and magically washes the sheets every morning before I wake up to keep me in the dark (which wouldn't surprise me), but this is a long-winded way to say I have no reason to believe I will piss myself in public.

The brain wants you to think what it wants you to think. And so I had been thinking I could let loose without any warning.

I was also feeling really grateful to be getting work during the pandemic (not sure if it will be over by the time this is out in the world, but if it is, and you are holding a copy or listening, please shout, "WE DID IT! BOWCHIKA WOW WOW!" at the top of your lungs and do a little jig. If we haven't, I'm sorry. Drinks on me. If you've managed to never hear about the pandemic of 2020, don't ask your parents. And I'm rich, bitch!).

I was really freaking out, so I called my therapist, Ellen. She tried to explain to me that I had never lost control of my bladder before, so why would it happen now?

"Yes, but I feel like I have to. I feel like I have to go right now, as we're speaking."

"I'm sure you do, but there's no reason to believe you will go now. Don't you normally do really well in high-pressure situations?"

"I thrive off them."

"Yes. But also, let's normalize it. Let's say you act out of character. What happens if you do go? What do you think would happen?" she continued.

"I'd be laughed at, and my career would be over."

"Or you could just excuse yourself. It's perfectly normal to go to the restroom," she said in a matter-of-fact way.

"I don't want to waste their time. People don't like their time messed with."

"Why don't you wear something, then? To make yourself feel better—just in case."

"Ellen! That's humiliating."

"No one will know."

I went to CVS that night with my girlfriend and bought Depend Silhouette Underwear. Since they were purple, and the woman looked happy on the box, it felt less humiliating.

I decided to throw out the instructions like I had with the pads years before, because it seemed self-explanatory. I was correct. However, I really wanted to know how reliable and flexible the diaper would be should an accident take place. I tried to think of versions of discovering that.

"What if we pour water in it?" I asked Amy once we got home.

"Nah, we need to know what it feels like so you can tell . . ."

"Okay . . . uh . . . then . . ." I looked at her. She gave me a look. "No. No. Absolutely not. I can't pee in it, because I don't want my body to think it's okay to piss my pants. That's the whole point," I continued.

"I'll do it for you," she said casually.

After drinking gallons of water for four hours (she is superhuman and can hold going to the bathroom all day), Amy put on the Depends and stood in front of me. She made eye contact and let it rip.

I should have proposed on the spot.

And lucky for her and my anxiety, there was no leakage.

The next morning, Amy drove me thirty minutes to the studio, because she has a car and it was a pandemic, and she is a genuinely altruistic person, NOT because I was that much of a needy person.

The producer texted me upon arrival, *Hey! We're running a few minutes late, can you wait for fifteen downstairs?*

Of course! No problem, I said, trying to be chill.

FUCK! The door slamming on me made me really feel like I had to go. I started entering every random-ass store, knowing full and well I'd be denied using their once-public, now "employees only" restroom. Can I just say the public restroom sitch in SoHo is bullshit—even not in a pandemic?

As I tried to plead my case, I was met with, "We can't let customers use the restroom." And, "Nope, sorry." And, "You're joking, right? This is a pandemic."

I know it's a fucking pandemic, and yes, I did read your sign, but sometimes altruistic people—which you clearly are not—make exceptions for medical emergencies.

I texted the producer back, holding my breath, *Hey, is it all right if I come up to use the restroom?*

Yes, of course!!

All you gotta do is ask, apparently.

Also, the fifteen minutes was up and to my surprise, I didn't leak. I walked into the recording studio (after getting my temperature taken) and immediately went to the vacant restroom. Bliss.

A trickle came out that didn't match the sensation that was pulsing in my abdomen, but I was very happy to be in that space. I came out of the bathroom and was told by an assistant that my studio was ready for me. I walked in, sat down, and put on headphones to listen. The studio had a glass window separating me from the engineer, director, and producer. They were wrapping up with another actor, so I had another ten minutes to wait. The more I got in the zone, the more the pulsing sensation (all the urgency but none of the pleasure) went away. After wrapping the other actor, the director took a two-minute break. When he left the room, so did I. To use the restroom. One last time. Just to be safe.

Droplets this time.

I walked back into the studio and didn't see Pete or Keke. They were nowhere. The director's voice came over my headphones and started the session. Oh yeah . . . it's *audio*—they splice the voices together in post.

Ah. I had worked myself up for the talent, only to find out that they wouldn't be here. *I'm wearing Depends! For you, Pete!* But I really needed to impress the director, producer, and the engineer, and I was sure they'd be thankful to avoid cleaning up a wet seat after my session.

It was game time. I made it through the session. Didn't need the help of my Depends after all—although they were there as a reminder that I would be okay. I didn't pee myself, unless it was from laughter, because we had a really good time, and I hit my target again.

"Yo! How'd it go?" John asked that night over FaceTime.

"Awesome. Really awesome, man. Had them laughing the entire time."

"That's beautiful!"

"Do I have permission to speak candidly?" I asked.

"Yes."

"I'm so happy it did because you know how I've been freaking out about that pee thing? Well . . . Amy . . . took one for the team last night to help me prepare."

His face grew red.

"Do I still have permission?"

"Yes."

"She put on a Depend for me to test its durability and let it rip in front of me. And—I don't know. It was so sexy. That's when I fucking knew. I'm never letting her go."

"God. No. Sophie."

"I'm telling you. You gotta try it sometime. It'll make you and your girl-friend closer. That or an enema."

His face was barely in frame.

Three hours later, we logged off.

I got up, put my arms around Amy, and squeezed her tight. To be honest, I don't know what the future holds, but for the first time in my life, I have a friend who's still here four years later. A few friends actually! I have a woman who loves me uncondi-tionally. I'm still a work in prog-ress, but I'm a happier and more functional one. Even if it means that I have to ahem, *depend* on something that's temporary. And I guess, Ellen, now everyone *will* know that I wore Depends, but when you listen to *Librarian and Cool Teen #2*, you're going to be so wowed that you'll forget all about it. (You won't.)

Look how far we've come.

Epilogue

The garage door rolled up, and I was presented with an entire two-car garage full of at least fifty moving boxes.

"All right, honey, you ready for your adventure?" Mom said with concern but slight amusement. "You get *tin* boxes, I cain't take any more than that."

"Why not?" I asked.

"It won't fit on the movin' truck, and I don't want to."

A beat.

"You really are a little hoarder, aren't you?" Mom continued.

I was back home in Mississippi at Papa and Grandma Sally's house. Mom had taken over their former house for a decade but had recently moved to Louisiana. The upkeep on two homes was hard. My task was to go through all the boxes containing my childhood memories and narrow it down to "tin" boxes. All fifty of them.

We had hauled those boxes throughout the years. Through every single house. They even stayed in the garage in my college house in Hattiesburg, much to my roommate's (and her boyfriend's and three dogs') dismay.[43]

I wasn't a hoarder. I was sentimental. There was a difference.

My stepdad, Ted, came over and stood next to me with his eyes squinted. He handed me a pair of working gloves.

"Be careful of the brown recluse and the black widows."

I closed my eyes, let out a "thanks for the lookout," and took the gloves.

I started looking through the boxes, barely lifting items, for fear my life would end then and there. It hadn't ended on the plane ride to Mississippi, to my bewilderment, but the brown recluse was sure to kill me.

---

[43] On second thought, you moved in your boyfriend and three dogs, so I don't feel bad about my boxes.

I opened up one box and sifted through found items: the Junior Miss medallion, a pair of gold heels, two bedazzled prom dresses. *Who the hell was this person?*

Then I opened up another box . . . and discovered my Bid Day card.

Roll Tide.

Next, I opened another box, which was filled to the brim with notes I had written to Emma or Anna or some random girl from my childhood, adorned with little hearts. *Gayyyyy.*

I was definitely holding on to all of those, and I put them in a "good pile." *I guess I don't need this* Teen Vogue *magazine, but it does have Emma Watson*[44] *on the cover.* I moved it from the bad pile to the good pile, making the executive decision.

I stood up and looked at the thirty-yard dumpster in front of the house. My mom had rented a dumpster intended for a warehouse of offices for all my shit, and I glared at its impending doom.

After about an hour of trying to divvy things up between "good piles" and "bad piles," much to my stress, all of a sudden, Ted came back into the garage and started taking things out of my good pile and putting them in my bad pile.

He had early onset Alzheimer's, and goddammit if that wasn't some type of sick joke for Susan. My mom had been through it.

Her first husband was a kleptomaniac, so they divorced.

Then there was my dad, which—god bless him—still didn't work out.

Then Buck, who SUCKED.

And finally, Ted. Sweet Ted. A lover of the great outdoors, who liked to woof like a dog because he thought it was funny, who now was standing there in his outback hat trying to help me. He would pass away within a year.

"Ted! Hold on there."

He stopped, frozen in his tracks.

"I'll take those," I said, trying to mask my panic. They were my old swap sorority shirts that I didn't have the heart to get rid of, for some ungodly reason.

"Why don't we go inside for lunch?" I asked.

---

[44] Emma, I wouldn't hate it if you took my book and placed it somewhere random for people to find. And like, let's get lunch?

He woofed and saluted me and then walked inside the house as the porch door swung closed. Then he walked back out and slowly walked to the shed instead, giving me a little wave as he passed through.

"Need help?" he asked.

"No, thanks, Ted. I appreciate it!"

I sat down on a box, sweating my ass off.

I was about to give up when I opened another box and saw the football jersey. And a pair of cargo shorts, slightly musty and crinkled. There was a picture of me smiling *avec confiance*. I did recognize *her*. She was fearless. She didn't take shit. I liked that kid.

I kept shrinking down the boxes, as much as I wanted to eye roll like a teenager and say, *You're really chapping my ass for making me do this, Mom.* She would come out every few hours, asking me, "Is that CD you haven't listened to since 2009 really important?"

"I'll let that one go," I said as I started to put it in the bad pile. "On second thought . . . it is the Rocket Summer . . . ," I said.

"Girlie, at this rate, you're gonna be here for a week! I'd love for you to stay, but I don't think you wanna be workin' that long."

I waved her off.

That night, I met Mom outside, grabbed a cigarette out of her carton for old times' sake, and we swung on the porch swing. I was finished for the day, but it would take me that extra week to complete.

"I didn't think this place would bring back so many memories," I said as I looked at the cows that I had been staring at since I was a baby. "I didn't realize I'd be so sad," I added.

"I know, honey, but I can't keep the house anymore," she said.

"I'll take it over."

"You gonna live in Wiggins, Mississippi? With Amy?"

I didn't answer. She already knew the answer.

"We had a good life here—why don't we think about that?" she said. I put my head on her shoulder.

"Lord, it really took you a while to get settled, didn't it?" she asked.

"It did."

"You were so frenzied. I wanted to help, but at times I felt helpless."

"I'm happy I went through everything. I think it all timed out exactly as it should've," I assured her.

"I'm just happy you're finally calm," she said.

And then, out of the corner of my eye, I saw Ted take my good pile and drag it to the thirty-yard dumpster while whistling to himself, happy as a clam.

"I think I'm gonna go help him," I said in my mom's accent.

"I think that's a great idea," she drawled.

Acknowledgments

There are a lot of people I want to thank who made this book possible, but first I'd like to thank the YOTEL hotel in Hell's Kitchen, New York.

January 11, 2019, I performed at the YOTEL. Yes, it's a real hotel name, and the place looks like it's straight out of *Blade Runner*. I don't know how I even ended on the lineup, seeing as the show was called *Poetry / Cabaret*. If it had been *Poetry / Cabaret / Comedy*, I'd understand, but that was not the case. No matter. I should also mention that it was the coldest day in New York in *years*, and I vehemently didn't want to go. I wanted to perform, but I did not want to trek from Forty-Second Street and Sixth all the way to the YOTEL (which was a solid four avenues away) in twenty-one-degree weather. For non–New Yorkers, just know that fucking blows. I told my girlfriend that I wanted to cancel, and she told me I couldn't. Case closed.

I showed up frozen and, after unthawing, had a really kickass time. The woman who went before me in the lineup was a poet and slayed. I felt connected to her art. However, her poetry was extremely serious, so when I got up onstage after her, I told the audience, "Now who's ready for some COMEDY?!" which actually did a lot better than you'd think.

After the show, I went up to the poet and told her how great she was. She said, "I loved your stuff too," and gave me her business card. "Let me know if you'd ever like to write a book sometime." And she disappeared into the wintry night.

My girlfriend tapped me on the shoulder and said as I turned around, "Now aren't you glad you didn't cancel?"

And that's how this whole fucking thing started.

I mean, it took another six months, and lots of convincing on many people's parts, but that's its origin story, baby. I wanted to include this tale because that shit DOESN'T happen. Or it doesn't happen to me. It's a Cinderella story, and it's COOL. And yes, I am so thankful I didn't cancel.

Hafizah. We met one snowy and cold-ass fortuitous night, and I almost backed out of that hodgepodge of a show. I'm so glad I didn't, because this book never would have happened. Thank you for listening to me and believing in this story.

Laura. You went through every single line of this damn book over Zoom. Pulling all-nighters, pulling all-dayers. I felt like I was back in college again. Thank you for pushing me. Thank you for trusting my voice and saying *yes and*—and for lightly pushing me to go in a different direction every once in a while. And laughing so hard at the rainforest café story. Thank you for going to bat when we needed more time and for putting your foot down when you felt like it was ready. Thank you. "It's cute."

Elsa. I have no words. How many quotes are scribbled all over my apartment from you? You taught me how to be a good writer. I didn't know how to write a book, and now I have a memoir because of you. I'm still hoping we get to hang in the Castro one day. Thank you for pushing me to be vulnerable and heartfelt and for making me fucking go there. I always felt safe to share my stories, and sometimes you were my therapist even though you didn't sign up for that. You held my hand and then you let go right when it was time. "Think of the thing that you don't want us to know about you and then tell us all about it."

Carmen. Thank you for picking up the baton and bringing this to the finish line. I loved working with you.

To everyone at Amazon who put in tireless effort to make this book happen: Emily, Emma, Anna, Adam, Stacy, Karin, Tara, and Jeff Bezos.

To Joey Soloway for giving me a chance to be part of your imprint. I grew up watching your shows, and to have your support was the biggest pinch-me moment ever. Thank you for giving me the platform to tell my story.

To my PR team, Sam and Kristin, and everyone else at Sechel. Thank you for pushing for me and believing in me every step of the way! You took a chance on me from the beginning, and LOOK HOW FAR WE'VE COME. Can't wait for more. LET'S GOOO!

To my Amazon PR team, Lucy and Amy. Thank you for selling the hell out of this book!! I know I wasn't the only book on your slate, but you made me feel like the only one.

Thank you to the entire Audible team! Thank you for guiding me through the insane number of hours it took to record this book.

And a special thank-you to Marla Kirban for being the best voice-over coach in the world. You always tell me when I do well, but you also tell me when I am god-awful, and that's my favorite part about you.

To Mindy Tucker for being the first person to photograph me as a comedian and for always making me feel like I belonged. My Alabama soul sister. Thank you, thank you, thank you for photographing such a wonderful cover. We've come full circle, girl! And Roll Tide!

To Emilia for making me look *real* pretty, and Merideth and Zoe for bringing the entire cover together. I'd frame it, if that didn't make me look like a narcissist! (Actually, I don't care and am gonna do it.)

To my friends Henry and Meghan, who read the book in the earliest of stages, when it wasn't a book. I'm pretty sure what I gave you was not great, so thanks for slogging through it.

Nick. Thank you for reading the entire book and helping me figure out a way to tie it all together.

Sami! My OCD partner in crime. Thanks for reading the entire book and then asking me to open up more about my OCD, then telling me to get on medication. And for being my ex.

Aaron Jackson! We drank at Julius like two gay witches creating a potion to make everyone fall in love with us! You were one of the first people who took me under your wing when I was writing this book, and I salute you! Thank you.

Thank you to Matt Rogers, for your amazing blurb and for directing *Riverdale Live* many moons ago! I've looked up to you for years, and having your support meant the world. I'm so happy you didn't say, "I Don't Think So, Honey."

Thank you to Isaac Oliver. We haven't known each other long, but you were a wonderful shoulder to lean on when I was a newbie to writing books. Thank you for reading my book and for your truly kind words.

Mom. We both know I would not be writing this book if it weren't for you. I know I will never be able to repay you for the time and energy and investments you've made, but I can't thank you enough for your support. Throughout the years, you've put me on your back and carried me over the finish line and are the best damn mother in the world. I told you I wanted to be a performer and a writer, and you never questioned it. You said, "All right, well, how we gonna do it?" You've never stopped believing in me. It feels so goddamn good to be able to say *we did it*. I love you.

Dad, thank you for teaching me real survival tips at a very early age. I'm more equipped for the apocalypse, and I'm thankful for it. Love you bigger than a dinosaur. And thank you to Deb for keeping him in line.

John. Thank you for listening to me talk about this book for two years over Negronis, via Zoom at 3:00 a.m., in a very legal café in LA, whilst tubing down the Delaware River?! Glad I found someone who also won't stop until he's on top! Like the "Piano Man" has said (but not exactly to avoid copyright infringement), "in life, you can go get what you want or you can just grow old," my friend.

Eric, thank you for getting me involved in the biz. "We're doin' it."

To my cousin Brittany: Thanks for helping me remember the Firestone house and going down memory lane with me. And for being a great cousin!

Thank you, Uncle Tony and Aunt Peggy, for giving me the scoop on the Santos fam!

To all my friends who've let me cry or rant or gloat about this book. Thank you. And special gratitude to John Trowbridge, Ben Warheit, Danielle Alfredo, Alex West, Eric Cunningham, Jessica Henderson, Ashley August, Marcia Belsky, David Odyssey, Brendan Fitzgibbons, Meghan O'Neill, Henry Koperski, Dave Mizzoni, Sami Schwaeber, Nick Pappas, Hope Prybylski, and Chandler James.

To the queer Brooklyn comedy scene: I fucking love you.

Thank you to the entire Lesbian Agenda crew. From the performers to James Harvey, who's our straight man paying his debts to lesbians, to the sound team, to Chris at the bar. Thank you to the fans of *The Lesbian Agenda* for selling out the show on countless occasions. And thank you to Matt and Union Hall. You constantly give marginalized voices a chance to shine, and you took a chance on me from the beginning. I found my voice in that basement.

Mark, thank you and the entire Broadway Video family for seeing something in my comedy.

Thank you to Gabe for making me gay.

Thank you to the many places I wrote my book child in: Guinevere Turner (you don't know me, but thanks for letting me and my girlfriend stay at your place in LA), Matt's place (again you don't know me, but thank you), Breakfast by Salt's Cure in LA, Madison & Park Coffee in LA, East One in Brooklyn, Stumptown in Brooklyn, the Marlton Hotel, the F train, Ben Warheit's pad (you do know me, and I'm glad to know you), Amy's childhood bedroom, the swamps of Louisiana, Papa and Grandma Sally's house in Wiggins, and my little nook in Cobble Hill, Brooklyn.

Jack, thank you for guiding me always and being the best cheerleader. This has been such a wild ride, and I'm looking forward to more adventures! Go Chiefs! To Richard, Max, Madison, and everyone at The Arlook Group: thank you for believing in me constantly. And thank you, Richard, for correcting me when I called your favorite deli a diner!

To my therapist, Ellen, and my psychiatrist, Miriam (I've never called you by your first name, but this is for your protection!): thank you for helping me every day to be less scared and for calming my swirling thoughts.

Thank you to my team of doctors, who I don't need but who put up with my constant hypochondria and countless messages on MyChart.

Thank you to all the professors I spent time with. From the ones who saw me floundering to the ones who saw me flourishing. Special shout-out to Robin, Monica, Lou, and Dr. Warrick.

Thank you to all the teachers at UCB who taught me "THE GAME" and how to be funny: Eric, Damian, Natasha, and Doug Moe.

Amy. You built me a desk. I've been working on this book for (more than) half of our relationship, and I can't believe how much support you've given me. You read my book. You made me pasta! You get out of the shower and only use half of the bathroom mat, so I can have a dry section for my shower. I am so lucky. And you make me want to rip off all my clothes and profess my love to you every day.

To Papa and Grandma Sally: I miss you both so much, and I know you would be traumatized if you read the book, but I sure am lucky we got to have all those adventures in the RV when I was a kid.

To Pee-Paw: I wish we had gone to the Philippines together. Thank you for meeting Grandma Carmen and for not listening to others when you were in love. I can't wait to go to the Philippines one day and learn more about your life.

Grandma Carmen, I love you. You're so young and beautiful! Please promise me I have your genes!!!

Thank you to the *F* key on my keyboard for hanging on by a thread.

Thank you to Nick Saban for giving me a sense of purpose for six months out of the year.

Thank YOU for taking a chance on me and reading this book!

Last but not least, thank you to OCD. You've been keeping me safe for so long, and now I'm keeping you at a *slightly* safe distance.

About the Author

Sophie Santos is a comedian and writer based in New York. She's written for TV shows on Bravo and MTV and currently hosts the satirical comedy show *The Lesbian Agenda*. Her writing has also been featured in *McSweeney's*. Sophie has appeared on *Jimmy Kimmel Live!* and *MTV News*, and she has performed at the Edinburgh Festival Fringe and the Kennedy Center. Follow her on social media for lesbian propaganda. For more information, visit www.sophiesantos.com.